MW01156531

for Dear Mazello,

You have been a

wonderful voice coach

BACTRIA PRESS

THE AFGHAN SOLUTION

Lucy Morgan Edwards arrived in Afghanistan as an aid worker at the height of the Taliban regime in Kandahar. She was an election monitor at the 2002 Emergency Loya Jirga and then a freelance journalist, writing for the Economist and Daily Telegraph. From 2004 - 5 she was Political Advisor to the EU Ambassador in Kabul. She is now based in Geneva where her husband is a Director of the International Committee of the Red Cross (ICRC).

& I will miss you

hugely.

Much Love,

Lucy

June '17

A devastating indictment of the intelligence and strategic failures that have led us into the current tragedy in Afghanistan. This book is also an insight into the Peace Plan that might have averted the conflict; something that western policy makers must be aware of as they seek to stabilise the situation and to extricate NATO forces from Afghanistan. A wonderful account … essential to understanding the history of this tragedy.

- WILLIAM PFAFF, author of *The Irony of Manifest Destiny:*
The Tragedy of America's Foreign Policy
and longtime columnist for the *International Herald Tribune*.

The Afghan Solution is an important and revealing book. Lucy Morgan Edwards has written a rich and compelling account of how Abdul Haq might have saved Afghanistan – and what the West can still learn from his singular vision of a post-Taliban nation.

- DAVID ZUCCHINO, Pulitzer-Prize winning journalist,
The Los Angeles Times

With US and UK military engagement in Afghanistan at a critical juncture, this book provides a timely reminder of the roads not taken and strategic options left unexplored. The cumulative effect constitutes a compelling indictment of state-building through external imposition. This book blends personal insights with a professional detachment and will appeal to the analyst, policymaker, practitioner and, not least, the decision-makers of tomorrow: the students of today.

- DR GRAEME HERD, The Geneva Centre for Security Policy

A deeply reported, well argued and deftly written account of the opportunities not taken since the fall of the Taliban. This important account is based on her own deep knowledge of Afghanistan; acquired as a journalist, EU diplomat and aid worker. It helps illuminate why the country is in its present mess.

- PETER BERGEN, author of *The Longest War: the Enduring Conflict between America and al Qaeda*

A fascinating insight into how political and territorial rivalry between Pakistan and Afghanistan is played out on the ground along the Durand Line; a British Colonial legacy that has plagued relations between Afghanistan and Pakistan since the latter's creation.

BAQER MOIN, former Head of BBC's Persian service and author of *Khomeini: Life of the Ayatollah*

This original and beautifully written book presents a case study in everything that western policymakers got so dreadfully wrong ahead of their Afghan adventure. It is vital reading for everyone who truly wants to understand this tragic conflict.

- PETER OBORNE, Political Editor, *Daily Telegraph* and author of *The Triumph of the Political Class*

By far the best account of Afghanistan during the period that I have read. It combines the pace of a page-gripping thriller with the insights of travel writing and political journalism at their best. There were times when I felt that I could smell and taste eastern Afghanistan.

- CONOR FOLEY, author of *The Thin Blue Line: How Humanitarianism went to War*

BACTRIA PRESS

Bactria Press, London.

Copyright © Lucy Morgan Edwards, 2011

Cover, typesetting, map and image production by Matt Swann
21stBookDesign.blogspot.com

A CIP catalogue record for this book is available from the British Library

Printed in the United States of America

Hardback ISBN 978-0-9568449-0-3

THE AFGHAN SOLUTION

THE INSIDE STORY OF ABDUL HAQ, THE CIA
AND HOW WESTERN HUBRIS LOST AFGHANISTAN

LUCY MORGAN EDWARDS

BACTRIA PRESS

This book is dedicated to my husband,
Philip

And in fond memory
of
Omar Nassih

An American businessman who has been assisting and lobbying for Haq around US Gov called this morning and believes that following an initial interest with Haq – which still exists – the hawks have won with their plan to attack and remove the Taliban with coalition forces.

Though there is no other source for this alarmist scenario it could explain the latency with which Haq has been treated.

I need hardly add that the Pashtun response will be one to unite and "all will be against the foreigner". The Haq option will be dead in the water and the US could well be in for a Soviet experience. In the Islamic world it would be a disaster.

'*Words from Washington*', SITREP, October 2001

CONTENTS

AUTHOR'S NOTE

Since 2001, I have interviewed hundreds of Afghans and others about the events described in this book. There are many others to whom I am indebted, but who prefer not to be named. Some names have been changed.

Much of the dialogue is from those interviews. Sometimes my interlocutors or I referred back to contemporary notes or letters or had a strong recollection of what was said. I have rendered such dialogue in quotation marks.

Quotations and information taken from other books, articles and other published materials are listed in the endnotes and bibliography. Permissions have been sought for the longer quotations made in the text.

ACKNOWLEDGEMENTS

This book owes a debt to many people beyond those already mentioned in the Author's Note. At UN Habitat, Samantha Reynolds set me off on this journey by first assigning me to work on UNCHS's 'community forum' projects and urban development programmes aimed at drought relief for vulnerable Afghans in Kandahar and Herat back in 2000. These later became the basis for what is now known as the 'National Solidarity Programme'. Chris Lockwood at *The Economist* encouraged me to report for him from Afghanistan both during and after the Taliban period. In 2002, Samina Ahmed at the International Crisis Group in Islamabad assigned me to undertake research into Transitional Justice in Afghanistan. This issue became a core theme of the book.

Of those Afghans and non-Afghans who have shared their insights and knowledge on both Afghanistan and Abdul Haq, I would particularly like to thank James and Joe Ritchie, Sir John Gunston, Ken Guest, 'RAM' Seeger, and Peter Jouvenal. Ken Guest and Sir John Gunston were particularly generous in sharing their very impressive understanding of battlefield strategy, Afghan history, the history of conflict in general and insights on the jihad. I owe them a great debt.

I acknowledge the hospitality, kindness and insight extended to me by Abdul Haq's family, the Arsala family, and would like to thank especially Haji Din Mohammad, Haji (Baryalai) Nasrullah Arsala, Haji Zahir Qadir, Majeed, Abdullah, Khalil and Khushal Arsala. I am particularly grateful to the family for sharing with me some of Abdul Haq's extraordinary letters. I am also indebted to Abdul Haq's former Commander's Khan Mir, Mullah Malang and Aga Jan for their descriptions of various of Haq's Operations carried out during the anti-Soviet Jihad and of his last mission and to Mullah Khaksar for his insights on Haq's Plan in relation to the

Taliban. Thanks also to Mahboub and 'Captain' for looking after me so well whenever I stayed in Jalalabad.

Malcolm Brinkworth at Touch Productions allowed me to use transcripts of interviews from his film, *Afghan Warrior*. And Peter Tomsen, former US Ambassador to the Mujahideen shared his insight and a letter Haq had written to him in 1994 on the capture of Kabul by Commander Massoud. Steve Masty shared insights with me about the jihad and Abdul Haq.

I acknowledge the work of the many writers and journalists who spent time in Afghanistan before me and produced books which have contributed to my understanding; in particular excellent work has been done by Ahmed Rashid, Barnett Rubin and Steve Coll. However because I have deliberately chosen a different tack, sometimes my reflections and discoveries may be perceived to be at odds with their viewpoint. Coll's book *Ghost Wars* ends at 10 September 2001, whereas mine takes the story forward through the Bonn Process. Where Coll's sources often relate the Tajik perspective of Commander Massoud - as well as the CIA and Hamid Karzai, I have focussed on the majority Pashtun angle and the potential presented by Abdul Haq. I also feel that Afghan writers and experts were rather quick to embrace Hamid Karzai as Afghanistan's 'leader' despite (as I have found from my research) the seemingly great ambivalence towards him by both Afghans and even journalists who had covered Afghanistan from the 1980s onwards. The fact that the Northern Alliance were willing to accept him at Bonn may have had more to do with his malleability than with his legitimacy or status as a 'National figure' or even his significance as a key member of the 'Rome Group'.[1] Yet this issue seemed to me to have been overlooked in many of the books written since 9/11. Although authors Ahmed Rashid and Barnett Rubin have produced an important body of work they have also, I feel, sometimes been rather too close to the political strategy adopted – both pre and post 9/11. See my footnote on this.[2] In relation to this I believe that - what has become - a tightknit group of Afghan 'experts' have focused much of their criticism on aspects of the US led military intervention (eg lack of resources given to Afghanistan after the decision to invade Iraq) rather than the political strategy. Barnett Rubin was apparently given diplomatic status by the UN to participate in the meeting held in Bonn at which the Agreement (for the political strategy) was thrashed out.[3] Though this book is not about one leader versus another; Abdul Haq 'versus' Hamid Karzai; the book is perhaps more critical of Hamid Karzai as a virtually un-assailable 'leader' of Afghanistan and more critical of the political chicanery of the Bonn Agreement and the 'Peace versus Justice Strategy.

Those who have supported me the most in this project are Cherry Spencer, and Sahar al Huneidi, both of whom encouraged me to take up the opportunity to work in Kandahar at the beginning and have remained interested in my Afghan adventures. This book has had a long gestation and during that time I have benefitted from the support of many friends but especially my father, Liz Scott, Emma Passmore, Kathryn Grusoven, Anita Gupta, Alex Grinling, Charlotte Marshall, Evelyn Partridge, the Reverend Maree Wilson, Rani Treichel, Elspeth Scott, Alessia Castelfranco, Anna Martinssen Pont, Amandine Roche, Diana Barrowclough, Lindsey Anderson, Miranda Rhys Williams, Iris and Thomas Ruttig, Poplar and Chippewa Cosmo, Zaved Mahmoud, Filippo di Robilant and Titziana Assal, who generously allowed me to use her delightful chalet in Grimentz to bring about an end to this long work. The staff at the Society of Authors have shown great patience in answering so many of my questions over the years while Susan Tiberghian at the Geneva Writers Group is eternally generous with her advice, warmth and encouragement. To all of them I owe a debt of gratitude.

I am also grateful to those who commented on early versions of the manuscript. They include Peregrine Hodson, Graham Herd of the Geneva Centre for Security Policy, Professor Charles Norchi of the Harvard School of Governance, Lara Santoro, David Ward, George MacPherson, Peter Morgan, Rachel Fountain and Amanda Baumgartner. For later versions: my father Quentin Morgan Edwards,

ACKNOWLEDGEMENTS

Dr Toni Pfanner, Lea Mattheson, Andy Sundberg, Antonio Donini and Norah Niland. I am grateful to the Royal Society of Asian Affairs and particularly to Briony Watson for her help in locating maps and to Diana Merylees for her kindness and encouragement. Also to Ben Evans for his editorial help and Matthew Swann for his help in the design and production of this book.

Lastly I must acknowledge the great support, love and patience of my husband Philip; without which the book could never have been finished. As well as the forgiving nature of my two sons, Oscar and Henry, who have endured hours of babysitting while their mother made this work a priority. I hope one day they will share in my passion for Afghanistan.

MAPS

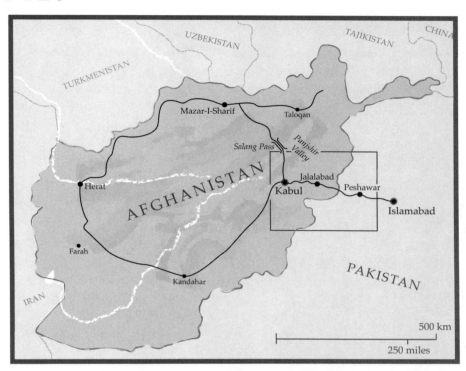

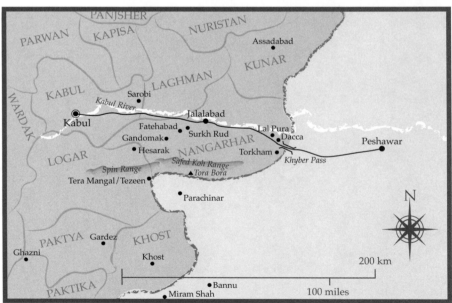

DRAMATIS PERSONAE:
PRINCIPAL CHARACTERS OF THE NARRATIVE AND THEIR POSITIONS IN 2001 - 2002

THE ARSALA FAMILY

An Eastern Pashtun family of eight brothers who fought the Soviets and the Taliban. They belong to the Ghilzai branch of the Pashtun:[4] their tribe are the Ahmadzai; their sub-tribe is Jabbarkhel. The most famous were:

Commander Abdul Haq – Famed Pashtun Commander of the Jihad and the only Commander to take the fight to the centre of the Soviet regime in Kabul. He is the principal character of this book. Assassinated in October 2001 by the Taliban.

Haji Abdul Qadir – Former Governor of Jalalabad, until the Taliban drove the family out in 1996. Governor again after their rout in 2001. During the early 1990s, Qadir was nominally head of the 'Eastern Shura' which comprised representatives from Nangarhar, Nuristan, Laghman and Kunar. He rose to fame as one of the most effective commanders in the East during the 1980s war against the Soviets. Awarded position of Vice President in the 'Interim Administration' (June 2002) but was assassinated within weeks.

Haji Din Mohammad – Governor of Jalalabad following Haji Qadir's assassination in 2002. The most pious of the eight brothers, he is the one that the rest of the family look up to. Governor of Kabul 2005-9.

Haji Nasrullah (known to me as Baryalai) – One of the younger brothers. After returning from Germany in 2001, he set up 'The Abdul Haq Foundation' and later a shura, both aiming to continue the community based work advocated by Abdul Haq.

Haji Zahir – Son of Haji Qadir and now Head of the Border Guard. Though only twenty-seven years old, he has already escaped a

Taliban jail with Ismael Khan and led a force at the battle of Tora Bora, where he captured twenty-two al Qaeda prisoners (and famously had them filmed by CNN).

Abdul Majeed Arsala – Haq's oldest son.

Hedayat Amin Arsala – A cousin who worked for the World Bank in Washington DC for twenty years and became Vice President after the death of Haji Qadir. Currently a senior minister in Karzai's government.

FORMER COMMANDERS CLOSELY ASSOCIATED WITH ABDUL HAQ

Jalaluddin Haqqani – Ex Khalis Commander (see below under section titled the 'Armed Opposition').

Aga Jan – based in Sarobi, a strategically important 'crossroads' between the east, the north east and Kabul. Famed for conducting important operations against the Soviets. Ex Khalis Commander.

Mullah Malang – well known for the brilliant operations he conducted against the Soviets in Kandahar during the jihad. Also has influence in areas as diverse as Badghis, Ghor, Daikundi, Ghazni, Wardak and Gardez. His men constituted the bodyguard of Mullah Omar. Ex Khalis Commander.

Abdul Salam Rocketti – Received his name as a result of his prowess in launching rockets against Soviet tanks during the jihad. Served under the Taliban regime as 'Corps Commander' firstly in Zabul Province and later in Jalalabad, where he was at the time of September 11. Ex Sayyaf / Khalis Commander.

Khan Mir – with influence around Paghman, north east of Kabul, from where he conducted operations during the jihad. Taliban Division Commander with 800 men. Ex Khalis Commander.

Arif Shah Jehan – Leader of Hazaras in Ghazni Province.

PRINCIPAL POLITICAL PARTIES

In reality, these 'parties' were polico-military factions associated with mujahideen leaders.

The Northern Alliance was a group of loosely-allied former mujahideen groups brought together by Commander Massoud. Its principal cabal, the Shura-e-Nazar (Council of the North), is associated with strongmen from the north-east, mostly from the Panjshir valley.

The original jihadi parties of the 'Peshawar Seven':

The three main (generally more hard-line) parties:

- Jamiat-i-Islami (led by Commander Massoud and the Shura-e-Nazar faction but whose Political leader was Professor Burhanuddin Rabbani)

- Hizb-i-Islami (led by Hekmatyar; NB when 'Hizb' split, Hikmatyar's more radical faction separated from that of Younus Khalis)

- Ittehad-i-Islami (led by Abdurrab Rasul Sayyaf; now leader of Dawat-i-Islami)

The four minor parties:

- Hizb Islami (led by Mullah Younus Khalis, associated with the Ghilzai Eastern Pashtun, with the Arsala family as its figurehead)

- Mahaz Milli Islami (led by the Gailani Family and associated with the former King, and the National Islamic Front for Afghanistan, NIFA, in Pashtun)

- Jabha-yi-Nejat Milli (Sebhagatullah Mojadedi, Pashtun)

- Harakat-i-Inqilab-i-Islami (Mohammad Nabi Mohammadi, Pashtun)

The two main Iran-based parties and alliances:

- Hizb Wahdat (Abdul Ali Mazari & Karim Khalili, Hazara)
- Harakat Islami (Asif Mohseni, Shia Pashtun)

The final significant party is Jombesh Mille, the Uzbek faction led by General Abdul Rashid Dostum)

PRINCIPAL MUJAHIDEEN LEADERS ('WARLORDS') OF THE NORTHERN ALLIANCE

General Abdul Rashid Dostum – Uzbek warlord based in Mazar, he recently returned from exile in Turkey.

Mohammad Qasem Fahim – Defence Minister and de facto Head of Shura-e-Nazar since the assassination of Commander Massoud on 9 September 2001. Associated with much extra-judicial killing when Head of Security for Massoud during the Mujahideen assault on Kabul (1992–96).

Ismael Khan – Tajik warlord and Governor of Herat.

Professor Burhanuddin Rabbani – Political leader of Massoud's party and Islamist scholar trained in Cairo.

Abdurrab Rasul Sayyaf – Ittehad-i-Islami – Islamist scholar trained in Cairo. Fundamentalist Wahhabist who set up training camps along the border with Pakistan in the early 1990s and, through his links with Saudi Arabia, brought many Arabs and funding to the region following the jihad.

'WARLORDS' IN NANGARHAR PROVINCE

Hazerat Ali – Police Chief and member of the Pashai, a minor ethnic group at Dar-yi-Noor (50 km north of Jalalabad). Although originally a commander of Haji Qadir, he has now become allied with General Fahim of the Northern Alliance and, despite his unpopularity in the East, is the principal ally of the Americans in Jalalabad. He led a band of soldiers at the battle of Tora Bora.

Haji Zaman Ghamsharik – Member of the Khogiani tribe in Chaprahar. Recently returned from exile in Paris to lead some soldiers at the battle of Tora Bora. Principal ally of the British in Jalalabad. Accused by locals of having orchestrated a massacre and pocketing money from the British poppy compensation scheme.

THE ARMED OPPOSITION

The Taliban – A stratified Pashtun group, believed to be supported by Pakistan, whose regime ruled Afghanistan prior to 9/11.

Jalaluddin Haqqani – Once a Commander of Hizb Islami (the same party of Younus Khalis and Abdul Haq), Haqqani became more radicalized and joined the Taliban where he led a front based in Miramshah, Pakistan, controlling the Loya Paktia and the Khost region of Afghanistan. Close to bin Laden whom he is thought to have invited back to Eastern Afghanistan in 1996, upon his expulsion from Sudan. Veteran Afghan journalist Kathy Gannon noted in 2005, "had he wanted to, Haqqani could have handed the US the entire al Qaeda network". Yet after 9/11 Haqqani, who had links with the CIA and Saudi's during the 1980s and maintains strong links with the Pakistani ISI, chose to continue fighting the US and NATO forces in 'Af-Pak' long after the toppling of the Taliban.

Sirajuddin Haqqani - Son of the elderly Jalaluddin, who will later lead the south eastern opposition 'front' against the Karzai government and US forces in Afghanistan.

Gulbuddin Hikmatyar – Radical Islamist ISI supported guerrilla, rival of Massoud. Recently returned from exile in Iran. Leading an insurgency from the areas bordering Pakistan's NWFP.

FORMER TALIBAN

Mullah Abdul Razzaq – Taliban Interior Minister who apparently ordered the killing of Haq after he entered Afghanistan, October 2001.

Mullah Abdul Samad Khaksar – Deputy Interior Minister who had switched his support covertly to Abdul Haq.

Mullah Ahmad Wakil Mutawakil – Taliban Foreign Minister.

Abdul Salam Rocketti – see section entitled 'Haq's former Commanders' (above)

WOMEN

Massouda Jalal – Female Presidential candidate in 2002 Emergency Loya Jirga

Dr Sima Samar – Erstwhile Chair of Loya Jirga in 2002, sacked by warlords. Since then, Head of Afghan Independent Human Rights Commission

Fatima Gailani – Head of Afghan Red Crescent after Qar-a-bec was finally ousted

Malalai Joya – Woman from Farah Province who challenged warlords at the Constitutional Loya Jirga in 2004. They threw her out. Elected to Parliament in 2005. Expelled by warlords after she criticised them for their human rights abuses.

INTERNATIONAL DIPLOMATS

Francesc Vendrell – EU Chief

Lakhdar Brahimi – UN Chief

Zalmay Khalilzad – US Ambassador

US SOLDIERS

Lt. General Dan McNeil – commander of the US led Coalition forces in Afghanistan in 2002

General Tommy Franks – head of CENTCOM during the U.S. invasion of Afghanistan and Iraq

THE CIA

Milton Beardon – Chief of Station, Islamabad, 1986–89

Gary Schroen – Case Officer, Islamabad, 1978–80; Chief of Station designate, Kabul, 1988–1990; Chief of Station, Islamabad, 1996–1999; Deputy Chief, Near- East Division, Directorate of Operations, 1999–2001

US DEPARTMENT OF STATE

Peter Tomsen – Special Envoy to the Afghan Resistance, 1989–92

ABDUL HAQ'S US BACKER'S

James and Joe Ritchie – American brothers who were brought up in Afghanistan. After making money as Chicago options traders, they initiated and funded a series of Loya Jirga meetings outside Afghanistan during the Taliban years. They attempted, through working with Haq and the ex-King, to support the process of providing an alternative to the Taliban for the people of Afghanistan.

Robert 'Bud' McFarlane – Former US National Security Advisor under President Reagan. Worked alongside the Ritchie brothers in attempting to find support for Haq in Washington DC both before and after September 11.

HAQ'S BRITISH SUPPORTERS:

Ken Guest – Former marine and cameraman who travelled extensively with the mujahideen from 1980-89 during which time he met bin Laden, Jalaluddin Haqqani and most mujahideen leaders.

Sir John Wellesley Gunston – A photographer during the jihad, who travelled extensively with the mujahideen during the jihad, went to support Abdul Haq in Rome after September 11, and then Peshawar before he left on his last mission, attended the Bonn Conference with Haji Qadir (as 'advisor') and the battle of Tora Bora. He also attended installation in December 2001 of Hamid Karzai.

'RAM' Seeger – Former Head of the Special Boat Service (SBS) who worked alongside Guest and Gunston in attempting to find support for Haq in Whitehall and amongst the British defence and intelligence establishment.

BRITISH SOLDIERS AND OFFICIALS

General Sir John McColl – Commander of ISAF troops in Kabul 2002. Former Head of MI6 (1989-94)

General Lord Guthrie – Chief of the Defence Staff (1997–2001)

Sir Richard Dearlove – Head of MI6 (1999–2004)

Lord (Paddy) Ashdown – former leader of the Liberal Democrat Party and International High Representative for Bosnia and Herzegovina (2002–2006)

Ian Duncan Smith – then leader of the Conservative Party

MISCELLANEOUS PEOPLE

Fazl Akbar – later Governor of Kunar

Dr Abdullah Abdullah – Panjshiri who became Foreign Minister in 2001

Ayoub Afridi – alledged drug dealer who lives on the Khyber Pass. Friend of Haji Qadir

Sher Mohammad Akhundzada – Governor of Lashkargah, Karzai ally

Engineer Arif – Massoud's Intelligence Chief. Became head of the National Directorate of Security (NDS), the Afghan intelligence service, after Kabul fell to the Northern Alliance

Mohammad Daoud – Northern Alliance Commander and ally of Fahim from Konduz, would become 'Drug's Tzar' of Interior Ministry in late 2004

Hamid Gul – former ISI chief

Mullah Izat – Northern Alliance Commander

Assadullah Khaled – Governor of Ghazni until 2005 when he was moved to Kandahar. Ally of Karzai family

Mustafa Khan – Commander of Haji Zahir

Jan Mohammad – Governor of Uruzghan, Karzai ally

Najibullah – last Afghan Communist President

Nader Nadery – Deputy Chair of Afghan Independent Human Rights Commission

Arif Noorzai – Karzai ally in Kandahar

Shah Shujah – Puppet King installed by the British in the nineteenth century

Amin Wardak – ally of Abdul Haq

Rahim Wardak – Defense Minister of Afghanistan, 2004–

Qari Mohammad Yousef – Commander of Haji Zahir responsible for capturing arabs at battle of Tora Bora. Later arrested by Americans and taken to Bagram.

Qar-a-beg – Panjshiri strongman who refused to budge from the sinecure he had taken as Head of the Afghan Red Crescent, following the capture of Kabul.

Dr Asef Qazizada – Deputy Governor of Jalalabad – 2002-5

Haji Rohullah – Salafi leader from Kunar, arrested by US and taken to Guananamo in 2002

Wuliullah – cousin of salafi leader from Kunar, Haji Rohullah. British allowed him to run 2002 poppy compensation scheme in Jalalabad

THE TRIBES OF EASTERN AFGHANISTAN

Ghilzai Pashtun
Ahmadzai
Khoghiani
Shinwari
Safi

IN NURISTAN:

Pashai (on the edge of Nuristan, and Kunar at a place called Dar-yi-Noor)
Parachi
Aroki
Gawarbati

ALONG THE BORDER:

Mohmand
Afridi
Utman Khel
Daoudzai
Mahmund
Bajouri

CHRONOLOGY

Year	Afghanistan
1973	**July:** King Zahir Shah overthrown by his 'modernising' cousin Daoud in a military coup.
1978	**April:** People's Democractic Party of Afghanistan takes power with a military coup (this becomes known as the 'Saur Revolution' and marks the end of two hundred years of Durrani dominance).
1979	**December:** Soviet troops invade Afghanistan.
1989	**February:** Soviet troops withdraw from Afghanistan.
1992	**February:** Abdul Haq convenes the 'Shura of the Commanders' in Chitral where mujahideen leaders agree to work together to secure the capital city. Massoud attends but neither Hikmatyar nor Sayyaf.
	April: The mujahideen commanders' accord is broken as General Massoud enters Kabul early and is made Minister of Defence on 5 May. Massoud and Hikmatyar's forces begin their assault on the city and the mujahideen government takes power amid continued fighting in Kabul. Disappointed with the inter-factional fighting now the Soviets have left, Abdul Haq quits Afghanistan.
1993	**February:** The Afshar massacre (of around seven hundred mostly civilian Shiites) is prosecuted in the Kabul district of Afshar alledgedly by the troops of Abdul Rasul Sayyaf and General Massoud.[5]
1994	**November:** Taliban capture Kandahar.
1995	**September:** Taliban capture Herat.

1996   **May:** Osama bin Laden, expelled from Sudan, returns to Afghanistan (where he had participated in the jihad between 1986– 89). He is apparently invited back by Abdul Rasul Sayyaf and is based at Chiparhar, in Nangarhar, which remains under Northern Alliance control until September.

September: Taliban capture Jalalabad and Herat.

2001   **September 11** attacks take place in the USA.

7 October: US-led bombing campaign of Afghanistan starts.

21 October: Abdul Haq leaves Peshawar and makes for Afghanistan.

24 October: Abdul Haq meets with Hisarak Talib commander

25 October: Arab Taliban forces converge on Tera Mangal and capture Abdul Haq.

26 October: Abdul Haq is executed by the Taliban.

13 November: Kabul falls to the Northern Alliance.

14 November: The UN Security Council agrees Resolution 1378 which mandates a 'transitional administration' for Kabul.

2–6 December: Offensive takes place at Tora Bora, from where Osama bin Laden 'disappears'.

5 December: The Bonn Conference takes place in Germany, after which it is announced that the Pashtun, Hamid Karzai, will head an 'Interim Authority' which will last until voting at an 'Emergency Loya Jirga'.

6 December: Kandahar falls.

2001   **20 December:** The UN authorizes the deployment of an 'International Security Assistance Force' (ISAF) to Kabul and its environs. Initially, ISAF comprises around 5000 soldiers.

2002   **April:** District and regional-level elections begin to select delegates who will attend the 'Emergency Loya Jirga'.

June: 'Emergency Loya Jirga' held in Kabul. It is set up to select the President of Afghanistan's 'Interim Authority',[6] election of the Cabinet, selection of the constitutional drafting committee, and decisions on the type of state Afghanistan will be. Its mandate will shape the state-building project for years to come.

2003   **December 2002–January 2004:** Constitutional Loya Jirga held in Kabul. It opts for a strong presidential system and a weaker parliament.

2004   **September:** Afghan presidential elections held in Kabul.

2005   **September:** Afghan parliamentary elections (This marks the end of the Bonn Process).

2009   US President Barack Obama commits an extra 34,000 US service personnel (including troops, engineers intelligence officers) to Afghanistan, bringing the total for coalition and NATO troops in Afghanistan to around 140,000 (and of US troops to around 113,000 troops; more than the USSR committed at the height of its engagement).

INTRODUCTION

Tera Mangal, Afghanistan, 25 October 2001

'*Al humdullilah*, we've caught the American and British agents!' they heard the man say in a thick, Arabic accent, and knew the Taliban were upon them. It was around ten pm and they were in the place named Tera Mangal, crouching on scree slopes dwarfed between slabs of vertical rock face which reached thousands of metres high.

Their Taliban captors moved out of the darkness and faced Abdul Haq.

Some minutes earlier, when the group first realised the Taliban were close, Haq had instructed his men to sit apart from one another so they would not all be seen. They had left their weapons back in Hezarac village after lunch with the elders and now had nothing with which to defend themselves. As early as that afternoon, when the Taliban were in each of the four narrow Passes that met high in the Hezarac valley, it had been obvious to them there was no way out of the narrow incline.

The steepness of the slope meant Haq had been forced to dismount the pony. He leant against the animal, breathing hard. Despite being known as the 'Lion of Kabul' for orchestrating tactically brilliant operations against the Soviet regime during the 1980s, tonight Abdul Haq seemed spent. The situation was clearly hopeless. He couldn't move fast and decided to give himself up before they saw the others.

The Arab cocked his Kalashnikov as the three other Talibs moved forward, their dark turbans momentarily silhouetted against the moon. They were nervous, undecided as to what they were about to do. Three had their arms held high, intending to stop the Arab firing.

'Move, go!' the Arab screamed as Abdul Haq stepped forward from the shadow, still holding the pony by its bridle.

'I need the pony, I can't walk without my prosthetic', Haq said and his voice, normally steady, wavered.

1

When I heard this story over three years later, in January 2005, I was told that the reason Haq could not walk was because his prosthetic was actually broken. He had lost his foot to a landmine during his quest to eject the Soviets from Afghanistan during the 1980s.

But that night in October 2001 the Talibs weren't listening. The pony was called for. He was helped onto the beast and led away, along with two of his commanders. Minutes later, thirteen shots were fired.

This was the capture of Abdul Haq as recounted to me, in Sarobi, by Aga Jan: the man who had been with him on this last mission, as well as countless others during the anti-Soviet jihad. There were varying accounts of what happened next. One was that Haq was tortured and shot in Rishicoor barracks in Kabul; the other, more credible, version was that a day later, the car carrying Haq from Hezarac reached Logar, on the outskirts of Kabul. A second vehicle – this one carrying the Taliban Interior Minister, Mullah Razzaq – sped towards it, from the city centre. And there, on a piece of tarmac in the open air, Razzaq grabbed a Kalashnikov from his bodyguard. Seconds later, the man Afghans knew as the 'Lion of Kabul' was shot dead.

**

On 5 October 2001, the London *Evening Standard* (see Appendix I) reported a veteran commander of the 1980s Soviet jihad calling for George Bush's imminent bombing campaign of Afghanistan to be delayed. The commander, whose name was Abdul Haq, needed time, he said, to implement his plan for an internal, peaceful toppling of the Taliban.

> 'Every time I meet commanders who cross the mountains in darkness to brief me', he said, 'they are part of the Taliban forces, but they no longer support them. These men will join us and there are many of them. When the time is right they and others will rise up and this Taliban Government will be swept aside'.[7]

Haq went on to add: 'The people are starving, they are already against them'.

But his voice, so authoritative when visiting Reagan and Thatcher to call for more support to the mujahideen during the Soviet war, was barely heard in the aftermath of September 11. The bombing started and Abdul Haq began his perilous mission. Two weeks later, on 25 October 2001, he was dead.

In November 2001, after his death, Abdul Haq's obituaries were dismissive, even overtly condemning. Not only was the manner of his death questioned but so too was his life and, implicit to that, his 'value'. When the *New York Times* described him demeaningly as 'a middle aged man on a mule'[8] or a 'privately financed freelancer trying to overthrow the Taliban'[9] the implication was that there should be nothing to regret about his loss. In London, an unattributed piece in *Private Eye* added snidely, 'Like so many erstwhile terrorists, Haq managed to reinvent himself as a "moderate" and a "peacemaker" – so successfully that his murderous exploits were entirely omitted from every single obituary'.[10]

Other pieces begged to differ and one, written by a cultural anthropologist and former US Diplomat to Afghanistan,[11] had a different take on the story:

> To hear them talk in Washington and Islamabad, you'd think there was some doubt. In fact, you'd think his death no great loss. Listen carefully. It's scared talk, the kind of stuff you hear from bureaucrats whose backsides are exposed.[12]

> Abdul Haq, they rush to insist, was on a mission of his own. Maybe he was, maybe he wasn't. Either way, it's shameful to demean him.

He added:

> There is some doubt about how the man died and where and when. We know he was 'questioned' and then executed. But was it by hanging with his body then used for swaying small-arms target practice, or was he shot in cold blood in a prison courtyard? It was in eastern Afghanistan – but Jalalabad or Kabul? It was two weeks ago – but late Thursday or early Friday? There's some doubt about who sent him

and who betrayed him. There could even be confusion about his name were it not so well known:

'Born Hamayoun Arsala 44 years ago, he became "Abdul Haq" – Servant of Justice – in the crucible of our Cold War's most decisive battleground'.[13]

***

As I finish writing this book, the Taliban has extended its control over large parts of both Pakistan and Afghanistan, both governments are weak and failing, and it looks as though the US and NATO will be facing strategic failure in the region.

President Obama's 'troop surge' and the strategy followed by the West in Afghanistan in 2010 remains broadly similar to that adopted at the outset in 2001.

Then, the US-led coalition provided financial and military support to the Taliban's traditional foe, the predominantly Tajik Northern Alliance which – since the killing by al Qaeda on 9 September 2001 of Commander Massoud – has been led by Mohammad Fahim. Prior to September 11, the Northern Alliance was an almost spent force, the Taliban having taken some ninety-five percent of the country.[14] I remember how in Kandahar during September 2000, the Taliban celebrated their capture of Taloqan – a city in the North East and deemed vital for the Northern Alliance supply pipeline – by removing the concrete barricades which had closed the road in front of the Taliban leader, Mullah Omar's, compound. Yet only a year later, in November 2001, when the US led coalition bombed the front line between the two sides, the Northern Alliance was able to take Kabul, the key 'power' ministries and, for a short time, the country.

Following the Bonn Agreement in December 2001 and the Emergency Loya Jirga in June 2002, the ethnic Pashtun Hamid Karzai became President. Karzai was essentially a figurehead to Northern Alliance warlords who were enabled to further consolidate their control over the machinery of state. For a while, there was peace of sorts but this quickly gave way to extreme corruption, a resurgence in opium production and eventually a breakdown in security. Seemingly defeated in late 2001, the Taliban only appeared to have 'melted away' and since 2003 their 'resurgence' has grown exponentially. Ironically they have exploited conditions similar to those which existed during their initial rise to power in 1995-6: popular discontent with the government's failure to provide jobs, security or justice, as well as a culture of impunity whose corollary has been widespread human rights violations. By 2009, the Taliban provided shadow governors and a parallel justice system in thirty-three out of Afghanistan's thirty-four provinces. Meanwhile the coalition has, in response, ramped up its military-based strategy with a 'surge' of 30,000 extra troops, bringing the overall number to over 200,000. There are also some 100,000 military contractors in Afghanistan.[15] Meanwhile the number of western troops killed in Afghanistan has increased relative to Iraq. And despite the $236 billion USD spent on Afghanistan by the US government by October 2009,[16] a successful endgame for the West looks increasingly unlikely.

The chief of US and NATO forces, General McKiernan, noted upon his departure from Afghanistan in spring 2009 that, 'ultimately, the solution in Afghanistan is going to be a political, not a military solution'.[17] And US General Michael Flyn said, 'Eight years into the war in Afghanistan, the vast intelligence apparatus is unable to answer fundamental questions about the environment in which US and Allied forces operate and the people they seek to persuade'.[18]

The West is floundering in Afghanistan and the prospect of strategic failure there by the coalition and NATO is today a very real proposition. The goalposts for withdrawal will be altered, leaving Afghanistan to its own fate. This will only empower those jihadists whom, in September 2001, we sought to overcome.

There is also now a tentative realisation that for a political solution to be durable it must also be 'internal': that is, arrived at and sustained by Afghans. Although the focus for the West's 'exit strategy' remains – in the absence of an effective political strategy – overly focused on building up the Afghan security forces, there is also talk of 'bottom up' governance at regional level. However, there is little real commitment to this, nor understanding of how to achieve it. Increasingly too, there is chatter about the need for a 'strong leader' who is able to work with all tribes, someone who has 'no blood on his hands'.

The idea that the 'war' to topple the Taliban in 2001 was a 'success' has only been challenged relatively recently. Many commentators often added that it was 'brilliantly executed'.[19] Afghanistan only failed, so the prevailing mantra went, because we went to Iraq. Sadly, this twin fallacy has obscured the root causes of why we have so comprehensively failed in Afghanistan.[20] And how the crucial mistakes were made at the *outset*, then compounded in 2002.

As I finished writing this book I attended a talk entitled 'Afghanistan–Pakistan: Mission Impossible?' in Geneva.[21] There, the Pakistani Ambassador to the UN stressed the need for the international community to utilise tribal structures to tackle instability in the region. But curiously, when I asked him whether today the Afghan situation might have been different had Abdul Haq not been ignored and subsequently killed soon after September 11, his reply indicated so much about what is at the heart of the problem. 'It was', so he said, 'the greatest tragedy that he [Abdul Haq] was sent on a mission by the CIA to Afghanistan to whip up support for a Pashtun government'.

This book is also an attempt to tackle some of the false 'narratives' which certain groups, countries, individuals or organisations have attempted to sustain – through conflation, misrepresentation or under-reporting of more complex nuances – about events, histories or individual stories. Often such narratives have sewn confusion in what is an extremely complex political situation. Sadly though, it is people and society, both in the West and where the conflict continues to take place, who continue to pay the price for this. Global security at large that will be undermined when the West eventually exits a far less stable and infinitely more complex Afghanistan than that they found in 2001.

This book is not really about Abdul Haq so much as about the strategy that the West *should* have followed in Afghanistan, the one we failed to take account of. For, as the Taliban Interior Minister told me, the Taliban killed him because 'everyone supported his plan in Khost, Paktia, Paktika'.

Thus, this book is also a first-hand witness account of some of the crucial facets of the West's post-September 11 Afghan intervention, intended for those who have an interest in why certain decisions are made and what the outcomes of those decisions can be. The book is written in narrative form because I take the reader to key events at which I was present. Many of these events became key turning points towards the outcome we see today.

The book's central thesis is the 'peace plan' which Commander Abdul Haq was working on when he was killed by the Taliban in October 2001. The book explores the reasons why Haq had warned repeatedly (in the aftermath of September 11) that the West should delay its imperative of bombing Afghanistan. And why Haq was thwarted in his attempt to put in place an 'internal' means of stabilising Afghanistan. I believe this is relevant both because of the enormous cost in both lives and treasure of the West's post-September 11 Afghan 'adventure' in Afghanistan. Also because of the failure to capture bin Laden at Tora Bora and now the likelihood of strategic failure by both NATO and the US-led coalition in Afghanistan. When one takes these costs into consideration, I believe that the story I have to tell is one that those groups who have recast the narrative to fit their own interests would rather you did not know about.

The book also tackles other related lines of enquiry: justice, impunity, Pakistan and the Pashtunistan issue, and the relevance of working with 'traditional' (i.e. tribal or quam based) structures to achieve lasting stability. On the issue of justice, I argue how the West's failure to indict former human rights abusers, instead making them its partners, has made Afghanistan a vastly complex theatre of operations characterised by a massive 'crisis of impunity'. It is now very difficult for Western forces operating within the country to know the difference between an insurgent, a Talib and a criminal drug dealer.

7

Other controversial issues dealt with in this account include: the fallacy of 'democracy' in a country where there is no rule of law; how the West essentially sold out Afghan women with its decision to use Northern Alliance warlords to conduct its war; how our intelligence agencies (principally the CIA and MI6) have failed to understand the most basic dynamics of this country, this region and the people who live there, thus pulling the West into a potentially interminable, unwinnable war whose 'objectives' change by the month.

Many of these problems had been written about by Abdul Haq in letters to Western leaders, sometimes as far back as the 1990s. These letters, most of which have never before been quoted, provide new insights into his thinking in the early 1990s, and are compelling particularly when one considers that he even warned of 'a cataclysmic event for the West' back in 1992.

This book is aimed at those with an interest in policymaking, whether that be military, diplomatic, humanitarian or peace negotiation. As far back as 2003, I remember an Afghan al Jazeera journalist commenting that, 'This is just a short interlude of peace in an otherwise ongoing civil war'. His words were prescient and today it appears that the West's 2001 military 'success' masked a military strategy that was more about emotion, fireworks, vengeance and Faustian alliances than about stabilising Afghanistan and building a viable state. A similar, apparently 'political' strategy was conceived at the Bonn Conference in December 2001. Some rather optimistically dubbed this a 'Peace Agreement'. It was not, for it did not include all parties to the conflict.

Despite the enormity of the West's costs in Afghanistan, and the increasing likelihood of failure, there has been a strange absence of interest in Abdul Haq and the 'solution' that he had conceived prior to September 11 for ejecting the Taliban and stabilising Afghanistan. Other Afghan commentators who have written about this 'solution' since 2001 have done so only fleetingly. Or worse, they have glossed over his role in working for an alternative to the Taliban in the years prior to September 11 (for which he paid with the murder of his wife and son in Peshawar in 1999).[22] Or they have mischaracterised his objectives; implying that Haq's objection to the US bombing of Afghanistan was limited to averting the bloodshed of civilians.[23] Or that he was simply trying to raise a force among the Ghilzai Pashtun, with the objective of avoiding a power vacuum in the east, where his family had been based.[24]

This book is about Abdul Haq's 'solution' in relation to: the history of the CIA and Pakistani ISI in the region; US and British intelligence weaknesses in 'Af-Pak' policy prior to and since September 11; the strategy and policies that were chosen 'instead' (many of which I participated in during the six years I spent in Afghanistan); the alternative 'Pashtun rebellion' option apparently provided by Hamid Karzai in the South; the consequences of ignoring the Haq 'solution' which include the West committing itself to an unwinnable war in Afghanistan and assisting the wider region to become a crucible of fundamentalist chaos.

Some may say that the relevance of Abdul Haq's story ended with his premature death at the hands of the Taliban in October 2001. I would not agree, firstly because I believe that history is important and also because it is only through knowing the past that we can understand the present. I also believe that if more of our strategists had understood the reasons why Abdul Haq was prepared to sacrifice his life to achieve this plan, then we might not have found ourselves in such an insoluble mess in Afghanistan today. With military strategists and Western politicians keen to find an internal solution for resolving the Afghan impasse, such that our troops can begin the drawdown, there will be renewed interest in the reasons why Abdul Haq was prepared to lose his life on the mission he attempted in 2001. And indeed, why he lost his life.

In Afghanistan, the storytellers' bazaar is notorious for its conspiracy theories and webs of inaccuracy. To wade through that, any serious researcher must 'triangulate' sources to obtain the most accurate picture possible.

I have felt it important to tell this story because Afghanistan is an enigma to so many Westerners who now have a stake in it: foreign civilians working there, military forces and their families, aid workers, diplomats and politicians. Today in Afghanistan, we are in a situation where, after eight years, we are still nowhere near what Winston Churchill defined during WWII as 'the end of the beginning'. This is a salutary lesson for those who as early as 2001 declared victory so prematurely. For, as the Duke of Wellington once remarked, 'The difficulties will begin where the military successes ended'. There are few who would argue this has not been the case in Afghanistan since the 2001 invasion to rout the Taliban.

But it did not have to be like that.

***

As the West was wondering how to be rid of the Taliban, the mantras chanted in unison by those charged with making policy after the September 11 attacks were that Abdul Haq – or 'Hollywood Haq' as he was dubbed by the Pakistani ISI, and ultimately the CIA and Britain's MI6) – 'does not have the wherewithal' and 'Abdul Haq has baggage'. Yet when the attacks of September 11 happened, Abdul Haq had for years been working with a group of commanders and tribal leaders around the former King. Their aim was for a peaceful toppling of the Taliban and a stabilisation of Afghanistan. By January 2001, Abdul Haq, who had been described as 'the legendary Pashtun commander',[25] felt the time was ripe.[26] By August 2001, he had pledges from his former jihadi commanders, many of whom were now strategically well placed within the Taliban, to move onto his side. He also had pledges from the King's group, the promise of defections by senior Taliban Ministers and Talib commanders in key strategic cities of the South and – at a historic meeting in Khoja Bauddin, Dushanbe, in July 2001 – this 'Pashtun hero of the war' met with Commander Massoud, otherwise known as 'the Tadjik hero of the war'[27] and they came to a 'mutually acceptable agreement'. Above all else, Haq desired a *united* Afghanistan and 'he was willing, if necessary, to be Massoud's deputy if that's what it took'.[28] [29]

He planned to implement his objective through consensus, through grass roots tribal unity and through tribal cohesion. His goal was, like Tzun Su over two thousand years ago, to avoid achieving his objectives through military force, with its unpredictable outcomes, if at all possible. Guile was a far superior weapon. And as a guerrilla leader in Kabul during the 1980s, he had used this plentifully, developing an underground network that had penetrated the Communist Army and civil service, targeting his attacks on power stations, munitions stores and key strategic outposts.

In the tribute piece written after his death, Whitney Azoy, an American anthropologist, outlined some of Haq's Olympian achievements:

> When the Soviets invaded in December 1979, he raided their convoys with, as one admirer puts it, 'little more than shotguns, deer rifles and dynamite'. He opened the first Resistance front on the immediate south and west of Kabul. Other brave commanders operated elsewhere; Abdul Haq would always concentrate on the capital city itself. He blew the Naghlu power station outside Kabul after months of meticulous preparation. He blew a seven level underground Soviet ammunition dump in nearby Paghman. The subsequent five-hour firestorm was famously videotaped 10 miles away from the roof of the British Embassy.

Azoy also indicated who his detractors were:

> In the holy war's aftermath, he helped organise a multi-party shura (committee of Resistance Commanders) in an attempt to avoid civil war. It wasn't because of Abdul Haq that such efforts failed. Look elsewhere for the culprits: among ambitious and self aggrandizing Afghan 'leaders' but even more among the Islamist cadres of Pakistan's ISI. While you're looking, ask yourself where the Americans were (ungratefully gone from the scene) and to whom America had entrusted Afghanistan's future (Pakistan's ISI).[30]

British cameraman Peter Jouvenal, who had covered Afghanistan from the early days of the Soviet intervention in the early 1980s, told me about the type of warfare conducted by Haq:

> His was a very different type of warfare, much more cunning and harder. Like the kidnap of a Russian advisor, not the firing of rockets. That's what made Abdul Haq special.[31]

This book looks at Haq's skills during the anti-Soviet jihad, particularly in Kabul where he conducted several operations believed ultimately to have shaped that war's outcome. It also revisits his candid criticism of the CIA's conduct of the jihad and how this led to his being vilified by both the CIA and ISI, and how that contributed to their assessment of his plan in the run up to and after September 11.

A key question under consideration in Afghan policymaking remains that of balancing power between the 'state', or centre, and the more traditional forms of governance provided locally. In Afghanistan during the 1970s, 'the centre was strong enough to maintain law and order, but it was never strong enough to undermine the autonomy of the tribes'.[32] It was in recognition of this state of affairs that Haq – who was from a leading tribal family or *khan khel*) – hoped to achieve his plan.

Although there has been some replacement of traditional village elders with jihadi ones, essentially not much has changed since the late nineteenth- century when the British General Sir Henry Rawlinson observed:

> The nation consists of a mere collection of tribes, of unequal power and divergent habits, which are held together, more or less loosely, according to the personal character of the chief who rules them. The feeling of patriotism, as known in Europe, cannot exist among Afghans, for there is no common country.[33]

This book aims to show what remains an enigma to most foreigners involved with Afghanistan. It takes the reader directly to the tribes and to the people who would have implemented Haq's plan. The same people the West must learn to work with if there is to be any hope of stabilising Afghanistan.

An underlying theme of this book then is the importance of finding Afghan solutions to the conflict. Afghanistan is a far more complex arena than Iraq, predominantly because it remains a largely traditional, tribal society which has never had properly functioning state institutions. Although much of the tribal means of governance has been fragmented by thirty years of war, it is still to the tribes that rural Afghans, particularly those in the south, continue to look for direction. Networks in the north, if not so tribal, remain largely 'clannish' in nature. Abdul Haq understood the importance of using the tribes – particularly the Pashtun tribes in the border areas and the south, which is the main hotbed of the insurgency – as a bulwark against the re-emergence of the Taliban from across the border in Pakistan.

Unfortunately, since September 11, Western policy in Afghanistan has been predominantly kinetic. Where alliances have been forged, they have tended towards the paying off strongmen willing to do the West's (or CIA's) bidding. The idea of building relationships through 'traditional' power structures (as opposed to 'tribal militias') has been an anathaema. The tribute piece by the American anthropologist continued:

> We don't know for sure what happened when Abdul Haq left Peshawar two weeks ago and crossed into Afghanistan. There are too many unknown details, many doubts about the official story. Just who was with him? Just what promises had been made and by whom? Just who betrayed him to the Taliban and why? We don't know – just yet. Inshallah (the Muslim for 'God Willing'), we'll get to that.[34]

Within weeks of Haq's death the war moved on, Kabul was taken and – in the tribulation and back-patting following that occasion – Abdul Haq and his warnings were soon forgotten.

***

I spent the greater part of six years living in Afghanistan. At the height of the Taliban regime, I ran community and urban reconstruction projects, the precursor to what is now known as the National Solidarity Programme (NSP),[35] in Kandahar and Herat. I lived, somewhat foolishly, under the threat of a fatwa against British and Americans issued by bin Laden. So when al Qaeda bombed the USS Cole, at Aden in October 2000, I left Kandahar for Quetta, crossing the Registan desert by taxi.

I returned to the region in the aftermath of September 11, eagerly naive to assist in the country's planned transition to democracy, working in a number of capacities: for the World Food Programme; as an election monitor for the initial 'democracy building phase' with the 2002 Loya Jirga; as a researcher on transitional justice for the International Crisis Group; as a monitor on the currency exchange project and as a freelance journalist. By late 2004, I was Political Advisor to the EU Special Representative and then to the Chief Observer on the 2005 parliamentary elections.

This book records what I saw in Afghanistan between 2000 and 2006, from the regime of the Taliban to the end of the formal implementation of the Bonn Process, a critical period. As the West's immediate post-September 11 'success' quickly unfurled, so I became more interested in the reasons why Haq had risked his life on this apparently doomed mission.

Abdul Haq was one of eight brothers who during the jihad were dubbed 'Resistance Royalty' by journalists. Mostly, the sobriquet arose from their charisma and individual effectiveness as commanders in fighting the anti-Soviet guerrilla war of the 1980s. But as *khan khel* (chief clan) of the Ghilzai Pashtun, the family also had a long history and relationship with the tribes of Afghanistan's four eastern provinces.

I was led to Haq's family, the Arsalas, by another journalist in September 2002 when researching a story on poppy production. Their base, Jalalabad, is on the trade route between Peshawar and Kabul, considered one of the foremost poppy-growing areas of Afghanistan. By 2002, Western diplomats dubbed the Arsalas 'warlords', considered them lynchpins in the drugs trade and failed to work with them in hunting down bin Laden at the battle of Tora Bora. The Tora Bora were the caves from which bin Laden had escaped in November 2001 and which the Arsala family knew intimately, having built them two decades before, as a base from which to fight the Soviets. Within fifteen years, the family's status had evolved from 'Resistance Royalty' to pariah.

For some reason, however, they trusted me. Between September 2002 and the end of 2005, I was invited in, taken into their confidence and allowed to stay in their houses for weeks at a time. I travelled to Kunar and Nuristan, to the drug smuggling bazaars of the Shinwar and the smuggling depots of the tribal areas. My friendship with them took me deep into the politics of the Pashtun belt, giving me an understanding of Afghanistan far removed from the Powerpoint presentations of the soldiers and diplomats among whom I later worked in Kabul. I witnessed the inter-warlord rivalries and Western intelligence mistakes that had led directly to Osama bin Laden's escape from Tora Bora. I also learnt the intricacies of rebuilding traditional structures of local governance, of smuggling, poppy and how the issue of 'Durand' – the historic difficulties over the border between Afghanistan and Pakistan – lay at the root of Pashtun nationalism and Pakistani politicking over Afghanistan. I was granted access to this family and to the tribal people of the Eastern Provinces that bore no relation to the lives of most foreigners living in the international compounds in Kabul. Possibly they trusted me because they knew I was there with an interest in their family, their history, in Abdul Haq and his role in the anti-Soviet jihad and in the Pashtun people. But also in how this tribal society worked and how it would react to the 'democracy' that the West was, nominally, delivering to Afghanistan. On the family's side, when I met them they were still reeling from the killings of both Haq and Qadir and had been sidelined by the West. I still wonder if it was for all these reasons that they allowed me access to their side of the story.

This book is both a temporal journey and an awakening about what is really shaping Afghanistan. In relation to this, I have explored the parallel 'private' US and UK efforts to find support for Haq in 2001, and have uncovered information about what was happening – primarily in the intelligence community but also among Afghan players – in the run up to and the months following September 11. This information is in the book but not yet in the public domain.

On the US side were two American brothers, James and Joe Ritchie, who had made their money as Chicago options traders but who remained impassioned by the country in which they had spent much of their childhood. For years they had financed a series of Loya Jirga outside Afghanistan, in an attempt to formulate an alternative to the Taliban. Ultimately they decided that Abdul Haq and the banner of the King provided the best means of toppling the Taliban regime.

Meanwhile, on the UK side, an independent effort to find support for Haq was being made by three former military men who had experience in 1980s Afghanistan. One had been a renowned Head of the British Special Boat Service (reforming it in the run up to the Falklands War), another was an ex-Marine who had covered Afghanistan extensively as a cameraman during the jihad and the third was an ex-Rhodesian army officer and Guardsman, a British Baronet who had also covered the Afghan War. They hoped – in vain as it turned out – to get British intelligence agencies to take Abdul Haq seriously.

Their stories mesh with those of Haq's former mujahideen commanders (many of whom had become 'Taliban'), members of the 'Rome' group (representing those Afghans and tribal leaders willing to unite beneath the banner of the former King), UN political staff, ambassadors, senior Taliban ministers, and tribal leaders.

The book draws upon previously unpublished letters, plans, sitreps[36] and faxes relating to Haq's plan and both US and UK efforts to find support for him within the CIA and MI6. There are also letters written by Haq to Western leaders during the early 1990s when Haq was attempting to warn – among other things - of the unchecked radicalisation taking place amongst 'foreign fighters' in the tribal areas.

As far back as 2001, I recognised that Abdul Haq provided answers to questions that – nine years into the current intervention in Afghanistan – are only beginning to be posed. Hence it is through Abdul Haq's story that I aim to explain the present by exploring the past, indicating where the mistakes were made and which route those with an interest in stabilisation for Afghanistan should be heading towards.

The book also raises related questions. For example, when did the US 'select' Hamid Karzai and why? Was there ever an intention to deliver democracy and rights for women to Afghanistan? Why did the West opt to subvert justice and accountability for a 'peace' with Afghan warlords that could never be sustained? The question is of prime importance, as twice now in their spectacular rise to power the Taliban have shown their version of Shariat to be a preferable alternative to the anarchy of the warlords. The re-ascendance of the warlords has probably done most to alienate ordinary Afghans from the West's intervention and impede the formation of a viable state.

Yet Abdul Haq foresaw the problems associated with the warlords taking power as far back as 1991 when – in a letter to the Saudi Ambassador in Islamabad – he prophecied:

> If these radical Mujahidin elements take power in Afghanistan, there will be war forever. There will be no peace and security, and we Afghan people will have to beg for food and support for the rest of our lives. From the other side, people will come to hate the names of Mujahidin and Jihad throughout the world, and think that the word means only killing, destruction, disunity and terrorism. It will destroy the image of Mujahidin and Jihad. Moreover, the students and guests of these radical elements will find many supporters in your country and, if not take full power, still engage in atrocities and chaos. This is neither good for you, nor for us, nor for Islam.[37]

In the aftermath of the 2009 presidential elections, this scenario looks to have taken hold. The opportunity of bringing these men to justice was ignored in 2001, when instead the West made them its allies in removing the Taliban. The result is what we see today.

After beginning this book I found myself talking to a former SIS man in Lamu, Kenya. His view of Abdul Haq seemed to typify that of the British (and indeed US) intelligence establishments when he said: 'He was dead within a couple of weeks so what did it matter?' With both Afghanistan and Pakistan now failing, causing attendant problems for the entire world, this book is about why it did indeed matter.

CHAPTER ONE

THE 'PEACE VERSUS JUSTICE' STRATEGY

The Tigers of Wrath are wiser than their Horses of Instruction

WILLIAM BLAKE

Kabul, June 2002

The evening was still and the dust had settled, now replaced by a light of such crystalline luminescence that the Mausoleum of King Amanullah stood like a cutout on its ridge above the city. On the other side of town, last-minute preparations for the Grand Assembly of Elders, known here as a Loya Jirga, were coming to an end. The buildings of Kabul's 1970s-style polytechnic had been steadily refurbished: glass puttied into shattered windows, fountains reconnected to water, coats of paint brushed over the strafe marks of machine-gun fire, landmines cleared from the long grass between dorms, piles of mouldering excrement swept from lecture theatres whose last residents had been Arab Talibs.

The delegates who would participate in the Loya Jirga had been elected in their districts and regions, and their thoughts were now pregnant with the responsibility of selecting Afghanistan's new President and the Cabinet of the country's transitional government. There was a distinct feeling that a new era of peace was about to dawn over Afghanistan, after twenty-three miserable war years. Despite some of the problems with bribery and intimidation in the first phase of the elections, the process overall had been fairly democratic and UN workers had expressed pride in achieving the election of over a thousand people[38] across Afghanistan.[39]

This Loya Jirga – the first Grand Assembly of Elders to be held here in twenty years – was the first step in the Bonn Process. The Bonn Process was the roadmap, agreed in November 2001, between the international community and a select group of Afghans (some now say too select) for the state-building and democratisation of

Afghanistan. It was not strictly a 'peace plan' because it failed to include all parties to the conflict, namely the Taliban.[40]

The tent where the Assembly would be held sat white and huge on the highest level of the site, dazzling in the sun against the ochres of the mountainside. The Germans had brought it from Munich, where it had been the principal beer tent at the Ocktoberfest, something the more conservative Afghan leaders coming here tomorrow would probably not be happy to know.

The screams cut through the still evening. A fellow election worker, an American, scurried up the steps shrieking that there were 'gunmen' on the site-level beneath us.

A UN political colleague walked towards us. When he heard gunmen had entered the site, his brow furrowed and he shook his head, storming away uttering expletives. His anger, so out of character for a man who was one of the 'elders' of the monitors – he had spent some twenty-five years in Afghanistan running aid projects for a Nordic organisation – was unexpected. Despite his seniority, it was obvious there was an undercurrent or an agenda of which even he was unaware.

Below us, ordinary Afghans – men and women, old and young – streamed quietly towards a large open-sided Indian *chamiana* tent with a carpeted floor. All seemed innately proud to have been elected; serious about the task they had come here to undertake: the 're-birth of their nation' in selecting its new government, and also serious about reconstructing Afghanistan after years of bloodshed and war.

However, something they had not foreseen was unfolding. Three shining black Landcruisers, codan masts still swinging after a high-velocity arrival, were parked on the level below us, surrounded by armed men. Through their open doors it was possible to see a stash of RPGs and Kalashnikovs; all strictly banned on the site. The Loya Jirga's atmosphere, so hopeful even within the past hour, was now bloating with latent violence, like a balloon filling with water until reaching bursting point, unleashing its force without being checked.

These Landcruisers had just borne some of Afghanistan's most ignominious characters into the heart of the site and – though we did not yet know it then – into the heart of the state-building project. Now milling at the edge of the *shamiana* was Prof (Ustad) Rabbani, a thin man who, though no shia, wore an Iranian-style turban. He had been Afghanistan's President during Kabul's 1992–94 'terror'. Behind was Fahim, who looked to me almost gangster-like and was scowling. A former Afghan female colleague who had taken me to visit the World Food Programme's widows' bakery programme in January 2002 had explained the significance of the Northern Alliance to the people of Kabul when I had commented naively that with Massoud's poster plastered around Kabul, people must feel a sense of relief in this new, post-Taliban era. She had reacted with passionate fury.

'These are *not* our people, they are from the Panjshir, *not* here. The people of Kabul *hate* Massoud because of what he did to us ten years ago! And of all Afghan factions, Massoud's soldiers were the worst!' But surely, I asked, these men were better than the Taliban? 'No', she replied, 'at least with the Taliban, we knew what the rules were!' She wanted to know why the West had made Fahim Defence Minister. Didn't we realise he was a terrorist' who had executed *thousands* of people when he was head of the KHAD? Taken them out to the airfield where they were killed? Her reaction unsettled me, particularly as she herself had been imprisoned by the Taliban just weeks before September 11, for contravening some rule.

Kabul's airport had desolate, open land around it. You could kill a lot of people there with no one watching. This evening though, the warlords continued filing into the *shamiana* to take their seats. Behind Fahim came Sayyaf. Then there was the thickset, bullish General Dostum.

A couple of women, no doubt emboldened by the atmosphere of intense international interest now in Afghanistan and believing that the rules precluded those with a history of human rights abuses from participating in the Loya Jirga itself,[41] unfurled questions at the strongmen like small arms fire. In short, why were the warlords, those responsible for destroying the country, here? The men stared back unflinchingly. Another woman challenged Rabbani to explain what had happened in Badakhshan for he had apparently bribed his way into a seat by buying votes with fake money printed by the Russians ten years before. As he attempted some explanation, there were peels of laughter from the women. A fellow election monitor, Amy, the daughter of an eye doctor brought up in Afghanistan during the Afghan civil war, was incredulous, having never witnessed Afghan women challenge those who had terrorised them. But at this stage the women – and I – still believed that the international community had come to Afghanistan in the wake of September 11 not just to rout al Qaeda, but to protect these women from the abuses to which they had been subjected for so long. Perhaps that is why they believed they had the ability to hold these men publicly to account. It was a defining moment for them. But it stopped right here. The warlords sat and faced the crowd defiantly and the uncharacteristic reaction of my colleague Nils was my first indication that all was not okay.

I decided to leave. But at the gate, British ISAF soldiers, virtually incoherent with tension, said the warlords had forced their way in. 'Put a fucking gun to the head of one of our lads', one of them spewed, his voice tingling with nerves. 'He was tellin' 'em they couldn't come in 'ere with them guns or cars, but the driver slammed down his accelerator and burst through the cordon. Fuck, this is fucking crazy', he screeched.

Outside in the car park scores of Hilux jeeps, laden with armed men, surged back and forth, like wild horses in a coral throwing up a miasma of dust. I dodged to avoid them, feeling intensely visible and alienated from this display of undiluted, aggressive testosterone. My elderly driver, Jan Mohammad, sat quietly at the far end of the car park, hunched over the wheel. He looked worried and, putting the car into first gear, commented that this perplexing, superfluous display of strength by the bodyguard militias of the warlords who had come to Kabul from the provinces was *bistiar gharrab* or 'very bad'.

We drove to the Intercontinental where I had arranged to meet a friend, a *Newsweek* journalist. The press corps were gathered there in a gloomy interior awaiting a press conference and my friend was re-capping with his interpreter the events of that afternoon. 'Khalilzad[42] must be out of his mind' he stormed, 'Why the *hell* make such a public display of US interference? He could at *least* have let the King say it himself?'

He was talking about a last-minute press conference which journalists had been called to attend. There, the US Ambassador, the Afghan-born Zulmay Khalilzad, had strutted menacingly up and down. Looking on were the UN chief, Lakhdar Brahimi and Hamid Karzai (who was nominally titled 'President' of the Afghan Interim Authority). But most surprisingly, in a quiet corner cowered Afghanistan's former King, Zahir Shah. The press corps were unaware why they had been called here until Khalilzad, raven-dark eyes scanning the crowd, exhorted, 'The King will *not* be running against Karzai as Head of State'.

He had apparently spun on his heels to face the press corps. An impregnable silence had fallen over the room. A protegée of Condoleeza Rice and Member of the Rand Corporation, Khalilzad had worked for UNOCAL, an American petroleum company that for years had courted the Taliban in an attempt to build a pipeline across Afghanistan.

The former King, now eighty-three years old, had seemed defenceless to the journalists. When he had returned to Afghanistan the previous week, ending twenty-nine years of exile, Afghans had gathered around ancient television screens in anticipation of his words. The older generation remembered his peaceable forty-year rule with fondness, and so it had been a momentous occasion to see him reach the bottom of the airplane steps on his walking stick. A microphone had been put in front of him, he had opened his mouth to speak and ... the sound system cut out. King Zahir Shah had mouthed words into nothingness and Afghans heard nothing of his sentiments about returning to the country of his birth after twenty-nine long years.

The relevance of the ex-King had become obvious to me days

earlier on Chicken Street where Afghans sold knickknacks and carpets. An elderly man stepped forward from a doorway to greet me and another election monitor. We were invited into his shop where Uzbek saddle bags, small rugs and old Gardener teapots were stacked. The frail old man offered tea, which my colleague accepted as we continued the discourse. The mood turned wistful: the man had tears in his eyes. Perry conversed with him in *dari* and explained that the man was happy to see foreigners again and that the last thirty years had been a time of pain for Afghanistan. Everything was okay until King Zahir Shah left, then things had become very black. King Zahir Shah emanated from Afghanistan's elite Mohammadzai clan of the Durrani Pashtun, rulers of Afghanistan since 1747. He had come to power in 1933 and presided over forty years of peace. It was only when his ambitious cousin, General Dauod, deposed him in 1973, while the King was in Italy for eye surgery, that things began to go wrong. Although Daoud had 'modernising' intentions, his was the first in a series of coups which would eventually plunge the country into war. I thought of what the old man must have seen in the years between Zahir Shah's departure and now: several changes of government and ideology, the arrival of the Russians, a ten year jihad to eject them, then chaos as the various factions vied for power before the Taliban arrived. At our guesthouse, during breakfast table conversations between Nils and the journalists, it seemed there was still hope the King would be brought back and Nils said:

> He would be a useful symbol, a banner beneath which opposing factions could unite, in memory of better days. Certainly the older generation are keen for this. Afghanistan is a very conservative society. The King could provide the glue that's needed. Better than religion.

Nils had explained that the problems would begin *after* the Loya Jirga. For it was doubtful the 'Three Musketeers' – Fahim the Defence Minister, Qanooni the Interior Minister and Dr Abdullah the Foreign Minister – could all stay in the key ministries. All three were originally from the Panjshir valley, so could not all feasibly stay in power. Fahim should step down but that would be difficult;

24

he was now the most powerful man in the country.

'The Panjshiris stepped into the corridors of power, taking over Kabul from its inhabitants, without the rest of the country getting a look in', Nils explained to the journalists, adding that Fahim had ensured the ministries were staffed by Panjshiris loyal to him. Hence the chiefs of Intelligence and Security are both from Fahim's village in the Panjshir. Fahim was also supported by Russia, Iran and the US, who needed to decide whether they preferred using him for their 'war on terror' or whether they preferred a truly democratic Loya Jirga. The latter would be better for Afghanistan's stability.

An American journalist commented that surely the shura-e-Nazar 'deserved' to take Kabul, having routed the Taliban on behalf of the West? I should perhaps explain that Shura-e-Nazar was the name given by Massoud to his mainly Panjshiri-led 'Council of the North', a sub-set of the Northern Alliance and comprising members of Professor Rabbani's Jamiat-e-islami Party. Throughout Kabul in the run-up to the Loya Jirga, the Shura-e-Nazar' were buying off votes in some areas, intimidating in others and generally working to control the elections. In response to the journalist's question, Nils sighed and asked them whether giving all the power to people from a valley representing less than five percent of the land area of the country was really sustainable? Afghanistan, he said, could easily end up like a federation, with the Panjshiris controlling Kabul. The problems would come when they tried to extend their influence into other areas. Then there would be fighting, and Pakistan, as well as neighbouring countries, would begin meddling again and things would get very bad.

***

The *Newsweek* journalist's comments about Khalilzad's bizarre behaviour at the press conference on the eve of the Loya Jirga, and its probable connection with the warlords' subsequent violent arrival at the Loya Jirga site was now obvious. Most of these strongmen had returned rather haltingly from exile to Afghanistan, in the wake of the Taliban's recent departure. The view of the UN political staff, who had come into contact with warlords and strongmen in the spring of 2002 during elections for the Loya Jirga, was that many of those who had returned would be subject to some sort of accounting by the international community for the abuses they had committed during the civil war of the early 1990s.[43] But this was not to be.

The following day Amy told me that after my departure those women who had dared criticise the warlords 'were intimidated to silence by *Amniyat*'.[44] *Amniyat* was another name for the Afghan 'intelligence' police, also known as KHAD[45] (Khedamat-e-Ettela'at-e-Dowlati) after the Soviet-style state security apparatus built up during the 1980s. *Amniyat* was made up of the sunglasses-wearing men who had attended the pre-Loya Jirga elections in Kabul with notepads, apparently to record potential troublemakers at the Loya Jirga.

How these security / intelligence men had actually entered the Loya Jirga site, which was supposed to have been secured, was perplexing. Only when we saw Engineer Arif, the Panjshiri chief of *Amniyat*, who was standing at the top of the site, did it become obvious that their presence was 'official'. Arif stood imperiously, with heavy-lidded eyes and radio in hand, directing his slick-suited minions around what was supposed to be a sealed meeting for the democratically elected delegates.

These men were loyal to General Fahim, now the most powerful man in the country.[46] Earlier in the year, he had awarded himself the title of 'Marshall' and today his intelligence police came to the Loya Jirga armed with Polaroid cameras, video cameras and the threat of later retribution for 'troublesome' delegates.

The UN chief, Lakhdar Brahimi, responded to the disquiet of the election monitors by saying, 'Tell them to go!' This was transmitted – rather imperiously – via an aide. Those of us who wished to stay, so the message was relayed, could do so, but we must be content simply to monitor the intelligence police; however we were 'on no account' to interfere in their behaviour.

Looking back at what has happened – and what flowed from

this event in June 2002 – it seems obvious that, as election monitors charged with protecting the integrity of the democratic process, we should, at that stage, have walked out. Although it was obvious that something was very wrong, I myself was not yet fully aware of the significance of what was going on. Perhaps, I thought naively, a larger and more purposeful plan for peace and stability was unfolding. But many of the monitors, particularly those who had spent more time in Afghanistan, as former aid workers, diplomats and writers during the anti-Soviet jihad, were very aware. One UN colleague had even quit prior to the Loya Jirga, telling Brahimi that he could not agree with the lack of representation of Pashtun elders from the south (for the UN had apparently deemed that they would be too closely associated with the Taliban).[47] For the rest of us, it was only when the Loya Jirga had finished that we could assess what had happened in the cool light of day.

This morning I was to check that *Amniyat* were not hassling the women in their dorms. There were reports they had even been into the rooms; a surprising contravention of Afghan culture. Outside the concrete building was a huddle of women, and amidst them a former Afghan colleague, Dr Massouda Jalal. She asked why *Amniyat* were present. Masouda was not just any woman. For several months, she had been preparing her campaign to stand against Karzai as Head of State. When she had first told me I hadn't quite believed her. But it was her firm belief that if women played a greater role in politics, much of the fighting might be averted. She was nervous. An intelligence officer stood close to her robes, bent over taking notes in a scruffy notebook. She told me it was difficult for her to talk because he would report on her.

Six months earlier, a meeting with the Women's Minister, Dr Sima Samar, had foreshadowed how things were going to unfold for Afghan women. It was a day sharp with cold, in January 2002 just eight weeks after the Taliban were routed from Kabul, and I had taken some Irish donors to meet some of the new Ministers. We had gone to Samar's office which was then in a Kabul suburb, Wazir Akbar Khan.

Samar looked vulnerable, sitting on a 1950s sofa and huddled in a black overcoat. The *chekhov* style stove did little to assuage the blistering cold rising from a concrete floor in the women's NGO. After six weeks as Minister, she complained that she still had no office. The son of Ismael Khan, Governor of Herat, had taken over the building reserved for her. The act was symbolic; for despite her being a Minister now he was a strongman and she did not matter. She said that she needed an independent place, so women could come without feeling harassed. Despite representing fifty-five percent of the population, women were still at risk, and in need of lawyers to take up their cases, as well as women's shelters.

A Hazara by origin, she had a reed-fine face, short dark hair and laughter lines around the eyes. She had just returned from Washington DC with the other new Ministers. She told me:

> In Washington, George Bush put his arm around me and said, 'Don't worry Sima, we are watching to see that the women of Afghanistan will be okay'. But the other ministers were watching him.

Behind her words was a degree of isolation, a plea for us to recognise that, despite the renewed interest in Afghanistan's women following September 11, an automatic progression in women's rights should not be taken for granted.

Samar somehow resembled Audrey Hepburn: was it the oversized coat, the cropped hair, or her slightness? Yet there was an underlying determination in her tone. She said she had been threatened on the plane back from Washington by the other ministers, who were asking her why she was trying to Westernise Afghan women? Now, here with me, she slapped the table and said:

> But I'm not asking for abortion rights. If I say 'access to education', is it Western? The *only* way we can change society is via education. Illiterate women think they are the *property* of men. We need equality, not privilege.

The Irishmen nodded sympathetically as she added that the big challenges in Afghanistan were education and employment. She wanted to give women skills so they were empowered. But it was important that the international donors act in a way that did not make the situation worse. She related an example of what irritated her about the weakness of donors in the face of the plight of Afghan women. A year ago the Taliban had announced that women and men should have separate hospitals. She was infuriated by the response of international donors, because the World Health Organisation (WHO) had agreed with the Taliban to 'build a *separate* hospital!' Samar said she believed that this had happened because the head of WHO was a Muslim, and added that when the Taliban closed girls' schools, UNICEF responded by closing boys' schools. 'It gave the Taliban the opportunity to *make* boys go to the madrassahs!'

Samar looked tensely into her teacup before going on:

> Even Karzai was scared to push women's issues: 'He's concerned other leaders will not tolerate progress. So donors *must* make aid money conditional upon women's rights being incorporated into projects'.[48]

The Irish donors, who would have several million pounds to spend on Afghan reconstruction, leant towards her, transfixed. But then she was off the issue of 'conditionality' and onto the problem of appointing fundamentalists to senior positions. She had protested angrily to Karzai about his appointment of the new Chief Justice: 'I had a *big* fight with Karzai about this; the man is almost Mullah Omar. How then could he protect women's rights or make changes?'

The men nodded sagely as she moved onto her third major issue: appointing unindicted former mujahideen to senior positions. In particular Mohammad Fahim, the Defence Minister, was 'also a problem', she hissed.

> In the Defence Ministry, they have ten Generals but seven are Tajiks, two are Pashtuns and one is Uzbek. None are Hazara. Yet it was Fahim himself who gave the names to the British government. He chose his people. How *could* the British accept this? You know in Cabinet each day the leaders say they will appoint people on the basis of the Resistance rather than education.

The Afghan 'Resistance' were those who had fought the Soviets during the 1980s. Many came from rural areas and were known as 'mujahideen'. Some Resistance leaders formed factional groups, normally on the basis of ethnicity. Their leaders, men who oversaw many commanders and dealt with foreign donors to the war, were usually called warlords. Energised with anger, Samar went on, 'But I was also part of the Resistance, only *I* did not kill anyone! And who bombed the West of Kabul? *These* men!'

One of the Irishmen finally spoke, asking for an explanation of the pictures of Massoud now pasted up on lamp posts across Kabul. The Iranians, she said, had printed seven metric tonnes of posters of Massoud and the Panjshiris were putting them up all over, 'even at a womens' conference!'

Today, at the Loya Jirga, some six months later, Sima Samar, who had initially been appointed as one of the three Joint Chairman found herself effectively sacked by Karzai. The warlords were apparently unhappy with her appointment.[49]

Leaving the Loya Jirga site that day, I saw an ISAF soldier arguing with an officer of *Amniyat*. Perhaps the soldier might have been forgiven for assuming that the intelligence men, loyal as they were to Fahim, had no business being here. But evidently no one had briefed him that Mr Kar Sym Yar, now effectively Chairman of the Loya Jirga, had received a visit from the head of *Amniyat* and several Panjshiri gunmen on the eve of the meeting, the same evening the warlords had forced their way inside the site. Kar Sym Yar had then been forced to sign an 'agreement' stating that the 'security' of the Loya Jirga was no longer in the hands of the international community, but in the hands of the Panjshiri dominated intelligence police.

***

When the Loya Jirga finally began the next day, it had been delayed by further private meetings between the US, the UN and the warlords or 'mujahideen leaders' as they now preferred to be called. The term was a reminder of their more glorious past, when they had dispatched the Russians, before turning on each other in bloody inter-ethnic conflict, laying waste to vast tracts of Kabul and to the civilian population.

Today they arrived in their glory; in strings of black Landcruisers whistling through the site, laden with guards and ammunition. Taking their seats they were recognisable by their head-dress: the Tadjik 'Lion of Herat', Ismael Khan, wore his trademark *keffiyah*; the Pashtun Governor of Jalalabad, Haji Qadir, looked monarchical in a gold turban; Dostum, the Uzbek leader of the north, wore a sharp Soviet-style suit and was accompanied by a bodyguard with a crew cut. Finally, the Pashtun Abdur Rassul Sayyaf was crowned with a vast white turban. They sat together in the front row of the meeting, united in their audacity. Behind sat the democratically elected delegates, now hushed to silence by the presence of those who had terrorised them during the civil war years within the past decade.

Most of the Loya Jirga Commission had wanted to disbar Sayyaf's candidacy because of his human rights record, particularly his brutal campaign against the Shia in Kabul during the early 1990s.[50] But as he took his seat regally a colleague whispered, 'After the first phase of the election he invited all the candidates for dinner and threatened to slit their throats if they didn't vote for him in the final phase'. Quoting William Blake, he added, 'The tigers of wrath are wiser than their horses of instruction'.

But who were their masters? Ourselves? The Americans? The United Nations? Sayyaf wasn't just any warlord with blood on his hands; he had opened the University of Dawal al-Jihad in the tribal areas of Pakistan using a large donation from bin Laden in 1980. It became a training school for extremists,[51] men recruited from across the Islamic world. The terrorists Omar Sheikh and Khaled Sheikh Mohammad, responsible for the kidnap and killing of American journalist Danny Pearl and involvement in both World Trade Centre attacks respectively were reputed to have spent time there and one former student even set up Abu Sayyaf,[52] taking Sayyaf's name in honour.

A week into the Loya Jirga, former King Zahir Shah was to make a speech. The delegates waited expectantly to hear the words they had missed when Zahir Shah's microphone had so mysteriously cut as he had stepped off his plane from Rome. The great tent was bathed in silence as the terrapin-like former King moved slowly towards the podium. At last on it, he gathered himself up to speak. His lips moved but his words were lost in the vast depths of the great tent. As the old King mouthed his words the delegates leant forward, straining to catch them. But oddly, the microphone which had worked perfectly just minutes before, had gone dead. It was the second time within a month. Again, King Zahir Shah's moment had passed, silently. Afghanistan's people were sorely disappointed.

As the days dragged on and the candidates sat silently in the tent, the real business of the Loya Jirga – the horse-trading – was being conducted without their involvement in a small tent marked 'VIPs only'. There, Karzai, the warlords, the US Special envoy and the UN chief Lakhdar Brahimi remained for much of the two week meeting, returning only periodically to the main tent after agreements on (unknown) key issues had been made. At the back of the tent an American Embassy staffer whispered, 'The Panjshiris are already handing out cards saying "Afghan Transitional Authority". Like they already know they'll be the new government'.

***

The die was cast for Afghanistan's future a day later at the Loya Jirga. The Shiite Ayatollah Asif Muhseni[53] called on delegates to re-name the country the 'Islamic Transitional State of Afghanistan'. In unison with Muhseni's suggestion Sayyaf swept to his feet, punching the air as his robes gathered around his legs. 'Everyone must stand to signal his approval for the motion!' Sayyaf shouted and the two front rows of mujahideen, including Karzai, rose quickly, eyes darting left and right, shouting 'right!' and 'Allah e akbar'. To be seen with your bottom still on a seat when an issue with 'religious' connotations was being debated was to invite persecution. But behind the mujahideen, ordinary delegates rose reluctantly, many forced into doing so by the intelligence police who swept the tent from behind. Incredibly, there was a lone voice of opposition from the warlords: Kandahar's jowly Governor Gul Agha Sherzai rose from his seat, wiping a bead of perspiration from below his black and grey turban: 'I think we've had enough war since twenty-five years ago in the name of Islam'. Undeterred by a collective gasp from the audience, he continued:

> This government has enough of a basis in Islam and everybody knows this is an Islamic government. We admire Islam and ... don't need to put its name on the transitional government.

But shouting broke out and men surged forwards, threatening chaos until the Governor of Nangarhar took to the podium, blue eyes flashing like headlamps beneath a gold turban. Grasping the microphone determinedly, Haji Abdul Qadir reminded the gathering that it was for 'Islam' that so many had sacrificed themselves during the jihad and the country would certainly be named an Islamic state. The motion was passed by a show of hands, few daring to dissent.

Outside the womens' dorms, Massouda was talking to another woman. She appeared unnerved and distracted. She was about to give a speech about her presidential candidacy but was scared of the reaction of the Mullahs to her candidacy: 'It is not in Sharia law for a woman to be able to run for president'.

She was hesitant as several black Landcruisers swept past. Dr Rabbani and General Dostum were leaving the site. But minutes later, Massouda, the first ever woman to run for President, gave her speech and said:

> The women of Afghanistan are champions. And they have to tell the world that even though they have been forced inside the home for the last five or six years, they can free Afghanistan and the world can trust them.

Afterwards, female and male delegates gathered around her. A male Professor of Medicine at Kabul University told her: 'We see women in government positions as very patient and trustworthy, we think that if a woman was leader, Afghanistan would progress much faster'.[54]

But the imam of Kabul's main mosque, Qari Abdurrahman Qarizada threatened Massouda with his words: 'Koranic law says women are too weak and unintelligent to run for president'.

The vote for president occurred by secret ballot, although in practice many factional leaders, having worked out deals in the side tent, forced the people from their fiefdoms to vote behind them. Haji Qadir managed to get most Pashtuns to vote for Karzai and so, despite visible support for Massouda (who got over one 170 votes), the overwhelming majority of votes went to the handsome young man from Kandahar who was already interim President of Afghanistan's Interim Authority.

In his first speech as Transitional President, Hamed Karzai said:

> The Afghan people want to get rid of warlordism. They want to get rid of the gun once and for all. And once again we have a strong mandate.

But he then disappeared with the US Ambassador, Khalilzad and Lakdhar Brahimi. They apparently went to the Presidential Palace to make further deals about Cabinet positions with the warlords. Meanwhile, security was tightened with new checkpoints and an earlier curfew across the city.

While the dealmakers were at the Palace, the delegates sat bored, impatient for the Loya Jirga to close and humiliated to have been excluded from the debate. One of them told journalists:

> I am really disappointed with the Loya Jirga. Governors and officials are telling people what to say in their speeches. I myself have been threatened into supporting Karzai and my first candidate was the former King Zahir Shah. This is just a Loya Jirga in name only. The main issues have not been discussed so far. If it goes on like this, fighting could restart because Karzai does not have the support of the majority of the people.[55]

The choice of Cabinet seats was supposed to have been decided by the delegates but now that it was clear how the meeting was being conducted, the horse-trading had moved unashamedly from the VIP tent to the Presidential Palace. This went on for most of the ten day meeting.

Finally, it seemed, there had been an agreement. So on the night before Karzai was finally due to announce the Cabinet, a British ISAF soldier explained about security arrangements for the next day. 'We're gunned to fuck', he declared nervously as a contingent of the Afghan National Guard marched past with Lee Enfield rifles swinging by their sides. Tomorrow, the tent would be filled with the more deadly armoury of the warlords' bodyguards.

***

Fahim's black Landcruiser tore through the site like a dust devil minutes before Karzai arrived the next day. He was a stocky man and descended the vehicle onto a red carpet on which the National Guard were lined up awaiting inspection. With his chin stuck firmly in the air and his thickset nose like a pile of squashed rugs, Fahim began to walk along the line of soldiers who towered over him.

The air inside the tent was thick with tension as everyone awaited Karzai. International diplomats and warlords alike had brought armed men. The whole event seemed like a superfluous show of testosterone as the bodyguards of opposing factions and international diplomats talked nervously into hand held radios, all the while eyes scanning the tent.

The new President had already delayed announcing the make-up of his Cabinet once and today the mood was of nervous expectation. Ordinary delegates knew that deals about which factional leaders had been chosen as Cabinet members had gone on elsewhere, instead of with their vote as promised by the Bonn Agreement. Still, they were unsure just who would be given government positions.

Finally Karzai swept in, cutting a fine figure in his long *chapan* silk coat, lambskin *karakaul* perched elegantly on his head. Taking his place on the podium, he began by making jokes to ease the tension. But he went on to announce his Cabinet haltingly. Those who had expected the Loya Jirga to rebalance the country's ethnic power were disappointed.[56] The hegemony of the Panjshiris was reinforced; of the three most powerful ministries – Defence, Foreign and Interior –the Panjshiris conceded one in name only. The only significant Pashtun to be offered a position was the Northern Alliance ally Haji Qadir, the powerful and charismatic Governor of

Jalalabad, who was made Minister of Public Works and one of the three Vice Presidents.

With the meeting closed, Brahimi and Khalilzad announced that its outcome was a triumph of 'peace versus justice'. When someone asked what this meant Brahimi explained, in a laboured way which rather implied the naivete of the journalist, that to maintain peace within Afghanistan, it had 'of course' been necessary to subvert the idea of justice. In later opinion columns, this was explained by adapting a Lyndon B. Johnson quote to refer to the warlords: 'It's better to have them inside the metaphorical 'tent' pissing outwards than outside the tent pissing in'.

But others disagreed with the view that those who had hoped for justice were simply 'naïve idealists'. One UN official admitted that the UN had ordered the Loya Jirga Commission (which was Afghan led) not to disallow Sayyaf's election. Although delegates were, under the rules of the Bonn Agreement, supposed to have signed an affidavit saying they had never participated in 'war crimes', because none of these people had ever been tried in a court of law, this could not be proven in practice. I witnessed Sayyaf make this point in response to a *Washington Post* journalist when – at an election at a school near the old British cemetery in Kabul[57] - she had challenged him on his past. As a result of this 'get out', those who had previously terrorised Afghans were allowed to lie about their past. Then they were allowed to attend the Loya Jirga and – supported by the *Amniyat* who intimidated and threatened democratically elected delegates – the warlords were able to shape the meetings' outcome and thus ultimately the outcome for the fledgling Afghan state.

Back then, in June 2002, as the monitors and UN colleagues met to assess the likely outcome of the Loya Jirga, another UN colleague commented, 'If I had been in Brahimi's shoes, I would have made a 'heavier' footprint and been more engaged. The chance to control the warlords is now lost'. The warlords, he said, would now return to their fiefdoms emboldened. They had now been 'legitimised' before ordinary Afghans in the eyes of the international community. In the following weeks, reports dribbled back to the UN of revenge attacks by these strongmen who, once back in their localities, singled out those democratically elected candidates who had dared speak out at the Loya Jirga. Sima Samar was forced into hiding. Brahimi and Khalilzad's notion of 'Peace versus Justice' seemed dangerously like renting peace. But for how long this peace could be 'rented' nobody was sure.

***

Within two weeks though an event occurred that set the stage for a further breakdown of stability. On a hot day in July, when the sun had reached its zenith on the far side of Kabul's dry riverbed, Afghanistan's Vice President was assassinated as he and his nephew left his Ministry building for lunch. Haji Abdul Qadir was also the Pashtun Governor of Jalalabad who had mobilised so many votes for Karzai only two weeks before.

When my interpreter Omar and I arrived at the Ministry of Public Works, a small group of journalists were already gathered around Qadir's bloodied Landcruiser. The site was not yet cordoned off and the vehicle had been driven into a wall, its bullet-ridden sides now resembled a cheesegrater. On the floor and front seats, where the bodies had been pulled from the car, the two men's ruby-coloured blood glistened. Bystanders said the assassins had rounded on Qadir as he was driven out of his Ministry's gates, not letting up their firing even as the car plunged into a wall. The killers then took their leave in one of Kabul's many thousands of yellow taxis, blending instantaneously into the traffic. Someone had clearly wanted Qadir dead and was taking no chances. 'Shame, he was a nice man', said my *Newsweek* friend quietly. His fixer then reached into the car to pull out Qadir's bloodied satellite phones and announced that in the last half hour before his death Qadir had tried, three times, to reach someone called 'Haji Z'. This was probably Haji Zaman, an enemy and rival of Qadir's from his home Province of Nangarhar, apparently driven out of the country by Qadir in the Spring. But the name which appeared on Qadir's phone did not belong to Haji Zaman.

Today had been Qadir's first official day at work as Public Works Minister. Oddly, the bodyguards normally guarding the Ministry were not Qadir's but belonged to the outgoing Minister. Someone said they had received instructions from the Interior Ministry yesterday to leave their weapons at home today. And several onlookers remarked that the assassins, who had been wearing the white *salwar kameez* of Nangarhar, Qadir's province, had been hiding in the bushes outside the Ministry for several hours waiting.

Three days after Qadir's assassination, at a registration of journalists at the Ministry of Foreign Affairs, the Panjshiri Press Officer, a small man with a splash of dark hair, a western suit and an east-coast American accent showed us into a minimalist 1970s-style office of leathered white chairs. His look was sullen, as though he really didn't have time to deal with us. The door was closed and we were told to turn off recording equipment while he spoke: 'I have just been to a Memorial Service, for a great man. For Haji Qadir'. He paused and looked around the room. The journalists sat in silence. The Press Officer continued, hissing to the group; 'I've been reading some of your stories on his death over this weekend. Most of them are bullshit!' He looked around, checking the effect of his words before going on:

> This was *not* an ethnic killing. Do I make myself clear? It had *nothing* to do with ethnicity and let me tell you people, I'm watching the stories you write and I don't want to see any more bullshit reporting, like saying this death had to do with ethnicity.

Though some of the press had said the killing could be ethnically motivated, others assumed it to be the result of a drug feud. When leader of the Eastern Shura in pre-Taliban days, Haji Qadir had apparently made a lot of money. No one was quite sure how, but everyone knew that poppy was the major crop grown in his province.

Haji Qadir had been the brother of another major Afghan commander: Abdul Haq. Ten months before, in the aftermath of September 11, the London *Evening Standard* had carried a story on 5 October 2001 about Commander Abdul Haq.[58] The headline read

'Rebel chief begs; don't bomb now, Taliban will be gone in a month'. A picture showed a large Afghan man named Abdul Haq. Another smaller photo showed him clasping Margaret Thatcher's hand. It was 1986 and she was lauding him for his role as a guerrilla commander in the Afghan-Soviet war. The reporter wrote that as well as being, 'one of the most respected mujahideen commanders in the guerrilla war against the Soviets', Haq was now 'a rebel commander at the forefront of a campaign to overthrow the Taliban'.

> The Taliban is collapsing from within, Haq explained, 'The people are starving, they are already against them ... but if the missiles strike, this will be delayed, even halted. Mr Blair has the influence to put the hand of restraint on America. I beg him to do it.[59]

But recent press articles had shown Blair leaving Moscow for Pakistan on the latest round of his diplomatic mission to shore up support for imminent US-led military action. He looked like a swotty schoolboy, frenetic and reactionary, desperate for approval. In contrast, Haq's face appeared calm, cerebral even. His 'strategy', the piece said, was to persuade the Taliban's own military forces to turn against their leaders in a secret war being waged against the hardline fundamentalist regime.

> Every time I meet commanders who cross the mountains in darkness to brief me, 'they are part of the Taliban forces, but they no longer support them'. Haq explained, 'These men will join us and there are many of them. When the time is right they and others will rise up and this Taliban government will be swept aside'. The only condition, he added, was that the struggle be one 'in which Afghans take the leading role'.[60]

With even the most liberal commentators in Britain subscribing to the idea of unleashing the full might of the West's military hardware on Afghanistan, the quiet words of this open-faced commander struck me.

That weekend the US-led bombing campaign began. It was Sunday 7 October 2001. A diplomat I'd known in Islamabad met me for supper. He now worked on the 'Afghan desk' in Charles Street, but like many Foreign Office officials, hadn't visited the country.

The FCO Security policy was so tight that the Islamabad-based diplomats were not, back in 2000, even been allowed to take a tourist trip up the Khyber Pass. But he had been fascinated by my stories of Kandahar. Tonight he was excited the bombing had begun. On the question of whether the strategy was really to use the Northern Alliance to oust the Taliban, he indicated that this was not the plan, even though, with most of the journalists behind Northern Alliance lines, this seemed unlikely. But he would not say just *what* the plan was because of 'security' constraints. So what was the plan?

'Pashtun Commanders', he sighed. 'We're going to use Pashtun Commanders. So you see we're *not* relying on the Northern Alliance'.

I asked if that meant they were going to use Abdul Haq, but he asked, 'Whose that?' I told him I had read about Haq in the papers the week before. He shrugged, 'Not so far as I know'.

'But who else is there?' I replied, 'He's the obvious one isn't he?'

'No, not as far as *we're* concerned'.

Haq's brother, Haji Qadir's strength had been as a pacifier, a bridge between the Northern Alliance and Pashtuns. During the jihad he had, unusually, been a Pashtun Commander representing the Northern Alliance in Kunar. This background had enabled him to push the Pashtun vote for Karzai during the Loya Jirga, while simultaneously keeping the Northern Alliance on board. As such he'd earned the sobriquet 'Kingmaker'. This was deemed important during those days as the Americans were busy fighting the Pashtuns in the South. But Qadir was seen as the last man after Abdul Haq with significant cross-tribal following. Now both he and Haq were dead.

CHAPTER TWO

REIGNITING FUNDAMENTALISM

Nothing on earth can ever justify a crime ...
if you grant an amnesty to the past, you are corrupting the future.

BENJAMIN CONSTANT, *Des Effets de la Terreur* (1797)

Kabul, July–October 2002

The soldiers directed us to some buildings on the far side of the compound, a short drive from the warlords' office. When we found two women huddled together beneath a tree, one rocking on her bare haunches, it was obvious we had reached the women's asylum.

I was here two months after the Emergency Loya Jirga. But what I was about to learn here would illustrate how those who had gained most from the Loya Jirga – Afghanistan's former mujahideen strongmen – were already imposing their stamp on society and the state-building project at large.

Today, a middle-aged minder with a stern face and the black skirts of a Sicilian widow bustled towards us. 'You must wait', she explained to Omar. Many of the women were apparently in a state of undress. Muffled screams came from the solid Victorian building.

Eventually the minder led us through a narrow corridor into the darkness and a vast hallway of stone, dank with the stench of urine. Gradually, the blur sharpened, revealing several ghostly figures: a cross-eyed dwarf woman and a girl wearing a shell necklace. They watched me intensely. The girl smiled faintly, showing fang-like incisors. Behind, in an opening between double doors secured by a chain, was an elderly woman whose lined face was suffused with deep furrows. Behind her, an upturned table and rags on the floor, clearly her sleeping arrangements in this vast and filthy grey space. She was naked. Suddenly the stillness was broken with ferocious intensity as the elderly woman battered the door with a club. Nothing seemed normal here, where an ordinary-looking elderly woman was not only reduced to living in such demeaning conditions, yet was also capable of reacting with such violent strength. In the next room, a dormitory where light flooded through glass-less barred windows, a stream of urine trickled across the stone floor and a row of battered metal beds did nothing to soften the hardness.

From beyond came the strangest cacophony of chatters and we moved through a door directly into a yard enclosed by a high wall. There, beneath a tree, sat a group of women. They were shaven and sat in the dust, each seemingly in a world of her own. Some rocked themselves, others sat still, legs folded, arms moving randomly. 'They cut and throw their *chadors* up there', the minder indicated tatters of coloured rags hanging from dead branches above like odd Christmas decorations. Omar looked startled but I knew these women's stories told of the brutality of Afghanistan. I wanted to understand what had brought them here. So Omar and I sat down with them on the dusty courtyard floor.

One woman's nose was bloodied and festering with flies. The minder, a black silhouette always hovering somewhere above us, explained how another inmate, a shaven thick-set woman called Nasreen, had sunk her teeth into it days before, tearing off the bulb of the nose. As we spoke, Nasreen sat alone against the yard wall, rocking. When I asked why, the minder explained that Nasreen had lost her family during the mujahidden infighting in Kabul. A rocket attack had occurred as the family ate supper and she had been spared because her father had sent her out to the kitchen to fetch a bowl of rice. All but her had been killed. Initially she had had eating disorders, but this developed into removing her garments, and more recently the aggression that led her to bite off the other woman's nose. Nasreen, it seemed, was just one reject of war and a society unable to deal with her. An old lady in a torn green dress entreated me, 'Write my name and take me out of the mental house to America'. The minder said the woman had been here twenty-five years and was unmarried because she could not walk. There was no wheelchair.

Another made an interjection which Omar translated. Six of her sons had died. After that, she had become 'ill'. The minder murmured absently. She was sixty-five, her husband had been killed by a rocket twenty years ago and she had five children. She told me that the women needed blankets and medication, because winter was coming. With treatment many could improve, but she had worked here fourteen years and now things were worse than ever: 'At least during Najibullah's government[61] we had water and electricity. The windows were broken during the fighting that followed'.

Marastoon, as this forgotten institution on an arid hillside beyond Kabul was called, once had a car that drove through the streets collecting the insane, bringing them here. 'The Taliban gave a bit more help than now', she added.

Walking back inside the shrouded corridor, there was a cell-like room with a small barred window high above the dirt floor. Within it was a 'lump' in the dirt; there followed a movement, and an old lady emerged. She gave a gratified smile, and pulled out a needle and thimble, which she held beneath her sacking cover. When I took her hand, she seemed pitifully grateful for human contact. She had been here twenty years, her name was Zainab and her smallest finger had gone, apparently bitten off by the same woman who had taken the others' nose. The old lady wore a dirty pink dress with a bow and was from Maidan Shah, a Pashtun area to the South of Kabul. She had come to be at Marastoon after her husband took a second, younger woman. When the two fought, this lady was brought to Marastoon, the victim of a society where women are expendable.

The shell necklace girl watched me sideways. She had been here for twenty years, having killed two men. 'Her son and another', said the minder casually. 'Then last year she killed two women here at midnight'. It seemed unbelievable. Here she was, walking around ready to kill again, needing psychiatric treatment which was unavailable. Preparing to leave, I noticed a closed door and, feeling the minder hiding something, opened it. Inside, a pale-faced woman sat on a bunk. Against the black of her *chador*, her face was unexpectedly beautiful, and it seemed that she should not be here.

Despite her obvious shyness, Omar's sensitivity enabled her to talk. She was called Raheela and she was twenty-five. Her parents were dead and she had been taken in by her uncle. But she didn't want to live with his family. For fifteen years, they had beaten and fought with her, even though she cooked them good food. Omar explained that the girl had gone to the Women's Ministry to ask for help. But they had sent her here. So, she had sought help and they had sent her to a dangerous mental asylum? Behind us, the shell necklace murderer stood watching, leaning against the doorway. Raheela commented that from night until morning it was impossible to sleep because everyone was shouting.

Having promised to help Raheela, I returned several days later with an Afghan-American doctor, a squat New Yorker who was a Mohammadzai Pashtun, one of the King's tribe. We were obliged to seek permission to enter from the Director of the Afghan Red Crescent Society who ran Marastoon. Outside his office, soldiers in fatigues mooched. The soldiers were the Directors' bodyguards. The doctor was shocked: 'Dangerous for the women', he remarked, 'a burqa is their only protection'. After a long wait we were shown in, and there sitting behind a large desk, was Qar a bec, the gold frames of his glasses catching shafts of light on the walls. He was a strongman who'd made no secret of his disdain for the election process in the Panjshir.

It seemed odd for him to be here in the Director's seat, as he was a warlord not a medical man. We drank tea and when I questioned him about the set-up, the lack of trained staff and equipment, he waved his arm beyond his head, saying there was no money for such things. He was vain and disinterested, only perking up when he heard of the huge response in the USA to the photographs of my colleague in this job, who worked for Getty Images. As a result of her pictures, American people wanted to send money to Marastoon. We suggested that maybe this could be used to buy the things the women needed. Taking a gold pen from his waistcoat pocket he wrote, presently pushing a scrap of paper towards me. It had his bank numbers on it.

Eventually, we were allowed to visit the women's asylum and as walked into the yard where the women sat together. Here, the doctor said quietly that this was a terribly sad place. We reached Raheela's room and the doctor spoke with Raheela in *dari*. Raheela sobbed that if no one could help, she would commit suicide. Eventually, the doctor said the Women's Ministry had sent her here, and told her, 'There are Panjshiri women there who can look after you'. But her Raheel's reply, as translated by him, was, 'Her mother had a heart problem and her father was an officer in the Communist government, so was killed by the mujahideen'. Later, Raheela told the doctor that if she cleaned herself, the other women would accuse her of trying to make herself beautiful. She would prefer to be in the women's prison where conditions were apparently better. The doctor told me that Raheel had said, 'She says they should change the name from Ministry of Women to Ministry of Injustice to Women'. As we left the building, he said that Raheela had left home because her uncle was raping her. It was the secret shame of the family, something that in Afghanistan could never be acknowledged.

We were obliged to leave the Marastoon compound close to Qar a bec's office. He fixed me with a threatening glare and gripped my shoulder until it hurt. 'You'll be kind to us with your pen won't you?' he said menacingly. The doctor translated, his head hanging low, but as our car bumped down the track minutes later, he growled angrily that the warlord touching me was a transgression of Afghan culture. He added that the warlord and soldiers were bound to be abusing the women. He explained that a warlord was running the Afghan Red Cross[62] because it was a lucrative post for him. 'Tons of money comes into the Red Crescent from other Muslim countries and if he's overseeing it, then well, you can guess the rest'.

Qar a bec had stood out during our elections in the Panjshir as purposefully disinterested, as though the electoral process threatened to undermine the position he had carved out for himself.

He tried to, three times. Fatima Gailani was appointed to the position but Qar a bec refuses to step down. And because Karzai has no power, he stays.

These were the words of Peter Jouvenal, a cameraman who had covered the anti-Soviet war in the early 1980s and has since stayed. As we drank tea in the garden of the guesthouse he had dubbed 'Gandomack Lodge' in honour of the famous battle of the first Afghan war where British had been soundly defeated by the Ghilzai Pashtun during their retreat from Kabul he told me:

> The Panjshiris only accepted Karzai as he has no power base; neither tribe nor political party. So they know they can manipulate him. If I made you president of Afghanistan you'd have a problem. Karzai's the same; he has no power so he has a problem. The Americans chose him as he was involved with pipelines, and so on.

Even so, with all the international community's Apache helicopters and F16s, it seemed odd that Karzai should not be able to get rid of a corrupt warlord at the Afghan Red Crescent.

I set about looking for a women's shelter for Raheela. This journey would enlighten me as to what had already begun to go so badly wrong with the West's intentions for reshaping women's rights in Afghanistan. The Deputy Women's Minister, Tajwar Kakar, who had dealt with Raheela's case personally, was not around. She had been in Australia for two months visiting relatives, her staff said. None were sure when she'd be back. UN staff were complaining that many of the new Ministers had simply taken off abroad on extended vacations, enjoying their new positions; instead of doing the important jobs they'd recently been appointed to at the Loya Jirga.

Our meeting took place upon her return, three weeks later. She was a grey-haired, rather stern-faced woman who disturbingly reminded me of a headmistress. She sat as though perched on a throne, and remembered Raheela's case immediately. 'She is a prostitute, so she is mad. That's why we sent her to the asylum!' I tried a different tack. Surely, even if Raheela were a prostitute, she needed assistance? Didn't the Women's Ministry provide shelters for women? She raised her chin, and said with venomous disdain, 'A women's shelter?' She had seen one in the USA and considered it very dangerous.

We don't want Afghanistan to become like that. In Afghanistan, our culture is different, every problem they [women] have they can discuss with the family.

This woman obviously hadn't come up against the dynamics of power relationships. Could Raheela really open up a conversation with her uncle about his raping her? Kakar was like Queen Victoria and – like the Queen who had denied the possibility of lesbianism – Kakar seemed to believe it unthinkable this girl was being raped by someone within her own family. If the family could resolve everything, why have a Women's Ministry at all? Even if Raheela were a prostitute, did that not still entitle her to some form of protection? From a visit to a prostitutes' day-care centre, a hidden place in the filthy backstreets of Kabul, it was clear the women had no other choice.[63]

But the attitude of the Women's Ministry reflected part of a trend that had been taking root since the Loya Jirga: the creeping re-establishment of fundamentalist Islam. It had begun with the reinstatement of the mujahideen warlords at the Loya Jirga and their demand that Afghanistan be named an Islamic state. The corollary? A return to Shariat as the basis of Afghanistan's legal system; a retrograde step considering the 1964 constitution had been more progressive, a mixture of Shariat and Western jurisprudence. This was the first nail in the coffin of judicial reform, and how close this would be to the Shariat system used by the Taliban just depended on who was interpreting the law.

The next nail in the coffin of judicial reform was the appointment at the Loya Jirga of the ultra-conservative Chief Justice, Fazel Hadi Shinwari.[64] Within weeks[65] he had reinstated the infamous Religious Police,[66] ironically hitherto associated with the Taliban, but in fact modeled on the Saudi Arabian 'Vice and Virtue' police force.[67] This move allowed the conservative elements associated with the mujahideen, men like Sayyaf, to crack down on the people, particularly women. They began issuing edicts to ban women from singing on television, to ban the showing of the weekly Bollywood film on Kabul TV, much to the annoyance of most Afghans. And in the Western city of Herat, the mujahideen Governor Ismael Khan[68] told women working in UN offices they could not shake the hands of foreign men and must continue wearing the burqa.

The words of the representative of the women's rights NGO, the Revolutionary Afghan Women's Association (RAWA), resonated. As long as the fundamentalists were in power, she said, the position of women would never change: 'They are against women and against human rights'. She was angry. They had warned the West about the fundamentalists during the war against Russia.

> Now we warn the West *not* to help the fundamentalists again. These people – Fahim, Abdullah, Qanoooni and Rabbani – destroyed the city, raped thousands of women and abducted young girls when in power from 1992 to 1996.[69]

Tense with emotion, she continued, 'These men the West has put in government are common war criminals!' But what about the proof needed to convict such men? For I had heard UN staff, perhaps parroting Brahimi, say the same when challenged about why the West had rehabilitated such men, instead of indicting them. I wanted to know how an Afghan woman would answer such a seemingly callous question. Frustrated, she shouted:

> It's like saying we don't have proof of Hitler or Mussolini! Our people have the documents and what does the damage around Kabul say about their crimes? Go and interview women around Kabul: many were raped by these men and Sayyaf sold our women to the Arabs. Because of this people allowed the Taliban to come, to save us from these bloody hands. This *shura nazar*[70] have no interest but their own power and as long as they have weapons the war won't be finished. The people were hopeful for the Loya Jirga until they saw these bloody criminals sitting in the front row. When the USA supported Hikmatyar we said this is wrong and warned them. Now we warn them not to repeat the same mistake.

Unlike the Nuremburg trials in 1947, or the attempt to capture warlords Milosevic, Mladic and Karadzic in the Balkans, the West clearly had no interest in bringing justice to Afghanistan, or even initiating the 'due process' required to evince that. Instead, those involved in such abuses were now its principal allies in the fight against the Taliban. She left, slipping the burqa over her clothes, blending in with the others in the white dust of the street.

Karzai's sacking of the former Minister, Dr Sima Samar at the Loya Jirga had set the ball rolling in favour of the fundamentalists. Samar was progressive and brave, and had highlighted the need for conditionality' on aid money spent in Afghanistan. This would have guaranteed the protection of women not just in the form of shelters but also have given them some chance of participating more fully in society. Now she had been replaced with Kakar, a woman the mujahideen establishment believed 'safe'. And the rights of Afghan women were effectively being washed down the drain.

'Khalilzad talked about a trade off between peace and justice at the Loya Jirga. Actually he's lost both', said a French-Iranian photographer I had worked with as an Election Monitor. No 'Johnny-come-lately' to Afghanistan, this journalist had covered the 1980's jihad as well as the Iran-Iraq war. He explained that Brahimi and Khalilzad had bowed to the warlords and now their factions would start fighting again. There was a real culture of fear here. And the recent deaths of those Ministers were not being investigated, he said. The 'Ministers' he spoke of were Haji Qadir but also Abdur Rahman, another Pashtun and former Aviation Minister. Rahman had been the keeper of General Massoud's funds in Moscow, but was stabbed to death on an airplane in an apparent argument with disgruntled Hajis who were supposedly annoyed their plane was late leaving for Mecca. The real story was much murkier and many Afghans suspected it related to Rahman switching his support from Fahim to the former King prior to the Loya Jirga.[71]

Samar, now Chair of the new Afghan Human Rights Commission,[72] had set up a Woman's Shelter. Maybe Raheela could be taken there? Days later, one of her staff reinforced what others were saying when he commented:

> The problem with the Loya Jirga was that it legitimised the mujahideen leaders. Prior to it, they'd kept a low profile. Now they have a lot of power and they've been able to change the agenda. Their intimidation

of Sima Samar at the Loya Jirga sent an implicit message of threat to educated Afghan women.[73]

This intimidation had resulted in Samar having to travel with armed guards, and live in hiding.[74] 'Something it was never necessary for her to do during all the years of Soviet oppression and war', he added bitterly.[75] It seemed that a huge opportunity had been lost at the Loya Jirga, an opportunity that, once squandered, could not be easily recovered. For it had set the direction of Afghanistan's fortune on a new dynamic. When I asked what could be done for Raheela, he said:

> The problem is that Sima is facing a great deal of pressure from the mujahideen to close her shelter, so it is not possible to take more women.

As Sima Samar had said back in January, in her meeting with the Irish: 'Even Karzai is scared to push women's issues too strongly, because he is concerned other leaders will not tolerate such progress'.

One late autumn afternoon, a member of the Afghan diaspora, who had returned to Afghanistan from Paris to serve on a panel charged with drawing up Afghanistan's new constitution spoke with me. I was doing some research on transitional justice for the International Crisis Group. Understated and with graying hair, Dr Fasili was clearly a man of intellect and had become a junior Minister in France.[76] But he was already dismayed by what he saw as interference in the democratic process. Referring to the warlords, he said:

> Now we'll face the problem of conflict more strongly due to the development of fundamentalism over the past twenty years, and the renewal of it in the last six months. There are the old chiefs, the Tanzims. They're the people holding power, the Islamic groups from the jihad period. All these factional chiefs were against the King during the Loya Jirga, because he is so widely loved here. The Religious Police were reinstated because of pressure from Rabbani and Sayyaf ...[77]

Ironically, Abdurrab Rasoul Sayyaf (Head of Ittehad-e-Islami) and former Prime Minister Berhanuddin Rabbani, retained power as conservative Islamist mujahideen. As such, both were against the modernising and 'Westernising' of Afghanistan. And their ideals were close to those of the Taliban. Fasilli continued, 'The West must be firm on these issues and ensure that aid is withheld, otherwise Afghanistan will return to fundamentalism'.

**

The Italian Ambassador was in the garden of his 1970s embassy. It was dusk and I was here because the Italians were leading on justice in the context of Security Sector Reform as mandated by the G8[78] issues.[79] He reminded me of a Lampedusa aristocrat when he said:

> Brahimi thinks legal reform is not possible in Afghanistan as the country is not ready for modern Western law. But it is one thing to be realistic and another to be so cautious that you don't *do* things.[80]

'Do things?' I asked. He paused, cupping long fingers around a cigarette and said, 'The real pressure to give the 'extra' fifty seats to warlords at the Loya Jirga came at the ninth hour from Khalilzad'.[81]

He spoke of the seats which had suddenly and inexplicably been issued to unelected strongmen on the eve of the Loya Jirga, the night the warlords had burst onto the site, which made a mockery of the work the election monitors had done to ensure that those charged with shaping Afghanistan's future at this key event would be the people chosen by ordinary Afghans. The Ambassador gave a knowing grin and whispered, 'You know it was Khalilzad who originally advised the Americans to back Hikmatyar during the jihad?'

Hikmatyar[82] was the renegade warlord the USA had tried – and failed – to assassinate earlier in 2002 with a Hellfire missile. Now Hikmatyar was being blamed for everything from the gathering insurgency in the south to small bombs being set off daily around Kabul. Khalilzad, the Ambassador said, had previous connections with UNOCAL, the US oil company which for years had been inveigling to build a pipeline across Afghanistan. He went on, now holding his cigarette like a dart,

Khalilzad made a *huge* mistake by marginalising the King. The King could have kept the Pashtuns happy and Karzai or the King could have been Head of State and Qanooni[83] Prime Minister. But … US policy is so short-term and has *no* respect for Afghan political evolution. By this I mean, why select Fahim or even Karzai as the men to fight al Qaeda for the war on terror, rather than concentrating on state building? The risk of a reversion to factional fighting within a few months is now very high.

The next day a Senior European diplomat told me;

'You know you *cannot* have stability without justice, or *at least* accountability'. And added, '

It was so cynical of Mr 'B' and the USA not to believe that an eighty-seven year-old man could have been a figurehead, one of the only people not seeking a position. It would have been so good for morale. It's a shame when governments act as cowards.[84]

The eighty-seven year-old he referred to was the former King, Zahir Shah.

***

A German lady had organised a meal with the Afghan Women Judges' Association. Even their representative dismissed the idea of protection for women: 'The situation is too difficult, such places cannot exist publicly because many men would not accept them'. Shelters' would loosen the ties that still bound women to the household. So shelters were politically impossible as any independence for women was looked upon as a direct threat to society. Particularly a society now returned to the mujahideen. Women who did not fit into the 'traditional family structure' remained vulnerable. Clearly the attitude of the new Women's Ministry was to see girls like Raheela as a threat. The easiest thing to do was thus to castigate her a prostitute, lock her up in Marastoon and throw away the metaphorical key.

I was increasingly concerned about where we could find

protection for Raheela and contacted RAWA in Pakistan to see if she could be taken to one of their shelters. It was a protracted process waiting for their representative to find me in Kabul again, because I could not call her directly for her own protection. The lady on the phone in Pakistan offered to help but it would be difficult for them to get Raheela away from Marastoon, as she was under the eye of Qar a bec and his men. During the days I was waiting for the RAWA lady to arrive, I met Caroline, a feisty British girl from a German Women's NGO, Medica Mondiale. She promised she would visit Marastoon and find Raheela, and two weeks later she arranged for Raheela to move into their house in Kabul. There, she took up a position of responsibility and seemed to gain some self-respect.

A few months after that first visit to Marastoon, US Defence Secretary Paul Wolfowitz visited Kabul in a blaze of publicity. Wolfowitz visited a newly refurbished, shiny women's clinic, hailed a triumph of progress for Afghan women. But maybe it would have been more appropriate if he had been photographed in the women's asylum at Marastoon?

News of Raheela came again in the spring. Raheela had been getting on very well and was helping out at the women's NGO where Caroline worked. But within months her uncle turned up and demanded she be handed over. How did he know where she was? 'The Women's Ministry told him', Caroline replied quietly. It was the last I ever heard of Raheela.

***

During September 2002, I was invited to visit the Salang Pass, a route constructed by the Russians in the early 1960s, linking Kabul with the north. An invitation had been extended through a fellow journalist from Hayat Muslim, a prominent Panjshiri. Muslim was about to leave for London as Afghanistan's Military Attache and was apparently a close friend of the Defence Minister Mohammad Fahim.

A french radio journalist called Anna, a cameraman and two aid workers came with us. Anna had covered Afghanistan extensively over the past decade and knew Muslim well, having often entered the country through the Panjshir. As we set out she seemed protective of her access to him, and their friendship, cultivated over several years. We drove through the Shamali Plains, stopped for tea in Jabal Seraj and continued up into the heights of the Hindu Kush, picnicking beneath the Salang pass at around three thousand metres. Behind us, an overhang in the road was held up by menacing concrete columns which shadowed the road for over twenty kilometres as it snaked its way into the Hindu Kush and towards the north. The pass had been built by the Russians in the 1960s, a mammoth feat considering one of the series of columns was over two kilometres long. The building of Salang seemed to foreshadow a long held Russian ambition to invade Afghanistan. It was the Soviet's principal supply and invasion route in; hence Massoud had concentrated his fire on Salang. When one stood below it, the whole Soviet plan seemed so obvious.

'So', I asked Muslim, as we ate a picnic of chicken wrapped in Afghan bread, 'why didn't the King foresee a Russian invasion when they built this?'

'The King?' he said venomously. 'He was just smoking pot and enjoying women!'

UN colleagues had explained why the US Special envoy Khalilzad had intervened to cut out the King before the Loya Jirga: because Fahim had threatened civil war, bringing his tanks to Kabul, if the King were made Head of State. The US response was apparently to say, 'We won't intervene if that happens'. And so the King was cut out, leaving many Afghans disappointed.

It was precisely because so many Afghans saw the King as a unifier, someone able to bring morale to sections of the country disenfranchised by the Panjshiri monopoly on power, that Panjshiri strongmen like Muslim, who were benefitting from the status quo, professed to loathe him. But the jealousy went back centuries, and related to the dominance of the Pashtun majority over the rest of the country.

Muslim appeared to be an easygoing sort of guy, always talking.

But he repeatedly told us how well the Northern Alliance had done to defeat the Taliban, and how the world owed the Northern Alliance a favour for this.

On the way home, he pulled over to intervene in a road accident, having recognised the car of a commander he knew. We were back on the Shamali Plains, north of Kabul, on a link road between the old and new roads. Anna and I got out of the car. It was almost dark and American Chinooks were flying back to Bagram from Special Forces operations in the south, their twin rotors silhouetted elegantly against a full moon. She lit a cigarette and blew out the smoke with a long sigh,

> God I've had enough of all his talk about how the Panjshiris deserve to keep all these ministries. It's disgusting and so transparent the way they're gorging on power.

CHAPTER THREE
THE POETESS OF JALALABAD

The sword only comes into the world when Justice fails.

JEWISH PROVERB

Jalalabad, September–October 2002

It was late September 2002, and I was visiting the eastern provinces to research the poppy story before heading for a week's R'n'R in Pakistan. Jalalabad, lying on the trade route between Kabul and Peshawar, was directly en route and lay in the midst of Nangarhar Province, one the world's richest opium poppy growing areas. It was also where I would begin to understand how the dynamics of the so-called political settlement, at Bonn and at the Loya Jirga, had impacted upon the majority ethnic Pashtun community and why they felt sidelined by the West.

A fellow journalist, an American called Louisa, would travel with me. She arranged for us to stay with the Arsala family, brothers of the late Abdul Haq and Haji Abdul Qadir. Louisa had met them when a member of the press corps covering the battle of Tora Bora in late 2001. At this time, in late September 2002, the Taliban were already re-grouping and waging an effective insurgency in the south. Pashtuns complained that much of the reason was their exclusion from the political settlement. While in Jalalabad, I resolved to find out more about what Haq had been trying to do and and why he had been trying to find an 'Afghan solution' to the conflict.

Louisa and I met early one morning in Wazir Akbar Khan, a Kabul suburb of 1960s houses, all lines, large windows and swimming pools. Only now the drains were choked, the pools empty and cracked and gaping rocket holes in some of the walls, having blasted into people's privacy, a stark reminder of the brutality of war.[85]

As we left Kabul heading south-east in the direction of the

Khyber Pass, and the border with Pakistan the light was still and grey. Our Toyota 4x4 was driven by a softly-spoken driver. At the edge of Kabul's grassy plains, he pulled in Pul-I-charkhi at a checkpoint where an assortment of scruffy huts perched on the rim of the Kabul gorge. A4-sized posters of General Massoud graced the huts on the first guard-post and soldiers searched cars ahead for weapons. 'They'll wave us on as we're foreigners', Louisa advised. A second guard post, twenty metres away, carried posters of a regal-looking man in a golden turban. His piercing blue eyeballs were angled to the side like a portrait whose eyes follow you around the room. It was Haji Abdul Qadir. Although both he and Massoud were dead, the posters glared at each other in a symbolic stand-off, the point where one power ended and another began; a tribal and cultural division.

'Thank God, we're in Qadir country!' Louisa exclaimed, disparaging of the Northern Alliance regional power-base we were leaving. The people of Jalalabad were still angry about Qadir's death. He was their 'best and brightest', taken the moment he went to do his job in Kabul. She added that people were pretty sure who had murdered him: 'Right in the centre of the most heavily guarded city in the country!' Haji Qadir's picture adorned checkpoints and shops all the way[86] to Jalalabad, which was then, before the arrival of asphalt in 2004, still four hours drive from here. Qadir had been Governor and head of the Eastern Shura[87] and clearly his influence, if not now his remit, still extended from the Khyber Pass to the very edge of the crater in which Kabul sat. It was a writ which ran significantly further than that of President Karzai, who people were already calling the 'Governor of Kabul'.

Dropping into the gorge, the sun went and we were in a chilly defile of cavernous flanks of stone. This was close to where the British had met their fate on the disastrous retreat from Kabul in December 1841. Akbar Khan,[88] son of the exiled Afghan King Dost Mohammad, had ridden through here, promising support to the British but simultaneously urging his horse higher into the passes to encourage the tribes in their slaughter of the retreating army. He was angered the British had exiled his father Amir Dost Mohammad and put Shah Shujah, the 'Puppet King', on the throne. Afghan sharpshooters rounded on the retreating army from the heights of the gorge, beginning a killing spree that would end in the deaths of sixteen thousand men, women and children of the British colonial force.

After Kabul gorge we approached Sarobi, a grim place of sun-bleached rocks. Four journalists had been pulled over and shot in the narrow walls of this pass when in a convoy heading for Kabul, to cover the capital's fall in November 2001. 'When I saw the suitcases with their Reuters stamps, I knew they were dead', Louisa mumbled grimly, 'they'd never have let their stuff go'.[89] We emerged into an open river plain of Nangarhar Province, an ancient landscape. The wide valley of the Kabul river, still shrunken after the fifth year of drought, was framed by a spur of rock. Pilgrims and traders of the ancient silk route had carried Buddhism through here onto China and Japan, leaving behind carved caves and monastery complexes of Ghandaran Buddhist civilisations. Nancy Dupree's 1977 guidebook[90] on touring Afghanistan[91] said the area was among the most sacred of the Buddhist world.

Today, the drive to Jalalabad was taking far longer than the two and a half hours estimated by Dupree when Afghanistan had intact roads during the 1970s. Alongside the Kabul river, the landscape was Babylonian; men knelt on mats beneath bulrushes, their bodies turned to Mecca as others made their ablutions in the river before offering their Evening Sura. Suddenly several pick-ups hurtled past us in the opposite direction, billowing dust. The first driver leant on his horn and swerved dangerously to avoid us. On each, ragged men gripped Kalashnikovs and rocket launchers to their chests. Louisa complained that these were the men of Hazerat Ali, who was probably making his weekly journey to Kabul to see Fahim. 'Traitor!' she exclaimed.

We arrived in Jalalabad at twilight and pulled up at a checkpoint on the city outskirts. Our driver was a Tajik and seemed nervous to be in a Pashtun area.

The city comprised wide avenues and curvaceous branches of eucalyptus and palm. The air was balmy and laden with orange blossom. Our descent from Kabul had been a thousand metres, and Jalalabad felt like a bridge between the dry winds of Central Asia and the damp subcontinent. 'There's a lot of shit goes down here, like the bomb last week', said Louisa, 'But at least this place feels real. Not like Kabul'. Driving into the city's heart, the intensity of sounds and smells increased. Thriving markets lined streets where men lounged on charpoys or stitched rush mats before open-fronted shops, small boys played billiards on vast green baize tables in the open, kebabs sizzled on small fires and the delicious intermingling of lamb and charcoal wafted through our car windows. Small two-stroke engine rickshaws weaved in and out of traffic, leaving a pungent trail of diesel, like a genie's wake. Under the covered hoods were women, their faces and bodies hidden beneath blue burqas.

Louisa beckoned the driver leftwards at a scruffy *chowk* (roundabout) marked with a blue sign which read 'Abdul Haq Foundation'. At a gated compound further along, two young men in the white *salwar kameez* of Nangarhar came out to help unload the vehicle, their bearded faces breaking into smiles.

Within was a calm oasis of green where several men in turbans sat on plastic chairs drinking green tea on a patch of grass. The scent of roses clung to the damp evening air and one of the four, a man dressed in white *salwar kameez* rose from his seat in the darkening light. 'I was worried about you on the road, you should have called!' he berated Louisa in a low voice, a broad smile having broken out on his fine-featured face. This was Haji Baryalai. He bowed his head, a tall man with a gun-metal grey, trimmed beard and a faint German accent.[92] We followed him into the green-painted brick house, removing our shoes in an entrance hallway and then up some stairs. 'Even some family members are not allowed up here', Louisa whispered. Photographs lined the walls: Haq and Qadir talking on radios, mujahideen *patou* blankets draped around shoulders, fighting jihad in the mountains of Afghanistan. One showed a young, much thinner kneeling Abdul Haq, a mop of scorpion tail dark curls on his head. Another showed an older Haq, plumper and with grey hair, standing next to Baryalai, who had a bushy beard and longer hair. 'Taken after he lost his foot', said Baryalai. 'That's when he put on weight'. But it was the man to Haq's left who caught my attention. The long, dark, henna streaked beard and Rasputin-like face was recognisable. 'Haqqani', said Baryalai. 'He was one of our mujahideen'.

Though I did not know it then, Jalaluddin Haqqani and his followers would in the years to come, provide the US-led Coalition (and ultimately NATO) with one of its most intractable problems in what came to be known as the 'Af-Pak' theatre of the post 9/11 Afghan War.

Upstairs was a sitting room, two small bedrooms and a terrace. A teenage houseboy showed me into one of the bedrooms. Its window looked out beyond the turquoise patina of a mosque to the mountains of Nuristan. I stepped onto the terrace and into the balmy night. A lone call to prayer was being sung out by some local muezzin. The others had come upstairs to drink tea in an adjacent room on floor cushions. When houseboys arrived bearing metal trays, they called me in from my quiet interlude.

There were photographs around the room and one in a window casement caught my attention. In the photo stood eight men, with Baryalai at one end, a serious looking Qadir and a chubby Abdul Haq. 'My brothers', Baryalai interjected, 'taken in 1989 when they lived in Peshawar. That is Haji din Mohammad, now Governor of Jalalabad'. Baryalai indicated the man in the middle of the group. He had high cheekbones and a grey beard.

A familiar looking print, around fifteen inches high and unframed, leant against the wall above a wooden desk. It was a facsimile copy of a familiar picture,[93] a man slumped over his pony, trudging across a barren rock landscape to bring the news of the slaughter, the worst 'signal catastrophe' of British colonial history, an event the Duke of Wellington had described as being caused by an arrogantly 'forward' foreign policy and bad intelligence. The place depicted in the picture, Fatehabad, was only half-an-hour's drive from here, on the old road to Kabul. Baryalai said:

> We have a relationship with you British. Our great, great-grandfather
> Mohammad Arsala was involved. Redbeard, he was called, and for
> this event he was given the Governorship of Jalalabad.[94]

Supper was chicken, chips, rice and small salads, eaten on the roof
across a spread of carpets and cushions. Above was a full, golden
harvest moon, lighting the sky behind the dome of the local mosque.
Baryalai's bearer, Mahboub, served us silently. A leprechaun-like
man, he was only four foot high but with a dark curly beard and
handsome straight features. Mahboub was from the Shinwar, a tribe
close to the Pakistan border, where the family had been based during
the 1980s jihad. At this time, Qadir had been the main commander
based in Shinwar, charged with running weapons into the conflict
from Pakistan. Baryalai explained that they'd had to walk across
the mountains from Peshawar, not along the road, and it would
take days.

Baryalai had moved back to Afghanistan from Germany to set up
a humanitarian NGO in Abdul Haq's name after his death. The aim
he told me was to carry on Haq's work, digging wells, rebuilding a
children's park which Abdul Haq began after he resigned his post in
Kabul in the early 1990s, encouraging farmers to switch their crops
from poppy. He added that some American journalists had been here
the previous week, visiting for the final prayers for Haji Qadir.[95]

***

As dusk gathered one evening that week, I chatted with two men who
worked for the Foundation: Sayed and the equine-faced Engineer
Sharif. Earlier that day, Sayed, a man in his twenties, told me how
his brother, killed in the early days of the Russian jihad, had studied
law at Balliol College, Oxford. The idea of a young man from the
inhospitable lands of Pashtunistan making his way to the refined
spires of Oxford seemed odd. Then he would return to his country
to fight alongside brother and cousin against the Russians, and be

killed. It seemed a waste of a life, an education, and a window on the outside world needed now more than ever in Afghanistan.

Sharif spoke excitedly about a poem, published two weeks before in the *Nangarhar Daily*. It was apparently by a woman called Mariam Nasseri and she was 'starting a revolution' with it, like 'a new Malalai' he said. Malalai had been a female poet who had galvanized Afghan men into defeating the British at the battle of Maiwand outside Kandahar in 1848.[96] Sharif and Sayed were convinced that today Pashtuns faced the same situation and twenty-five year-old Mariam Nasseri would galvanise men to the sword. Sharif thudded the table as he spoke:

> The poem is called 'Strangers in our Land'. We don't need these guests in our country. America wants to keep Afghanistan as the second Israel in the region. We are not Taliban or al Qaeda, they are finished now! Ninety-five percent of people of Afghanistan do not support this government. It is not a real government.

From an adjacent minaret a single muezzin began the call to prayer. Sharif brought out the poem, on a well-thumbed scrap of newsprint out and quoted the words by heart:

> How can the younger generation look upwards,
>
> They are alive, but their country is ruled by Jackals.

The rest he read first in Pashtu, before translating line by line, with some interjection by Sayed.

> No one can express what the truth is
>
> Or who brought this situation to the country?
>
> Powerful hands keep our mouths shut
>
> And the young generation fails to defend its country
>
> Those not able to remove the communitys' pains
>
> Should take the clay pots, as Gooder, with the women
>
> And the young generations will keep bracelets on their hands
>
> For they are living under an invaders dominion

This is not our constitution

For Pashtuns defend freedom with blood

Sayed explained:

> Today's Afghan men are weak. This is why she says they now live with their eyes cast downwards. They were once 'lions' in their heroism, but are now allowing themselves to be ruled by mere 'jackals'.

The 'jackals' were perhaps the men of Hazerat Ali: chief of the speeding troops we had met on the road and a local warlord from a minority tribe, the Peshayee (also known as Shahee), who were from a valley north of Jalalabad, towards Kunar. His picture was plastered on buildings and on the Landcruisers his men drove. Sharif told me that Ali was just a proxy for General Fahim and this was one reason why locals distrusted him.

The next day Sharif told me that Nasseri was 'too proud and too beautiful to wish to meet you'. He lowered his voice, and continued:

> The poem says no one is able to express what the truth is, and who brought this situation to the country, but this is *especially* the case for Pashtuns in the south and east of the country. You know, these days we just don't know who the enemy is. At least during Russian times, when we were fighting the jihad, we knew *who* we had to fight.

He shook his head dejectedly. Within a few weeks there would be a concrete example of what he meant.

***

A family of Afghan refugees stayed at Baryalai's house on their way to the Pakistan border at Torkham. They had come back to Kabul the previous spring, with the many thousands who were hoping to rebuild their lives in Afghanistan. Now, they were returning, with a heavy load, to Pakistan.

'Qadir's murder was a turning point for us', said the head of the family, Najibullah Hussein. Prior to this they had retained hope for the future of Afghanistan, but now believed things would destabilise further. Qadir had been the last strong Pashtun, a link between the Pashtuns and the Tajik dominated Northern Alliance, he said. 'Now, there's no leader and no hope for Pashtuns in the new government. Things will get worse'. Fifteen years before, when the Soviets left in 1989, thousands of Afghans had returned, leaving homes and businesses in Pakistan. But they had to flee again when fighting broke out between warlords. Hussein did not want to take the chance of that happening again.

Weeks later, when travelling to Kabul on a local minibus from Jalalabad, I saw at first hand just why Pashtuns were beginning to boil over. The bus had to pull over at the Pul-I-charkhi checkpoint on the outskirts of the city. There, Tajik guards forced the passengers to hand over all newspapers written in Pashtu, telling them sharply, 'Now you're in Northern Alliance territory so you'll do as we say!' Other grievances included, the 'random' (which is how they appeared to Pashtun people, at least) arrests of their leaders by the Americans. When the Kuchi leader, Naeem Kuchi, was arrested and taken to Guantanamo thousands of his followers came to Kabul to protest.

Haji Qadir had died within the past nine weeks. I'd covered his funeral in Kabul as a journalist. It was a ceremony mostly of Northern Alliance warlords. They had arrived at the Eid Gar Mosque in a plethora of Landcruisers with dark windows, driven at breakneck speed. After a short service, they left and Qadir's body was flown by helicopter to Jalalabad. An AFP journalist told me his coffin passed through the streets on a gun carriage pulled by a Soviet-era APC[97] as his mujahideen wept openly. But Qadir had not been buried next to his ancestors and Abdul Haq at the Arsala's simple family plot in Surkh Rud. Instead he was taken to the Mausoleum of former Afghan Kings and buried at the feet of Kings Habibullah and Enayatullah in Jalalabad's city centre. Even as he was lowered into his grave the people had chanted: 'Haji Din Mohammad, Haji Din Mohammad'. They did not want a minion sent down from Kabul to be their next Governor; they wanted another Arsala.

CHAPTER FOUR

'I'D RATHER BE A LION FOR ONE DAY, THAN A JACKAL ALL MY LIFE'

> What follows is true about Abdul Haq. His family – among Afghans one always starts with family – has for centuries been notable among the traditional Ghilzai Pushtun leaders of Eastern Afghanistan. Local people had always looked to this family for energy, courage and organisation. They were not disappointed by Abdul Haq.
>
> WHITNEY AZOY

Jalalabad, October 2002

For several days Louisa had slipped off to meet someone, leaving me on my own at Baryalai's. I was busy reading on his terrace, utterly absorbed by Robert Kaplan's book *Soldiers of God*. Kaplan had spent much of the 1980s travelling into Afghanistan with the mujahideen as a journalist.[98] His account enabled me to understand more about this family's place, not just in the region but also in the hierarchy of those fighting the Soviets during the 1980s. He offered the type of information that the coalition, and indeed the international community, seemed oblivious to, particularly when it came to the search for bin Laden a year before at Tora Bora. He would also explain the ability of this family to mobilise the tribes of the eastern provinces. I would gain my first insight into how this dynamic worked a day later.

The Arsala's place in the Pashtun tribal structure was impressive. Arsala khel is a subdivision of the Jabar khel, a predominant landowning clan of the Ahmadzai of the Eastern Ghilzai Pashtun. The Arsalas were considered *khan khel* (or chief clan) of the Ahmadzai and had been appointed to this coveted position by no less than the Mughal Emperor Akbar himself. The Jabar khel had since the mid eighteenth century been in conflict with the Durrani Kings, who were also Pashtun and ruled Afghanistan from their base in Kandahar. This conflict lasted until the deposing of the former King Zahir Shah in 1973. It is thus a strange irongy that Abdul Haq, a member of the Jabar Khel, intended to orchestrate the return of the ex King Zahir Shah to Afghanistan in the name of peace and unity.

The Arsala's originated from the mountainous district of Hezarac, close to where the British, retreating south-east from Kabul in 1842, had met their end. In relation to this, a great- grandfather known as Redbeard had earned himself the Governorship of Jalalabad for his part in the slaughter. The fame of the Arsala brothers by the late 1980's was a direct result of their effectiveness in leading insurgencies. It also related to the individual charisma of three of the brothers; Haq, Qadir and Haji din Mohammad grew to become figures of national importance.[99]

As with all mujahideen at that time, the brothers were associated with a Resistance 'party'. To maintain control of the USA's Afghan war booty, the Pakistani ISI had ensured the factions of the Afghan Resistance leaders were divided into six groups which became known as 'parties'. The 'six' became 'seven' when Abdur Rashid Sayyaf's arrived with support from Saudi Arabia, keen to promote its brand of Wahhabist Sunni Islam. In reality the 'parties' were politico-military factions which could then be played off against one another.[100]

The Arsala's 'party' was known as Hizb-e-Islami-yi-Afghanistan,[101] and was led by a rural mullah called Younis Khalis.[102] Hizb–e–Islami-yi-Afghanistan differed from those of the other Resistance leaders, the Islamist militants, in that it was made up almost entirely of Ghilzai (eastern Pashtuns) living in the area between Pakistan and Kabul. It represented the *ulama* of the Eastern Shura and, according to Kaplan was essentially a party run for the Arsala family, with Khalis its figurehead. Its most powerful figures were Haq, Haji din Mohammad, and Abdul Qadir, the Nangarhar Commander. And in the Khost area, Jalaluddin Haqqani.[103]

With Khalis spending a lot of time inside Afghanistan, Haq's eldest brother, Haji din Mohammad became de facto head of Hizb.[104] Much of the vigorous military activity of Khalis's mujahidin was in effect cross-border raiding, 'for they could hit their targets during brief missions from Pakistan'.[105]

Although absorbed by Kaplan's book, I noted that with each of Louisa's departures, Baryalai emitted sarcastic comments about her going to see the 'military man'. This military man, I learnt, had played a role in the battle of Tora Bora, the cave complex to which al Qaeda had retreated in November 2001 and the last place where bin Laden was heard talking over a radio. He had also been imprisoned by the Taliban for several years and orchestrated a jailbreak from Kandahar prison, alongside Ismael Khan, causing the Taliban, to forcefully search all the houses of foreign NGOs in a bid to find him.

Early the following morning, a large, cream Landcruiser with massive, kitsch spoilers came to fetch us. It had once belonged to Haji Qadir. Two sub-tribes of the Ghilzai were fighting towards the border with Pakistan, and Zahir had been asked to intervene. Louisa and I could go and interview the people whose problems might make a story for publication. The driver took us to a compound beyond the turquoise patina dome of the Sikh mosque. Inside high stone walls, a verdant lawn and rose garden sat incongruously with red Hilux jeeps and lingering fatigue-clad soldiers. Masculine tension pervaded the air. The house stood behind, two storeys high, dark green and cream like a birthday cake iced in layers.

A houseboy led us upstairs. At the landing, a short man with a flaxen, trimmed beard stood to welcome us. His eyes were wide-set and with the same piercing quality as Qadir's, but tempered with laughter and unconcealed puppy-like excitement at our arrival. He invited us to come up for 'milk tea and eggs'.

We were led into a room where unsmiling turbaned men sat on a dark blue new floor littered with red-corded cushions. They ate from shared plates of fried eggs and shifted along as we sat. One, so large the others had allowed him a full side of the room, nodded to acknowledge our presence. He had intense dark eyes, a white beard and steel grey turban. He leant forward to say in broken English:

> The King once came to this region but I told him, 'We already have a King here in Nangarhar and it is me, as I am the King of the Shinwar people'.

Afghanistan's rather effete King, Zahir Shah, would be dwarfed by this huge man. His comment indicated the tenuous nature of these Tribespeople's loyalty to the centre. Plus there was a sense of nobility about him. Maybe it was the turban, associated since ancient times with the sacred, with justice, possibly even with Kingly power.

Their penetrating eyes made me empathise with the idea of wearing a burqa. 'So today you'll see an argument about land which has gone on for forty years', Zahir explained, his English thick with an Afghan accent. He explained that the kuchi, a Nomadic tribe, had settled during the 1960s on land belonging to the Mohmand.[106] Tensions had run so high that last week the Mohmand had burnt four hundred of the Kuchi's houses. We were dispatched in Zahir's Landcruiser to where the dispute had taken place. Several Hiluxes, bristling with soldiers, followed close behind and Zahir's brother Qader came as our escort. The landscape between Jalalabad and the Mohmand looked more intact than any in Afghanistan: rows of mature eucalyptus, olive and citrus had somehow avoided the obliteration of war; the detritus of agricultural collectives developed by the Russians.

Reaching the Mohmand tribal area, the landscape was a sun-bleached open land. Tattered men stepped from the burnt shells of houses and pathetic, angry people stood alongside their charred belongings. An elderly man with pale blue eyes and dark hair stepped forward and Qader translated quietly. People had come from Mohmand villages across the dry river valley and 'fired' on their houses. The old man held out a blackened copy of the Quran, wringing his wrists in anger. 'This is a sacrilege against Islam'. We stood in the glaring sunlight. Qader pointed out the man's wife, still crouched behind a burnt bedstead in her black *chador*. He explained the kuchi men were truck drivers and away when the Mohmand came.

It was shocking that two groups living beside each other could maintain such hatred for generations. Kipling was right in asserting that at the heart of every Pashtun blood feud lay *zar, zam, zamin*: gold, women and land. Qader explained that the two tribes had sent a case to Kabul before the Taliban came, but it was overlooked.

> When my father became Governor again, he agreed to call a Jirga between the elders of both tribes. But was killed before it could happen.

He spoke calmly and I wondered if the villagers were aware this was a son of their former Governor, Haji Qadir. He went on to say that his uncle, Haji din Mohammad, the present Governor, would have to leave his responsibilities in Kabul and return here to a meeting of the elders of both tribes.

Later that evening at Zahir's house, one of Mohmand leaders, a tanned young man with blue eyes arrived. He had come to see Zahir, to defend the actions of his tribe, and stood on the doorstep explaining why his tribe had burnt the houses. 'That village does not belong to Kuchi', he said defiantly, arms crossed. He continued:

> Several times we ask them to leave. We have documents six hundred years old showing the land is ours. We are Muslims. But our population is getting bigger day by day and we have less land. To solve this the Government must ask the tribal people. They have a list of which land belongs to which people. We will accept a decision by the Jirga, but not the United Nations.

Nangarhar Province's population had grown vastly since the war, with many refugees moving down here from Kabul during the inter-factional fighting of the early 1990s. Now people were also returning from Pakistan and needed land to farm, but fertile land was limited. The man turned away, irritated.

***

Louisa returned to Kabul, and I stayed on in Jalalabad intending to leave for Peshawar two days later. Baryalai said he had business there and could take me with his driver. In the meantime, Haji Zahir sent a houseboy around with a message inviting me for tea. So I returned to his house, where the soldiers still lingered watchfully among the roses and uniformed Police Chiefs awaited audiences on the stairway. Their eyes bore into me as I climbed to the first floor. Today the house was a blaze of activity: carpenters scurried past with tools, working on rooms upstairs and on the landing was propped gauche Pakistani gilt rococo furniture.

Inside the room where we had breakfasted, I could see Haji Zahir propped on an elbow, supported by navy-corded floor cushions, unconcerned by the frenetic activity around him. He ate cashew nuts, tossing their shells into a glass dish on a red Afghan carpet. A man stooped over his feet, and as I walked around I realised he was clipping his toenails. 'Come and sit', he beckoned. I took my shoes off shyly, sitting cross-legged as Zahir sat up. Green tea was offered. A tight faced personal secretary came in and out relaying messages, stooping to deliver rushed whispers into Zahir's ear or handing over paper chits. Zahir unfolded these with chubby fingers while the secretary stood behind stiff as a courtier, nose in the air and hands behind his back, throwing disapproving glances in my direction. Occasionally Zahir pulled a gold pen from the pocket of his *salwar kameez* and scrawled replies. The secretary took these and backed out deferentially, head bent with mutters of 'Haji Sahib'. The whole thing reminded me of the court of Henry VIII. Zahir exuded an air of regal indifference. He even had the same sturdy frame and flaxen beard as the young King. A large rectangular ruby encased in diamonds sparkled on his left index finger. 'It belonged to his father', Sharif had told me admiringly. A houseboy shuffled in with a kettle and poured green tea into a glass. We chatted about Kandahar, and I told him how our house dog had grabbed the radio of a Talib who had come desperately searching for Zahir in the houses of the foreign NGOs when he had escaped from jail. He had gone to Mashad, Iran. Zahir told me:

> I went there after 'scape from jail. But from September 11, my father called Iran for several days looking for me. We had not spoken for nine months.

There had been an argument between Qadir and his son. When Qadir rang Zahir after September 11, he told him there would be a change of government soon and he needed him to return to Jalalabad to secure it once more. Zahir spoke calmly, occasionally drinking from a glass of green tea.

> I offered to go from Nuristan side but my father said 'no we already
> have people there and you must go from Peshawar side'.

I wondered if this was the time Abdul Haq was making his mission
into Afghanistan, from the same place. As though reading my
thoughts, Zahir said:

> This was the most difficult side and from where the Taliban first arrested
> me. Later they captured my uncle Abdul Haq there and executed him.
> I told my father, 'I am your son and if you need me then I am doing
> what you ask'. So, I crossed into Afghanistan in the back of a taxi from
> Mashad. We drove to Zahedan and then Quetta. We stopped to pray
> in a mosque and as I knelt to wash, one man said, 'Ah Haji Zahir you
> come from Iran?' He was spying for Taliban. I was afraid as Quetta is
> not far from Kandahar and the Talibs knew me by face. So I said I was
> just going to Quetta for half an hour. I stayed one night in Quetta and
> caught a flight for Islamabad next day. But I did not use my name.
> Luckily they did not use passports for local flights then.

He went on to say that when he arrived in Peshawar he only had
a few hundred dollars, not enough to buy the satellite phones he
would need to contact his commanders inside Afghanistan.

> I was talking on phone from Landi Kotal, at the top of the Khyber, and
> after five minutes the line was cut. The same with another commander.
> ISI were tracking my calls. A friend said, 'Are you crazy? There are ISI
> spies in local clothes searching for you'. So I took a taxi up the Khyber
> Pass and went to Ayoub Afridi[107] for help and shelter.

Afridi had grown rich on poppy, the trade of the frontier. I had seen
his walled compound at the top of the Khyber Pass on my first visit
to Peshawar. So vast you couldn't destroy it with a tank. I saw it
on my first trip into the arid mountains of the Khyber Pass, part of
the swathe of land between the two countries known as the tribal
area and thus officially out of the Pakistan government's control.
It was a place where lawlessness, retribution by blood feud and
the smuggling of drugs and arms were commonplace. As our van
had lurched past the concrete walls of a vast fortress, the guide

had commented, 'Mr Afridi's house'. Whoever Mr Afridi was, I'd thought, he was leagues apart from ordinary Pathans. The walls were half a kilometre long on one side alone.

Zahir continued, 'He took me into a basement. The room was lined with dollars. He said to me, "Take what you need. I don't want to see this money back"'. The scene sounded like something out of a Bond movie. Maybe Afridi was trying to generate goodwill with the Ghilzais, to assure himself of future poppy supply.

> By this time my father had flown from Germany to Tajikistan and was in the Panjshir valley. I found a friend at Luargi who gave me guns on credit. Kalashnikovs. And satellites I got from Pir Bash.[108] I called up my commanders from the Pakistan side of Torkham,[109] people at army bases in Kunar and Nuristan.[110]

He flicked cigarette ash casually into an ashtray of lapis lazuli.

> I left Peshawar deep in the night to avoid being tracked by the ISI and crossed into Afghanistan at Shalman. Walking twelve hours across mountains at night with ninety-five friends and soldiers; a lot of soldiers but no guns. So I told some to stay on the Pakistan side until we had guns. We made for Yacobi and arrived at Dacca base.[111] There were some small Taliban soldiers there, about thirty persons. They were sitting and we came and took their guns and cars. I told them to leave and go home. After five minutes at Dacca, my sixty soldiers and commanders came and at each crossroads between Torkham and Jalalabad my soldiers from surrounding tribes joined our convoy. Over a thousand came from Nuristan alone. When we arrived to Jalalabad we had six hundred men with us. The Taliban had fled. The elders had told them to go, that they were no longer wanted'.

'And they did, just like that?' I asked, surprised.

> Yes of course. Hazerat Ali came from dari noor,[112] I came from Peshawar and Gen Saeed Agha came from Kunar and Nuristan. Some of our soldiers also came from Khoghiani and Hezarac and we captured places from all sides.

'Didn't the Americans help you?' I pressed. He turned to one side, looking out of the window into the yard below where his soldiers lingered around the Toyota trucks, waiting for him. He continued:

> The US turned up only one week before Tora Bora began. Hazerat
> Ali's men began looting houses. My father arrived to Jalalabad from
> Panjshir in a helicopter and I told him to arrive at Bessud Bridge.
> Because the airport was now under the control of Hazerat Ali.

Ali had been one of Qadir's commanders during the jihad but was
now, apparently, Fahim's proxy down here. Some suspected Fahim
of Qadir's assassination, because the latter stood between Fahim
and power. Zahir continued, 'Haji Zaman[113] stayed in Peshawar
until later. I closed the border so he couldn't come'. As I wondered
who Zaman was, Zahir interjected, 'A week after my father arrived,
he was made Governor again'.[114]

***

Haji Zahir was now chief of the Border Guard for Nangarhar
Province. His men were therefore now under the auspices of the
Ministry of Defence. One afternoon, he took me to his 'office' at
Torkham, one of the main crossing-points with Pakistan.

The car hurtled through the fruit markets of Jalalabad and the
bodyguard fed Zahir cigarettes in quick succession. Behind us
Zahir's brother Qader drove a black Lexus and four red Toyota pick-
ups bulging with bodyguards, struggled to keep up. I remembered
Sharif commenting that Zahir had the same temperament as Qadir.
We drove beyond the citrus towards the border at Torkham on a
road shaded by eucalyptus. On one side, the Hindu Kush framed
the landscape, vermillion beneath the sky. We passed brick kilns
the shape of stacked birthday cakes and little girls in magenta pink,
carrying eucalyptus fronds in their arms.

Zahir's camp was at Dacca, at what had once been a British camp
close to the mountains bordering Pakistan. We arrived, a long convoy
of cars, and I saw how under the awnings of canvas tents, kettles
sat alongside Kalashnikovs. It could almost have been a cub scouts
campsite. Except that soldiers milled casually, some lying on *charpoys*

beneath a white hot sun, until they realised Zahir had arrived.

We descended from the car and Zahir pointed us to a reed structure. We sat on *charpoys*, looking across an arid, stony landscape. In the distance, swathes of pale green ran along the Kabul river. Beneath our reed shade, soldiers running around us like minions, we could almost have been rich tourists on a Kenyan safari. A boy brought small glasses of sweet green tea. Zahir became suddenly shy and introverted. Later I wondered if this was simply propriety again, in front of his men. Moments later, he stood, speaking Pashtu. The men sprang to activity, feeding a belt of brass cartridges into a cannon. Seconds later, a crack and a plume of smoke in the mountains several kilometres away. Still, the soldiers worked at double speed, winding the belt into the gun as Zahir stood behind, grinning. A second crack boomed, followed by the sound of rockfall, this time in the mountains even further beyond the road where lorries wended their way towards Torkham. Zahir had clasped his hands together and his eyes sparkled happily. Life in Afghanistan was good if you were a commander. However, within weeks an episode occurred which demonstrated that life as the scion of one of Afghanistan's leading families was not always so easy, particularly when the Americans were in town, hunting down the 'remnants' of al Qaeda.

***

It was already October and the snows would be coming soon to the northern areas, making flying into Gilgit difficult. If I didn't get to Pakistan soon, I might miss my chance. I was to meet my *Daily Telegraph* colleague for a few days relaxation and hoped to see the glistening snows of Rakaposhi at Karimabad before winter set in, blocking the passes. Baryalai said I could stay overnight in his house there.

As we drove out of Jalalabad, a long convoy of Toyotas with blacked-out windows passed us at an intersection. They drove in convoys, red Hilux jeeps carrying searchlights and loaded with scruffy soldiers clutching Kalashnikovs to their chests. These were

Hazerat Ali's men and Sharif told me that at the time of the Russian jihad, when the Arsalas had been leading the mujahideen fighters based at Tora Bora, Ali had been Haji Qadir's cook. Now he'd been elevated with US and Panjshiri largesse. Spitting tobacco into a drain at our feet, Sharif had said:

> Ali wants to be everything; religious leader, community elder and warlord, but he is not qualified for these positions. He is not educated and does not have the respect of the people.

From Baryalai's Landcruiser, I watched Ali's soldiers then noticed three larger, pale silver vehicles amongst Ali's vehicles. On top of the silver SUVs, men sat in camouflaged fatigues. They caressed rotating anti-aircraft guns and looked self-consciously Tom Cruise-cool in wraparound Ray Bans. They were American Special Forces, but for all their expensive equipment and 'cool presence' – what with the allies they had chosen – they seemed completely out of their depth here in Jalalabad. Baryalai caught my gaze and said, 'We don't know what they're doing, coming and going to the Kunar Valley'.

CHAPTER FIVE

A 'CATACLYSMIC EVENT FOR THE WEST'

Peshawar, October 2002

We were in Torkham, the busy border crossing of the Khyber Pass, by one o'clock and Baryalai's bearer accompanied me to get my passport stamped. With his dark bushy eyebrows and furrowed brow, 'General' could easily have been a character in *Carry On up the Khyber*. We were on our way to Peshawar and – although I did not yet know it – would find a pile of letters which Abdul Haq had written to Western leaders warning them of the unchecked fundamentalism then developing in the tribal areas during the early 1990s.

Inside the Pakistani passport office, banana leaf fans hummed beneath a red tin roof and a crowd of men pushed forward towards a green baize desk. Men in small fez caps sat at the desk using ancient typewriters, tapping information slowly from piles of paper. Above hung a musty print of the Qa'ed-e-Azzam: Pakistan's founder, the cross-eyed Mohammad Jinnah. We were cocooned in a time warp, sometime around 1947. Suddenly, an older man pushed his way agitatedly through the crowd, rasping something to the man behind the counter. The Pakistani bureaucrat shrugged, looking directly at me, 'He says the brother of Haji Qadir is outside, don't keep him waiting'.

As he spoke, one of his colleagues threw my passport towards me. I took this to be a deliberate sign of contempt for my association with Qadir's family. Possibly the man was an ISI agent. Back in the car Baryalai said, 'Normally people don't recognise me, I try to keep a low profile'. But no doubt his grand dark blue Landcruiser, and the picture of Qadir adorning its windscreen, had attracted attention. The tribal people seemed to hold Qadir's family in esteem, even if the Pakistani bureaucrats did not.

Baryalai's driver wended his way through the gathering dusk and I could make out a steep profusion of railway lines, bridges and tunnels in Victorian engineering with sturdy embankments for such mountainous terrain. Baryalai interrupted my thoughts, 'If you imagine how much work and expense was put into it by the British, then you understand how important Afghanistan was in those days'. The Pass had been created during a time the British felt they needed Afghanistan as a buffer, to protect British India from the ambitions of an expansionist Russia.

We drove into Peshawar at nightfall. The concrete bazaars, which had sprung up since the Afghan war, were still colourful and frenetic with activity, despite the return of roughly half a million refugees to Kabul during the summer.

'Look to the left', Baryalai pointed out a patch of ground. But all I saw were large clods of upturned wood and earth. This, he told me, had been a refugee camp but was recently razed by the Pakistan government who wanted to get rid of the Afghans now. He continued:

> But still two million remain. They've seen this situation before, in 1991 when people returned to Afghanistan, having given up businesses and homes, thinking the Russians had gone. But the civil war began soon after and they had to return here.

It was seven o'clock in the evening when we arrived at the Abdul Haq Foundation office, in the newly built suburb of Hyattabad, an area named after a Pakistan Peoples Party (PPP) Minister assassinated while speaking at a meeting in the area. The PPP was the party of Benazir Bhutto, whose father had been executed unfairly by the Islamist General, Zia al Haq.

The stone-walled compound enclosed a large building, a verandah and lawn. As the Landcruiser pulled in, several men moved out of the dusk, greeting us with eager smiles. I later realised they were Afghan and had fought alongside the Arsala brothers in the jihad. The house had a large central stairway, and attractive dark red Afghan carpets. The walls were lined with pictures of the Arsala brothers in their mujahideen years, standing on mountaintops with *patou* rugs wrapped around hunched shoulders, conferring with their mujahideen fighters. One picture of Haji din Mohammad showed him talking into a walkie-talkie and beneath someone had written: 'HD Mohammad, now Deputy President, as mujahiddeen fighter'. In fact, this was incorrect for although he had been offered the position of Vice President in the aftermath of Qadir's assassination, din Mohammad had declined. Another photograph showed a group of men gathered together in the mountains, standing on a red carpet in the open air. 'The meeting of the three hundred commanders in 1991', Baryalai said, adding that Haq brought the Commanders together for talks, and he, Baryalai, had been 'secretary' of it. The mujahiddeen were about to take Kabul from Najib's communist government and Haq was trying to unify the factions before they entered the city.[115] Baryalai added:

> His attempt to bring unity amongst the leaders failed because Massoud took the city, breaking the agreement to hold back. When Hikmatyar fought him for control, the civil war began.[116]

Like Osama bin Laden, Hikmatyar was still at large. 'Now the Americans are trying to find him, in the mountains over there', Baryalai waved his arm backwards in the direction of what I later knew to be Nuristan and the Kunar Valley.

> I even offered the CIA names and addresses of Taliban leaders and al Qaeda. They're all living around Peshawar, but the Americans were not interested.

He emitted a gentle sigh and called the houseboy to bring green tea to a sitting room just off the hallway. I might have thought he was exaggerating if I hadn't heard similar stories from Afghans perplexed that the Americans had seemed so disinterested in capturing bin Laden.

I sat on one of the sofas and imagined the activity in this office almost a year before, when Haq had met with tribal leaders and senior Taliban in the weeks following September 11. Perhaps this was also the house in which Haq's wife and small son had been slain during April 1999; killings that were rumoured to be the work of the ISI. Haq had told others he believed the killings an attempt to dissuade him from continuing with his plan to dislodge the Taliban.

Later, Baryalai drove me across town to the Pearl Continental Hotel. We sat at the roof restaurant, where coal-fired braziers spat sparks into the clear night and guests on *charpoys* and Afghan rugs enjoyed succulent mounds of barbequed lamb. Baryalai explained that he had left his hotel and family in Germany to return to Afghanistan after September 11 because he wanted to fulfil Abdul Haq's dream of 'peace and unity' in Afghanistan. He said the people had looked to his family for leadership for many years and it was his duty therefore to return. The difficulty was that his children had been brought up in Germany. 'They're interested to come to Afghanistan but shocked at the deaths of their uncles. They're not used to these things', he said, dismally. The American intervention was a disappointment. 'They brought us the Panjshiri government, the Loya Jirga, Hazerat Ali and Haji Zaman', he said.

Locals whispered that Zaman had taken money from MI6 and bin Laden simultaneously at the time of Tora Bora. They reckoned he'd even led bin Laden across the mountains to safety in Pakistan. 'Ask *your* people. *They* backed him', Baryalai opened a palm towards me, tensely. '*They* chose him to fight at Tora Bora and backed him because the ISI *told* them to. MI6 took *all* their information from ISI'. Baryalai was not the first Afghan to tell me this and given how blatant ISI's relationship with the Taliban had been during my first visits to Kandahar and Herat in summer 2000, when ISI men travelled quite openly with us on humanitarian flights to 'manage' senior Taliban in Afghanistan's most remote cities, it seemed pretty incredible for MI6 to have done this.

Baryalai explained that Qadir had needed to take Zaman to the border to ensure his protection, so unpopular had he been.

> 'Most of the problem', you have to see, is the *perception* by the East, the South and even parts of the North that the Karzai Government is a 'top down' thing. If American and Panjshiri support for Hazerat Ali continues, it could encourage local people to turn to support Hikmatyar
> . There's already increased insecurity in the Eastern provinces in the form of small bombs, landmine incidents and grenade attacks. It relates to a resurgence in support for Hikmatyar.[117]

Although it was pleasant sitting beneath the stars of an early October night, I was shattered. We drove back to the house and at the top of the grand wooden staircase, Baryalai said he wanted to show me something. We went into a large room where there was a sofa, an armchair, and an antique colonial desk. I sat and Baryalai's bearer, 'General', arrived bearing a tray of spicy milk tea and then stood, hands clasped behind his back looking on expectantly as Baryalai rifled in the desk drawer. 'You need to concentrate', Baryalai said, handing me a clip file with a dusty cover. Inside were jammed dusty letters and newspaper clippings documenting Haq's past as a mujahideen fighter. Further on were letters Haq had written in the early 1990s. 'He wrote most of these after his decision to resign as chief of the Gendarmerie', he said. Haq had been training an Afghan police force for the mujahideen government in exile. It was his suggestion, Baryalai explained, that security would be needed when the mujahideen moved into Kabul, to take it from the Afghan communist government headed by President Najibullah. The government managed to survive some three years after the departure of the USSR from Afghanistan.

I flipped through the letters. There were several typewritten addressed to someone called Ambassador Peter Tomsen, written in 1992. Tomsen had been US Special Envoy to the mujahideen. A paragraph at the bottom of the page caught my attention,

> On its current path, Afghanistan runs the risk of becoming fifty or more separate Kingdoms. Foreign extremists have begun to move in, buying houses and weapons. Afghanistan may become unique in being both a training ground and munitions dump for foreign terrorists and at the same time the world's largest poppy field.

Other letters were addressed to President Jimmy Carter, President Reagan, Margaret Thatcher and a Saudi Arabian Ambassador based in Islamabad. Haq was obviously a man of stature, with good contacts. Newspaper clippings showed him meeting with Thatcher; the same photo I'd seen in the *Evening Standard*. Another showed him standing near Reagan. The piece accompanying it explained he'd gone to Washington DC where he was feted by Congress and Ronald Reagan as a 'freedom fighter'.

A letter written to the Saudi Ambassador, typed on notepaper headed Hezb-e-islami, Afghanistan, and dated August 1991,[118] (see Appendix II) began:

> Whoever controls Kabul controls the nation ... this is why Kabul is the major centre for the struggle between mujahideen and the regime.[119] This is why when Saudis come to Afghanistan they go to jihad in Kabul ... This is why Sayyaf and Hikmatyar want more control in and around Kabul. From one side they are poised to take political control, from the other side they bring most arabs with them. From both sides they gain influence in arab countries and get more financial support. ...Usually these radical elements don't talk a lot about jihad. Instead they talk about their politics and their radical brand of theology, how to bring revolution to their home countries and how to build support for what they call a 'pure' Islamic state. They brainwash them.

Reading this letter reinforced the idea that Sayyaf had used Saudi backing to gain power; the type of power which had produced the hysterical fundamentalism I'd witnessed at Sayyaf's election in a Paghman mosque on a Spring day only six months ago just before the Loya Jirga. More importantly, this letter also demonstrated clearly just who was behind the original terrorist training camps. Possibly the very same training camps which had produced some of the September 11 hijackers. Certainly one of his camps had produced Omar Sheikh, the killer of journalist Danny Pearl.

In a letter written to Tomsen after the fall of Kabul,[120] Haq expressed concern about the arrival of foreign fighters, the proliferation of fake ID documents and the setting up of terrorist training camps in the mountains of Tora Bora and eastern Afghanistan. These were things the West only began talking about in the wake of September 11. The letters were a repository of warnings about the type of 'jihad' already developing unchecked in Afghanistan in the early 1990s. Haq's recognition of what this portended for the world, transfixed me. 'Is it good?' Baryalai asked several times. Nodding silently, I read on.

> After their training these visitors go home, defend their trainers and act as ambassadors for these radical elements ... If these radical

mujahideen elements take power in Afghanistan, there will be war forever. There will be no peace and security and we Afghans will have to beg for food and support for the rest of our lives.

In those words Haq had predicted what was now going on in Afghanistan, despite the presence of the coalition and NATO, and all the attendant military spending of both.

'If these radical mujahideen elements take power in Afghanistan, there will be war forever', Haq had written. Yet at that summer's Loya Jirga, I'd seen Western powers effectively *giving* back to 'radical mujahideen elements' the power they had first seized during the chaos of the early 1990s. Only this time iced with the West's legitimacy for good measure. While democratically elected ordinary Afghan's had stood by muted, or in fact, stunned into silence.

'Without action', Haq continued, 'There will be a cataclysmic event for the West'. Haq had written these words in 1991. Even then, he had effectively predicted September 11. Sadly for the world, he had done so at the time when Western governments, delighted with their cold war 'victory' over the Soviets, were closing embassies in Kabul, shutting off their interest in Afghanistan. Even as the last Soviet convoys pulled out during February 1989 and the Afghan communist government of President Najibullah, which survived until 1992, came to an end, the forces of Massoud and Hikmatyar began their fratricidal campaign in Kabul. Haq's hopes for an agreement between rival factions faded as fighting continued between the factions and commanders who set up checkpoints in the countryside to rob and attack civilians. The irony was that even as the Soviets left, foreign Islamic fighters began to arrive in order to train for jihad in Afghanistan.

These letters reinforced the notion I'd had of Abdul Haq that day back in September 2001, when I'd first read his story in the London *Evening Standard*. He was indeed a man with prophetic qualities, having foreseen September 11, the use of his country as a base for fundamentalists and terror, as well as a centre of global heroin production. Yet at a time when it may still have been possible to deal with these issues, no one had thought fit to listen to him. There was probably too much backslapping going on as the Cold War came to an end amongst those who'd enjoyed pulling the strings of a distant covert war.

With the American strategy here effectively handing control back to the mujahideen, the 'warlords', Haq could be correct in asserting there would be war here forever.

'Still people will come to hate the name of mujahideen and jihad throughout the world and think that the word means only killing, destruction, disunity and terrorism. ... Moreover the students and guests of these radical elements will find many supporters in your country and if not, take full power, still engage in attrocities and chaos. This is neither good for you, nor for us, nor for islam'.

'Meanwhile foreign help is diminished these days and the radical elements turn to assistance from Libya, Iraq and their other friends in the arab world'.

In this letter, Haq proposed a programme run by his own men in Kabul and Peshawar:

... to pick up these men and send them to the real jihad they came for, not propagandise them with political terrorist activities. When they return to their home countries they will talk only of jihad. That way, the radical elements lose lots of friends. The arab mujahideen, when they return home, no longer gain publicity for them, recruit supporters or raise funds. You will have fewer problems and so will we ...

More sensible elements deserve your support so that people see them as leaders, for your interests, for those of Afghanistan and for islam. We must strengthen Kabul so that the radicals cannot have it.

In another letter, Haq emphasised the importance of traditional structures:

Afghans have strong traditions and poor education makes many people even more reliant on old ways. Whenever we were invaded, the Ulema [religious leaders] issued edicts, tribal leaders provided supplies and leadership, and the people fought. Afterwards they found political solutions together through these traditional elements of power. Before the 1979 invasion, Soviet inspired social reforms fractured the old system.[121] When the Soviets invaded the people fought but without traditional leadership, so political resistance parties were formed in Pakistan and Iran. Despite their unfamiliar structures and ideologies, the parties helped our nation fight, but they agreed on nothing else.

In a letter to Jimmy Carter dated 6 January 1992, Haq wrote:

> Today elections are impossible so I suggest we try and resuscitate the traditional system once again. Today the elements of power and tradition are Ulema; tribal leaders, resistance commanders; intellectuals and political party leaders and good muslims in Kabul. Each have shuras and committees ...

> In helping create the political parties, America and other foreign nations built up anti-democratic Afghan fundamentalist groups which are now almost out of control. But by building on our own traditions, Afghans may yet be able to overcome these dangerous idealogues and restore peace and security.

The following day, Baryalai put me on a bus to Islamabad where I met up with the Pakistan-based *Daily Telegraph* correspondent for some R'n'R. We flew to Gilgit, staying at Karimabad, in a place aptly called the Eagles Nest opposite the great peak of Rakaposhi. It was already cold and the air was thin. I read Hopkirk's *The Great Game* and imagined the Victorian colonial adventurers who had passed through these great mountains before me, devising, gathering intelligence and plotting against their Russian counterparts in a bid to protect the Raj. Meanwhile my colleague fiddled continuously with his short wave radio, eager for news about the UN Security Council's resolutions on Iraq. He had just returned from Baghdad, where he had covered Saddam's prisoner release from what would become the infamous Abu Ghraihb. Now he was impatient to be back there, and like many of the more ambitious young journalists I'd met here in Kabul, eager for the war to begin.

CHAPTER SIX

THE 'LION OF KABUL'

It was thought that the forceful impression Haq made on President
Reagan and Prime Minister Margaret Thatcher was pivotal in the
subsequent American decision to supply the Mujahidin with Stinger
missiles in 1986.

ROBERT KAPLAN, 1994[122]

Afghanistan, 1980s

Within weeks Baryalai invited me back to Jalalabad to attend
Abdul Haq's one-year memorial service or *shahid*[123] as it is called in
Afghanistan. At this stage, Haq's historic relevance to these people
came into relief for me. I would learn that his importance had been
two-fold: as a Pashtun commander with a brilliant capability in
asymmetric warfare, but also as a tribal leader able to work with
all of Afghanistan's different ethnic groups. These twin qualities
had been sadly lacking amongst other mujahideen leaders, yet
had played a key role in Haq's quest of ejecting the Soviet regime
from Afghanistan. They might also have been critical factors in his
bringing about an end to the Taliban.

On the day of the *shahid*, I approached a partially-destroyed
building with Sayed, a local translator. Feral-seeming, fatigue-clad
soldiers milled around the gates, eyeing me. This was the Institute
of Pedagogy, where the ceremony would be held.

Within the compound, several hundred young women sat
neatly in rows beneath eucalyptus and palm. Their bleached white
chadors were protection from the still-strong October sunlight,
making them look like nuns. They were in fact, schoolgirls. On the
stage, a man sang prayers. Beside him, posters of three dead men
– Haq, Qadir and din Mohammad's son Isatuallah – were draped
over a podium alongside the Afghan national flag. I took a seat as a

buxom woman, presumably the headmistress, took to the podium. She stood beside flashing Christmas lights, speaking about Haq's good work, saying that after ousting the Russians, he returned to his Province to build a children's park in the town and support education for all, including women.

Minutes later, along came a man with leonine features, a white beard and grey silk turban. 'Haji din Mohammad', whispered Sayed and sighed with disappointment as din Mohammad took a seat next to Hazerat Ali, who was younger than I had imagined and wore a cream *pakhal*. He was now 'Corps' (or Security) Commander in Jalalabad, yet looked childishly sulky as accolades were read about Abdul Haq.

In recent days, I had asked locals in the bazaar their view of the situation in Jalalabad. One said, 'Why are the Americans supporting this man [Hazerat Ali], and making him too strong here, when he is not educated to be a leader?'

Today a Westerner sat on the stage, and looked rather incongruous amongst Haq's brothers and former mujahidden commanders. He wore cream cowboy boots and did not look the UN official 'type', but was sharply dressed with a dark jacket thrown over white *salwar kameez*. 'James Ritchie', Sayed said, nodding in the direction of the American reputed to have financed Abdul Haq's last operation. Aloof, fair-haired and handsome, his face was set in a scowl.

Din Mohammad moved gracefully to the front from where he paused to look into the crowd. He was taking his time, reflecting with an aura of gentle paternalism. In a low, quiet voice he began to speak, gripping the podium with both hands. The schoolgirls leant forward listening intently, tears in their eyes.

'He's speaking about the events leading to Haq's death at the hands of the Taliban', Sayed explained. I felt like an intruder at a family funeral. For not only had these people clearly known Haq and his brothers, but they also understood that for din Mohammad, the death of Haq was only part of his sorrow, as his son Isatullah had also been captured and killed by the Taliban. After Haq's death, Isatullah had been driven to a military base in Kabul where he was shot, his body thrown into a well. The posters of him adorning buildings in Jalalabad showed he had been good looking. Later, people told me he was din Mohammad's favourite son, was also exceptionally talented and 'the only one of this generation likely to do any good for the people' as Sharif commented later.

The ceremony continued, Sayed translated the Pashtu words gravely. On the stage, hands clasped together above his chest, was Haji din Mohammad. He began his speech quietly, but as he went on, the pent up emotion released as his voice begun to crescendo. Sayed whispered:

> Everything is expensive in Afghanistan, but blood is very cheap. After their deaths, din Mohammad didn't speak for seven months. Until the Loya Jirga.

The soldiers of Hazerat Ali moved almost indecipherably through the crowd. Ritchie's face remained fixed upon din Mohammad. His jaw was tight. I wondered why he was here and how he had become involved. He was apparently a Republican, and had made his millions as a Chicago options trader.

A further ceremony was held, this time for the men, at the Abdul Haq children's park. Perhaps two thousand men had gathered on a treeless expanse. Many sat shoeless on mats, their Nangarhari style turbans with a raffia fez within to aid air circulation, gave relief from the sun. An umbrella was held over one of the speakers. He wore a black turban and with a dark *chador* covering his shoulders, and stooped like a wounded hawk. As two men helped him towards the stage I winced for his dignity. For it seemed they were dragging him through the dust up to the podium. There, he began a speech in *dari*. He had apparently come from Kabul with a group of Shia men to give homage to Abdul Haq's life. They were Hazara people, from Afghanistan's Central Highlands. When the ceremony ended the men rose quickly and moved as one molten mass towards the plethora of Landcruisers. Then the long convoy made its way out of Jalalabad and onto a road snaking through fields and villages until it reached a place called Surkh Rud (Red River), close to which was the Arsala family's small village.

We drove out of Jalalabad and for several kilometres, ragged-looking men lined the road besides crenellated adobe compounds. The men stood upright like soldiers and each had a Lee Enfield rifle hanging vertically by his side. This was a sign of respect for the family, Sharif told me, 'To show they're guarding them when they visit the village'. It was like a feudal gesture of honour. Within several kilometres was Fat-eh-abad, where the remnants of the retreating British had been slaughtered in 1842. We arrived at a small hamlet and parked behind the line of Landcruisers which glistened in the sun. There was a wheat field on one side and, on the other side, a stone wall. Behind this I could see men moving around as though following something, mumbling citations or prayers. I noticed the two mounds of stones, side by side. Beneath these, I realised with some shock, lay the bodies of Abdul Haq and Isatullah. Their graves were disarmingly simple, particularly when considered in relation to the numbers who had come here to honour them.

The elders circled the compound, walking behind two ceremonial wreaths of gaudy plastic flowers which were being carried. In the centre of each wreath was a framed photo of Haq and Isatullah. The men jostled and pushed as they walked, crying openly, each trying to be as close to the wreaths as possible, as though the proximity conferred access to the dead men's souls. When the wreaths were set to rest, one on each pile of stones, the crowd moved away. Now the brothers – din Mohammad, Baryalai and the grey bearded Kassim – lined up in a row with heads bent and hands clasped. Moments later, I gathered the prayers must be over because, as quickly as they had arrived the men now left in Landcruisers coiling white dust behind them.

Baryalai told me to follow him into the village. Some way along a simple mud track, he stopped at a stone entrance. A wooden plaque was marked: *Arsala khel* (the Arsala clan). Nearby, children played beneath the tamarind trees, sheltered by a stone tower. We moved through the entrance and into the calm of a sweet-scented walled garden and sat in a clearing on *charpoys*, surrounded by orange trees and the sound of birdsong. A man with squinty eyes brought us tea and some of the mourners joined us. 'Was the family home here?' I asked. Baryalai answered with a grave tone:

Yes, just across the road. But it was destroyed by pro-communist sympathisers around the time our family went to Peshawar in 1973. This garden was made for our family by our brother Daoud after the war.

***

It was late afternoon the next day when the ancient Soviet M-18 helicopter finally left Jalalabad's small airport. I was crouched over, intoxicated by the strong petrol smell, sitting on a modified airplane seat with Baryalai to my right. This was a machine captured from the Soviets and, judging by the bullet hole through the thick glass porthole window to my left, had seen some action. After taking off, we flew over the city and up the Surkh Rud (Red River) past the Arsala family village and higher into the mountains towards Kabul. Someone pointed down and visible under the helicopter, which now swooped on its side, was a convoy of old Soviet tanks parked in a circle around a hilltop. When I asked what was going on below us Baryalai said that Hazerat Ali's brother was digging up old antiquities to be sold via Pakistan into the international art trade. People had come to Baryalai to tell him about this and to complain. But he said, 'there's little I can do because they're the American allies'.

Someone shouted for us to hold onto our seats as the helicopter roared, climbing higher. Below were saffron coloured mountains. The group of Shia elders sat facing me. Their crippled leader clutched his prayer beads and Baryalai told me the man had been wounded in the jhad, and still had two bullets still lodged in his spine from a battle at Maiden Shah. We touched down at Kabul airport at dusk. The shells of blown out and destroyed aircraft stood haunting in the mist near the runway. As we awaited a car Baryalai chatted with several of the elders. I wanted to ask the Shia about Abdul Haq and why he had come to Jalalabad to honour him. With his disability, the journey would have been a huge effort. Although there would be another ceremony for Haq in Kabul the next day, other government Ministers had been conspicuous from this one by their absence.

I looked into the Shia's face and a surly man from the Ministry of Foreign Affairs (MFA) translated, 'His name is Saeed Hadi Hadi and he was a Hazara leader, now based in Car-te-ce, the main Shia district of Kabul'. The Shia's face was concentrated as he replied:

> He came because first Abdul Haq was his close friend, second they were together in jhad and third, because Abdul Haq sacrificed himself for peace and freedom of Afghanistan.

***

The contrast between Abdul Haq's modest grave and that built by Haji Zahir for his father was considerable. Haji Qadir lay at the feet of King Habibullah in Jalalabad's central park. His grave was ornate and would later be covered by a gaudy mausoleum. Such manifest differences between the brothers only increased my interest in them. It was not just the graves, but also the vast compound Qadir had been building at the family's village of Surkh Rud that spoke volumes.

Qadir had begun building the compound during his first reign as Governor of Jalalabad during the early 1990s, as the mujahiddeen tore Kabul apart. Qadir held the position until the arrival of the Taliban in 1996 when he fled to Peshawar, then the Panjshir, leaving his house half built. So the Taliban took it to store armoury, safe in the knowledge the Northern Alliance would not bomb it. Today, even from the mound of stones where Haq was buried it could been seen across the fields: a vast mass of crenellated walls and armoured watchtowers. When months later Haji Zahir gave me the tour, I saw that the place was several hectares large, more the size of a university than a family home. The effect was a hugely ostentatious cross between Fatepur Sikri[124] and JR Ewing's 'Southfork'. In fact, there was something distinctly JR Ewing about the dead Qadir with his determined, flashing blue eyes and his iron charisma at the Loya Jirga.

'One house for each son and one for each wife', Zahir announced proudly, as we looked at the nine huge buildings, each with stuccoed fronts and fake doric pillars. There was also something grotesque about such opulence here in the fifth poorest country in the world.

***

Abdul Haq, meaning 'Servant of Justice', was the name he took at the onset of the jihad. Born in April 1957, his original name had been Hamayoun Arsala and he was the fourth of the eight brothers, born to the second wife of his father. The family had been sent to Helmand during the 1960s, where Haq's father worked as an official of the King. So although Haq's earliest years were there, his schooldays were spent outside Jalalabad, at the village near Fat-e-abad, in the hamlet of mud-walled compounds some 30 kilometres from Jalalabad, tucked into the shade of the Safed Noor (Black Mountains). The rest of this section deals with Haq's initial training with Jalaluddin Haqqani in Loya Paktia, his role during the Soviet jihad, and the background to that period. Also the role of the CIA and Pakistani ISI, for whom the memory of Pakistan's war in Bangladesh ultimately shaped the Pakistani General's response to the Soviet jihad.

Haq was fifteen years-old by the time of the 1973 coup, when former Prime Minister Mohammad Daoud ousted his cousin King Zahir Shah and forty years of peace ended sharply as the King and his family were sent into exile.[125] At this stage Haq could not have realised that Daoud's coup was to ignite a series of developments leading to the Soviet invasion of Afghanistan in 1979, the exile of two-thirds of the population and a bloody war which continues to this day.[126]

Daoud wanted to democratise the state, hence he had the backing of the left-leaning urban elite, educated urban folk like the family of my interpreter, Omar. Daoud began a process of land reform but made the mistake of persecuting anyone with anti-communist views.

Although some mistakenly called him the Red Prince, believing him to be a satellite for the USSR, the irony was that Daoud was a Pashtun Nationalist and looked to Iran and the West rather than the USSR for support.

Alhough still a schoolboy, Haq was already against any form of totalitarianism. After the family's flight to Pakistan, he left high school early in order to begin resistance activities against Daoud's regime.[127] Early on, he objected to communist teachers spreading propaganda against Afghan culture and Islamic values as well as favouritism to leftist students. He moved back into Afghanistan to begin a resistance campaign alongside his brothers when only seventeen. Haq moved to Kabul early, against the advice of his family who were concerned about the danger. He began developing an underground network in the civil service and army, and plotted a coup against the regime. It failed, several officers were arrested and Haq was captured on a bus escaping to Paktia.

The Daoud regime sentenced Haq to death and he was taken to the hexagonal-shaped, Pentagon-style prison called Pul-I-charkhi on the edge of Kabul. Thousands of political prisoners and students were taken here during the 1970s and 80s, never to be seen again. Thinking he was about to be hung, he gave away his watch, radio and money before being led away, blindfolded. Incredibly, Haq's family were able to negotiate a $7,500 bribe for his release.

The end of Daoud's regime marked the end of the Durrani dynasty. The date, 27 April 1978, has since become known as the Great Saur Revolution[128] and this second coup was orchestrated by men trained as soldiers in the USSR. Noor Mohammad Taraki was installed as President of the Democratic Republic of Afghanistan. His government, comprised mainly of the Khalq faction of the People's Democratic Party of Afghanistan (PDPA),[129] was more radical in response to opposition than Daoud's had been, and many professionals fled for Pakistan and the USA. The pace of reform sped up and measures included the imposition of a ceiling on landholdings, reducing rural indebtedness, providing a minimum age for marriage and introducing a secular education system.

Now the growing impulse for resistance was linked to the speed, brutality and insensitivity to religious and cultural norms with which the changes were introduced. Taraki was infamous for his use of the KHAD and there was an acceleration of the disposal of people deemed to be dissidents. Many were executed at Kabul's airport. As with King Amanullah's rapid secularising programme of the 1920s, there was a backlash from the rural population. Angry country folk took up arms against the regime and there was a call to jihad. Government forces simply responded with greater violence. But behind Taraki was a politician named Hafizullah Amin, whom the Soviets never trusted. Amin had been educated at Columbia University, and the Kremlin believed he could be a CIA agent.

In this atmosphere of repression, Haq resolved to take up the call to arms. After his release from prison, he went to Loya Paktia in the south-eastern Pashtun belt to work with a well established mujahideen leader against the Taraki regime. This leader was Jalaluddin Haqqani[130] who led a separate front for the Party of Younus Khalis, further west along the border with Pakistan.

Jalaluddin Haqqani would develop a network (now led by his son Sirajuddin) that would later become more radicalized. It was associated in the early 1990's with the building of training camps in the borderlands between Afghanistan and Pakistan, then with Osama bin Laden (whom Jalaluddin invited back to eastern Afghanistan in 1996)[131] and later with the Taliban. Today the Haqqani network is an extremely significant front in the insurgency against NATO and the government of Hamid Karzai. Operating from North Waziristan inside the Pakistani tribal areas, the Haqqani's association with Pakistan's ISI make tackling it extremely difficult for NATO.[132]

But in the months of 1978 while Haq was with him, Jalaluddin taught Haq how to fight and to use and repair different types of ordinance and machine guns.[133] Later Abdul Haq returned to Jalalabad to began guerrilla operations.

It was December 1979 when Haq and his men learnt the Soviet Army had invaded Afghanistan to save the communist government. They heard the news by radio from the caves of Tora Bora, which the Arsala family had converted into a base for resistance.[134] Haq warned his men the fight had just begun. Several weeks later, they heard the deafening noise of Soviet tanks arriving in Jalalabad. Barbrak Karmal, a moderate PDPA member, was installed as President by the Soviets.

In his book *Charlie Wilson's War*,[135] George Crile says of the Soviet invasion:

> The full might of the Communist Empire had descended on this remote, primitive third world country. Giant II-76 transport planes were landing in Kabul, the Afghan capital, one after the other, disgorging tens of thousands of combat troops. Columns of tanks were moving in the cities, while MiG fighter jets and helicopter gunships filled the skies.

Violence against ordinary Afghans increased dramatically. In the cities, intellectuals and suspected insurgents were rounded up and executed, and thousands of university students disappeared, many into the mass graves that have recently been discovered around Pul-I-charkhi prison. In the countryside, villages and farmland was bombed, supposedly to drive out the resistance.[136]

> The Soviets killed a larger percentage of Afghans than the Nazis killed in World War II...' 'if Europeans or Americans suffered the same level of violence they would more likely seek to compromise with their occupier...'. ...'But 'The Afghan Mujahiddeen, numbering over 100,000, were the first group of insurgents to drive out a Russian army since Czar Peter the Great began his empire's southward expansion three hundred years ago.[137]

Despite the amount of firepower directed at the Afghans, they never resorted to terrorism. But the fight did not come without a cost.[138] Over a third of the pre-war population (five-and-a-half million Afghans) became refugees, forced to flee to neighbouring Iran and Pakistan. The situation was so acute that during the 1980s Afghans accounted for fifty percent of the world's refugees. Within the country itself, another two million of those who stayed were forced to migrate. No other conflict apart from the 1971 Bangladesh war had created more homeless people since WWII. 1985 was the bloodiest year for

Afghanistan and the NGO, the Swedish Committee, reported that over half of all farmers who stayed in Afghanistan had their fields bombed, over a quarter had irrigation destroyed and livestock shot by Soviet or Afghan communist troops.

In response to the Soviet invasion, in Eastern Afghanistan the Arsala brothers organised themselves. Qadir became the main Commander in Shinwar, the hostile desert-like area between Peshawar and Jalalabad, and one of the main supply routes to the mujahideen. Haji Din Mohammad became de facto head of Khalis's party, spending much time in Peshawar, raising funds and organising the transfer of resources to the mujahideen in the field. Abdul Haq took the fight right to its epicentre, to Kabul[139] where the communist regime was headquartered. He was the only mujahideen leader to do so. Alongside Ahmad Shah Massoud and Jalaluddin Haqqani, Abdul Haq became one of the three great commanders of the anti-Soviet war.

He had decided to take the fight to the centre because he realised the communist regime was not threatened by rural insurgencies. So he developed tactical guerrilla fighting units around the city and his resistance fighters grew from four men to over five thousand. Despite his small band of men, and limited supplies – they were supplied only with what they could capture and what sympathetic residents gave them – Haq was successful in attacking government outposts, power facilities and the army. One night they listened to the radio and heard a BBC announcement say that 13,000 resistance fighters were operating in the Paghman area. They were only eighteen men at the time but had to announce a large force or risk being humiliated.

In Kabul, he developed an underground network with a guile that enabled him to penetrate the regime's army and civil service. And it was some of his operations, including in 1987 blowing the largest of the Soviet munitions dumps just outside the city at Qarga, which ultimately turned the war. Yet despite his ability to develop effective guerilla fighting units, he was never properly recognised by the Afghan Resistance Movement, which denied him the munitions and support he needed. Partly this stemmed from the movement's roots, its relationship with Pakistan's ISI and Haq's candid criticism of that.

From the early 1970s, the Afghan resistance movement had been based in the frontier town of Peshawar, inside Pakistan. The movements' inception had begun with a trickle of support from the CIA. But things changed when Pakistan's right-wing military dictator General Zia al-Haq came to power in a 1977 coup. The democratically elected government of Zulfiqar ali Bhutto was overthrown and Bhutto summarily hung in a public garden. The elfin, monkey-faced General now proceeded with the job of creating a pure Islamic society in Pakistan, 'that perennially undefined and therefore unfinished task which has given political legitimacy to many despots in Muslim countries'.[140]

With the USSR's Christmas 1979 invasion of Afghanistan, General Zia and his officers recognised the potential for a sharp increase in US military and financial aid to their fledgling fundamentalist regime. An Afghan war financed by the US would also assist Pakistan to achieve strategic depth against India. Pakistan's recent memory of having to surrender 90,000 soldiers to India during the 1971 Bangladeshi war had left the Generals deeply humiliated.

The tactic would be to present Pakistan as 'a needy frontline state against Communist aggression' and for Zia 'to make himself invulnerable as a dedicated anti-communist, an Islamic Holy Warrior'.[141] This would also bolster his reputation with the religious parties of Pakistan who he was encouraging in their mission to Islamise the country by building religious schools, known as madrassahs.

President Zia was in a position of immense strength with the USA when the Soviet Union invaded Afghanistan over Christmas 1979, the reason being that Carter had recently targeted General Zia as a result of human rights abuses, cutting off US aid and military cooperation with Pakistan.

> Now with the Red Army sweeping into Afghanistan, Carter had to do a 180- degree turn to win Zia's approval to use Pakistan as a base. Zia drove a hard bargain; the CIA could provide the weapons,

but they would have to hand them over to his intelligence services for distribution. America's spies would have to operate exclusively through Zia's men.[142]

The US desire for a covert operation also gave Pakistan's generals immense power[143] and sewed the seeds for problems later on. A Russian journalist[144] who covered the war extensively said, 'The Pakistani military regarded the entrance of Soviet troops into Afghanistan as "Brezhnev's gift"'.[145] Indeed the ISI's monopoly on America's largesse was effectively a 'private pipeline to power'[146] for the army and intelligence establishment, enabling Pakistan to use the Afghan war (and the USA's desire to rout communism) to meet its own ends. With Pakistan controlling the purse strings and deciding on the tactics of Afghan guerrilla leaders, Afghanistan would become a client state of the radicalised regime.

Abdul Haq recognised the problems inherent to this approach early on, and his candid criticism of the CIA's covert policy lost him friends in both the CIA and the ISI. It also ensured he was belittled by them and cut out of the largesse received by other, less scrupulous mujahideen leaders. And it probably contributed to his death.

CHAPTER SEVEN

'THESE DAYS, WE DON'T KNOW WHO THE ENEMY IS'

Jalalabad, 2002

In autumn 2002, the key question remained Osama bin Laden's whereabouts. It was less than a year since his 'disappearance' from the caves at Tora Bora. I heard that the Arsalas had been cut out of the consultations over strategy at Tora Bora and – unlike the preferred warlords, Haji Zaman and Hazerat Ali – were unsupported during the battle. So Haji Zahir commanded his men during the Tora Bora operation, unpaid by the Americans. Yet he was the only commander to capture any al Qaeda prisoners (for which Hazerat Ali later tried to claim credit).[147] It seemed – despite their history during the jihad, their strength with people in this area and the fact that they knew the caves intimately – that the Arsalas were well and truly *pariah* as far as the CIA and coalition were concerned. An episode just outside Jalalabad would confirm this, as well as indicate the CIA's seeming inability to dis-aggregate useful allies from those who were just keen to be in their pay or indeed those who were trying to improve their standing with the new Northern Alliance 'power' in Kabul. Since then I have often wondered how much this attitude to the family contributed to bin Laden's escape from those caves. 'Bin Laden could easily have been caught at Tora Bora', people in Jalalabad told me, shrugging with bemused disdain when I asked why the operation had been such a disaster. Haji Zahir's view was:

> The Americans consulted Haji Zaman and Hazerat Ali but not me. They could *easily* have caught him but made a fatal mistake! I'd have told them to close all routes around the caves and Tora Bora *before* they began bombing. It's basic military practice!

His gaze fixed on mine from behind an index finger held vertically before his nose.

> But they didn't close routes, and bombed for ten days *before* allowing soldiers to go in! So al Qaeda had a clear ten days to escape!

Many reckoned that bin Laden and his men had left Tora Bora via the exit at a place called Parachinar.[148] He was rumoured to have been led across by Haji Zaman, the warlord supported by MI6.

***

Although Haji Zahir sometimes wore the *pakhal* traditional to the men of the Panjshir – where both he and Qadir had joined forces with the Northern Alliance to fight the Taliban – he remained a man of the East. But these days Zahir was having to keep a low profile in Jalalabad. One day, soon after my departure to Pakistan, the Americans found themselves and their armoury used in a local rivalry which had its roots in Kabul, at the Ministry of Defence.

On the night of 2 October 2002 – not three months after Haji Qadir's assassination – some forty humvees, tanks and trucks made their way through the darkness towards the Pakistan border. Some of the heavier American vehicles had been stationed above Jalalabad, at Sarobi, for several days. Others were flown in by Chinook from Bagram, landing at Jalalabad airport which was now controlled by Hazerat Ali. At around three am they joined a further convoy driving out towards Dacca, the camp where Zahir's border guard were stationed, the same place he'd taken me soon after our first meeting. His commander at the base that night, Kari Mohammad Yousef, told me six months later that the raiding party had included around fifty US Special Forces soldiers clad in black ski masks, 250 soldiers from the newly created Afghan National Army (ANA) and Hazerat Ali's men. Zahir's soldiers were disarmed, gagged, tied up and beaten with rifle butts.

Later that night, Ali's men burst through a checkpoint guarded by Zahir's men without using the 'word of the night'.[149] So Zahir's men fired on their vehicle and they fired back, killing one of Zahir's soldiers. The inference? With such open support from the US they could do as they wished. These events took place while Zahir was in his Jalalabad compound and his houseboy informed him that night that the Americans (the 82nd Airborne Division) had parked several vehicles outside his compound. Soldiers were taking notes, measuring up his gateposts and the height of the walls. When, the next morning, Kari Mohammad Yousf informed Zahir of the previous night's events, Zahir told him to ask the Americans what had been the problem. But when Kari arrived at the 82nd Airborne's office he was promptly arrested and taken to the jail at Bagram airbase. 'They made me stand for a whole week with no rest', he complained later. The Americans released him after two months, when they realised he had been the Commander who had captured twenty-two Arabs at Tora Bora.

The day after their raid, the Americans came to Zahir's office and accused him of an alliance with al Qaeda and the Taliban. When they insisted they wanted him to come to their compound for questioning, he screamed at them in frustration that he had been imprisoned for *three years* by the Taliban

> I'll *never* give myself up to you, to be sent to Guantanamo! If you want me, you'll have to get beyond my soldiers to find me. And take me dead!

An American sergeant finally outlined the reasons for the raid: 'We had intelligence you had a Chechen on your camp'. It was true there had been a Chechen on the camp, but Zahir, taking Louisa's advice, had made several reports on him to the State Department earlier that year, explaining that the Chechen may previously have been linked to al Qaeda but in the absence of any provision for such a person in Jalalabad town, he was using him as a 'cook'. The man was deaf and dumb. He received no response to his letters.

A few days later, Zahir, still gripped by the grief of his fathers' death, but forced to be wise beyond his twenty-eight years, told me:

> In these days we are 'listening' and 'looking', but not 'saying'. I wish my father was still alive. If he was here this wouldn't be happening. I tell you they are taking down the walls of the compound, soon they will be in the house!

His eyes were cast downwards and I wondered if this was an allusion to the coalition presence or a displacement of the old order.

Possibly the Americans had presumed that Hazerat Ali – being non-Pashtun and 'Fahim's man' – was their 'real' ally down here and not Haji Zahir, or indeed any member of the Arsala family.[150] At Dacca, I'd thought Haji Zahir a playboy. Now it seemed he was a pawn in a wider game involving the US and 'their' chosen allies. But nobody here had told the Americans, or the British for that matter, the rules.

***

I finally met Haji din Mohammad. I had scheduled an interview to gauge his views on the poppy situation and he invited me to dine with him and a nephew who had flown in from California. We met in what had been Qadir's house in Kabul. The nephew was quietly intellectual, but told me his mother was the sister of the Arsala brothers. She had wept bitterly at her home in California when she heard of Qadir's death, clutching his picture to her chest all night. Her husband, the boys' father, had been killed by the Soviets while fighting with the mujahideen.

Din Mohammad led us upstairs, into the only curtained room in the empty 1960s-style house in Wazir Akbar Khan which Qadir had been about to furnish before he died. Din Mohammad, always considered the most conservative of the eight brothers, was the one the others had looked up to during the jihad, when he had run the office of Younis Khalis's Resistance Party Hizb-e-Islami[151] in Peshawar. Tonight his grey silk turban hung in a tail over his white *salwar* as he sat cross-legged with us on the floor.

A Samovar was brought for us to wash our hands and his eyes creased with humour when I exclaimed how cold was the water. He apologised it had been hard for me to contact him; he had been to Saudi on *Haj* with President Karzai and afterwards had visited Abdul Haq's five children, now living in Dubai with an aunt. There was something protectively paternal about him and as we dined he diverted the conversation to an anecdote. He had been riding a tandem bicycle with Haq's young boys[152] and, putting his foot into the chain by mistake, filled his shoe with blood. He hadn't wanted the boys to know or they would worry. Later, when I asked about the British poppy compensation scheme,[153] he commented,

> We are *still* waiting for the promised compensation for the people of Chipahar [district] ... they did compensation for emergency but not for long-term ... now they have some experience, maybe they will think about a better way.

Yet the people of Chipahar, he told me, had actually asked for a dam project *instead* of the British compensation. This had been waived by the British despite the fact that the water table had recently dropped four to five metres. Even drinking water was now a problem. The people needed reservoirs to stabilise the water level because over eighty-five percent of the population were involved in agriculture. He added, 'It is not effective to struggle against poppy cultivation using military or a police force before alternative means for farmers to earn a living are established'. I understood he was referring to pressure being exerted by the British on the Afghan government to destroy poppies using local security forces. When he said that there was even talk of aerial spraying, I remembered how Soviet-inspired land reforms in Afghanistan had stimulated rebellion. He continued, 'The sooner we rebuild our country so there will be no drugs menace and no terrorist activity'.

His words were a stark reminder that the drugs problem would not be eliminated in Afghanistan until the West had also pulled its weight in terms of reconstruction to help rebuild the local economy.[154] Yet at this time, late in 2002, very little of the reconstruction money promised in January 2002 by the international community at the Tokyo conference had arrived. Only one billion USD had so far been spent, and much of this on resettling returning refugees.

***

That October 2002, at a lunch party in the spacious grounds of the Turkish Embassy, journalists, aid workers and diplomats bathed in a 1970s stone pool and ate a buffet lunch in the luxuriant grounds where the Turks had geese and a horse roaming. We sat on the lawn, plates balanced on our knees and an American diplomat got talking with me. She worked for the State Department and was interested to hear about Jalalabad. It was now a full year after September 11, yet State Department staff were *still* barred from travel to the Provinces. This, she said, was because the 'Pentagon wanted to "lead" on Reconstruction'. 'And they are calling what are essentially still "security operations" in the south, "reconstruction"', she added. Now this was confusing. So I simply answered her question: 'Well, as you ask, I can tell you there are problems in Jalalabad'.

'With Haji din Mohammad?' she snapped. Now it was her turn to be perplexed. When she heard about the raid on Zahir's men and the unhappiness of the locals with Hazerat Ali, she gave me her card and said if I heard anything maybe I could let her know. A week later a UN political staffer said to me:

> Din Mohammad is a religious man, yet without the intimidation of a man like Sayyaf … When you hear him talking about the need for sustainable forestry in Kunar, you know he tackles these issues with sensitivity and integrity.

I trusted this man's opinion. He was the son of a well-known Afghan intellectual and historian[155] and had been based in Jalalabad earlier that year. Drumming his fingers on the desk, he added, 'But an Afghan Government Intelligence report has just been released, saying Haji din Mohammad is supporting Hikmatyar and al Qaeda'.

When I told her about the intelligence report, Louisa said,

> It's true that if Qadir were alive this would not be happening. I'm sure Fahim and Qanooni killed him … because he stood between them and power. Qadir, so respected by Pashtuns and Panjshiris alike, must have been *such* a threat to them.

She paused, wiping her brow.

> If the US end up taking Haji din Mohammad because of this stupid report … there'll be an uprising in the Eastern Provinces and it'll encourage people to turn to Hikmatyar because he's against the

Americans. They're just driving the people to that. Don't they realise those people *chose* Haji din Mohammad? I witnessed them chanting his name at Qadir's funeral, before Qadir's body was even in the *ground*. The people chose him and if the US removes him there'll be hell to pay!

The next day Kabul airport was closed. An Italian security officer told me a clutch of stinger missiles had been found in the hills and it was believed Hikmatyar had put them there.

So I decided to visit the State Department lady. She met me at the gate of the Embassy. Unsmiling US marines looked down from watchtowers behind rolls of barbed wire and a bulldozer was parked behind the gate to prevent unwanted entrants. Oddly, she seemed nervous of taking me to an office so we sat outside the white plastic luxury caravans where the Embassy staff lived and discussed the problems with Jalalabad. The wind whipped between us and the sound of electronic trumpets blasted out a tinny version of 'The Last Post' through a megaphone. She bolted from her chair, standing to attention, cutting the conversation mid-sentence. I was taken aback as it was bizarre watching her standing there amidst the windy caravans, just her and me. Finally, awkwardly, I stood too until the mawkish sound ended. She sat down.

I'm sorry, it's just that last week a new Colonel here lost it with me, shouting me down in front of fifty colleagues for not standing to attention.

What? I asked.

Yeah. He screamed, 'Don't you have any *respect* for the victims of September 11?'

***

I returned to Jalalabad to interview Hazerat Ali in the garden of his house. It was dusk and the smell of two-stroke engines mingled with jasmine. Metal platters laden with grape and pomegranate were brought to us as we sat, both a little shy of the interview about to occur. I noticed how close were Ali's eyes, like a squint-eyed spaniel but carrying a tinge of menace. 'So why didn't you sort this out with Haji Zahir in the normal way?' I asked, talking of the Chechen incident. The 'normal way' in Afghanistan meant over tea and nuts rather than with American B52's. Ali frowned. 'Even if my brother is sympathetic to al Qaeda then I will not defend him', he said with deliberate obscurity. His manipulation of the facts indicated the probable origin of the so-called 'intelligence' reports denigrating the Arsala family. I probed further but Ali would say no more. But he didn't deny being behind the Chechen incident.

Baraylai called from Kabul. He would not be back for several days but I was welcome to stay on in his house. One morning at eleven, Baryalai's Shinwari houseboy, the impish Mahboub, came upstairs. Zahir had apparently sent a car for me. Downstairs awaited a pick-up full of bodyguards, RPGs balanced on their knees. We drove out of the city and towards Samarkhel, where we stopped. This was a checkpoint manned by Zahir's soldiers. He was there for I saw his bald head among a sea of fatigue-clad men. He was walking towards his convoy of cars and looked like a medieval king surrounded by knights. The driver pulled away before there was a chance to say hello. So we continued out of town, beneath the tamarind trees and into the open scrubland towards the border.

This time we stopped at 'Dacca' in the foothills of the Khyber Pass. It had been a British guard post during the 19th Century. Now it was a collection of buildings to the left of the road with a checkpoint on a steep hill above. We drank tea beneath a rubber tree, Zahir to my left and his solders milling about us. He told me he'd been to a funeral on the way here and that for security reasons, he'd now switched into one of the six red SUVs used by his soldiers. After tea, we drove on to Torkham and the border where Zahir had another office. Perched high on the hill opposite was a checkpoint where he told me his soldiers had recently fought a battle with the Pakistanis for over forty-five minutes, with the deaths of eight Pakistani soldiers. Zahir was annoyed the Afghan government had apparently 'given' the hill to Pakistan thirty years before in exchange for electricity and water for Afghan offices at Torkham. 'But I would *never* have done this', Zahir emphasised.

Steep crags of the Khyber Pass faced us. We moved into a small office building near the main border crossing; another of Zahirs' Border Guard offices. On a bleached wall at the far end were framed pictures of Qadir, Karzai and Massoud. It was like a protection policy which shouted, 'Hey, we're allies with all these men, so you can't touch us'. A man came bearing thick, Lahori-style *chai*. Zahir said that he and the man had been together in Kandahar jail for three years. And he began the tale of his famed escape from Kandahar jail:

> My father left Afghanistan in late 1996 as the Taliban took Sarobi. Sarobi was an important crossroads in Afghanistan; with routes from the Khyber to Kabul and cut-through up to the north-east, to Panjshir and beyond. The Taliban had taken it surprisingly fast. He screamed through the border here at Torkham in his Landcruiser as the Talibs arrived.

Behind Qadir, other elders of the Eastern Shura didn't make it and some of Qadir's commanders were apparently killed in a bomb attack, he said. I had heard this story from people in Kabul and – as is often the case in Afghanistan – there were several sides to the story. One was that Qadir had blown up these other commanders himself. But later, after repeated questioning of many people, the consensus view seemed to be that the bomb attack had been orchestrated by a rival mujahiddeen group.

Following his escape, Qadir and his family returned to the Hyatabad home they had occupied as exiles in Peshawar for almost twenty-five years. And the Taliban swiftly took all but the north-east of the country. From Peshawar, as they had with the Soviets, the Arsalas then allied with Massoud to fight the Taliban.

'After the winter my father asked me to lead an incursion of rebel commanders from Peshawar', Zahir said. It was April 1997 and the aim was to open up a southern front to distract the Taliban, to relieve pressure on General Massoud. Qadir would lead a front through the mountains of Nuristan, to the north-west of the Khyber Pass, and Zahir would lead a front from the south of the Khyber

Pass, through the Shinwar. In both regions the family still counted on local support. 'When he called me I was surprised. Because I was due to go to "Jap pon" (Japan) the next day, on business.[156] But my father said, no you must do this'.

So Zahir left for the border with his men in dead of night.

> ISI had word of our expedition and tried to shoot me the morning before I left, as I was driving with my cousin, but I escaped and they injured my arm. We went in through Afridi[157] country but the Taliban had threatened villagers they'd kill their every last *chicken* if they let Haji Zahir pass by.

Even so, Zahir had occasional friends in the Shinwar willing to give them shelter.

> But the people were very afraid. And after seven days of very little food I had only forty men left out of three hundred. They had deserted due to the cold and conditions. We went through rivers and walked all night, wading from nine pm until seven am.

Zahir was wounded in a shoot out.

> My radio battery died and I was behind a rock and reached round for the medical bag and the Taliban shot at me. I was trying to radio my commanders to come to help from different mountaintops. But my men carried me on.

Finally, one morning they were surrounded as they slept beneath a pile of large rocks on a hill.

> But we looked so wretched the Taliban didn't realise it was me. They said 'Look at these poor bastards' and 'don't worry guys, we'll release you when we get down below'. I thought I could escape but the Governor of the district was waiting below and when he saw me shouted, *'al hamdallullah,* it's Haji Zahir'. So the Taliban took me to the Governors' Palace in Jalalabad. One said, 'Six months ago you were King of Jalalabad but now you're our prisoner'. Mullah Omar told them to take me quick to Kandahar and so they drove me there in a convoy of sixty vehicles, Toyotas, to ensure I didn't escape.

He spent over three years in the city centre jail. Only twenty-eight years old, he looked more like forty-five: the top of his head was bald and he had dark circles under his eyes.

> It was the shackles I wore for three years: ten kilometres chains. And the lack of food as each day we only had half a bread and just one cup of tea. I got very thin but when ICRC did a mediation and prisoner exchange between Taliban and the Northern Alliance my father was allowed to send me, money, twenty-five lackh, and then I bought more food.

He was able to do so because the Taliban kept the money and sent someone, writing out a chit for Zahir's food or cigarettes to deduct the amount spent. He said:

> They were simple but honest people. But they beat me often saying, 'You are Pashtun so why are you fighting for the Northern Alliance?' But they didn't beat Ismael Khan.

He lived in a cell with two other men and was allowed out once a day to wash and pray. Four days after his capture, as Zahir was washing in a small *kareze*,[158] they told him to come. A Judge, the Taliban Intelligence Chief Kari Hamid Gul and Corp Commander awaited him.

> 'On Friday we are going to kill you', they said. Mullah Omar had made an edict and it was announced by public radio. The Taliban Foreign Minister, Mutawakil, announced that Ismael Khan and I would be executed after prayers the following Friday unless my father stopped fighting with the Northern Alliance. So I told the guard I'd pay him $2000 if he got me a radio for two nights to hear what they intended to do. I heard my own father say on the radio in response to Muttawakil, 'I am not stopping my mission for my son and if you kill my one son I have seven more to take his place'.

Zahir sighed. 'I was not happy about this, he said. I was not surprised. Qadir must have been a tough father. It was a retort on a par with Stalin's when offered up his POW son by Hitler: 'I will not swap a Private for a General'.

> Then Dr Abdullah said by radio to the Taliban: 'If you kill Haji Zahir then we promise that on the same day we'll send the boxes of all

eight hundred of our Taliban prisoners held in Panjshir valley back to Jalalabad in boxes'. And so the Taliban didn't kill us.

He wiped his brow.

Ismael Khan called me '*Pir*'[159] when I told him a few days before the two of us were due to be hanged that I'd dreamed we would one night ride two horses in the river. This signaled to him we would be free and eighteen months later we were.

He paused, looking somewhere beyond the window.

But the Taliban taunted me, saying 'See, your father doesn't care for you'. So I said, 'He is my father. I respect him and whatever he says I agree'. I was proud of him for not bending to them. He was like a lion.

After a year in prison, Zahir and his cellmates attempted their first escape, scraping cement from between the bricks each night. But after weeks of painstaking work they found a metal grid inside the wall.

So we had to try another wall. Eventually we broke through and found ourselves in an alley. But with a nine metre perimeter wall beyond. I had to ask for a stick for my 'broken' leg. We made a rope ladder from *salwar* and the hemp used to carry yoghurt sacks. Then with two men and a third on top we scaled the wall.

The attempt failed because two Panjshiri prisoners heard them drop and told the Taliban. The second escape attempt, eighteen months later, was altogether more dramatic.

Each evening I was allowed out of my cell to do ablutions before prayers. I noticed a man beside me and said 'salaam' to him each night. It was odd how he always came and washed next to me.

After a while, Zahir realised the man was a guard and though Kandahari, he was not for Taliban.

After a few weeks he offered to take letters to my father in Panjshir and family in Peshawar. But I knew the ISI would follow him, and realise as soon as he came to their house, as ISI was with Taliban. So I said if he could go to Iran, Ismael Khan would help.

So Khan wrote a letter to his son. The guard's father took it to

Mashad, in Iran. But the money was not released. 'Ismael Khan is tight with money', Zahir laughed, making the shape of a fist. 'Now', he added, 'Ismael Khan is making $1 million dollars per day from the border whereas we are making only 1 million Afghanis per day [about $30,000].[160] But we give all to central government'.[161]

He laughed yet the issue was an embarrassment for Karzai, whose influence on outlying regions was so weak he was now dubbed 'Governor of Kabul'. In Kandahar jail, the weeks passed. The man came back and told Zahir that he'd not been able to get the money from Khan's son. But luckily Dr Rabbani, the President of Afghanistan in exile and a friend of Qadir's, came to Mashad. The father of Zahir's guard met him and asked for help.

> Rabbani immediately bought a Landcruiser for $20,000 and the guards' father drove it to Kandahar. When it arrived the Guard bought me a note in jail explaining what the escape plan would be.

The men would bring them Kandahari clothes, a *salwar* and turban, to change into. Electrical cables would be cut and new shackles with keys brought for them to wear after removing the old ones with pliers. The guard would come in the early hours and open the three sets of gates. Then, on the night, they would don the clothes and follow him literally walking out of the jail.

> I was scared because there was a little rain that night and so the Talib guards had moved their *charpoy* right onto the platform outside my cell door and so I had to creep past them sleeping.

Outside the gates, they met the guard who took them across a sleeping Kandahar to the place where the taxis leave for Hilmand to the west. The car awaited them. It was still dark, but the man said they had to wait for his son. They waited ninety minutes and, although Zahir was getting more irritated, he didn't ask why they were waiting. Eventually the sun came up and the son came. At this stage Zahir asked why he'd been so long. He said that if he had left his duty early and not re-shut all the gates again the Taliban would have realised: 'His action gave us an extra five hours to escape because the next guard only came on at ten am'..

They drove to Hilmand and at Lash-Kah-Gah, the town of the great opium bazaar, turned off into the desert.

> By now I was certain the Taliban would catch us with helicopters from the sky. But thank God a few drops of rain came and it was too cloudy for helicopters.

One of the districts here was controlled by an anti-Taliban commander, so they tried to make it to there. They were lost in the desert for three days trying to cross into Iran near a desolate place called Zaranj. When they got to the place of the 'bridges made by sand over thousands of years', the father of the boy knew they were in the friendly commander's territory. They came upon an old man and his son collecting relics. 'The rain made it perfect conditions for them to do this', Zahir explained as an aside. They asked them to show the way and the old man warned them there were still landmines left there by the mujahideen.

> But we were impatient and insisted he came on with us in the car. Within minutes, we hit an anti-tank mine. Ismael Khan was lying half in and half out of the car and it was destroyed. So I took him out. He had a huge shrapnel wound in his leg. Thank goodness the commander of the district arrived soon after and rescued us.

Zahir said the commander wanted to take just him and Ismael Khan and not the old man and boy. But Zahir did not accept this. So they all went to Iran together and then on the plane to Mashad.

> When I arrived my father called me from the Panjshir where he was fighting the Taliban. It was the first time we had spoken in three years.

Zahir remained in Iran, but had a falling out with his father, Qadir, over some money Qadir loaned him for a house in Iran which Zahir apparently lost in a bad deal. The two did not speak until after September 11. He was tired now. We made ready to return to Jalalabad and lunch.

***

A few days later, Engineer Sharif and I drank green tea together at Baryalai's 'Green Castle'.

> At least when we were fighting the Russians we knew *who* we had to fight. But when you're fighting your own neighbours, things are a *lot* more complex.

He put down his cup and looked at me.

> The Americans were so *stupid* for the way they treated Zahir, after his *bravery* at Tora Bora.

'Is that why people resent them giving Ali so much power?' I asked. Sharif hissed:

> It's because Hazerat Ali takes their *money* and does what he's *told*. But the Arsalas, they won't be the running *dogs* of the Americans.

CHAPTER EIGHT

'AFGHANISTAN WILL BE THE WORLD'S LARGEST POPPY FIELD'

If the British help us make factories and roads and education,
then the people will not be interested to grow poppy.

AFGHAN FARMER, October 2002

Jalalabad, Shinwar and Kabul, October 2002 & May 2003

'Afghans have only themselves to blame; they're just criminals growing poppy to support warlords!' Julie snapped. She was an elegant Islamabad-based British diplomat whose hospitality I had enjoyed in the autumn of 2000, after my evacuation from Kandahar. But today she was tired, having worked long hours since September 11 providing briefings for London. Even so, I knew she had visited neither an Afghan poppy farm nor even the Khyber Pass! British Foreign Office security policy would not allow this, so Osama bin Laden's 1999 fatwa[162] threatening death to US and British nationals who dared step into Afghanistan had worked. Now British diplomats were gated in leafy, suburban Islamabad. So how could Julie have *any* idea of the situation? Here in Jalalabad, a year after those comments, made in October 2001, I was about to be enlightened. I was to learn how the family could use their influence with the tribes to reduce poppy cultivation in Nangarhar Province. Ironically, they were still perceived by the international community as little more than drug dealers.

Baryalai, under the auspices of The Abdul Haq Foundation, was organising a 'drugs awareness seminar' in conjunction with the UN and religious leaders from around the Province. The aim? To use religion to persuade farmers not to grow poppy. One of President Karzai's first initiatives on coming into office was to announce a decree banning the growing and trafficking[163] of poppy. In reality,

113

and as the world was about to find out with the publication of UN figures on poppy output for 2002,[164] getting rid of poppy would not be a corollary of ejecting the Taliban.

Although the Taliban had used poppy as a means of financing themselves, their August 2000 edict banning production had been remarkably successful. Only 185 metric tonnes of resin was produced in 2001, and most of this came from the Northern Alliance controlled area. The Taliban's successful ban was a measure of their control over even remote rural areas and poppy was about to be a litmus test of Karzai's hold over regions beyond Kabul.

At the seminar, elders and farmers had gathered beneath a roof of reed shading them from the harsh midday Nangahar sun. They looked regal in an array of turbans of differing greys and silver twisted silk and listened as a Mohmand tribal elder listed the problems facing his tribe. Dressed in white *salwar kameez*, with a straw fez beneath his turban, he spoke from a podium with a small speaker. Sayed translated:

> We understand if poppy production is illegal and are ready to cooperate with the government and international community to accept a ban but our problems cannot be ignored. The Mohmand tribe needs security and for the central government to provide job opportunities and education for poor communities.

Another complained, 'We need a retaining wall to protect our lands which are being denuded by the Kabul and Kunar rivers. My people are now in debt'. Much discussion centred around financial assistance promised back in the Spring by British Foreign office staff. Sharif leant forward:

> The British came from Kabul promising compensation in return for destruction of the poppy crop. The farmers agreed, the destruction took place, but the money hasn't turned up. So now they feel tricked.

Over the following months, the poppy issue revealed facets of British and US involvement in Afghanistan which could potentially become as significant a mistake as the Soviet's land reform package. These had pushed rural people into open revolt, accelerating the pace of resistance, and ultimately the USSR's humiliating departure from Afghanistan.

At a lunch after the meeting, several farmers invited us to see their farms. At a place known as 'Twenty-Nine Streams', farmer Nazim gul was nobly dressed in a grey and black silk turban. But the land was bleached lifeless by the sun with no water for several kilometres. What was used had to be carried in by the women. Irrigation systems built in the 1970s by the Russians had been decimated during the fighting that followed their departure, when the mujahideen had tried unsuccessfully to take Jalalabad from the Afghan communist government.

Gul grew wheat, cotton and maize for home consumption on his plot of land of only seven *jiribs* (1.5 hectares) but said his family's life depended on income from poppy, the best cash crop. Not least because wheat needed water. The price[165] for poppy then was considered excellent, at around $700 per kilogram. For 700kgs of wheat, he earned only $100.

The irony was that the Taliban had banned poppy production very successfully in Afghanistan in the year 2000, albeit with the threat of force. The ban had restricted output, hence by 2001 farmers were keen to plant again to benefit from the high price. The farmer grew upset, telling me about the British scheme;

> They destroyed our poppy with sticks and then tractors, about fifty
> people came to our village from Jalalabad, but no cash was paid to us!

He would probably plant again in a few weeks because although a decree had come from President Karzai banning poppy cultivation, there had been no concurrent support from government. 'A ban is not sustainable without jobs or salaries'. Afghanistan was a country with no welfare state. The war had narrowed options for making a living by destroying irrigation systems and roads so the perishable fruits Afghans had once sent to India were no longer viable.

Gul's house was a simple adobe structure with a flat roof perhaps two metres square and devoid of the possessions typically to be found, such as carpets, radios or crockery. His wife offered us green tea but it was dusk and we had to return to Jalalabad. Outside a handful of goats were tethered. The only colour in the deadened landscape was the brightly-dyed dresses of his daughters. The family came outside to wave as we stomped over the baked stony ground to our car and invited us to stay next time we were in the area; their hospitality a contrast to the misdirected attacks of the international community in general and the British – who had just taken on responsibility for poppy – in particular.

The reason I had been been received with an unwelcome smirk at another farm that afternoon was becoming obvious. I had been sent around the corner to talk with the womenfolk in a farmyard. Behind a screen sat the farmer's wife on a *charpoy*, dark plaits hanging either side of her weathered face. When my interpreter commented on my 'Britishness' she had cocked her head and begun a litany of comments in *Pashtu* along the lines that the British were tricky. Until now my British ancestry had been met with a wry smile and comments like 'Pashtu and English people have a long history together', a reference to our part in three Afghan wars, but said with a degree of respect. This dissatisfied lady referred to Britain's less gallant history in the poppy scheme of April 2002.

Although the seminars were aimed at reducing poppy production and increasing farm incomes, there was still no prescription as to how this could be done. The British government had decided to take the lead on controlling the Afghan drugs situation largely because Afghan poppy was, according to the UN, now accounting for over eighty-five percent of heroin on Britain's streets. But in the end, the need to put food on the table and market forces would prevail. Baryalai said of the British scheme: 'The money paid would be based upon land area of poppy grown. But many farmers received nothing'.

Despite the fact the market price for poppy was then $700 per kg of paste, and farmers could harvest an average 14 kilograms per *jirib* (meaning they would be out of pocket entering the British scheme), many did so out of 'honour' according to Baryalai. They had even agreed to destroy their lucrative crop just before harvest. Yet having done so, they received nothing. No wonder they were seething.

Local commanders associated with the US and British backed warlords, Haji Zaman and Hazerat Ali, had encouraged the farmers to over-declare the amount of land they had. And the commanders would pocket the difference. The irony was the fraud might have been controlled had the British worked with Haji Qadir, because the Governor's office had land ownership maps against which the claims could have been verified.[166] 'But the British had wanted to do their own thing', Baryalai sighed. 'One surveyor was even killed for refusing to cook the books'.

The NGO chosen by the British to run the scheme was the Welfare and Relief Committee (WRC). The man who ran it was the cousin of someone named Haji Rohullah from Kunar. But Rohullah was a leader of the Salafi sect, a Wahhabist group believed to have links with extremist groups in Saudi Arabia. The Americans had arrested him two months back. And WRC was an NGO based in Pakistan. It seemed odd that an international NGO had not been chosen to run such a controversial scheme or at least to monitor the work of WRC, to whom the British had subcontracted this important work.

On asking Baryalai whether Qadir's reputation as a 'drug lord' was fair he shrugged and said:

> My brother was no saint, but how does the Governor of a province go about collecting money from drug traffickers? But my brother was stupid in making friendships with people like Ayoub Afridi. That has made people associate him with drugs.

Early in 2003, six months later, I finally interviewed the FCO official now in charge of Jalalabad's failed poppy compensation scheme. As time passed, more and more checkpoints were set up at the embassy. Now it was necessary to stand beneath watchtowers and search lights, knocking and awaiting the opening of a slot within the vast iron gate. An Afghan guard would nonchalantly ask what was wanted and then, after making instructions to write the name of the diplomat on a piece of paper, would invariably slam shut the slot in ones face. Those visiting the British Embassy remained on the wrong side of the closed iron gates, in a tumbleweed-empty street, unable to see their car. As much as ten minutes might elapse before, permission having hopefully been granted, it was possible to step into British territory.

Within, green lawns fronted a classically shaped building. This was the Doctors' House to the old Colonial Hospital. The remains of what had been Britain's most grandiose embassy in South Central Asia lay scattered over the wall. Built by Lord Curzon during his tenure as Viceroy of India in the early 1900s, the building had been handed back to Pakistan at Partition but was later fire-balled by an Afghan mob in 1995 in retribution for what they saw as Pakistan's support for the Taliban. I had once come here to interview the Ambassador about the Embassy's history for a news feature. That day the Ambassador had asked me, 'Have you read this book, *The Mulberry Empire*?'.[167] It was a novel.

> It has very good descriptions of Kabul. I have to say though, I'm not much interested in Afghan history books but the descriptions in this one really make you believe you are in the back streets of Kabul a century ago.

But today the place looked more like a military camp than an outpost of the Empire, its lawns spread with men working out using weights and benches. Eventually, it became obvious they were bodyguards, not FCO staff. At this stage, such 'close protection' squads and private security operators as existed in Kabul still kept a relatively low profile. But already British diplomats and even spies, ventured out only in convoys of Landcruisers, behind blacked-out windows[168] and with scores of bodyguards. Sadly, the Fitzroy McLean-era of envoys seemed to have been replaced by the era of 'suburban man'.[169]

On this bright May morning, the diplomat suggested we sit in the garden. He began confidently:

> Blair is very keen on the drugs issue here as UK and domestic policy isn't working. So now we're 'in country', the PM is very keen to tackle the supply side of the drugs situation.

From the level of an Afghan poppy farm, this seemed akin to pushing water uphill. He went on;

> As the poppy was already in the ground last year we decided to compensate, as by then the farmers couldn't grow anything else.

It seemed plausible, except that I had seen the outcome in Jalalabad.

So a rate of compensation was set and eventually raised.

Across the lawn, the Embassy's *hazara* bearer shuffled towards us, carrying a silver tray. He wore a crisp white Nehru jacket and was famous, having looked after the Embassy during the civil war years when all western powers had pulled out of Kabul. He was named Zahir Shah, after the King. On his tray, was a coffee filter and cups. The diplomat continued airily:

> Undoubtedly there was a lot of fraud … but you see most of the eradication was done by Afghans with Brits not in the field due to the security situation. So I guess there was a lot of room for connivance by the surveyors and commanders.

Zahir Shah, whose wrinkles were deep as furrows, began pouring the treacle-coloured coffee into white porcelain teacups.

> Jalalabad was done in conjunction with WRC.[170] That's an Afghan NGO closely connected to the Eastern Council that Haji Qadir was involved with.

The accusation was too thinly veiled to let go. 'You mean Qadir took money from the scheme?' I asked. The diplomat replied emphatically, 'Of course, he was one of the biggest drug dealers in the country!' When I asked if they had information regarding Qadir's drug dealing activities he replied, arms crossed very tightly across his chest, that 'everyone' knew it. I asked for specific information, given that Afghanistan was a country of rumour and counter-rumour. He shifted uneasily in his seat.

> Qadir was up to his *eyeballs* and so's his son! Didn't you hear how the son raided an opium bazaar?

The event in question, he said, happened the previous April, in 2002. Haji Zahir had raided a bazaar, apparently seizing two tons of poppy paste, cash and cars from a bazaar in the Shinwar tribal region at a place called Ghani Khel.

***

The story didn't seem to add up so I returned to Jalalabad. The gate guards at his house said that Zahir had left for his office across town.

The office was a grand building set in elegant gardens of cypress, along the river from the Governor's Palace. The place had been President Najibullah's winter residence, but today its entrance was flanked by two crudely-painted pictures of soldiers in swimming-pool-blue paint. They stood stiffly like cardboard cutouts and one was apparently Abdul Haq. This was the office of the Interior Ministry's Border Guard, of which General Haji Zahir was head. Inside, real soldiers sat on *charpoys* beneath a rubber tree, guarding the entrance to a building behind.

I was shown inside, led through a room full of turbaned men where a military commander sat and into Zahir's office. He sat behind a huge desk in mid-discussion with three elders. His voice was raised, speaking Pashtu furious and fast, his broad brow deeply furrowed, his index finger prodding the air to reinforce a point. After a few minutes, all three elders, apparently satisfied with their audience, got up to leave. Swiftly, the first three were replaced by five more, marshaled in from the adjacent room. Each time one group of elders left, Zahir rang a bell on his desk and another lot trooped in. The discussion moved fleetingly from one topic to another but just now concerned *khandaqs* (water holes) at Samar Khel, on the outskirts of Jalalabad.

An Afghan bodyguard stood behind Zahir, back to the wall and wore wraparound sunglasses, t-shirt, ordinance vest, trainers, three-quarter length trousers. With his short hair he resembled a US Special Forces soldier, though he was, in fact, Afghan. The desk had no phone or computer, just two empty filing trays, a handheld radio, a miniature Afghan national flag and plastic flowers, and behind, the obligatory picture of Karzai. Occasionally, when Zahir raised his arm, Qadir's diamond and ruby ring flashed, giving him a kingly appearance.

Some of the elders looked frail despite the stamina their long walk to get here must have required, yet all were deadly serious.

They wore grey or white turbans, or occasionally the flat woolen *pakhaul* characteristic of the north-east. After the arrival of each group a boy would carry in trays of *chai sabs*, which the elders took. They reached for the plate of boiled sweets, unwrapping them simultaneously, wrappers crinkling together. Their eyes fixed upon Zahir's face as a representative led the conversation. When it was time to go each group left with *'salaams'* and *'Mukhtarams'*; their *patous* swung and their heads were bowed with gratitude. I sat quietly on the sofa watching the flocks of elders come and go so fast there was little time to ask for an explanation of their business.

During one audience, a white-turbaned man raised his voice and waved a fist at the bodyguard. He was apparently the 'King' of the Shinwar people I'd met on my first breakfast meeting with Zahir. Another old man sat opposite me wearing a white fez, hand on heart as he remonstrated with Zahir, almost crying. But Zahir still looked relaxed and said they were:

> Coming from Bar Dars [the borders] to share information or for help with their problems. From Kunar, Nuristan and Laghman.[171] They are not using their own Governors to deal with problems as these are weak 'Karzai' men.

The reference to Karzai was delivered with an edge of weariness; an indication the Governors had been appointed more for their loyalty to the President than their legitimacy with the local population. By contrast, the fact many of these elders had apparently travelled several days to see Haji Zahir indicated their trust in him.

'So are you recreating your fathers' Eastern Shura,[172] with you as its head?' I asked. He frowned and said, 'The people prefer to come to our family because they know us'.

During my visits to Jalalabad I had, in fact, seen elders in the houses of Zahir, Baryalai and Haji din Mohammad. They came from most tribes between the Khyber Pass and Kabul, from beyond the fertile orange blossom plains of Nangarhar, into the mountains on both sides of the valley, and across the Passes of Nuristan, and Kunar in the north, and the Spin Gar range and Paktia to the south.

However, their loyalty was not automatic. The tribal people

held the Arsala family continually to account and the relationship had to be continually won; a duty undertaken with gravity and sensitivity. Elders, poets and ordinary people come to the homes of Baryalai, Zahir, and Haji din Mohammad to sit for hours drinking tea or praying in unison with them on lawns or carpeted floors. They asked advice on local problems or brought news of events in outlying districts.

Today, when the last of the elders had left I asked Zahir to explain what had happened over the Ghani Khel opium bazaar. He looked down, shaking his head sadly. 'Go and interview the people. Ask them yourself', he said. But could he first explain why the British should be saying such things? 'I don't know', he sighed, but began the story.

> It was April 2002 and Karzai had just issued the edict banning the cultivation and trafficking of poppy. So my father, who was Governor, asked me to go and close this bazaar in Shinwar. He'd already asked Hazerat Ali and Haji Zaman but both refused as the Shinwar people are so fierce. So, at midnight he asked me.

He beckoned to his bodyguard who put his head close, so that Zahir could whisper an instruction to him. He continued:

> I only had six hours to find eight hundred soldiers .We went to the place next morning at six o'clock and closed all ze ways to the town. Blocked the roads. I took Nangarhar tv with me and they filmed the whole thing.

The bodyguard, who had slipped out of the room, returned with a cigarette which he handed to Zahir.

> And then we went into the bazaar and we open the shops and take the poppy paste. Two tons we find. And we took the smugglers cars with us and went back to Jalalabad. There, I handed the paste to my father, the Governor and said, 'Now this is your responsibility'.

Qadir had apparently put the paste in the vault beneath the Governor's Palace. Zahir returned the cars to their owners within two weeks 'after the people came to Jalalabad and give the proof [of ownership]'. And the poppy paste?

My father telephoned me from Kabul during the Loya Jirga[173] saying, 'The British are coming to Jalalabad to collect the poppy paste'. But they did not come and then two weeks later my father was dead.

Remembering the violence with which Qadir had been killed, I shuddered for Zahir as he went on, talking now about the British FCO staff: 'They came weeks later and took the paste'. 'They did'? I asked. 'Yes', he sighed. I asked if he would mind if I visited the bazaar myself and he said, 'I've told you, go and speak to anyone. Ask *them* the story'.

So the following day I set out with an interpreter. 'The more dangerous people of the eastern region', said Morad, the interpreter, as we headed south-eastwards towards the mountainous Shinwar region. It was en route between Pakistan and Jalalabad, which was why Qadir's mujahideen had taken cover there during the jihad. After an hour or so, we took a dirt track off the main road. Ghani Khel was reputedly one of the largest opium bazaars in Afghanistan, a place of mythic hostility. However we arrived to find a village in the foothills of the mountains. It was poor and constructed of mud walls. We went first to the District Office, a simple room where the Administrator sat behind a bare desk beneath pictures of Haji Qadir, wearing his golden turban and President Karzai. I asked him about Zahir.

Yes, Haji Zahir came here in April 2002 with his solders. He stopped in the main square and spoke with detail about the government's procedure, the Poppy Edict.

The poppy edict, banning the cultivation and trafficking of opium was something I'd forgotten about. Perhaps the British diplomat had too, since he'd failed to remind me that the edict had coincided with Zahir's haul of the bazaar.

The man, whose name was Abdul Sugur, went on, 'He took his soldiers and opened the padlocks of all these small shops and took out the paste'. He made the shape with both fists of a hammer being banged on a padlock to force it open.

'And the cars?' I asked.

'Yes in the beginning he took but after he transferred some smugglers things to Jalalabad he gave them back to the people'.

'Is Haji Zahir *gilam jam*?' I asked. The word meant 'carpet baggers' and was an expression applied to raiding mujahideen who'd poured into Kabul and looted it after the collapse of the Communist regime.

'No, he is very good man!' he said starkly, adding: 'The British when they came to issue the cash, they cheated and did not give for right people and now the government has cut peoples poppies!' He thumped his fist angrily on the desk.

> This was a *very* strong place and people had own Kalashnikovs and so the British did not want to come. So Haji Zahir came in quick and closed.[174] Central government sent out a message many times *not* to grow poppy but the people they disagree. At last the central government contact Haji Zahir and made a document for *him* to take action. He came here very strong with hundreds of soldiers and closed and collected the things. Many times the Governor had told the village chief 'please inform your people', but *nobody* obeyed and at last he decided to take action.

The Governor he mentioned was of course Haji Qadir. Another man, a Judge called Jima Gul, added, 'The British wanted to come but they were too afraid'.

The men explained that the traffickers came to Ghani Khel from Iran, Tajikistan, Pakistan, with opium being taken over the mountains from here, or the Kunar or Tagau Valleys by donkey. 'There are a thousand different paths and ways to reach Pakistan from here'.

A third man, a clerk called Abdul Shaker said, 'If the British help us make factories and roads and education then the people will not be interested to grow poppy'. Minutes later men crowded round me in the bazaar area. I asked what happened to the cars. One man, giving his name as Sher Wali, replied:

> Yes Haji Zahir closed my shop and took my poppy and private car, but two weeks later when I went to Jalalabad and give my name, my father's name, he give back my car but not poppy.

Now, they said, there was no specific place to sell the poppy. They made money by selling ghi oil, flour and sugar.

The British story was so out of kilter with what these people were saying. It seemed odd that the British would not have understood that Shinwar, being where Qadir had based himself during the jihad, was a place where people were loyal to him. So why on earth, if the family were huge drug dealers, would the Arsalas wish to steal cars and poppy paste from these men? Back in Kabul it was surprising just how far the British story of Ghani Khel had spread. At least, amongst the diplomatic community that is. Two weeks later, I interviewed the French Ambassador, an effete-looking man who began his 'audience' with me by talking of the Presidential campaign.

> Dr Rabbani and Ustad Sayyaf kicked off the campaign last week when they visited Kandahar. They are very clever; power doesn't come if you sit all day. Karzai is just a dignitary put there by foreign powers. Sayyaf, now he is one of the best orators of the Oriental world and the best of the Arabic world. A good scholar and good in Farsi but a Pashtun. He wants an Islamic state based on the true interpretation of the law which he knows so well. You know it's like la *cité antique*, the model of the perfect city.

As he spoke the words of a friend and Pashtun interpreter, Hanif, came to mind:

> Sayyaf is one of the worst destroyers of our country. And to remind people of this Kabul TV has been playing a speech he made back in 1992 when he told people, 'We have to raze the temple to build the mosque'. He said this right before he began razing the western side of Kabul.

Hanif was talking about the Afshar massacre of Hazara people, which Sayyaf had apparently led with Massoud during the civil war years.[175]

The French Ambassador continued his eulogy, striding ahead as he spoke, wrapped in his own ideological world:

> If I were an Afghan and had to vote for Rabbani or Sayyaf, I'd vote Sayyaf as for an Afghan its better to have an intelligent man. Though

as a Frenchman I'm not ready to accept religion in the constitution ...
Fahim is Karzai's only supporter.

I knew the French still had a tradition of supporting the men of the north-east, even now that Massoud was dead.

'Wasn't Qadir also a supporter of Karzai?' I asked.

He looked at me over the rim of his glasses. 'If I'd gone to Qadir's funeral I'd have been standing over the grave of one of the worlds largest drug dealers!' He spat the words with such venom that I assumed I was about to be given concrete evidence. But instead, he said:

'*Don't* you *know* how his son raided a bazaar, seizing two tonnes of poppy paste?'

'And have you been to this place?' I asked quietly.

'No'.

'So where did this information come from?'

'The British!' he snarled, 'They've spent a *lot* of time down there you know'.

The fact that unsubstantiated rumours circulated so easily within the diplomatic community was a little shocking. Thanks to their security regulations, it seemed diplomats didn't get out of Kabul much. Certainly the Afghans said they didn't visit Jalalabad these days. Their information also circulated in a far more hermetically-sealed environment than that of journalists who did not travel around with large convoys and armed guards, and whose facts and opinions were at least subject to peer review once their articles had appeared in print. Clearly flustered by my intervention the French Ambassador added, 'Well, *any* Afghan who grows poppy is a *criminal* and should be jailed!'

It was depressing to think those representing the international community had such limited sympathy for ordinary Afghans, even less an understanding of the desperate situation people faced here. Later, in Baryalai's Kabul office I found him sitting with Dr Asef Quazizada, Jalalabad's Deputy Governor. They had come to Kabul to see Karzai with the representatives of Baryalai's shura the following day. The shura was growing in stature and becoming known nationally as a good example of traditional governance structures.

Dr Asef, a kind faced man with a shock of dark hair under a *pakhaul*, had lost half a leg during the jihad. Uneasy after my interview, I asked Dr Asef what was the main problem with the British compensation scheme.

> That? Oh it was very dangerous time because they [the British] give the money to Haji Zaman and to Wuliullah directly.

Zaman, I'd heard rumoured from various people in Jalalabad, was MI6's warlord of choice during the battle of Tora Bora.[176] 'They gave the money *directly*?' I asked.

> Yes, and because Wuliullah was Survey Officer he had control. So if one farm had two hectares he wrote five to six hectares and three hectares he give to himself and only two to the farmer. Now he's back in Pakistan. He left because of this.

What was quite extraordinary in this case though was that the FCO had not asked another NGO to audit WRC, the NGO chosen by the Foreign office to administer the £70 million worth of British taxpayers' money which had gone missing prior to letting them manage so much money. Auditing was standard practice amongst aid agencies. Now people were saying that WRC was a Pakistani-based NGO. That would fit, given that Zaman had reputedly been recommended to the British by the Pakistani intelligence, the ISI.

In telling me the WRC was linked to Qadir, the diplomat had perhaps been trying to throw me off track. What was he was so scared of? Maybe something to do with the fact the man who had run the NGO charged with administering the scheme – Wuliullah - was a cousin of the Salafi leader, Haji Rohullah, whom the Americans had recently arrested in Kunar and taken to Guantanamo, on suspicion of links with al Qaeda. With Wuliullah heading up WRC, one might not have been far wrong in saying that British taxpayers money was, albeit indirectly, in danger of being funneled to those supporting terrorism. Baryalai's boy filled my glass again, jolting my memory.

'Dr Asef', I began. 'What happened to the poppy paste that Haji

Zahir took from Ghani Khel bazaar?'

'That? Oh it was locked up beneath the Governor's Palace until the British came and took it after Qadir died', he said, unaware of my investigations into this, much less the accusations levelled by the diplomatic community in Kabul.

'And do you have proof?'

'Oh yes, the British signed for it when they took it away', he said gently.

I hadn't thought to ask such an obvious question. 'They signed?'

'Of course', he replied graciously.

Later Zahir passed me a copy of the paper with the signature of a British diplomat dated 21 July 2002. I still have it. It gave the diplomat's name and noted in both *dari* and English: 'For receipt of two tonnes of poppy paste'.

Having collected the poppy paste themselves, I wondered why the FCO (or was it the MI6, for the spies normally camouflaged themselves behind the status of 'diplomat') felt the need to spread false stories? But there was more to this. The interesting aspect was how it related to Britain's role at Tora Bora, and just how closely the British had embedded themselves with their chosen warlord – or was it Pakistan's 'chosen' warlord? – Haji Zaman. Asef continued:

> Qadir was angry about the embezzling of funds from the poppy scheme and told the British to find their own house. But even so, Charlie stayed with Zaman for two weeks after the Loya Jirga last spring.

'He did?' I asked. 'Charlie' was the British official, or MI6 agent, apparently responsible for the disastrous scheme. The issue came up again one evening with Zahir when I returned to Jalalabad.

> The British blocked my father from being Interior Minister at the Loya Jirga.

'Why?' I asked.

> Maybe because he threw Charlie out of the Governor's Palace in May due to problems with the poppy scheme. My father shouted at him, 'It is two fifty pm. By three o'clock I want you out of Jalalabad!'

128

The affair – and the British failure to come up with compensation money – was a huge loss of face for Qadir who, as Governor, had brought the farmers on board with the scheme, promising them money in return for their destruction of the 2002 opium crop.

'If British do mistake in Afghanistan *first* mistake is to support Haji *Zaman*!' Zahir, sitting cross-legged on the floor after supper, thumped his fist angrily on the carpet.

> *Every* time British are in Jalalabad they sit in Zaman's house with him and Wuli Wullah from beginning until Zaman left Jalalabad. It is clear Wuliullah –who British gave the £70 million poppy compensation money to – is a cousin of Haji Rohullah[177] who is working for ISI.

Zahir was talking fast and angrily now about the head of WRC, and cousin of the Salafist leader arrested by the US. Zaman had been asked to leave Afghanistan during May 2002 after being suspected of laying a bomb under the car in which Marshall Fahim and Haji Qadir were passing, during Fahim's visit to Jalalabad. Even the diplomat I'd spoken to at the Embassy, the one who'd made the allegations about *Ghani khel* had admitted to me, 'Zaman had to leave Afghanistan because he was working against the central government'. The order for Zaman to leave Afghanistan came officially from Kabul. Zahir, looked directly at me and said:

> Two days before Zaman had to leave Jalalabad my father tell British you must leave Zaman's house and get your own house! You people, you British spend *more* dollars on Haji Zaman, thousands of weapons you buy for Zaman. When he came back [from Paris] he had *nothing* in his hand! We hear Rohullah boast, 'I took three million dollars from British and I give to Zaman'. I guessed this must be the compensation money meant for the farmers who'd destroyed their poppy under the scheme. They failed the poppy scheme as millions of dollars was taken by Rohullah, Wulliullah and Zaman. The British told us, 'If you destroy poppy then for one hectare we give you five dollars', but they didn't give us one dollar for our soldiers, nor oil for the commanders even though we destroyed 18,000 hectares of land in Surkh Rud! When Zaman left Jalalabad you British were crying. Yet Charlie lived in Zaman's house. The first time your people start your mission here

they bring Rohullah who is al Qaeda and Wuli Wullah and Zaman who is known to be threat. *This* is why your mission failed!

Again, Zahir thumped the floor and I remembered the woman in the fields who'd shirked when I'd said I was British. Zahir continued:

First when British start this mission and my father was Governor they didn't discuss with him but did *direct* with Zaman. Zaman promised to destroy the poppy and started with his own district, Khoghiani, but failed. So the British told my father we had to destroy it. The people allowed us even though they would not allow Zaman onto their land. So why did British talk with Zaman instead of talking direct with Governor? If they deal direct with Governor these things not happen. Yet even when Charlie knew Zaman was lying and has no power with people, he's *still* not asking the Governor's help?

The Arsala family had become a pariah, ignored by the British over everything from capturing al Qaeda at Tora Bora to resolving the poppy dilemma. The world at large had paid for the failure to capture Osama bin Laden at Tora Bora and now British taxpayers and Afghan farmers had paid richly for this next mistake.[178] I could understand why Qadir had been furious. Zahir told me later he had shouted at the British Ambassador in front of Karzai about what fools the British had been over the poppy scheme. Beside me now, Zahir was really angry,

In film we took for Nangarhar TV of raid on Ghani Khel last year my face is *black* from the sun. *Why?* Because I was out each day with stick with my soldiers destroying poppy. It cost us money to pay our soldiers! The British paid Zaman and Ali to do it, but they stayed in their beds.

Six months later, I met a brother of the diplomat who had apparently lived in Zaman's house running the poppy scheme, and been dismissed from Jalalabad by a furious Qadir. I had gone to meet someone at a tennis club in west London. She introduced me and when he heard I'd been in Afghanistan asked in a languid drawl whether I had met his brother, Charlie, whose last name was the same as the one the Afghans had mentioned.

'No', I said.

'Well actually he's on the inside if you know what I mean. Goes to all sorts of places'. He glowed with pride as we sat drinking tea beneath a chestnut tree. But I was remembering an interview in Jalalabad with a man called Gamshareek, the elderly white-bearded editor of *The Nangarhar Daily*, 'What was Zaman like?' I asked.

A huge murderer. You British like murderers. Every time he had opportunity, he killed for money. I want democracy in our country. We are proud of those who died for our country, like Abdul Haq. But if you have sympathy for us, bring us law and constitution. The future of Afghanistan doesn't need Commanders like Zaman and weapons. It needs pen and education. Commanders cannot rebuild Afghanistan but pen can.

CHAPTER NINE

'FIRST YOU CALL US FREEDOM FIGHTERS, NOW WARLORDS'

> In Kabul the rule of Shah Shujah proceeded smoothly against a
> backdrop of British bayonets.
>
> *Afghanistan, Highway of Conquest*

Bagram, Herat and Jalalabad, April - May 2003

'Today the "Coalition of the Willing" is at the Gates of Baghdad,
bombing Saddam Hussein's Republican Guard', I wrote in my
diary on 3 April 2003 on a plane flying back to Kabul, as beneath us
Afghanistan's snow-covered mountains sparkled.

I was returning to coproduce a documentary for a British
television station, Channel IV.[179] It was to be an update on progress,
or the lack of it, in Afghanistan eighteen months after the invasion.
My companions were the filmmaker Paul Yule and the presenter,
British political journalist Peter Oborne.

The atmosphere at Gandomack Lodge had changed and although
the antique Lee Enfield rifles collected by Jouvenal still lined its walls,
the journalists had left for Iraq during the Autumn. In their place had
come consultants, engineers, 'democracy experts', diplomats, NGO
workers and contractors. Over an ample Gandomack breakfast the
next morning, we met a British engineer who had come to work on
the new US Embassy. 'A fuckin' huge project', he boasted, elbows
outward as he cut into a sausage, '$300 million dollars worth'.

It was more than the US had so far spent on Afghan reconstruction
in the eighteen months since the fall of Kabul. Most money committed
to Afghanistan was being soaked up by military operations. Paul
was keen to make a triangular journey around Afghanistan, driving
from Herat via Kandahar to Kabul. Peter and I were not so sure.
Since our return I'd learnt that three foreigners had been killed on the

same road only a week before: two US soldiers in Helmand and an International Committee of the Red Cross (ICRC) delegate in Zabul Province. The ICRC delegate had apparently been dragged from his car. A translator relayed that those who captured the delegate had called to ask their chief, Mullah Dadullah in Pakistan, what to do with him as until now it had been taboo to kill aid workers, particularly those working for the ICRC which was considered a neutral party in the conflict. But today, with the Iraq war having just begun, Dadullah's reply was, 'Kill him'.

The official UN advice was now not to travel by road. But in the Presidential Palace we found a markedly different response. 'So would you say it is okay for us to do this trip?' Peter asked Karzai. Smiling blithely in his elegant silken *chapan*, Karzai told us that it was 'perfectly safe' to make the trip. His preference for spin over safety in what was clearly a rapidly deteriorating security situation unnerved me.

As late as early 2003, the insurgency had still been fairly minor, involving only small pockets of Taliban. However, an event I'd covered for the *The Economist* in January 2003 had surprised me. Coalition forces had brought in AC130 gunships to bomb caves following intelligence that as few as two or three Talibs were hiding out at Spin Boldak, the border crossing where I'd occasionally stopped for tea when making the drive from Quetta to Kandahar for my work with UN Habitat (UNCHS) during the Taliban period in 2000. Bringing in gunships seemed nothing more than an expensive stunt, akin to using a sledgehammer to crack what at that stage was still a very small nut. Yet the effect would be to fan the insurgency. I remembered the sepia-coloured photographs of the young men pasted on the walls of a restaurant I had stopped at once during the Taliban period in Spin Boldak. Their motivation had been to oust the foreign infidel from their land. These photographs dated from the 1980s and my Kandahari colleagues had fingered the faces in those frames lovingly, proud that their brothers had not died in vain. That fight had been to oust the Soviets, the next generation would deal with NATO and the Americans. I wasn't even convinced that the allegiance of many of these young men would be to the Taliban. It seemed more a commitment to honour their history of ousting every invader from Ghengis Khan to the British.

We visited Bagram airbase, home to the 18,000 or so 'coalition', but mainly American, troops who were arriving in time for the daily eight am 'pick up' of journalists for the coalition press conference. We left our car at the gate and climbed into one driven by an African-American soldier. He would clearly rather have been back home in the US. 'People think the war in Afghanistan is over and look to Iraq', the soldier explained wearily to Peter. 'But this is still a full on combat zone', he added despairingly, driving us into the base. We passed scores of soldiers jogging, M16 rifles slung over their shoulders.

Despite media assertions throughout 2002 to the contrary, it was obvious to many of us based in Afghanistan that the war was far from over. Early in 2003, an American soldier was now affirming this. It would have been a revelation to hear a political officer or diplomat say as much at this stage.[180] Close to where we had to register as press was a vast, sealed aircraft hanger. One of the Afghan journalists pointed to it and said, 'That's where they're detaining people and two men even died there before Christmas'. There was something menacing about the building which was strictly a 'no go' area and the Afghan journalist turned out to have been correct. Two Afghans held in detention by coalition forces, one probably an innocent taxi driver, had indeed been murdered there. Carlotta Gall, of the *New York Times* was already onto the story, but it would be two years before it was fully in the public domain.[181]

Half-an-hour later, we stood in the glaring sun as coalition spokesman, Colonel King, wearing a peaked camouflage cap, presented his press conference. He paused to assure himself all eyes were on him, before his voice boomed out

> Operation Valiant strike ended two days ago. And at Spin Boldak last night eight enemy were killed, fifteen others detained.

An Afghan reporter whispered in my ear, 'Mullah Omar has been distributing papers calling Afghans to react like the Iraqi people and defend their country'. Colonel King went on:

As far as we know they were Taliban. Now eight killed, that's relatively successful as they no longer have positions they can hold or access to supplies.

Each day at the Bagram press conference, figures of 'the dead' were given out in relation to the previous nights' engagement. The higher the toll, the greater the Americans' deemed the operation to have been a 'success'; it was the same routine employed apparently in Vietnam. It seemed a particularly myopic 'metric' of the military campaigns' success, nothing to do with the battle of perception or the winning of peoples' 'hearts and minds' to support the new government. It was also likely to inflame Afghan anger since every insurgent killed had relatives who would mourn him. Often the so-called 'Taliban' cited by the US were simply locals carrying an old rifle[182] for most Afghan households had one tucked away. Coming to the end of his spiel, Colonel King announced confidently, 'We'll be here till we beat the Taliban'.

'When'll that be?' I asked cheekily.

He laughed and said, 'I don't know'. As he turned away, I thought I heard him mutter quietly, 'Somebody else'll be making that decision'.

***

We drove to Jalalabad to research the poppy story. Hanif Sherzad, our interpreter, was famous in Afghanistan because he read Kabul TV News. He and I drove in his Toyota Corolla while Peter and Paul went in a 4x4 with armed guards. On the edge of Kabul we reached the Pul-I-charkhi checkpoint. The posters of Haji Qadir and Abdul Haq had gone. When I had last passed through here, in the opposite direction, coming by minibus from Jalalabad back in January, some of the Panjshiri guards had confiscated Pashtun newspapers from the other travellers saying sharply, 'It's our city now'. This was only one example of how ill feeling was being incited by the Panjshiris, some of whom now thought they 'ruled' Kabul against the Pashtun majority who now felt completely unrepresented.

Hanif, a Pashtun, was originally from Jalalabad and was now expounding on US policy in the city. 'It's a *big* mistake you know. One day you'll see the pay-back', he said, frantically trying to keep control of the wheel as the Corolla bounced along the rutted road. 'They are a very *small* minority, the Dar-I-noor'. He pinched his thumb and forefinger together to emphasise. 'Really, it's a *tiny* valley on the way to Kunar'. He was talking about Hazerat Ali's tribe, the people who had recently disarmed Haji Zahir's soldiers. Kunar is the valley bordering Pakistan where Hikmatyar 's followers were rumoured to be hiding out and where much of the fight against al Qaeda would focus from 2004 onwards.

Hanif had recently been in Gardez working with ABC News.

> I saw one of our American journalists ask an ordinary citizen of Gardez, 'What do you think will happen when US forces leave the country?'

Hanif banged his wrist against the wheel.

> You know, the man replied. 'If today you leave the country, tomorrow the Taliban will return and I will first and foremost join them!' And when the ABC reporter asked why, the man replied, 'Because I studied in Peshawar and Kabul and what reconstruction have you done? You promised us jobs. *Where are* they!?'

Hanif also had his own opinion on the war in Iraq.

> I have no doubt that the America will break up if this is their way. Even our communist PM, Taraqi, said, 'The will of the people is the will of God'. If all these peoples around the world are against this war then the will of the people will prevail.

We were late arriving in Jalalabad. The Panjshiri guards Paul had hired to accompany us broke down and we had to wait for them on the road. So far they'd been more of a liability than an asset, and now we were in a Pashtun area they were nervous. The journey had taken five hours whereas normally it should take three with the new road. By the time we arrived at twelve thirty, Baryalai had tired of waiting and gone to a wedding in Surkh Rud. Spring was more advanced here than in Kabul; the gardens in Jalalabad were greener and the aroma of orange blossom clung to the air.

Peter and Paul installed themselves at the Spin Ghar hotel, which was dirty and still haunted by the menacing guards of Hazerat Ali. I stayed at Baryalai's place, and later that evening Baryalai told me there had been a small demonstration against the Iraq war at Nangarhar University, but Hazerat Ali had arrested the Deans of various faculties and thrown them in jail. Baryalai shook his head, 'Hazerat Ali is just doing this to show loyalty with the Americans. How can he do such a thing without recourse to court, judge or legal system?' The Shura Baryalai had set up in January and which was gaining significance. I asked what were its main activities and who it represented? He told me it was not supposed to 'represent' any one group. It was more a consultative council of locals interested in participating in decisions on issues ranging from reconstruction to security issues, dispute resolution or even to finding recruits for the new Afghan National Army. Even at this stage in 2003, there was concern that so far the ANA was recruiting a large proportion of its soldiers from Tajik areas. Again, the Pashtuns felt left out and voiceless. This was not surprising though, given that Fahim and the Panjshiri clique occupied the bulk of senior positions. The shura was trying to address this issue. Baryalai emphasised that those who participated in the shura were not people paid to do so. Baryalai rubbed his forehead as he spoke:

> They come because they're interested to do something for our region. More and more people come to me now due to this type of problem with Hazerat Ali. And our shura is seen as a challenge to his people. So a report recently came from Kabul through the intelligence. It told them to investigate me.

Flyers or 'Night letters', apparently from Pakistan, had also been distributed throughout Jalalabad city calling him an agent of the US' because he had not publicly condemned the Americans.

> So we are being squeezed now by both sides; Pakistan and central government …

He looked tired, and explained that there were 'invisible forces' in Pakistan orchestrating pressure on him because he had spoken out in the Districts against rockets being sent into Jalalabad city. He had warned this could escalate, leading to the type of chaos that had made fertile ground for the Taliban's arrival. 'He and Zaman even helped the Taliban escape', he said, speaking now of Karzai. When I commented that this must be a bit far fetched he said that Karzai and Zaman had to retain favour with the tribes, as the foreigners would not be there forever. Baryalai continued:

> Karzai's problem is that he has no support. Neither from his own tribe nor from the mujahideen either. Because he spent too much time in offices and not enough *fighting* the Russians!

The mujahideen had accepted Karzai as President precisely because with minimal tribal support and no political party, he could never threaten their hegemony. Now he was also losing popularity, not just because rural people were not seeing the promised 'reconstruction', but because Karzai's many promises to tribal leaders from different parts of the country had not been unfulfilled. Now people were openly calling him 'Shah Shujah' after the nineteent-century Puppet King installed by the British.

I asked about Jalalabad's Buddhist remains at Hadda and the thousand minarets, and he told me sadly that it was all destroyed.

> I've not much hope in the war against opium. So much was lost during the past twenty-three years here but especially the culture. We've nothing left, we've destroyed everything. Just as the Iraqis have nothing left.

In Baghdad, the National Museum and Iraq's National Library had been looted the week before. Today, I'd found a message on my satellite phone from Jon Swain in Baghdad saying he was leaving, he'd had enough of it all. The incompetence of the Americans had left the city polluted and burning. I told Baryalai about the message and he said with a tone of defeat,

> To rebuild a country you have to work with the system that is compatible. You cannot just *adapt* the USAID system from Bosnia to Afghanistan. You have to work with the system *here*.

Some acquaintances back in London were arguing that the interventions in Afghanistan and Iraq were morally imperative 'humanitarian interventions'. The implication was that 'morally imperative' would equate to a successful outcome, whatever that meant. After all, hadn't Bosnia been? In the face of the complexities and nuances of Afghan society, however, it was not at all clear that Afghanistan would follow in the steps of the international community's forays in other places.[183]

Baryalai's attempts to revive the traditional shura system in Jalalabad had been met positively. The shura would be comprised of men recognised in the community for their wisdom rather than their political allegiance or force of arms. As such, there would be no remuneration attached. They would emulate the traditional system of consensus that had been partly destroyed during the Soviet occupation, by the targeted killing of village elders and intellectuals, and the support by outside powers of factional leaders. In the approach that Baryalai was attempting to re-formulate, local governance decisions were made after hours of tea drinking and debate by village elders. It even took many weeks of discussion with local elders for decisions to be made about the remit and scope of the shura. But the work paid off because eventually this shura was used as a blueprint by the Ministry of Rural Development for other shuras apparently intended to be set up around the country, particularly in relation to counter-narcotics efforts, in which Baryalai's shura had been so successful.[184] However, I heard that despite giving lip-service, Karzai did very little to promote this concept and was often obstructive, possibly seeing this legitimate, traditional Afghan form of governance as a threat to his autonomy.

The filming of the documentary continued. One of the reasons Peter wanted to visit Herat was to deliver a missive to Ismael Khan, the city's Governor and self-styled Amir, the mythic figure I had wondered about since hearing of his escape from the Taliban's clutches and Kandahar jail. So having arrived in Herat by plane, Peter, Paul and I spent one hot dusty day following Khan's convoys on a trail through villages whose streets were lined with children singing songs from the Holy Q'ran, with little boys on one side of the road and girls on the other, all wearing bright white chadors. Finally, in the mosque at Ingil District, a place where five hundred had been killed by Soviet bombing, Khan made a long sermon of both memorial and encouragement. 'A *much* greater orator than our politicians', Peter whispered.

***

When Peter and Paul left for London, I returned to Jalalabad. My interpreter and friend, Omar, offered to drive for he and his mother, who was from the Khoghiani tribe based near Jalalabad, were going there to visit her brothers' family.

To our left, the shining peaks of the Hindu Kush framed the Panjshir valley beyond us as we approached the descent to Sarobi. We were discussing the UN's new scheme aimed at disarming Afghanistan's militias, known as DDR ('disarmament, demobilisation and reintegration'). It had been launched the week before by Lakhdar Brahimi in Kabul and I was telling Omar how an Afghan BBC journalist had asked a seemingly innocent question: 'Isn't it paradoxical the UN is launching this 'disarmament, demobilisation and reintegration' programme while the Americans, just last week, were still arming warlord militias in the north?'

Brahimi had brushed the question off, but today Omar commented passionately:

> *This* is the problem. The US are dealing *everywhere* with Commanders. It brings the country down. It's good to give dollars but give that to the Finance Ministry, to the government or the ANA, not to warlords. Who will care about the ANA when everyone has guns?

In 2003, the ANA was the still 'new' Afghan National Army. The international community was hoping it would become the main force in the country, enabling foreign troops to leave.

***

At Haji Zahir's compound the next morning he said of my visit to Ismael Khan: 'He is your new friend and my old friend'. He went on to relate how Karzai had recently called all the Governors together in an attempt to force them publicly to hand over customs money to the central government. But General Dostum and Ismael Khan had apparently come to Zahir's house in Kabul to beg him not to agree to this.

'And what did you say?' I asked.

'I say "in time of mujahideen I am mujahideen bu in time of democracy I am democratic man", and so we must support this government'.

I took a handful of kishmesh, not quite sure of his point.

> Dostum is making $40,000 USD per day from customs duties not handed to the government, while Ismael Khan, with the Iran trade at Herat, gets $800,000 per day! In Jalalabad we only get $30,000 per day. But all this we give to central government!

He sounded angry, and flicked ash into a lapis bowl.

> The Western powers will soon remove Ismael Khan from his post. You remember my words. First they will remove Khan and then others.

'But isn't it good if they get rid of the warlords?' I asked. He scoffed.

> First you call us 'freedom fighters', now 'warlords'. Yet in war against Soviets we were heroes, now we're just villains!

Some members of the family – in particular Zahir and previously his father Qadir and also Haji Din Mohammad - maintained a national network of alliances with other 'ex-mujahideen' and warlords. Such men remained extremely unpopular with the more 'progressive' urban Afghans. It was disappointing to learn that this network of 'friends' included men like Sayyaf who, along with Massoud, had apparently been heard giving orders to his Commanders as the Hazara people at Afshar, a suburb of Kabul, were targeted in a massacre in February 1993. So I asked Zahir why he was so friendly with Sayyaf.[185] Zahir boomed:

> He was very good friend of my Father! He and my father was the only

141

> Pashtuns who stayed in Northern Alliance area and continued fight against Taliban and did not relent!

Sayyaf also represented another difference between Abdul Haq and Haji Qadir. For even as Qadir had fought alongside Sayyaf with the Northern Alliance, Haq had urged the West to beware of him, and emphasized his link to the training camps on the Pakistani border and the arrival of foreign fighters.[186] From one camp the self styled 'Sheikh al hadith' (Sayyaf) had peddled fundamentalism among foreign fighters, whom he encouraged to visit the region through his Saudi contacts. Two of the most notorious terrorists, Omar Sheikh and Khaled Sheikh Mohammad, the former accused of killing American journalist Danny Pearl and the latter of being a mastermind behind both attacks on the World Trade Centre had spent time at Sayyaf's vast camp.[187]

Zahir called Raz, his wiry and scruffy manservant and babbled something in Pashtun to him. Moments later Raz returned, placing two Polaroid photos in Zahir's hands. 'Look', he said. The pictures showed men placing a golden turban on Zahir's head. 'They're elders from the tribes of Khoghiani, Shinwar and Mohmand'. Perhaps this was a symbolic gesture, the mythical mark of leadership accorded him by ordinary people. So I wondered out loud how he was getting on these days with the Americans. Zahir told me:

> I'm more friendly now with one of their commanders. One (of them) came to see me recently and said, 'Why do you never come and visit us?' So I replied, 'I'm not needed anything from you'.

Perhaps the subtext to this was that Hazerat Ali went to see the Americans a lot because they were his paymasters. Zahir continued, still fingering the photographs. 'Now they want me more and more for their work'. They had, apparently, changed their opinion of him after travelling around the region, meeting with commanders in Kunar, Nuristan, Laghman and Nangarhar who said they were allied with Haji Zahir.

Learning this, it was obvious how this place differed to Kabul. The West would never impose its ideal of 'one man, one vote' here in the east and south of Afghanistan where the web of alliances, deals, paternalism and religion was not just complex but medieval. Where the tribes mostly looked to a leading family for leadership, trust and inspiration. The hopes I had held initially for a Western-style secret ballot democracy in Afghanistan, while I was monitoring elections in the run-up to the Emergency Loya Jirga back in Spring 2002, were now looking quite naïve.

***

The following week evidence of the existence of Afghanistan's nationalised 'ex-mujahideen' networks became more obvious. It was a late summer's day; Zahir was visiting Kabul and had asked me to travel to Paghman with him for a picnic: 'We're going to see Mullah Izat. He's invited me for lunch at his garden in Paghman'. Paghman was the valley outside Kabul where Sayyaf was based. Reading my thoughts Zahir said with a wry smile, 'It's okay, Izat is not like Sayyaf, more like me'.

We drove out of Kabul with Zahir's soldiers not riding postillion today, but tucked tidily inside two of his red Toyota pick-ups. 'I'm not wanting to make big show here in Kabul', Zahir answered. He still, I knew, saw Kabul as hostile territory after his father's violent death. We headed towards the blue mountains of Paghman. Soon, we were overwhelmed by dust and the roar of a cavalcade of fifteen vehicles, led by four Landcruisers, passing us.

'That's Rabbani', Zahir sighed. 'But where's he going? He can't be going where we're going!'

'But I thought he was a friend of yours?' I said. 'He paid for you to get out of jail didn't he?'

Rabbani had just launched a political party called the National Party (Nowzat e mille) and Zahir told me that the week before he had asked Zahir to join.

> He wants support of the eastern region which he knows I can get. He is expecting mujahideen to band together. But if I should join his party, why not make my own? The people don't have trust in him. He's done nothing for them!

With all the uncertainty clouding Qadirs' death, Zahir was steering a line independent of the Northern Alliance and particularly the Shura-e-Nazar. The mujahideen were already manouevering, as evidenced by the French Ambassador's talk of Sayyaf and Rabanni kicking off the Presidential election campaign, to be held a year from now, in 2004, in Kandahar.

Two days later I visited the office of an old Loya Jirga colleague, the head of one of Afghanistan's 'pro democracy' Political Parties. I have changed his name and not mentioned that of his party to protect his identity.

I arrived to find Musa reading Mr Brahimi's latest report to the UN Security Council. He was not impressed.

> You know Mr Khalilzad and Mr Brahimi, they deal with Fahim. Now Mr Brahimi is saying that ISAF must be extended outside Kabul to deal with the security problems. But it was *him* who gave power to the warlords at the Loya Jirga last year. Yet now *he* is blaming the breakdown in security on the international community's failure to extend ISAF!

He slapped the report down disdainfully. His alert face was clean-shaven, except for a small handlebar moustache.

> It's a good excuse for Brahimi to go on about extending ISAF to areas outside Kabul but it was his and Khalilzad's actions that gave the warlords more power in their regions.

He shook his head, before adding prophetically.

> Anyway if they extend ISAF to the areas outside Kabul it will make this into a guerrilla war. The Americans should be doing that job.

'But should people like Fahim have been completely excluded from the Loya Jirga?' I asked, playing devil's advocate.

> Maybe they should have participated – even though it was against the rules agreed at Bonn – but they should *not* have been given full voting rights and allowed to intimidate democratically elected candidates.

***

Musa and I had worked together on district level elections for the Loya Jirga in April 2002. With his own political party and dedication to the cause of democracy, he was the type of Afghan many might have assumed the West would work with in bringing its vision of democracy to Afghanistan: a brave man soundly committed to following through on the democratic ideal articulated so loudly after September 11. At thirty-eight, he was also buoyantly youthful. He held steadfastly to the view that Afghanistan could make the transition from war, chaos and brutality, towards a peaceable democracy. As a police officer during the communist regime, he had also risked his life during the Taliban on reporting human rights abuses to the UN. Today was the first time I had seen him looking crumpled.

I asked him about the issue of Ambassador Khalilzad's pronouncement that the Loya Jirga had been a triumph of 'peace versus justice'. He frowned and said:

> The effect was to show the people that the warlords were legitimate. This has been bad for the central government.

He said that his own party were doing well, because people had been so disappointed by the fundamentalists' decision at the Loya Jirga to make Afghanistan an Islamic state. Since then, membership of the Republican party had increased sharply. 'If the country becomes an Islamic State, there is no chance for democracy', he said. He was very disappointed though that the bill legalising the formation of political parties had yet to be passed.

> So until the party law is agreed we cannot operate freely and open offices across the country. That gives the jihadi parties an automatic lead in preparing for the elections as they are *already* formed. So *all* these new democratic parties *cannot* become legal?

This meant that only the so called 'parties' of the mujahideen, in other words the 'seven' groups fostered by Pakistan as politico-milit022ry factions during the jihad period, were presently 'allowed' to operate in Afghanistan. Musa nodded, 'They don't need an election law to begin operating but anyone else who wishes to form a political party does'. He then reiterated what we both knew:

> When the warlords came to the Loya Jirga they had less power and
> people protested against them. But after Mr Brahimi and Mr Khalilzad
> allowed them to participate, which was against the rules of the Bonn
> Agreement, and gave them full voting rights, they left with *more* power.
> Really, Khalilzad and Brahimi are just thinking of *their* benefits. They
> made a fundamentalist Loya Jirga for Afghanistan last year in which
> they shared government posts between the fundamentalists. This is
> leading to a fundamentalist constitution for Afghanistan and then
> next year, fundamentalist elections too.

His words reinforced the idea that it just didn't make sense that
President Karzai, the US, the UN and the international community,
who had publicly legitimised the warlords at the Loya Jirga and
effectively reinstated them in their fiefdoms, now stood back
wondering what had gone wrong and why security was breaking
down in the regions. It was just too simplistic to blame everything
on the Taliban. The international community was beginning to
wonder why the Afghan National Army was failing to become a
unified force, the drugs trade was spiralling out of control and the
insurgency in the south was gathering pace. But having effectively
put them there, now the international community had no leverage.
If the warlords and strongmen didn't *feel* like handing over customs
duties, didn't *feel* like disarming their militias (re-armed by the
Americans since 2001) and didn't *feel* like renouncing their lucrative
and opaque role in the drug trade, who could stop them?

The international community was glossing over what were, after
all, rather fundamental problems, focusing instead on the larger
imperative: US domestic policy. Hence the objective was to hold
swiftly punctuated elections. This would give the American voter
the impression that democracy had 'arrived' in Afghanistan. Never
mind that there was no rule of law in the country to make such
'democracy' viable.

To illustrate the problem of holding elections in a country with
no rule of law, I refer to an incident that occurred on my return
from monitoring elections in the Panjshir valley in April 2002. We
had left the mouth of the Panjshir, arriving at Jabal Saraj at dusk.

The village comprised ancient wooden houses and was formerly a Northern Alliance stronghold at the top of the Shamali Plains. The driver gesticulated towards his parents' house across a wheat field, so I suggested we stop for tea.

Minutes later, we sat with the drivers' father on the floor of his house. He was unhappy about the elections here a week before. He told us that the people were not able to vote for their chosen Commander, because a neighbouring, more powerful one named Abdur Rahman Maulana, put forward his two candidates. So they were elected. The old man looked dissatisfied, pulling on his beard. But I was wondered impatiently what was the point of having elections if the Afghans weren't even going to vote the way they wanted? It was a secret ballot after all. When I made a remark to this effect, the old man responded in *dari*, talking fast and furious, throwing impatient glances my way. When his response was translated, it was along the lines of what would these people do once the election teams leave? Who would protect them? For his security would be threatened if he did not vote with the powerful commander. The interpreter cast his eyes downward and it was obvious to me that this was not the West. There was no rule of law here. Of course those with power could dictate terms.

Leaving the town at nightfall, our driver pointed out Maulana's compound on the right, a large military base. I had seen Maulana at another election, at Saed Khalil, a few days before. He had lumbered nonchalantly into the mosque at the end of proceedings to claim his prize. He was a dark-haired man in his mid-thirties and I'd been surprised by his red toenails and henna-patterned feet. He looked like a pirate, someone who lived outside the rules. He waited complacently for the announcement of his name and then, making no acceptance speech, turned to leave. A heavy gold watch hung from his wrist. We streamed out behind to find a black Toyota Hilux waiting outside, its engine running, packed with bodyguards and ammunition. I'd been suspicious then, now I understood what had happened. Why there had been no vibrancy or debate in that election? Abdur Rahman Maulana, a man not even of the district, had it tied up with fear from the outset.

Despite the climate of fear and intimidation in many places beyond Kabul, diplomats still talked confidently of strengthening President Karzai's remit in the regions and reconstructing the country. But Musa, like many Afghans and indeed like Abdul Haq, believed that the opportunity to do this had been lost forever once the decision had been taken to re-arm the Northern Alliance (and other mujahideen and militia groups). From then on, any chance for a democratic settlement in Afghanistan was lost. When, in 2001, the Taliban faced defeat, many warlords and their commanders had literally driven back across the border to reclaim former fiefdoms. Now they had reappointed themselves as police and army commanders, provincial governors and even Cabinet ministers.[188] From these positions they could continue their often drug-related or corrupt money-making activities much more easily. Their integration into the Afghan state enabled them to operate with impunity, even though many had a history of war crimes. Outside Afghanistan there was intense international interest in the capture and indictment of Milosovic and Karadzic in the Balkans. Meanwhile inside Afghanistan, similar characters were being rewarded with government positions.[189]

Thus it seemed that the British Foreign Secretary, Jack Straw, had things the wrong way around when in 2002 he commented on this flawed strategy:

> The more we can get people in who have occupied positions of *force* and *strength* in the past but who now say 'we're committed to a political process' and the more we can close off the options for people who resort to violence, the *better* the future of Afghanistan will be.

In such a context the outlook for brave Afghans like Musa, people attempting to form small democratic parties, was lamentable. The international community had done nothing to protect them. There would only be increasing tension with the warlords and their politico-military factions, which rather oddly were named 'parties'. Ironically, on the other hand, by the time of the 2005 parliamentary elections – on which I worked for the EU Election Observation Mission - the international community and Karzai would have engineered a 'single non-transferable vote' (SNTV) voting system which – by its 'divide and rule' nature – would mitigate *against* political parties. Musa finished his phone conversation and said:

> The problem *really* began when the Americans allowed the Northern Alliance to take Kabul in November 2001. This broke the Bonn Agreement and signalled that international rules could be broken. Unfortunately we *cannot* cooperate with them [the jihadi parties] as they have not obeyed the laws and just want weapons. Until there are *no* weapons and *no* warlords the people will worry … Free elections without disarmament are impossible. The heads of [political] parties should *not* be involved in war crimes. Anyway, we are also mujahideen but not like them.

The failure of the West to support people like Musa seemed a lost opportunity. Such people really believed –somewhat naively it now seems – that in the wake of September 11, Afghanistan was facing a rebirth with prospects of a democracy supported by the international community. On the issue of the Constitutional Commission, Musa said:

> It is headed by Shahrani, a fundamentalist and a mullah. How can *he* make a democratic constitution! … The UN has allowed Karzai to fill the Constitutional Commission with representatives of politico-military factions, i.e. the warlords, while excluding the democrats.[190] They have *even* removed the word 'democracy' from the Constitution.[191] They inserted the word 'Islamic' so the country will be an Islamic republic. But it would be better to have a constitutional monarchy for Afghanistan. Basically, the constitution is private and controlled by the mujahideen. For them, Karzai is the perfect leader because, having no power of his own, he is forced to do what they want.

His words echoed the warnings of Dr Fasilli, who had warned six months earlier that the drafting of Afghanistan's new constitution had effectively been hijacked by the mujahiddeen. He stood up, clearly upset.

> The Shura-e-nazar parties have *lots* of money. The difference is those who want *real* democracy, no one gives them money. We pay for our offices and tea from our own pockets.

CHAPTER TEN
PLAYING THE AL QAEDA CARD

Trust a snake before a Harlot

And a Harlot before a Pashtun

TAJIK PROVERB

Jalalabad, Lal Pura, Goste and Fatemena, August 2003

'You have to come back to Afghanistan now', said Zahir down a crackly line. 'I can't say why by phone, but there are problems. You must visit villages along the border, ask the people yourself and write about it'. I did not know it then, but fighting had broken out along the Durand line in summer 2003. Apparently the Pakistani Army were making incursions into Afghan territory, backed by the US who wanted Pakistan to seek out al Qaeda.

Zahir told me that a thousand men had been in his house that day to celebrate the wedding of Abdul Haq's eldest son, Majeed, to Haji din Mohammad's daughter. I thought how sad it was for Haqs' son that as both his parents had been murdered, neither would attend.

London in high summer was unpleasant, even more so in the heat of the row between the BBC and Tony Blair's cabal of officials about the 'sexing up' of the intelligence dossiers on Iraq. Now presided over by Blair's spin doctor – an increasingly maniacal Alastair Campbell at Number 10 – it seemed no depths would be left unplumbed in the struggle to divert attention from the failure to find weapons of mass destruction in Iraq. The previous weeks' casualty had been Dr David Kelly, an honourable-looking weapons expert and civil servant mysteriously found dead on the edge of an Oxfordshire woodland. There was something deeply unpalatable about what was going on.

Relieved to have an excuse to return to Afghanistan, I booked a flight and returned to Kabul where, in the shadows of the 1960s airport building, one of Zahir's cousins awaited me. During the long drive to Jalalabad he refused to be drawn on the reasons for my visit. But apparently a British junior minister[192] was seeing Zahir that day to discuss drugs.

Today we sat beneath the mulberry trees in the damp, clinging July heat. It was Friday, the day of prayers and rest. Haji Zahir's convoy had driven past the family's village, into the flat land below the black mountains, towards Khoghiani district. 'Visiting neighbours', he had explained, as he parked the white Landcruiser close to some adobe houses, his soldiers trailing out behind us from a clutch of red SUVs. We were shown to *charpoys* in the shade and I sat opposite him, wilting quietly in the heat.

> This was once the house of a big Malek, he was so rich he had over one hundred cows just for milk, and he was a great friend of Zahir Shah who used to come here.

Zahir smiled, clearly relaxed among his own people. Tea was brought by an elderly man. 'Just imagine, King Zahir Shah sat on a charpoy here, thirty five years ago!' he said. Groups of elders arrived, nodding respect silently, before seating themselves on cushions spread on the ground along the sidelines.

> They are elders of the village and also soldiers when we need them. Zahir explained as I wondered how long it took news to trickle through the adobe villages of his arrival?

Abdul Haq's remaining sons were there: the three youngest were round-faced boys aged ten, eleven and fifteen with a predilection for Diet Coke. They sat beside Zahir and gazed at him fondly, as though to a father. The oldest was the newly-married eighteen-year-old, Majeed, who sat apart on a *charpoy*. Behind him, a white goat was tethered along the adobe wall of the maleks house. Cattle stood in the shade, flicking their tails and behind the wall was a group of cyprus trees.

A red Toyota SUV arrived and out came bodyguards unloading steaming tin pots. Lunch. After some preparations behind a reed screen, the men filed out like medieval courtiers. They bore pewter dishes of rice, stew and salad. We ate with the elders from the village on a long mat beneath the trees, some of the villagers looking on, quietly drinking tea. To my right, a row of small birdcages hung from the tree covered with cloths. Inside were nuristani doves.

One of Zahir's men came and whispered into his ear. A map was brought out and examined by the two with gravity. Zahir crossly gave me the latest update on Pakistani movments around the border:

> The central government told me to defend, not to fight the Pakistanis. But the people believe the Pakistanis have boats and may cross the Kunar river and make further incursions. They've already done so in Shinwar, Mohmand and Khoghiani [Tora Bora] tribal areas

'So what do the Americans have to do with it? I asked.

> They came and told me, 'We're going to carry out an operation in Mohmand in three days', and I offered them my bases. They didn't use them. But when they left, they left the Pakistanis there; now Pakistan is in Kunar and all down the Durand line to Spin Boldak.

He flicked his wrist in annoyance at the crumpled map which lay across his lap. 'But Fazl Akbar, a 'Karzai man', has denied it three times. So I'll have to go up to Kunar and Nuristan soon'. He was talking about the new Governor of Kunar. His pen skated back and forth over the map and its crosshatched border markings.

> You know the problem is that the Americans are using British maps. But we're using Russian maps. *That* has correct borders on!

That Zahir was managing this situation with little support from Kabul was evident later that afternoon when we arrived at the kitsch fort Qadir had started building at Surkh Rud. Zahir's bodyguards streamed out of the 4x4s, ran across the compound to the concrete shell and, moments later, returned ferrying boxes of ammunition. This was the ordinance the Taliban had stored in Qadir's property, knowing it would not be bombed by the Northern Alliance. 'They're taking it to my checkpoints in the tribal areas', said Zahir, a thumb in his jacket pocket.

I've spent $300,000 from my own pocket in these six weeks. The government has offered me one million Afghanis and they keep phoning to check if I've received it. But I tell them, I'll send it back together with another million!

This was my first indication that summer of the Durand issue. The previous week, as news of skirmishes between the Pakistani government and Afghan forces filtered back to Kabul, a mob had ransacked the Pakistani Embassy protesting the violation of Afghan territory by Pakistan. That summer talk of Durand seeped into everything; from the Pakistani press (*The Khyber News*), to the intelligence reports which Zahir had brought by messenger each day from the frontier, to the talk amongst elders, UN staff or Zahir's family. It seeped into our meals, our teas, the interviews I did along the mountainous areas of the Durand line, with the Governor, elders and tribal leaders in Jalalabad. They all believed Pakistan was here due to a tension between the two countries that went back over a hundred years.

The genesis of the problematic 'Durand Line' was the 'Gandamak Agreement' which was signed in May 1879 between British Major Louis Cavagnari and the Afghan Amir Mohammad Ya'qub Khan during the Second Anglo Afghan War of 1879-80. Britain would maintain a diplomatic and military presence in Afghanistan and control its foreign policy, as well as being granted jurisdictional control of the three strategically important frontier districts of Kurram, Sibi and Pichin.

When the Gandamak Plan failed to achieve peace, the British opted to leave Afghanistan, though not before ensuring it remained a buffer between their own Indian empire and that of Russia. To ensure this they decided to annex the unruly Pashtun tribe. Hence, Afghanistan's eastern border would be moved inwards and westwards by about 150 kilometres at the narrowest point. The effect was to enlarge British India's North-West Frontier Province and split the Pashtun tribe which had latterly been concentrated in Afghanistan. 'Durand' – as the 1893 agreement between Amir Abdul Rahman Khan[193] and Sir Henry Mortimer Durand, Foreign

Secretary of British India, became known – formally adjusted 'the eastern and southern frontier of His Highnesse's dominions, from Wakhan (corridor) to the Persian border'. The problem was that Article 4 of the agreement, as follows, was never undertaken. This stipulated that the:

> … frontier line will hereafter be laid down in detail and demarcated, wherever this may be practicable and desirable, by a Joint British and Afghan Commissioners whose object is to arrive by mutual understanding at a boundary which shall adhere with the greatest possible exactness to the agreed map, and have due regard to the existing local rights of villages adjoining the frontier.

So while the limits of Durand were set on paper, the border was not itself demarcated. And this would become the focus of a bleeding sore in relations between Afghanistan and, upon the partition of India in 1947, the country which was created as Pakistan.

Haji Zahir, like many generations of Pathans, never recognised Durand, believing Abdul Rahman had made a personal agreement in return for money. While some Afghans believed it was only to last one hundred years, others believed the conditions so unfavourable that many had never recognised it. Today, although he was still only twenty-eight years old, the tribes along the Durand line were looking to Zahir to resolve the problem along the twelve hundred mile stretch of border which he managed.

***

The town on the far bank was reminiscent of an Arabic trading post on the East African coast. As our wooden vessel took to the fast waters at a collection of wooden huts in a parched place known as Lal Pura, the soldiers regarded me blankly. They had wild kohl-rimmed eyes and some leant against Russian-era rocket propelled grenades, red hair coiling vertically outwards beneath umbrella-shaped woollen caps. The crazy scene was more 'The Raft of the Medusa' than Afghanistan. They were mostly Nuristani and the boxes of ammunition and supplies they carried would be passed to comrades manning checkposts in the direction we were headed towards the heights of hostile border areas. I was visiting the mountains with Haji Zahir's 'Barder' Police (Border Guard) and Lal Pura village was within kilometres of the Khyber Pass, one of many gateways to the unruly tribal areas belt of sun-bleached land lying sandwiched between Pakistan and Afghanistan.

The Corps Commander, a solemn-faced man named Mustafa Khan was in charge of thirty-six checkpoints along this fifty kilometre stretch between the Shinwar and Mohmand districts. After a month of keeping the Pakistani government forces at bay I could see that he was tired; his eyes were like saucers.

We descended the boat to sit on *charpoys* near the water's edge while a car was found. A line of men stooped beneath heavy sacks, moving supplies from a rusting truck on the sandy riverbank to a wooden vessel. They moved determinedly beneath their load like an army of ants, white powder spilling from torn sackcloth. Heroin? I sat upright, thinking I had penetrated the smuggling district, but it was urea from Pakistan, shipped via this route to avoid tax.

'Smuggling?' I asked.

'No, not smuggling. Business!' the cousin corrected me. 'Because this is *tribal* area and they are not allied to any government'.

About thirty *barders* (borders) soldiers now clambered on top of the ramshackle Toyota from which the urea had just been unloaded, reminding me of a Guatemalan taxi I'd once taken over the Mexican border in which people hung off every orifice. There were few vehicles this side of the river and this one, they explained, had been brought over by the Soviets and then captured by the tribal people. Now its sole use was to ferry goods across this 'no mans land'. The cousin motioned for me to climb inside and we set off, driving into open desert past the occasional abandoned village, stumps of houses being all that remained after bombing by the Soviets, silent now except for remnants of tree cover. As we headed into the parched hills, I noticed a profusion of buffalo carcasses littering the route. 'They come from India, through Pakistan and to here and die from the heat crossing the mountains', explained the driver, a merry man named Liqat. After forty minutes of sweltering heat he dropped us where several *charpoys* were arranged beneath the shade of trees, explaining he was now driving to Pakistan. When he collected us later that day for the trip home, a buffalo was strapped to the truck floor. 'So it won't die of heat', he said, as though this should have been obvious. The buffalo were raised in Pakistan before being smuggled into Afghanistan for eating.

This was Fatemena village, Mustafa Khan's base camp. In fact the 'village' had been abandoned years ago after Russian bombardment. Today Khan's soldiers lounged on *charpoys* away from the midday sun. Khan pointed solemnly to a parched mountain several kilometres distant from here. 'During six weeks my poorly armed men have through good morale managed to push Pakistani government soldiers back 6 km from here'. As Mustafa Khan spoke, the soldiers clamoured to look through a set of Russian binoculars mounted on a tripod, scanning a peak which Khan said his men captured at three am the night before, having scrambled up it just as Pakistani government soldiers were being dropped by helicopter the other side. 'Now', he said, 'the Pakistani's are trying to cut off my supply route'.

When I understood that the Afghan Border Police were up against Pakistani military spending which included a $3 billion USD 'reward' from the American government two months ago for its' part in the war on terror, Mustafa Khan's achievements seemed more remarkable. The US contribution to Pakistan was in marked contrast to the paltry $1.8 billion received by war-decimated Afghanistan for 'reconstruction' during 2002.

We drove up the incline of a ravine towards the frontline, Mustafa Khan behind the wheel of a ramshackle anti-aircraft lorry captured from the Taliban. We descended and scrambled by foot through a cutting towards a checkpoint. Several soldiers, pleased to be diverted from the monotony of awaiting enemy fire, welcomed us. They had laid a row of mortars in a neat line, next to which was a rocket launcher from which they could fire to the end of the escarpment. Some fifteen kilometres away, they pointed out another

Top - Dubbed "Resistance Royalty" by foreign journalists during the 1980s jihad, the Arsala brothers provided some of the most formidable Commanders of the Afghan war. Here, Haji Qadir wears a white fez and stands on Abdul Haq's right side. Haq wears a blue salwar.

Bottom - Abdul Haq as a young Mujahed.

both © Nasrullah Arsala

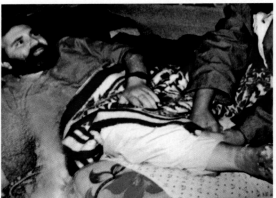

Top left - Abdul Haq.

Top right - Nasrullah 'Baryalai' Arsala.

Middle - Abdul Haq recuperating in Wardak Province after the loss of his foot to a landmine.

Bottom - With his mujahideen on an operation. Haq stands on the left side holding a stick.

all © Nasrullah Arsala

Top left - The ex King, Mohammad Zahir Shah.

Top right - Aga Jan, Haq's famed Commander in the strategically important Sarobi area.

Bottom - The Taliban Deputy Interior Minister, Mullah Khaksar.

Top left - 'RAM' Seeger after his period as Officer in Command of the UK's Special Boat Service (1974-76), which ex marines have credited him with having re-shaped in the run-up to the Falkland's War. Seen here with the Sultan of Oman, whose Special Force he Commanded during 1977. © 'RAM' Seeger

Top right - Ken Guest, second from right, with Jalalludin Haqqani's Jadran tribe Mujahidin during attack on hill top base at Taraghry, 7th March Afghanistan 1981. As it is early in the Soviet-Afghan War majority of Haqqani's force were still armed with bolt action rifles from World Wars One and Two and mostly wearing traditional leather bandoliers with .303 ammunition. © Ken Guest

Bottom - Joe Ritchie, who with his brother James tried to get serious support for Abdul Haq's Plan in Washington DC in the run up to - and the aftermath of - September 11. © Touch Productions

Top left - Assadabad, Kunar in December 2002 with the Governor and Central Bank employees as we counted and then burnt old 'afghani' notes.

Middle - Small child on Kabul to Jalalabad road near Sarobi.

Bottom - Arrival in Khost by Soviet era Mi8 helicopter to undertake currency exchange operation - 2003.

Top left - On the Durand Line at Yacoby, the Afghan border guard defend themselves against apparent Pakistani incursions.

Top right - The body guards of Haji Zahir.

Bottom - On the way to Dur Baba smuggling district, in the Shinwar region.

Top - Author with Haji Zahir on the Afghan side of Torkham border post.

Bottom left - Haji Zahir and elders in discussion in his garden in Jalalabad.

Bottom right - Dacca, a guardpost of Haji Zahir's border guard, was once a British outpost.

Top left - Haji Zahir at the fortified compound Qadir had begun building during his first tenure as Governor of Jalalabad.

Top right - Afghan soldier with flower and kalashnikov.

Bottom left - Haji Zahir and elders from Loya Paktia and Paktika.

Bottom left - A picture of Haji Qadir looks down on the crowd at a ceremony of Shahid for Abdul Haq.

Pakistani position, the highest in the area. Under canvas in the dead ground, an elder with henna-coloured side-burns, a grey beard and white fez sat on a charpoy and prodded a knarled finger towards me. 'For a hundred years they are *not* here. This is *our* territory', he said and jutted his chin dismissively towards the Pakistani position.

> They had vehicles and heavy artillery and told us to agree for this territory to become Pakistan, in return for electricity, roads and bribes to elders.

The Pakistanis had been here weeks earlier, before Mustafa Khan pushed them back. The old man pushed back his white fez and said:

> The local people take weapons against Pakistan, but elders (three maleks and one maulavi) take money plots in Hyattabad to capture Afghan territory. Why, after fifty years?

Hyatabad was the Peshawar suburb where Afghan resistance leaders had built villas. He looked into my face as though somewhere in it some he would find some meaning that might enlighten him, possibly relating to the legacy of British history on the North-West Frontier.

> But I am Afghan and we'll *never* sell our soil to Pakistan. If the Afghan government was stable, we should say to Pakistan that our territory goes *all* the way to Attock.

Smacking the lap of his salwar, he added, 'That's part of Afghanistan and they should give it back!'[194]

I wondered about Afghanistan stretching all the way beyond Peshawar again, even to Attock where the rushing waters of the River Indus severed the two lands of India and Central Asia: a natural and historical boundary. Attock was also the location of a fort, where Benazir Bhutto's husband, Asif Zadari, was rumoured to be in prison on corruption charges. If the Afghans still believed their border lay 150 kilometres to the East, it was understandable that men like the old man would be angered to see Pakistani government forces pressing westwards over the Durand Line. And simultaneously Pakistan's anxiety was understandable, for if the Afghans desire were met, the territory of Pakistan would effectively be halved. The old man went on:

> There were Americans here, eighty to a hundred of them and twenty
> vehicles, one week before. They came several times to patrol, coming
> alongside the Pakistanis, bringing twenty helicopters and fifty tanks. I
> asked what they were doing and their Commander said, 'the Pakistan
> Government told us that Mullah Omar is here so we've come to capture
> him'. But I told them there is no al Qaeda here and after several days
> they left.

He picked up the fold of his kameez and stretched it neatly across
his lap.

> The Pakistanis said, 'We are searching for al Qaeda. But al Qaeda
> is only a good name! Anything you can do using *name* of al Qaeda!
> When Pakistanis came they said Americans invite us here to capture
> al Qaeda. I don't know about politics, just that this is my soil and I
> will protect it! I am Afghan and will never sell my soil in exchange for
> anything![195]

Before we left, the old man asked if I would like to visit his house for
tea so he could show me the skull of a British soldier killed by his
grandfather. I declined politely. But wondered if the skull was a last
vestige of the third Anglo-Afghan war. It was always a revelation
to see how much these simple people were so conscious of their
history; certainly far more so than Prime Minister Blair, who was
about to commit the British to a major escalation of our post-2001
role in the south, in Helmand.

Back in Jalalabad, others reaffirmed that Pakistan was simply
using the excuse of capturing al Qaeda as reason to take more
territory from the Afghans. People were also furious that President
Karzai didn't react more strongly to such audacity. When Kabuli
men had mobbed Pakistan's embassy that summer, Karzai made a
public apology to President Mussharaf and promised the culprits
would be jailed. People questioned whether it was his weak hold
over the country and lack of military capacity that had engendered
such a limited response? Or, whether as leader only of a 'transitional'
administration, without a remit to renegotiate borders, maybe he
wasn't in a position to challenge Pakistan's interpretation of where

Durand's fuzzy limits lie. An elder at Jalalabad's Loya Jirga shura office told me:

> This is a transitional government which can't decide borders so the USA should keep the integrity of Afghanistan as we don't have an army or government. Pakistan is cheating the US, telling them al Qaeda is on its borders.

Unknown to US generals, the Afghans and Pakistan were fighting an old battle. Days later, a UN officer based in Jalalabad admitted: To be honest I haven't heard of al Qaeda or terrorist activities in that area and they haven't captured a single terrorist.

Pakistan and the US were apparently undertaking a joint operation called 'Combined Resolve', aimed at controlling the tribal areas and hunting down al Qaeda. But during a meeting in the Kasr Palace, Jalalabad's Governor Haji din Mohammad confirmed:

> It *is* a problem. Pakistan has crossed the zero line in several places, by several kilometres. But the real issue is the Durand Line. Pakistan wants to use it as a negotiating tool. There is no al Qaeda in Mohmand area. This is a good *excuse* for the Pakistanis to come inside. They want territory. Talk about al Qaeda is just propaganda.

I went up the hill and past a road which CIA staff had blocked off, renamed and signboarded 'Chocolate Alley', because, the Afghans said, the CIA liked to hand out 'chocolate' to local children from there. Today I was visiting the tribal areas chief, a whippet-thin man named Faraydoon Mohmand, head of the Mohmand tribe. 'Pakistan is using the name of al Qaeda for its own benefit; to get control of the land and to have money from the USA', he told me in a room surrounded by sepia photos of him as a young military officer. The people of his area, the Mohmand tribe, had always supported the family of Jalalabad's Governor Haji din Mohammad.

> So why should we support al Qaeda or the Taliban? This situation is creating a problem between Afghanistan and the USA, as they are bringing our enemies to this country. This is an issue of sovereignty, a national issue, but if the central government does not react, the tribes will take it into their own hands.

***

The border dispute illustrated the twisted chicanery of complex relations between Afghanistan and its southern neighbour. Although the Durand issue lay at the root of the problem, following Pakistan's annexation from India in 1947, this had metamorphosed into the 'Pashtunistan issue'. Both mirrored Pakistan's insecurity about her existence. As Haq recognised, both had contributed to the festering sore at the heart of Pakistan's 1980s strategic and regional policy. A sore which continues to emit venom, yet whose existence often seems invisible to those advocating a regional policy to dealing with Afghanistan's problems today. The following paragraphs explain why the issue remains as toxic today as it was during the 1970s and 80s, when Pakistan preferred to back biddable Afghan mujahideen leaders (such as Gulbuddin Hikmatyar) whom they knew they could rely on to support Pakistan's strategic interests.

As Baryalai had explained, Afghanistan's relationship with the Soviet Union really began after the ejection of the British and the 1919 Treaty of Rawalpindi. It deepened following Partition and the emergence of Pakistan. Afghanistan and Pakistani relations were soured from the outset after the Afghans did not immediately 'recognise' Pakistan as a new nation at a meeting of the UN in the early 1950s.

Then came the inevitable disagreements over the independence of the Pashtun belt. For the Pashtun tribal areas of the North-West Frontier Province had enjoyed quasi-independent status in relation to British India since 1901. After Partition, Afghanistan hoped they would gain independence but instead some areas were subsumed into the newly created Pakistan, which then had to deal with tribal uprisings. In 1949, after the Pakistani air force responded to one such uprising with an air strike, the Afghans reneged on all previous treaties creating a frontier with British India, and pushed for the idea of an independent Pashtunistan, on the Pakistan side of the Durand Line.[196] Pakistan responded furiously, cutting off

Afghanistan's access to the Indian Ocean and blockading petroleum. The Afghan government was forced to sign a free trade and barter agreement with Mosco; in exchange for petrol, Afghans would provide wool and raw cotton and the Soviets began oil exploration in Northern Afghanistan. Relations between Afghanistan and the USSR deepened further when diplomatic ties with Pakistan were cut once again and the Pakistan-Afghan border was closed for two years until 1963.[197]

During his tenure both as Foreign Secretary in the 1960s and President following the 1973 coup which deposed the former King, Afghanistan's President Daoud had brought Afghanistan closer to the Soviets than to Pakistan. This relationship was the culmination of a long post-WWII balance between the USA and the Soviets, both of which had competed for influence in the country, often by undertaking aid projects.[198]

During the early 1970s, Pakistan's generals knew that Daoud, an Afghan nationalist with a devotion to the cause of a 'Pashtunistan' state, hoped the lands taken by the Durand Agreement would revert to Afghanistan. Naturally the generals had no wish to reopen a debate over claims for land potentially reaching the old British fort at Attock.

It was for this strategic reason that Pakistan and the ISI preferred to back Islamist leaders, such as Gulbuddin Hikmatyar , during the jihad. The intention was to make Afghanistan an Islamic state and find a leader to serve their cause in Kabul. This would also assist in creating a bulwark of 'strategic depth' against India, the constant threat to the south. Hence Afghan nationalists like President Daoud and later Abdul Haq, men with an ideological following were a threat to the Generals. The Generals preferred leaders they could control with the pursestrings, men like Hikmatyar and Sayyaf. Hence the Generals used US dollars during the jihad to buy off Hikmatyar - for he could then be counted on to form a pro-Pakistan government in Kabul – and later, Sayyaf.[199] Crucially, this would also obviate any need to renegotiate Durand and risk losing Pakistani territory. It was for this reason that, of all the seven mujahideen leaders, Hikmatyar received some eighty percent of the overall funding given by the CIA to Pakistan for the purpose of running the Soviet jihad. And probably why Abdul Haq, who could not be 'bought' but spoke out against the policy was ridiculed and dubbed 'Hollywood Haq' by the ISI.

At this point it is important to note that Abdul Haq, although an Afghan 'nationalist' was *not* a 'Pashtun nationalist'. He was not pushing for an independent state of 'Pashtunistan'. This was ironic, given the way he was treated by the ISI, as he was not a threat to Pakistan.

Abdul Haq was one of the few Afghan Resistance leaders who recognised how the twin unresolved issues of 'Pashtunistan' and 'Durand' lay at the heart of Pakistani politicking over Afghanistan. He understood how the two could have devastating consequences for Afghanistan and eventually global security. During the post-September 11 American-backed hunt for bin Laden, both issues were being resurrected. However, President Mussharaff also now faced a growth in support for the Islamic fundamentalist coalition Islamist Mutahed-e-majlis-amal (MMA), which won elections in 2003 in the NWFP. So not only was Mussharaf's military regime having to balance his position as an ally of the US in its Afghan 'War on Terror' with his pro-Islamist Generals and the ISI, but now he faced a resurgence of radicals in his midst. Some thought this a good reason for Mussharaf's crackdown on Pakistan's tribal areas. 'They're not exactly his best friends', said the UN spokeswoman, referring to the MMA.

Still, in the summer of 2003, Pashtuns like Haji Zahir felt Pakistan was not just using al Qaeda as an excuse (at least in Nangarhar Province) to take control over the unruly tribal areas and leveraging off the ignorance of the foreigners. No, Pashtuns like Haji Zahir knew in their blood that Pakistan was using al Qaeda here as an excuse to gain Afghan territory as a bargaining chip to press Kabul to close the debate on Durand. President Mussharaf, in a gibe at Karzai over his lack of control over outlying areas, called him 'Governor of Kabul'.[200] Yet the irony was that, while fighting Zahir's men over checkpoints in Afghanistan's eastern territory, Pakistan was apparently turning a blind eye to the regrouping and training of hundreds of Taliban on Afghanistan's southern border in the Baluchistan triangle near Quetta. A regrouping that didn't even have the excuse of being in tribal areas beyond the Pakistan government's writ.[201]

***

By late 2003, it was apparent that the 'real' war against al Qaeda as well as the search for bin Laden, now almost a mythical character, was happening further south along the border, in a hostile place closer to Quetta called Waziristan. By Spring this was known as a new 'jihadi highway' where Chechens, Arabs and Pakistanis flocked to fight jihad. After almost three years, the US didn't seem to be making any headway in finding Osama, despite indication in spring 2004 from the US military that bin laden would 'definitely be caught' by that Autumn. US intelligence agencies still seemed so convinced that Pakistan really was their unalloyed ally that they were caught off guard in October 2003. *Time* magazine described an incident where the Pakistani military, supposedly fighting on the border in tandem with American troops, actually opened fire on the Americans.[202]

If US Commanders had studied British history in the area they would have seen tremendous parallels between their own attempts post-September 11 to stem an insurgency and find bin Laden and the story of two other Holy Men who had caused trouble: Mullah Powindah in 1894, and then, during the 1930s, the Fakir of Ipi.

Following the Durand Agreement of 1893, the Pashtun tribes east of the Durand became more turbulent in opposition to the British who were then ruling India. Increasingly, a feeling of nationalism began to replace ethnic and tribal loyalties. Waziristan was one of the most problematic areas, along the border, a place where 'people were as unyielding as the rocks that covered the landscape'.[203]

The story of 'The Fakir of Ipi' began on a summer day in 1936 when a Waziri tribesman entered the district town of Bannu in the Province of Waziristan. There, he was captivated by the wife of a

Hindu merchant. Taking her with him, he brought her back across the administrative border and married her in a Muslim ceremony. When her original husband brought the case to court on a charge of kidnap, the case of Chand Bibi, as she had chosen to be called, took on the significance of 'a pretty face that moved, not a thousand ships like Helen of Troy, but at least two British divisions'.[204]

The verdict came down in the Hindu's favour and Muslim tribesmen smouldered over what they saw as an affront to their version of Muslim law.

> Several thousand Wazirs ambushed the Indian Army's Bannu brigade, killing and mutilating 130 officers and men and making off with a bumper crop of rifles and ammunition.

The whole episode may have quietened down but for the Fakir of Ipi, a priestly Wazir who for years had gone quietly about his holy duties without attracting much notice. It was only with the Chand Bibi case that the Fakir's unassuming exterior was exposed to show how beneath there 'bubbled a hatred for the unbeliever certifiable in its intensity'. Using the name 'Islam Bibi' as a rallying cry, the Fakir showed himself to 'possess the skills of a Field Marshall and enough rabble rousing charisma to mobilise a tribal army'.[205]

The Fakir of Ipi, who was named Haji Mirza Ali Khan, headed up a group of Mullahs and managed to stir up rebellion amongst the Madda Khel and Tori Khel section of the Waziris. When British troops arrived they came:

> ... festooned with automatic weapons, girdled with field guns and howitzers, chaperoned by flotillas of tanks and armoured cars, shaded by the umbrella of the Royal Air Force.[206]

Nevertheless the British were forced to send three Divisions into action and, by the time an uneasy peace was made in 1937, had suffered over a thousand casualties. The debacle of the Fakir of Ipi had cost the British some £50 million (no small sum in 1937) and led to the deployment of fifty thousand British and Indian troops.

Despite their superior firepower, the British found the tribesmen, who were now armed with long range rifles, more mobile and tribal fighting very difficult. The Fakir of Ipi was never caught and remained safe near the Afghan border at Shawal. From there he remained a thorn in the side of the British, and later Pakistan, until his death in 1959.[207]

In his book on the Fakir of Ipi, Warren said; 'The attempt to pacify Waziristan had been the last of several major incursions into tribal territory during the hundred years of Britain's presence in North West India. On each occasion the tribes and the mountains won a strategic victory. The Waziri Campaign was eventually called a 'school for soldiering' by Sir W Barton.

Like the incursions fought by the British in the 1930s, by 2003 it was already apparent that the coalition too were caught up in a similar game in which the Pathans, with their superior knowledge of the mountains, hatred of the infidel and guerrilla skills, would ultimately win. And Pakistan, having already received some $3 billion USD in military aid from the US, was benefiting too.

There were other similarities between the Fakir of Ipi's insurgency and that which began to put itself on the radar in 2004. As with al Qaeda and bin Laden, part of the strength lying behind the Fakir's motivation was his faith in the ideal of a Muslim society:

> The extent to which Islamic fundamentalism lay at the core of the Fakir of Ipi's motivations is only too apparent. He desired a status quo in which muslims lived beyond the interference of a western style administration directed by non muslims.[208]

And as with bin Laden:

> It is commonly believed that anyone who gives information about him or about those who go to see him will be instantly struck blind. All illness and misfortune seem to be attributed to his displeasure. Not a single malik, tappa or lambarder has come forward voluntarily, with any information.

This was possibly due to the close-knit nature of Pashtun society, and in particular its emphasis on Pashtunwali, the Pashtun code which values hospitality and looking after ones guest.

The insurgency along the border in Waziristan, as well as by

2004 throughout southern Afghanistan, was clearly a war furnished by a varying concoction of forces. Pakistan's policy of apparently denying support to the Taliban while simultaneously allowing them to regroup on Pakistani territory outside Quetta and giving shelter to their fighters, increasingly caused people to accuse them of 'implausible denial'.[209]

CHAPTER ELEVEN

'NO ONE COULD HOLD A CANDLE TO HIM': A PRIVATE US EFFORT TO SUPPORT ABDUL HAQ (PART I)

Jalalabad, August 2003

It was not until August 2003 that I finally talked properly with James Ritchie, the man who alongside his brother Joe, had financed Haq's last trip into Afghanistan. The Ritchie brothers were patriotic Americans, 'signed up' Republicans who had made a lot of money as Chicago options traders before turning their attention to helping the country they'd been partially raised in. During the Taliban era, they financed several Loya Jirga meetings outside Afghanistan – in Istanbul and Bonn – under the auspices of the 'Council for Peace and National Unity'. The objective was to bring Afghans together to discuss their country's problems. The meetings culminated in the Rome Process, at which key leaders agreed to work together under the banner of the King to provide an alternative to the Taliban. But around the time of September 11 and indeed earlier in the year 2000, things did not go the way the Ritchie brothers would have expected. Much of this related to disconnects within the US military, intelligence and diplomatic establishment.

The first of several meetings I had with James Ritchie was held at the office of his NGO on land adjacent to the Peshawar road. Ritchie was undertaking projects to grow saplings for propagation elsewhere. The land – which had belonged to an agricultural project set up by the communists – was bordered by mature eucalyptus. Behind it were gravel sand banks marking the confluence of the Kabul and Kunar rivers.

We sat in the clammy heat of his upstairs office. Ritchie was a tall man with a golden-grey stubble beard. I had seen the grave of a 'Ritchie' in the British cemetery in Kabul; 'killed in 1978 in an auto accident near Kandahar'. I later leant that this was Ritchie's father.

He seemed irritated so I began by asking him about his agricultural projects. 'They won't fund agricultural education here so how on earth are we supposed to build capacity amongst the population?' he said, referring to USAID. I asked him about the failed British poppy scheme. Eyes glaring, Ritchie hissed his reply:

> If they'd just *pissed* the £70 million away it would have been better. But instead they managed to increase poppy cultivation, upset the people and give money to people who should *never* have had it. Yet how much money did they spend on agriculture in Nangarhar Province last year? Nothing!

'And do you think the US will really carry out their threat to aerial spray?' I asked

> The thought of the US doing aerial spraying is *unbelievable*. So we destroy their economy and now the only viable thing they have left is poppy and we want to destroy that too.

An elderly man came into the room with a tray of green tea. He set it down on the table and began pouring the sweet, pale liquid into glass cups. Ritchie stopped for a moment to watch, as though calmed by the process. Then he said slowly:

> The relief effort in Afghanistan did more damage than the Russians. The reason? We did it all through Pakistan and completely overturned Afghan society. Warlordism is not a characteristic of Afghan society. It was never there until the jihad'.

I turned to the subject of Haq and the events surrounding his death: 'So are you saying they murdered him?' 'Basically yes', he responded, talking about possible CIA complicity.

> Because they didn't follow my instructions concerning the 'spy plane'. The one they sent in to look for Haq. In a hostage situation you don't give away your presence. But they deliberately fired a shot even before Haq was arrested by the Taliban, so making damn sure he'd be done for!

I took out a notebook.

> The instructions must have come right from the top. They didn't want Haq around, so they fucked him up, they fucked him down and they

led him to his death! At all crucial points they pushed him in there. They led everyone to believe he was the well-funded Pashtun leader. In other words, they made him a target and they didn't give a shit.

He sighed.

You know *even* a well connected journalist I know with contacts in the US government, told me that when I'd called in asking for help, the CIA had said, 'Let the one-legged bastard walk out of Afghanistan!' *That* was their attitude!

Later, we drove back into town together. The freneticism of Jalalabad's market streets calmed him and by the time we swung down the street where Haji Qadir's daughters were living he seemed more serene. 'Have you read *The Da Vinci Code?*' he asked. I hadn't.

It's very interesting on the masculine/feminine codes of society. These people seem to have something of that here. Man, there's something special that holds this place together.

As he spoke, he thumped his right fist on the steering wheel.

God if they had *Die Hard, Live Fast* and all that crap culture imported here, this place would have totally caved in after what's happened here the last twenty years. But something more, maybe it's in their society or culture has held the place together after what they've had slung at them.

We met again a few days later, again at his office. I pulled some English 'Prince of Wales' biscuits from my bag. 'Here, I bought these for you', I said, profering them. He took them from me.

'What are these, MI6 cookies?' he said, chin jutting forward.

I was not quite with his flow. 'Come on', he continued, eyes fixed upon me coldly, 'What's a young English girl doing hanging out in Afghanistan? Whose paying you?'

His tone was cutting. I looked at him, neatly dressed in a white *salwar kameez*. With his angled features, he could have been attractive, but unlike many good-looking men he did not use them to his advantage. Instead, he seemed embittered.[210] I told him I didn't work for MI6, nor anyone else.

'Then how come you know so much about me?' he challenged

and I reminded him that he'd been in the press a lot during October 2001, that we'd met in October 2002 and I had heard more about him from the Afghans.

After that we had a more relaxed chat. Despite his hard exterior he seemed a man of conscience, who wanted the truth of Abdul Haq's story to come out. As such, he wanted me to record our interview. 'But it has to be somewhere I feel safe', he said. I asked if he was scared of bugging. 'No, it's just that I may need to cry, or kick the wall. I have to access areas very deep inside'.

He suggested we continue that night, in the Koh I noor foundation, the Jalalabad house of Haq's youngest brother, Haji Daoud. Later and after sharing a meal with Haji Daoud, the three of us sat in a circle on some of Daoud's fine Afghan rugs. 'He's very artistic', Zahir had told me of Daoud, who was his uncle. Unlike the rest of the family, Daoud had sienna-coloured hair and played an Afghan instrument, the *Rubab*. He had been castigated for this by some of his elder brothers who felt it beneath the family. But Daoud later told me he felt it important to guard against the dying out of Afghan culture and had also taught his two sons to play. It was him who had planted the orange groves and made the garden in the family's village.

The air conditioning roared but did little to assauge the steaming August heat, or the tempo of our conversation and Ritchie's anger, for he had ratcheted up his aggression. Maybe it was being on familiar territory and with an audience?

'You must be the *sister* of John Gunston?' he said in a voice laden with malice which left me bemused.

'John Gunston?'

'Come on, you're an oddball. John Gunston's sister'. He eyed me intensely and I was confused. 'Then what's an English girl doing wondering alone around Afghanistan? You're something to do with Gunston aren't you?' he continued, determinedly.

A young man came in bearing a tea kettle and three glasses and began pouring for us. Moments later there was a knock at the door. Zahir's cousin had come with a driver to collect me, but the meeting

– delayed by supper – had barely begun. I sent the cousin away then tried to steer the conversation back to Haq. Ritchie's staring eyes continued examining me, trying to ascertain who I really was, until I felt very bare. 'OK, so whose payin' you?' he drawled.

I needed the interview, he knew this and seemed to enjoy playing cat and mouse, digging at me for reasons I could only guess at. I wondered why he had so little trust. He sat calmly opposite me, with Daoud to one side looking very uncomfortable. But Ritchie hadn't finished his lashing yet and growled at me.

> I don't know who you're reporting to, but yesterday after talking to you I decided I didn't give a *damn* because the British intelligence services need to know this story. Because in the mid '80s they *wanted* Abdul Haq. But the CIA told them he was *their* asset. Do you know what I mean by 'asset'?

He shouted the last word and I felt the full force of his anger. I needed the information in order to piece together as much as possible about Haq's final hours and the circumstances leading to his death. So I began by asking Daoud, who was the youngest of the eight brothers, a little about Abdul Haq. He spoke hesitantly at first, his voice was gentle, honeyed and he spoke in the present tense. He had travelled with Haq a lot, and worked with him in the office for four years. So the two had been 'very close', he said.

> We had a big loss when he passed away. I wish he was alive for this situation we have now. When I see his pictures I am crying for him. I never cry for others. But for Abdul Haq I cannot stop my crying. When Haq was coming the people knows he's coming like a mountain. But he never said 'do this'. He does not want to bother people but does himself. We know why he's gone, why no one asked. My point is this. When he start this struggle to do something for his people, his country, rest of world. A lot of problems is creating here. All [problems] was from here. He was against these things fifteen years ago. He said, 'I am a Muslim, an Afghan, a Pashtun. I have own ideas. Don't take from other people. During war with Russians, he was a careful person. When he was a commander he never threw rockets by the people or by the civilians. He said, 'I was fighting against troops not the civilians'.

171

He never did that. He did fight with Russians or army people. At that time I spend more time with him during war with Russians round Kabul, Jalalabad. He was older than me by five years. We was friends, riding the bicycles, etc, when children.

'So what did he mean', I asked. 'When he talked about 'needing to put in place an "alternative structure" before he died?'

He says we should not fight, should trust. Should connect with tribes and civilians. Always *connect* with your people. When he died Hazaras were more upset than Pashtun! And *they* celebrated his memorial in Quetta.

There was a pause during which Ritchie began talking about bin Laden.

The fact of the matter is if they *wanted* him, they could have *had* him. It's difficult for me to imagine that when times were peaceful in Afghanistan ... *before* September 11 they couldn't have located him! Hell, Daoud could have located him!

He turned to Daoud and laughed. For the first time that evening, Daoud smiled.

Ritchie went on, the malice now dissipated.

He was only seventeen years old when he said he'd take the fight to Kabul ... and formed a network there like nobody. Massoud may have been King of the Panjshir if only he'd get out of the mountains. But Haq was the guy in Kabul. In '85 he was only twenty-eight years old yet being carted around by Prime Ministers and Presidents ... but I've heard very few people express themselves better.

'And when did you meet him?' I asked.

In '98. I was sponsoring an Afghan conference in Germany, a Loya Jirga precurser and they'd had three meetings before but this had 250 Afghans from all over the world. If you look at the list of Afghans who came to this meeting, I'll bet you half are now ministers. He was the one who organised that meeting ... and Karzai put it together too. The Northern Alliance were just members like everyone else ... there were Taliban there too. It was really a good meeting. The objective was to put together a Loya Jirga so people could decide the Taliban was not the right government to have. Although Haq was the driving force and one of the strongest speakers I've known, he generally never spoke at these meetings. He'd sit at the back or not go. But when he did speak people listened and the ones who didn't have huge agendas usually agreed. He'd basically let others speak. He was brilliant for doing that. Not like his cousin for example. Hedayat Arsala, the guy that looks like this actor, the one in the 1984 Orson Welles thing. The proud, educated guy of the family. They can't stand him. He's Vice President now. But Haq, here's this young kid whose a street fighter and gets rich and famous and can also talk and has power. Is charismatic. Wants everyone to get along. But would only go in as low key as you could possible be at these meetings.

'Are you saying his cousin was a contrast to that?' I asked. 'His cousin Arsala wanted to be the next president. Probably still does', Ritchie sighed.

It wasn't til a year later in Rome that we really got to know one another - November 1999 - and started to do things together. But you know the Royal family screws everything up. Royally! I don't know why this meeting never went anywhere. Maybe as we could get no support from the US or anyone. There was just *no* interest. They wanted to have a Loya Jirga and put the King in charge as head of it and go to Afghanistan. And if the Taliban didn't agree they could have had it in Pakistan. All sorts of Talibs would've come. If they'd have had a Loya Jirga in 2000 or '99 the number of Talibs who'd have gone would have broken the back of the movement as the 'real' Taliban were really fed up. But of course Pakistan would'nt have supported that. So if you want to get to answer as to what we've done wrong now, well, we were doing the same thing wrong in '99 and '98. We support Pakistan and they *are* the Taliban. It was also the same thing we did in '92 to '94. When the muj came and we supported Pakistan's people. The UN had put together a peace plan and the *entire* thing was called off by Pakistan. It was when the mujahideen were about to go into Kabul … Haq had trained and put together a police force (with the UN) for Kabul so he would've been in charge of security. But President Nawaz Sharif and the head of ISI didn't agree. They wanted a rotating presidency so they'd stay in charge. Hikmatyar would be PM. They were trying to keep Hikmatyar and not let anyone have the Presidency long enough to get the upper hand. They've always held the purse strings, and had control of what our agents did. The whole thing started with Zia[211] and Charlie Wilson. We [the US] were not friends of Zia. He took over in a coup. We were suspending all aid. But the same thing's happening now that's happened again and again. The reason the US fails in Afghanistan is that in working *so* close with Pakistan. They just keep on going down the same old blind alley! First of all we give 'em three billion bucks. Crazy. We want to rebuild Afghanistan but we give *Pakistan* three billion and put only a few hundred million in here! Mad!

Having come to the end of this, he sat back scowling and reflecting. Then he said:

Qadir had approved the Indians putting a consul in Jalalabad just a week or two before his death.

He took a sip of tea and looked at me again, 'The British intelligence certainly had *their* share of responsibility and this guy Gunston was here'. I made a mental note to try to find Gunston.

'The Afghans speak of him affectionately', I put to Ritchie, although I myself was yet to meet this Gunston character.

'Really?' Ritchie's response was tinged with a mixture of sarcasm and disbelief.

Well, I guess he travelled with them during the jihad and anyone who came over and put their neck on the line they have some affection for. After Rome, Gunston turned up with Special Forces guys or officers. I wasn't sure what they were doing. Gunston said he was an old friend of Haq's and knew people who could put this together. He was staying in the house. Trying to put together a plan, going over numbers etc. He put together a $10 million dollar package for trucks, weapons etc.

The interview was to continue the following afternoon, only this time at Ritchie's house. When I arrived to find a large place behind the main thoroughfare out of town he was not there. But an old man waved me in saying, '*Pass miya her*', indicating he would come soon. The house had been rented from some Arsala relatives who had left for the US when the Taliban came. The garden was spacious and lush, with many trees and terraced flowerbeds. As I admired it, the old man returned with tea.

When Ritchie arrived, we resumed discussion of the events surrounding Haq's capture and the response to that by the US military and intelligence. He seemed more at ease today and paused every so often as he recollected.

> The fact of the matter is the night he was captured, it was in *desperation* that I was calling people in the USA. I called my brother and got hold of Bud McFarlane. He gave me a number he said was CENTCOM and it was actually the CIA. So I called them. But I would never have *dreamed* their operations are so separate from the military, that if I called they'd keep it secret from the army. I'd assumed they were operating in concert with one another. Good Lord, there's a war going on! My requests were for some kind of assistance to him. But the entire night they either didn't even contact the army or the army lied about the fact that they knew about it. One or the other. This is something that comes out later, after his death when I went to CENTCOM and discussed it with them.

He paused, sighed and rubbed his palms tightly against his thighs.

> So, initially they told me they couldn't send help for him 'til they'd gone in with a Predator and surveyed the situation. It was maybe two hours later. So for an hour-and-a-half or two hours, we located them on the map. We knew where they were as they'd been in contact with us by satellite phone. There was a large helicopter landing site right near where they were. I said to the Americans, 'Look if you send a plane there, the enemy'll be able to hear it', and they said, 'Absolutely not'. But the damn plane was so noisy the people on the ground thought it was a helicopter flying over! The Americans got there with the drone and said they could see nothing on the ground. But we had their location precisely as Isatullah had called and given me his GPS points. For Isatullah an emergency pick-up would have been completely simple and the same is true with Haq. We'd spoken to him on the phone so picking him up was a no brainer. You could do it in thirty seconds. They were not together. Isat was running so they were getting further and further and Haq was hiding. We had three phones: Haq, Isatullah and Haji Qassem each had a phone. Obviously if they

175

had wanted to land they could have secured the area but that would have involved a risk.

He choked a little and I wondered if he was crying. 'Do you think the Taliban were tipped off by the Pakistanis?' I asked.

I don't know. But I'm sure the Pakistanis were helping them. The Taliban could have known Haq and his men had passed that way from people at the border. There were a lot coming from all directions [Sarobi, Jalalabad, Logar]. It's hard for me to believe the Taliban would have just gone and killed him because ... I don't think they were that much animals.

He began talking of Haq's elder brother.

So Qassem had run away quicker than Isat. After his jihad days he knew where to go and made it to the top of the mountain. He called and said there were four vehicles coming on the road. Yet these people – the CIA – are *still* saying they can't see anyone in this valley from their Predator. I don't know what they can do but I know there were a *lot* of people down there. And the US is flying over the valley so everyone can hear them. But say they can't see anyone! Then they decide to drop some bombs!

His voice rose, the tone one of rage and disbelief.

Now *I* don't know *what* to say when they ask if they can do this ... I say, 'First off he can't run, he's *too* fat and only got one leg. Secondly, if you're going to drop bombs you may kill him, what's the *point*?'

He paused.

I talked to them *numerous* times Thursday night. I can't remember exactly the second time. They asked me about dropping bombs, but I told them what Qassem had said: that there were vehicles coming from this way. They said they'd check it out, left me and came back saying they could only find two vehicles. A little later he [the agent] calls me and says 'Can you get them on the phone quickly? We're going to drop bombs'. Then he says, 'It might be too late; I think they are lining up; ah, they're dropped'. So the third time he was basically not asking me but *telling* me they were going to bomb. He was just making sure I didn't hear about it from anyone else!

Ritchie's voice tailed off, his passion spent in the retelling of the story.

'So what was the point of dropping the bombs?' I asked and he sat back, crossed his arms and began with icy deliberation.

To me, *that's* the sixty four thousand dollar question. They said they'd hit a vehicle and killed everyone in it but they killed *no one*. The vehicle was brought to Jalalabad later and Qassim saw it and it had a big hole in it. But it did injure some people. The Americans said they could not get resources out there at this time and were running low on fuel and had to go home. Then … I don't know I spoke to Isat a number of times. Din Mohammad spoke to him too, may be too many times as he had to save his battery. I can't believe how calm din Mohammad was. Just like he was talking to him from down the street, you know. And Isat was telling him to send the helicopter with the ladder which dropped down, saying 'I'll jump on it'. Din Mohammad was laughing.

Ritchie hung his head. For a long time, none of us spoke. Isatullah had been din Mohammad's son, the one who apparently showed most promise. A moment later Ritchie went on, saying bitterly:

The answer to the question, 'Why did we screw up?', is a body. He *is* the story. *Why* did they do that? *What* was the policy? *What* was the strategy? This was *not* an isolated incident but the culmination of a lifetime for Haq in terms of his rejection by the ISI and the US. The same old song. Just the second or third verse.

I nodded and he went on.

The British used Massoud and Pakistan didn't like that. Massoud said, 'Afghanistan was invaded by the Russians from the north, and now by the Pakistanis from the east'.[212] The Pakistanis didn't like people being around him. You see Abdul Haq was a very strong figure who could have been way more useful – and popular – than Massoud. In the early '80s, it was Haq who was the hero. He was barely out of his teens when Reagan had him at some black tie affair. So *why* did they suddenly cut him out, kill him or at least act in such a way that it was not only not helpful but actually extremely harmful to his predicament. The kind of action you would *never* take if an American citizen had been in that situation. I just can't understand it. Here this guy was, unarmed and in enemy territory, and preaching the message we wanted and we [the US] had publically said we were going to support him, preached the message [to Pakistan] that we were supporting him and then – in his hour of need – we spit on him. If that isn't following your policy right to the bitter end I don't know what is.

'But the war wasn't going well at the time Haq died', I said. 'So why didn't they support him?'

They were in with the Northern Alliance by then. I just can't understand why they would withhold support from the Pashtuns up to when they *really* thought they were in trouble. I mean they had a month to plan this thing!

He looked at me, palm outstretched in mock questioning.

OK it's a short time to get aircraft carriers there. But Abdul Haq had been selling this thing for years. I told you we'd gone to Rome right? We'd been planning a Commanders' meeting for some time. We'd talked to, he'd talked to, the State department trying to get visas for some Commanders. That was *before* September 11. Then after September 11, it was like well we'd better have this Commanders meeting *immediately*! So I went to Rome on 14 September. The US was supposedly working on visas but they just didn't do it. So Abdul sat there in Rome almost two weeks, waiting! In retrospect it seemed they were trying to put a stick in the spokes. You can get someone a visa! It was only for ten people! They were from all tribes!

He paused, head in his hands.

So Abdul Haq got tired of waiting for these people to come and left. And right after he left, they all miraculously got their visas. I met with them in Rome. Zaman came. I didn't realise he'd been invited by Mustafa Zahir [the King's grandson] *not* Abdul Haq. Of course the question would be who is *really* inviting him to the meeting? Just *who* put the idea in Mustafa's ear to invite him as that guy is nothing but trouble. Nothing but trouble! He was basically like a spy stuck in the meeting.

There were numerous things from that time that to me indicated they'd chosen their guys and had *no* interest in supporting anyone else. At the time of Haq's death they were getting nowhere and right after it I went back to DC and had only been there a day when I got a call that Tommy Franks[213] was flying up to DC. Bud Mcfarlane thought the sole purpose was to meet me. After all, we'd been told by another General that we had more intelligence than the whole CIA put together! Maybe that's true. As the people they wound up supporting was just a joke. Asked if I could meet with some of their guys running the operation, I said, 'Absolutely, tomorrow if you like'. We flew down there that night to Tampa to CENTCOM. Around November 4, we were met at the airport by Jeff Kimmons who was the J2, the General in charge of security. We went in first thing next morning and were met by J2 and J3, the General in charge of operations – Jene Renwardt – the guy on ops now in Iraq). They had a bunch of other guys there. It was huge ... stupid. We went in like the war room. Two screens on the wall. They had pictures of Afghanistan and a few pictures of key personalities, warlords. When I finally got a turn to talk I was pissed about what had just happened. I asked what was the deal, saying, 'You won't bring help and just do what I ask you not to do!' There was a CIA rep there and supposedly the guy who was supposed to come hadn't been able to due to security reasons. This guy was a notetaker and all he was there to do was to listen. He knew *nothing*. Could only shrug his shoulders. It was basically because they didn't want to talk. Renwardt says to me, 'What are you talking about?' and they all looked at the CIA agent. They had never been communicated to about the Haq thing by the CIA. He said he was just here to take notes. I couldn't help but be sarcastic. Renwardt said, 'Here's my card, if that ever happens again, call me'. And he slapped it down several times on the desk in front of me saying, 'If it happens again, call me!'

Ritchie sighed.

Well, I said, 'It can't happen again, can it? He's dead!' A number of people, there were very interested. I mean after all, we had all these Commanders with satellite phones *in country*. All they had were a bunch of people in Peshawar. People who wouldn't *dare* go in. Haq also had people in Peshawar who had to hide out from ISI. I said they needed to get a safe house in Peshawar and to get these commanders [of Haq's] coordinated. The army guys were literally, 'Let's go'.

I checked my machine was still recording, and he went on.

So I got on a plane two days later to go back and got as far as Dubai. When we got off the plane someone was messaging my phone saying, 'Don't go. We've been contacted and you're endangering your life and those you talk to if you go there'. The message was supposedly from the CIA. From someone Bud trusted. So I thought I shouldn't go. So I stayed in Dubai a few days. Finally called the Kimmons guy. J2. He told me they didn't have jurisdiction in Afghanistan as 'on the ground' was CIA territory. There was a disagreement between the CIA and army and the CIA didn't want me involved. I don't exactly understand the division of labour. I sat there for five to seven days. And I'm getting calls from Haq's commanders – who were all lined up and ready to move, inside Afghanistan – asking what to do. I was sitting in Haq's coffee shop in Dubai one day when I got a call from Khan Mir. He's Haq's Paghman commander. He called me from Paghman at night. Said the Taliban were right there, some running out of Kabul. They were all leaving Kabul. He said which Talibs were here and which were there and what should he do? He said where the Pakistani Talibs were, where the Afghan Talibs were and where the Arab Talibs were. So I called Renwardt. I got his staff that answered the phone and told him the situation and said it was urgent. But Renwardt never called back! When I asked if he got the message he said, 'No'. It was just a few days later. But when he said that … I realised. The military don't drop their messages! I didn't know what to do. There were some of Haq's Commanders in Peshawar afraid for their lives. We needed to do something. But these guys fled and hid. Nothing was *ever* done to give them a safe place to operate from. Though I asked Kimmons about it, the only message I got was that *they* [the CIA] were taking care and basically I was to 'butt out'. But I can't remember if that was Renwardt saying they were in charge … every time I gave information it seemed to get people in trouble. ISI was simply blackballing. A CIA person relayed through Bud that I should not go back. There is no question that at the time I was there there were death threats against myself and Haq according to Haji din Mohammad. After Haq's death he told us someone said they'd had a plan to get the two of us. At the Friday mosque they whipped people up and they brought a big demonstration against his house, against 'the American'. There were four buses, the police had to come and block the streets. Haq knew that would happen. We left that day and went to Islamabad. He knew something was up. It was organised by ISI or the Taliban. But ISI *is* the Taliban, they're one and the same. That's the irony. We're paying off Mussharaf and the first thing we do is offer him one billion dollars. You should talk to Benazir. I had a *long* talk with her after this. She has a *very* interesting perspective.[214]

So then I came back to Peshawar and that was the night the Taliban fell. Then it was one thing after another: Kundoz, Shiberghan, Tora Bora. Sarobi was still dangerous. But Aga Jan was there! Do you know him, he's one of Haq's main Commanders? He's the guy there, knows the people. Yet they're sitting there [the US] supporting people in Peshawar. Then the journalists were killed on the road. But *still* they wouldn't help Aga Jan put a security force on the road. Their alternative was to support the Northern Alliance. I presume that's what they wanted to do. I just *don't* understand it. Why at this time they were working with Zaman and Wardak but *no one* who had any pull in Sarobi ? It's a *key* place you know: controls the north, south, east and west, coming and going from Kabul.

He shook his head again and I made a mental note to find Aga Jan, the commander who had such sway in Sarobi. Ritchie paused, watching me write in my book, then said slowly:

Haq's death has removed the chance for peace for Afghanistan. Now there's no one left who could hold a candle to him.

CHAPTER TWELVE

A PERSPECTIVE ON BRITISH POST-SEPTEMBER 11 STRATEGY AND INTELLIGENCE: THE UK HAQ EFFORT (PART I)

London, September 2003

Back in London that September, I decided to find out about the ethereal Englishman Ritchie had tried to link me with at first: Sir John Wellesley Gunston. The Afghans had often asked me, 'Do you know John Gunston? He was at Tora Bora ...' or 'He's working for MI6'. The irony was that, rather than working for MI6, I would find Gunston to be very critical, not simply of MI6 but of many of the most celebrated figures of the British military, intelligence and political establishment when it came to the post-September 11 'Afghan policy'.

I found him referred to in Kaplan's book:

> The two were introduced to each other in the lobby at Greens hotel. Haq listened silently as Gunston related his experiences (with Hikmatyar and Massoud) giving names, dates and descriptions of various weapons and battle formations in the clipped, technical style of an army officer. He talked about how the Soviets used transport aircraft to provide battlefield illumination during night engagements. He went on to describe the actual configurations of the flares. Unlike the other journalists, Gunston was able to judge the fighting ability of the mujahidin as a military professional and was quite direct in his criticisms. 'You have a very good memory', Haq told him somewhat cryptically. 'Get in touch with me if you want to make more trips inside'.[215]

Later Kaplan describes Haq organising a clandestine visit to Kabul for Gunston in 1988.

> Something no other western journalist had done with the Mujahidin since 1985. Haq told Gunston not only that he could get him into Kabul but that he could also arrange meetings for him there with the regime's army officers and KHAD agents who were secretly working

for the mujahidin. 'I know you wont crack up and tell everything if you"re caught', Haq told him. Gunston swore it was the first time in his life he was humbled.[216]

For someone who had been accused of operating furtively, he wasn't hard to find in the London phone directory. 'Yes, I know who you are, I've been reading you in *The Telegraph*. Good stuff!' a boyish voice said generously.

When I said I was interested in writing about Abdul Haq, he said:

> You're onto a good one! He was a *great* guy and the *only* hope for a decent solution post-September 11. He called me and asked me to meet him in Rome in Sept 2001 where he was working with the King. He had *loads* of resistance leaders who paid their own way to join him, from Farah and Hazarajat to Nangarhar. They looked for an Afghan solution and an ethical representation. It is quite exceptional for it to come from a Pashtun. Actually he was more of an Afghan than a Pashtun.

He suggested I meet with him so that he could furnish me with news cuttings and maps. And soon I rang the doorbell of a Victorian house by the River Thames. There was a voice through the intercom, the door was buzzed open and I was alone in a library style room with polished parquet flooring. Each wall was lined with leather-bound, gilt-embellished antiquarian books. At the far end, a TV and stainless steel kitchen area. Presently, the thump of feet could be heard coming down wooden steps. A man with floppy brown hair tumbled into the room. He was dressed in cords and a Viyella checked shirt in the English 'country' style.

'I was leaving for Dubai and then the east', he smiled. 'So you just caught me'. He was off to Kabul to try to 'get the Pashtuns to work together' in a Pashtun jirga initiative. It seemed a good idea, particularly as even now, in late 2003, there was still no Taliban reconciliation initiative. He gestured me towards a leather sofa as he made coffee, talking enthusiastically.

> They're a great family but not all knights. Haji Qadir was a playboy. Well, he lived that element. Yet he was the old order, whereas Haq was the new order.

'Old order?' I asked. 'Well, Qadir liked to have his potentate around him. He was a great guy'. His view resembled the picture Kaplan had painted of Qadir: a sort of medieval knight upon whose arrival in a village during the jihad would prompt a huge feast with the local goat being slaughtered. Gunston told me he was Qadir's advisor at Bonn, that he had advised him how to deal with the Brits and the US. Qadir had asked him to go to Tora Bora with his son Zahir.

Haq was of course dead by the time the Bonn Conference took place. Gunston spoke about Tora Bora:

> At one stage we almost went to war with Hazerat Ali. Dear old Zahir is like Abdul in the early days but has his father's temper. I see him as 'the Hope'.

As we spoke, he occasionally quoted from Afghan history books, asking if I had read this or that, pulling books from the shelves, fingering their pages. Gunston went on:

> A lot of people decried Abdul as they owed allegiance to other Commanders or groups. By this I mean Western journalists who went 'in'. But it depended who you were with. During the war it was easy to become partisan.

'So why was he so unpopular with the Americans?' I asked.

> Certainly people like Beardon would call him 'Hollywood Haq'. It was clear that the guys they [the CIA] liked were the ones who would take orders from *them* or the Pakistanis. But Abdul had difficulties with the Pakistanis who'd ask him to carry out murderous operations.

He waited for me to catch up.

> Look, Afghanistan today is teetering on a *knife edge*. The US has inherently destabilised the natural order of power amongst the ethnic races.

His voice was measured and as he spoke I glanced up at his shelves to see, rather auspiciously, a leather volume of Belous' *The Tribes of Afghanistan* sitting adjacent to Ludwig Adamec's *History of Afghanistan*. The leather-bound scarlet and gold volumes indicated an appreciation, at least, of books. The historical references he peppered into every anecdote demonstrated not only his voracious appetite for reading, but also his interest in history. Unlike the British Ambassador I'd met in Kabul, a man who – despite enjoying the grandeur of life in Curzon's Embassy with its huge retinue of staff – did not seem as interested in books about Afghan history as I felt he should have been. Gunston continued at full pelt, as though unburdening himself.

> OK, so initially they didn't care. A CIA guy even said to me, 'We're here to kill ragheads and you're trying to sell us a stable Afghanistan. We don't care, we're here for *payback*!' And that was in October 2001!

I recalled how, only months earlier during a late night discussion in Islamabad, an American diplomat who was friendly with a girl I'd known had commented savagely, 'We're not here for nation building. That's bullshit. We're here for revenge'. I repeated this to Gunston, who commented dryly.

> So this guy understood. But the British, I'm afraid to say, compounded the error. They supported the US *without* a sense of our history and experience in Afghanistan.

He put down his glass, 'And do you want to know why?' I struggled to pull out another notebook, nodding.

> Well, firstly, in September 2001, the guys dealing with Afghanistan – I was asked to brief an anti- terror branch of the MOD who briefed the PM – well these guys, they just quoted from the Ashdown article which, incidentally, was written by a mate of mine.[217]

He broke off laughing. I'd read the article, the only piece of journalism written after September 11 that seemed to understand the nuances inherent to the Afghan problem. Gunston was now relaxed enough to be pretty direct.

> So I went in to brief 'Six'. It was amazing. Their knowledge was *zero*. They knew about the Falls Road,[218] but that was about it!

I leant forward.

> From '95 or '96 onwards, MI6 scaled down their interest. Our MI6 people were basically 'let go'. *Just* as the Taliban took power in '96. So they were left with a twenty-three year old running the Islamabad office! And as you know that meant not just Pakistan but Afghanistan

too was run from there. It was outrageous!

I had known many of the embassy staff in Islamabad. Most were in their early twenties, some working as spies but masquerading as diplomats. Often in their first or second job abroad and with a penchant for meeting up with their British chums on Sunday afternoons for group DVD sessions or curries at the Marriott. Gunston continued:

Since September 11, the US has gone in all guns blazing and created a government that has alienated forty-five percent of the Afghan population. It cannot work. Initially the US didn't understand there were 'good' and 'bad' Pashtuns. It was like, they wear turbans so they're all just 'ragheads'!

He shook his head.

The problem is the international community don't understand that the Taliban is a *stratified* group, made of different supporters – hardliners, religious zealots and nutcases – but subordinated by al Qaeda and their money. Many decent Afghan nationalists supported the movement because the Taliban brought back law and order. The majority wanted stability, peace and prosperity. Not the *Arabisation* of the government.

'Is *that* why did Haq opposed the bombing campaign?' I asked.

Haq's fear over the bombing was that they'd alienate forty-five percent – i.e. the single largest entity – of the population. The Brits should have known but were inherently foolish-minded in September 2001. Instead, they and the Americans just identified Afghans they could do business with – Karzai and Zaman – dismissing Abdul as 'Hollywood Haq' who spoke large but didn't deliver. The reason? It's a label that goes back to ISI and the 1980s when ISI considered Haq too 'independent' to give weapons to. They preferred to work only with people who'd do their bidding.

'Did you witness Haq's "independence" yourself?' I asked.

I spent two years 'inside' on twenty-four trips between '83 and '89. And also spent time with Hikmatyar's group, Massoud and NIFA and can tell you that Haq was *the* most significant commander in the Kabul area during the Soviet war. Despite not having the resources he needed due to problems with the ISI. He was against the big show operations with no material benefit and possible collateral damage. So *not* ISI's favourite. Plus of course they disliked the fact he was eloquent with the press and criticised the CIA's unquestioning support for running the Afghan war through the ISI. That's what came back to haunt him during September '01.

He then suggested we go up to his office where he could copy me some of the news pieces relating to Haq from the time of the jihad and then September 11. He also gave me some photos taken by himself as a young freelancer during the jihad. As he pulled them out of drawers he annotated verbally the operations to which each picture related. There were many of Afghan mujahideen carrying RPGs and machine guns, stalking behind rocks. Also, news cuttings and photos, some of Abdul Haq, dating from the 1980s. When we returned to the ground floor he said:

> At time of his death, *Private Eye* published a small piece saying he was a 'murderous terrorist' and responsible for planting bombs in 1984 killing eight or nine people . But I was with him then and no such operation took place.

He pulled it out and I read. The piece began with a sarcastic take on some of the things journalists who had known Haq had written about him, and went on:

> In a war where few have emerged in glory, Abdul Haq was one of the good guys'.

> And so said every leader writer, too: the death of this decent and civilised chap, they agreed, was a 'severe blow' to the war against terrorism.

> But, as we pointed out in the last *Eye*, Abdul Haq was himself a terrorist. He took pride in having planted a bomb at Kabul airport in 1984 which killed 28 people – most of them schoolchildren. In an interview a couple of years later he was asked if he had any qualms about killing civilians and children, "I don't care", he replied, showing the charm which so enraptured hacks like Bruce Anderson.

> Like so many erstwhile terrorists, Haq managed to reinvent himself as

a "moderate" and a "peacemaker" – so successfully that his murderous exploits were entirely omitted from every single obituary.

Gunston interjected:

Of course the piece in the *Eye* was conveniently unattributed. A dirty tricks smear. Probably because I had pressure put on the intelligence services in October 2001 to support Abdul so when he died it was in their interest to diminish him.

As I digested the enormity of this, he said:

Look, you see the *manner* of his death spelt out his *value*. And that wasn't all. In December 2001, the *Daily Telegraph* said MI6 were responsible for the fall of Kabul, Jalalabad and Ghazni. Nonsense! They were simply taking credit where it wasn't due. In fact, din Mohammad asked me to get help from 'Six' to pay for buses to get their people to Jalalabad from Peshawar. He also asked for them to stop bombing the villages and killing their people. I told MI6, 'You guys have a window of opportunity to support Haji din Mohammad and be part of it'. But they didn't call him.

Baryalai and Ritchie's assertions about Gunston working for MI6 now looked pretty weak. Even so there was an air of privacy, even secrecy around him. Over the following months I visited him several times and he was always very forthright about Haq, but clearly had 'other projects' going on.

He furnished me with documentation about Abdul Haq's plan for toppling the Taliban. And told me that a former head of the Special Boat Service (SBS), Major 'RAM' Seeger,[219] had accompanied Gunston to Haq's Peshawar office during October 2001. Seeger's job was to put the plan devised by Abdul Haq into an intelligible format, so that those in the UK[220] with the potential to assist would understand the dynamics.

The documents included situation reports (hereafter 'sitrep') from the period from September to October 2001. Some of these, Gunston told me, had been passed to the SIS. There was also a fax addressed to General Lord Guthrie (see Appendix III) briefing notes on Haq and the various Commanders (Taliban and otherwise) who had pledged support, various summaries of the plan, notes on the requirements for money, arms, transport and so on, as well as updates.

But it was a neatly typed-up sitrep marked 3 October 2001 (see Appendix IV) that first caught my attention. I later realised this had been typed by RAM Seeger, whom Gunston had been working alongside together with an ex-marine named Ken Guest, in an attempt to secure support for the Haq strategy in the immediate aftermath of September 11. I will come to Seeger and Guest's perspective in a later chapter.

The sitrep dated 3 October was numbered with points one to twenty-four it was an outline of the reasoning for the Haq option strategy. 3 October was of course still four days before the US-led coalition began its bombing campaign of Afghanistan. When the sitrep was typed up, Haq would not have known that the bombing would begin so imminently, hence perhaps the sitrep was more hopeful of success than it would have been had this information been known then. Nevertheless in the introduction, the sitrep said that the plan was dependent on the charisma, reputation and pledges of support from Taliban commanders and could unravel through lack of material support but that the critical effect would be the actions of the US and its allies. By this, I took the point to mean, a bombing campaign.

The second point was about the 'prizes to be gained from a successful outcome' (i.e. of Haq's strategy). This would include a 'relatively bloodless overthrow' of the Taliban, the capture of Kabul by Pashtuns, isolation of al Qaeda, an 'acceptable broad based-government of all ethnic groups', and, as a result of all the above, a 'terrorist-free' Afghanistan.

The sitrep explained how Haq's plan was mostly dependent on large-scale Taliban defections, which they believed were possible, particularly because some 'major players' had apparently pledged support and the regime – as I had seen myself even in Kandahar – was unpopular, not least because the Pashtuns were fed up with hosting al Qaida's Arabs. The fifth point explained the importance of not having a US-backed Northern Alliance capture Kabul and impose a 'Tajik dominated government on the country' which would of course 'not be acceptable to the Pashtun majority' who were then likely to rally to the Taliban, thus prolonging the civil conflict and strengthening al Qaeda. This of course, is exactly what the US-led coalition had done! In recognition of the difficulty of having the Northern Alliance take Kabul, the sitrep thus proposed a Pashtun counterweight to the Northern Alliance to ensure a better distribution of ethnic power, and to increase the likelihood of the evolution of a more widely acceptable government. This point was underlined with reference to the civilian population's memory of recent Northern Alliance atrocities committed in Kabul during the early 1990s. The sitrep floated the idea that al Qaeda (and by implication, the Taliban) was more likely to lose legitimacy in the longer term if the government was overthrown peacefully.

Under the heading 'Outline Plan', the sitrep went on –in the sixth point – to say that Haq's plan was to cross the border with two small hardcore groups of around two hundred 'lightly armed mujahideen' because:

> ... any larger initial group would arouse attention and provoke Pakistani interference. Once safely across the border, 'these groups would be quickly increased by groups of volunteers travelling independently from Pakistan or areas inside Afghanistan. The first of Haq's groups would start from the Mohmand tribal territories and after crossing into the Kunar valley converge on Jalalabad. The second group would start from Terrimangul and head for Teezine and Sorobi which are Haq's tribal homelands and from which he is confident he could draw much popular support. Large scale defections would be expected as soon as the Taliban units were approached or confronted. Pledged defections by Jalalabad commanders would ensure the capture of this town and access to heavy weaponry (tanks and artillery) and uniformed soldiers. Areas of arab resistance would be bypassed.

Reading this, I remembered the campaigns Haji Zahir had described, particularly his return to Jalalabad after exile in Iran post-September 11. Then, he had described coming into Afghanistan with a small column of followers. As they had marched they had called up previously forewarned commanders who had fought with the family during the jihad. These commanders would then mobilise foot soldiers, who would join Zahir and his men. By the time the column reached Jalalabad, it would be many thousands strong. The foot soldiers came from the tribes along the route, from Shinwar, Mohmand, Kunar and as far away as Nuristan, where the men wore pancake shaped *pakhals*.

The seventh point of the sitrep added that simultaneous to the advances from the East would be: 'two uprisings from within Afghanistan – the area north west of Ghazni (Wardak) and the area south of Ghazni but north of Kandahar'. Presumably these would have been orchestrated by commanders who still retained loyalty to Haq due to their history of fighting together during the jihad. Many of these commanders were apparently now embedded with the Taliban.

The eighth point stressed that once begun, Haq estimated his plan could be over within three weeks. He would begin his plan on his home ground, at Tera Mangal/Teezin. Terrimangal lay to the north-west of Jalalabad and was where the family had originally come from, centuries before. The elders there retained loyalty due to this historical link. Haq must have followed this plan, because 'Terrimangal' (also known as Tera Mangal') was where he had been captured by the Arabs.

The next section was titled 'Afghan support for Haq' and the ninth point:

> It is not possible to gauge the actual and potential support for Haq
> with any certainty but the indications are that it is real.

I reflected on my own experience of Jalalabad – with the number of elders and tribesmen I had seen coming to the compounds of the Arsala family, my visits to the Shinwar, the Mohmand and the borders, the weeping school girls at his *shaheed* and the reaction of people to the unpopular US-backed warlords – his support was real.

The sitrep continued and the tenth point ten said:

> We have met and talked with two commanders from the areas around

> Ghazni: Mullah Malang (renowned ex-DRA former mujahideen and more recently ex-Talib commander) and another commander from Wardak. We have also met and talked with two Talib commanders from Sorobi and Hisarak, the leader of the Mohmand border tribe and several other veteran mujahideen commanders.

These areas mentioned were all critical crossroads and strategically important places in the Taliban/Pashtun heartland of the south.

I knew Mullah Malang from my visits with Baryalai and later, when I worked for the political side of the EU. Then my colleague – who was later expelled from Afghanistan in December 2006 for apparently trying to 'do deals' with the Taliban - allegedly on behalf of MI6 – was already using Malang as his point of contact. During the anti-Soviet jihad, Malang had been renowned for his effective anti-Soviet operations around Kandahar.[221] Critically to Haq's plan though, one of Malang's mujahideen during the jihad had included the young Mullah Omar. And with Malang's other former commanders now apparently comprised Mullah Omar's bodyguard. As Malang was a Talib who had recently defected, and was to have played a key role in Haq's Solution, he was a pretty high value defection!

Another possible 'defector' mentioned was a leader of the Mohmand tribe. He was also one of the people I visited whenever I travelled to Jalalabad. He was a true product of the frontier, yet bore an air of sophistication. Whenever I met with him we would discuss issues affecting his people and those in the region at large, e.g. the issue of Pakistani incursions over the Durand line, or whether the stories of the US spraying poppies were myth or fantasy. He always told me of the problems in a most measured and intelligent way.

The tenth point said that Haq was 'acutely anxious of the need to get things right'.

> He realises he has only one chance and as a consequence most of his efforts have gone into building alliances and establishing support. He is confident that he will attract more than enough men and that the problem may in fact lie in attracting too many. He is planning on a basic force of about 5000 volunteers, this being the largest practical

number he can control and supply. Defecting units of course would be additional to this.

The next heading was titled 'Outside Influences' and the four sub-headings beneath it were: ISI, the USA, al Qaeda and the Ex-King. Firstly, it said, Haq had:

> ... recently been visited by the ISI and is currently meeting with them again in Islamabad. He describes their mood as nervous and uncertain. They have expressed the desire to let bygones be bygone and the view that the Taliban has no future. They have not however (as yet) committed themselves to any sort of concrete support.

As I write this I realise that this is where Haq made his greatest strategic miscalculation. He knew himself that his history with ISI was one of distrust. Many had told me that the ISI were suspected of being behind the murder of Haq's wife and small son in their Peshawar house in 1998. The reason cited for that was Haq's genesis of an anti-Taliban plan. So why, I wondered, had he allowed himself to trust them this time? It was possible that he thought that - with the weight of an angry USA about to bear down on the region - that he and the Pakistanis might have joint strategic interests for Afghanistan? Certainly with the US led bombing campaign about to begin - setting the scene for a Northern Alliance takeover of Afghanistan - this joint strategic interest ought to have been a consideration for Pakistan.

The third 'external influence' mentioned in the sitrep was thus the USA. Since Haq's death the Pakistan's have, as I saw myself when I questioned the Pakistani Ambassador to Geneva,[222] been behind rumours that he was supported by the CIA. Prior to his death, Ritchie told me, the CIA themselves had spread rumours that they were supporting him. The sitrep said:

> American Embassy personnel have visited Haq several times but according to him have not come up with anything concrete. Haq is worried that a deployment of American troops would result in increased support for the Taliban as Afghans closed ranks against the foreign invader. From what we have seen and heard we would support this view. At present the main foreign invader is Al Qaida

but this situation could change quickly. On the other hand, the threat of American action against the Taliban and Afghanistan weakens the government and encourages all moderate factions who want a peaceful Afghanistan to oppose them'.

The last heading under 'outside influences' was 'Al Qaida' and here it said – somewhat presciently given bin Laden's subsequent escape and disappearance – that al Qaeda had:

> Purchased 15,000 camels and a large number of kochi [nomad] tents. This suggests that they are preparing for a long march through inhospitable terrain. Bin Laden has been reported to have visited Jalalabad and has subsequently moved to Kandahar and is now believed to be hiding in the mountainous area north of Kandahar and west of the Ghazni road. The same Taliban source also quoted al Qaida members as saying that they had struck but one of ten planned targets.

As to 'freezing out' al Qaeda, the sitrep added that:

> Mullah Malang expressed the view that if Haq was successful and the Taliban were overthrown, the arabs in al Qaida (less the obvious terrorists who would be arrested) would be invited to return to their own countries. NB. This would be the easiest course of action for a new Government to adopt but might not suit the USA. A possible *quid pro quo* for material assistance might be an undertaking not to do this.

Why, I wondered, might this not suit the USA? Surely they might still have been able to capture some of these operatives once the tribal people made clear they were no longer welcome in Afghanistan?

Under the last heading of 'The ex-King', the report said that although the ex-King was still 'very acceptable as a figurehead for the creation of a new Afghanistan', his family and followers, having no experience of the country, were not. I presumed this to mean that Haq wanted the ex-King for the purposes of putting in place his 'structure' and the relevance of the ex-King was to secure this as the 'umbrella' or glue for a multi-ethnic accord. This was reiterated by the next point which said:

> Haq intends to run his operation in the King's name for the cause of a united and peaceful Afghanistan. He does not wish to adopt a special name or cause specific to his efforts.

A heading entitled 'Difficulties and Dangers' indicated what the weak points might be and said:

> Haq's operation will be running on borrowed money and a shoestring and very dependent on the resources he captures and / or are handed over to him by defectors. The uncertainty of this reliance is aggravated by the needs of his plan for speed, momentum and co-ordination. The dangers are that lack of transport and radios will result in poor coordination and delay. His men will also expect to be fed and clothed. To a lesser extent they will also want to be paid and it is possible that much of his potential support will fall away when it is realised that he has no financial backing.

As I re-read this point, I wonder how much coordination of knowledge there was between Gunston, Seeger and James Ritchie, who was, after all, apparently financing the operation. Could it be, I wondered, that the two groups trying to promote Abdul Haq and his plan had not been very coordinated in their commitment? It must be remembered though that both were private initiatives, although there is no indication that the British individuals were giving money themselves, but trying to secure political, and ultimately thus financial support. Time was also short.

The next point recommended that in terms of civil administration in Jalalabad, Haq's brother Haji Qadir would make a suitable provisional governor. As we know, he then was. But the British and Qadir had had their differences. It seems that their differences were so great that one has to wonder whether it was in their interests to have Qadir dead. Certainly the British 'ally' in Jalalabad, Haji Zaman, who was a long-term foe of the family, was thought by many Afghans to have been behind Qadir's assassination. The sitrep finished with the following statement:

> Not to provide discrete support to Haq's enterprise would seem to be needlessly risking the huge gains that could result from a successful outcome. The obvious needs are money, vehicles and radios and possibly some discrete specialist support (e.g. FACS and stand off fire support, signallers, advisers etc).

Gunston told me that the Brits had offered to donate a grand total of 'four satellite phones' to the Haq effort.

***

Gunston invited me for lunch at the Special Forces Club in Knightsbridge. Pictures of SOE agents lined the walls on the staircase. There was a desperately sad photograph of four-year-old Tania Szabo receiving the George Cross from the King on behalf of her dead mother, the renowned Violet Szabo. Some of the women whose pictures I was looking at had achieved extraordinary things during the Second World War, undertaking what was then called 'non-conventional warfare'. Yet an innocent-looking watercolour of a brick kiln had a particularly brutal resonance. Underneath a plaque explained how four SOE female agents had been burnt alive in it after their capture by the Gestapo. In the bar we ordered lunch.

Gunston told me that on a strategic level Haji din Mohammad had been coordinating the movement of people and tribes and dealing with Younus Khalis and his son.[223] This had been important in ensuring a dissolution of the Taliban and the re-establishment of a new order. He was infuriated by the lack of support for din Mohammad by the British. 'Yet they had the *cheek* to claim they were part of this', he said, shaking his head.

> Kabul was a *nonsense!* The problem is that these so-called 'spies' report back to their political masters and therefore people say it *must* be true. It's just like the politicisation of intelligence over the David Kelly affair.

He asked the barman for ketchup and went on, telling me that General Guthrie had been used as emissary of Tony Blair. 'But I told Guthrie to use Abdul, and said, "He has the ability to engineer the collapse of the Taliban"'. Guthrie had responded to Gunston's request for help by saying that he was seeing Dearlove the following day and asking Gunston to send a fax.

Dearlove was then Head of MI6. Gunston had sent him an outline of Haq's plan, indicating who else had been briefed. When Dearlove wrote back to Guthrie he had apparently said, 'I want to assure you that the PM is working hard for the good of Afghanistan

... We're looking into it'. Gunston sighed.

> It was a lost opportunity that *should* have been explained. But was *denied* as they'd already chosen Haji Zaman. Oh, and the Americans had chosen Karzai.

I knew that was true. For I'd been staying at the Serena Hotel in Quetta in October 2001, while Karzai was still hiding out in the desert near Kandahar and the *Newsweek* correspondent asked if I wanted to accompany him to interview the Karzai brothers in Quetta. Gunston went on:

> Plus of course there was an active element in the US who were *denying* Abdul. As for the British and MI6, well they chose Zaman and ignored Abdul, Haji Qadir and Haji Din Mohammad.

The US 'element' which had ignored Abdul were, he told me, the CIA.

> A guy called Milt Beardon, CIA station chief in Islamabad from the mid 80s, leader of the group who ignored Abdul, calling him 'Hollywood Haq'.

I'd seen Beardon being interviewed on the Haq documentary.[224]

> He's still trying to undermine him. Yet Beardon basically ran his side of the war from Islamabad and a *telephone* connection to the ISI!

Later, when I read parts of Beardon's book,[225] it seemed obvious to me he wanted to undermine Haq's part in the Soviet war and particularly an operation which had turned the war in favour of the Afghans and the West: the blowing up of the Soviet army's seven story underground munitions store at Qarga.

Gunston said that Beardon ran Abdul Haq down 'because of his outspoken criticism of CIA policy of working directly with the ISI'. He illustrated this with reference to 'a very funny bit in *Charlie Wilson's War* which showed ISI's iron grip'. Abdul Haq, he said, had been intending to take Charlie Wilson – who was Chair of the US Government Appropriations Committee and responsible for having massively increased spending on the Soviet war – into Afghanistan. However, General Gul, ISI chief, himself cancelled the visit, infuriating Wilson, who apparently shouted down the phone to Gul saying, 'This is *my* war, *I'm* paying for it. And if I want to see it I damn well will!'[226]

Changing the conversation, I asked Gunston if he knew who had killed Qadir?

> Fahim. But now the Panshiris say Zaman. Afghan history begins at the bazaar of the storytellers and then you have to wade through the conspiracy.

I asked how he had become involved in the plan to support Haq and he said:

> I briefed MOD and called Haq during the meeting. In August, my son and I had gone to meet Abdul Haq in Dubai and he said he'd be in Rome with his commanders on 19 September and asked me to come. He said, 'I've been approached by Taliban elements and they want to work with me'.

He paused, looking out of the window.

> Look, to know why Abdul's plan was significant, one has to understand that the Taliban are not a homogenous force. They're made up of a slim majority of Arabists and hardliners. But most are decent Afghan nationalists. The bulk wanted peace after the mayhem of the Najibullah and Mujahideen time. And although Abdul was a patriot, he wasn't a nationalist who was about to start causing problems for Pakistan over the Durand line. In this respect they were short sighted not to support him.

> Abdul had been approached by the [Taliban] Eastern Corps Commander, a man called Rocketti. Now Rocketti had been one of Abdul's commanders during the jihad. He'd earned the name 'Rocketti' for his skill then in launching rockets. Yes, he'd had a chequered past, but now he was earnest in what he wanted. Like other Pashtuns there was concern, after September 11, about the return of Jamiat.

> You know, Massoud came as the 'Lion of Panjshir' and left as the 'Lion of Kabul'. These guys took Kabul to the cleaners. With that memory in mind, not just the Taliban but decent Pashtuns wanted a Pashtun who'd bring peace. They wanted to turn their forces over to use *against* the remnants of the Arabs.

So Rocketti was ready to call it a day with the Taliban and move over behind Abdul and what had formerly been the Rome Process. Behind the King. To work for a multi-ethnic new order in Afghanistan. In mid-September 2001, Rocketti and the 'Eastern Command' and 'Three Division' commanders in Kabul, as well as the Divisional Commanders in Hezarac, Gardez and Ghazni, told Abdul they were with him. These were all Taliban commanders who after September 11 went to Peshawar, or sent Abdul word there, that they would turn over their divisions to him at the designated time.

My eyes widened as Gunston went on: 'Do you understand? He'd broken the back of the Taliban. Just look at the map!' It was true. The places he'd mentioned – Ghazni, Gardez and Hezarac – were all former Taliban strongholds, lying in an arc throughout the southern part of the country. If the commanders running the show down there had already met with Haq and promised to come over to his side, then clearly they'd been persuaded by his view of the future. Not just that it was a better alternative to a Tajik-dominated government: these were discussions Haq had already begun years before with the Rome process. Gunston continued;

> I went to Peshawar and while I was there a Taliban minister came to meet Abdul and stayed two days. I don't know who it was. Everything was secretive and they came during the night to avoid detection by the ISI. Another commander came from Maiden Shah. I went to Rome and met guys from Farah and Hazarajat. They were all with Haq's plan.

So, as with the Hazaras I'd met at Haq's one year *Shaheed* service, it was obvious to me that other ethnic groups and not just Pashtuns were clearly with Haq's plan. Gunston went on;

> Abdul wanted the King to be the unifier to avoid ethnic clashes. Abdul was one of very few Afghans who could achieve this. A national figure, his credibility was intact not just because of his record as an effective commander against the Soviets but because he walked away in 1992. Even though he was Head of the Police then, he didn't want to be involved in the civil war that took place as other commanders divided the spoils of Kabul between themselves.

I knew from talking to Baryalai that Haq had been training the mujahideen gendarmerie. He had trained up his men in the tribal areas and Pakistan and then waited on the outskirts of Kabul for the communist government of Najibullah to fall. When Kabul finally fell Haq had tried at first to bring order. But when other mujahideen leaders took up ministerial positions for themselves, allowing their soldiers and factions to loot and destroy the city, Haq had withdrawn, going first to Pakistan and then to Dubai where he set up an unsuccessful oil business. At the time he'd said to his family, 'I didn't fight jihad against the Russians in order to do this to my people'. Gunston continued:

> I went to Rome then London and spoke to [Paddy] Ashdown who bought into Haq's plan and agreed to push it. I then got in touch with MI6 chums and briefed people. They used names like Havelock and Grenfell and were rather 'grammar school'.

Gunston was moving into his element now.

> They [the MI6] didn't understand what the hell was going on and got their information from CNN! I went to the FCO and spoke to the anti-terror and Afghan desks. The former was fascinated but they'd already chosen Zaman. The problem was the US was in the driving seat and the Brits had just handed them the keys.

I knew this to be true from the angered frustration of my diplomat friend in Islamabad. After September 11 she had complained about how everything was being decided by the US. When the British Foreign Secretary, Jack Straw, flew into Islamabad he went straight to the American Embassy for a breakfast meeting, before even being debriefed by his own FCO staff. The Americans made the decisions and the British just 'toed the line', she sniffed. Gunston said:

> The CIA had denigrated Abdul. Although the Northern Alliance gave the US direct access to Bagram and were into the Panjshir by September, it got so bad that even though the Brits visited Haji Qadir in Jabl Siraj, by the time Tora Bora happened they'd decided to ignore him completely. It was due to the Zaman issue.

'And the British support for Zaman?' I asked. Gunston sighed.

> Yes, Qadir was absolutely despondent. In London, MI6 just said, 'OK, give us his number and we'll call him if we're interested'. They had *no* idea of the importance of 'face' in Afghanistan. You *can't* talk to a man

like Qadir in such a way. I tried to explain to them that they should tell him, 'Look, we're busy but we'll get to you when we can'. God, these MI6 guys, they were in their mid-20s and knew nothing!

He overbit his lip and shook his head, rolling his eyes.

So I took 'RAM' Seeger with me and we went to see Abdul in Peshawar. He had a plan with the idea of turning the four main vertebrae of the Taliban military axis; Jalalabad, Gardez, Ghazni and Kabul. It would have decapitated the Taliban military command overnight.

I must have looked confused.

Look, Pashtun battles are done with the 'big flag' and a 'loud drum'. But the 'deal' is actually done two nights before over green tea and nuts. Abdul needed to field a force and he had forces. After September 11, his office was full of defectors, former mujahideen commanders he'd known when fighting the Soviets and tribal leaders. And he was in touch daily. There were *lots* of Taliban and former mujahideen in Pakistan.

I imagined Haq seated behind the antique colonial desk in his office in Peshawar receiving these clandestine visitors.

We emailed this initiative to the Brits and they got it. An MI6 man called William turned up in Islamabad from the UK. 'RAM' and I kept out of the way as he didn't want to meet us. Abdul said to him, 'I need to trust you that you are not working with Zaman'. You see Zaman had bought an office and claimed to the Brits he had 200 commanders. It was bullshit, he'd just arrived from France.

So, this was what the diplomat I knew had inferred during our dinner in London after September 11 when he had said that the plan was to use 'Pashtun commanders'. But had no idea who Abdul Haq was. Why had British diplomats (and possibly intelligence operatives) not known who they were dealing with? There was no excuse for them not to know who Haq was. It cannot simply have been that, even as the bombs began falling, the British had already chosen their man: Haji Zaman.

When I put this 'Zaman possibility' to Gunston, he looked at me and said:

Yet Abdul had this whole *string* of Taliban commanders plus senior Taliban ministers ready to defect, to move over to his side with very little fight. In these key Taliban cities of the south.

He'd been trying to say to the West, 'don't bomb, or you'll turn people against you'. What he *really* meant was that a bombing campaign would result in the soldiers he needed – i.e. the Afghan Taliban defectors – running back to their homes leaving al Qaeda manning the guns.[227] Because it wasn't al Qaeda he'd done the deals with, it was the moderate Afghan Talibs, i.e. the very men he'd fought with against the Soviets. Many of whom he'd actually commanded back in those days. He wanted to destroy the Taliban from *within* as he knew they were ready to collapse.

This was the nub of everything; the reason Haq had begged Blair and Bush not to bomb Afghanistan. Because, as a Talib colleague from my days in Kandahar had told me before September 11, even in Kandahar, the Taliban's ideological base, people had begun breaking Taliban edicts like watching their TV sets. Why? Because many of the more fanatical Taliban were not even Afghan, but Pakistani. I myself had witnessed peoples' contempt for the Arabs when, during my work there in Summer 2000, I had made a trip to Kandahar's 'Gen'ral Post Office' to make a phone call to London. My driver, himself a former jihadi commander, had been asked who I was by one of these men. He then told me questions were being asked by 'Arabs' about the fair-haired foreigner (albeit I was wearing a *chador*). When I asked my driver how he knew the man was not Afghan he sneered, 'By the way he spoke'. He added contemptuously, 'We don't want these people here, they're not Afghan'.

For these reasons I had guessed that the movement was brittle, waiting for the final strain that would cause it to snap. Abdul Haq had understood this and was trying to say so. Later on Haq's Paghman based Commander, Khan Mir, who, after September 11, who was 'embedded' with the Taliban's interior Ministry, himself in Command of some eight hundred men would reiterate to me the importance for Haq's strategy of the West 'not' beginning a bombing campaign.[228]

Gunston continued, exasperated.

> Now, instead of a multi-ethnic democratic government, we have an ethnic imbalance and a return to warlords! Most of us working in Afghanistan knew the Taliban had overrun the country easily during the early 1990s, because people were fed up with the infighting and corruption of the warlords.

> It's *crazy* you have this today, yet in Rome[229] there were Pashtuns, Tajiks, Uzbeks and Hazara leaders. They were *all* ready to buy into the process. *All* these guys were ready to work under the King's banner for an ethnically balanced Afghanistan. Now you have the Panjshir nonsense in Kabul.

He sighed.

> I saw Guthrie and the Tories but they were *useless*. I met Ancram, Hugo Swire, IDS [Ian Duncan Smith] etc, but the Tories were already giving uncritical support to the government and the US. The Americans had of course 'bought them off' by allowing IDS to meet Bush, which he was so chuffed about. So, when I briefed them, they weren't interested as it would have been seen as being critical. IDS said to me, 'What shall I do?' I said, 'Can you get this info out to the people who matter and can help?'

> I briefed Guthrie, Sir Colin McColl, the Tories and Paddy Ashdown (who was dealing with both MI6 and the PM). Lord Cranborne was the first to come back. He said, 'People don't believe he's got the ability and wherewithal'.

Then Gunston said in a low voice:

> Cranborne, you have to remember was close to the Labour party as he did the 'deal' with Blair to keep some of the Lords when Blair was disbanding the House of Lords.

> Abdul wanted to go in [to Afghanistan] under the King's flag, as the honest broker. Not as a Pashtun nationalist or as a Khalis commander,[230] but as an Afghan for the Afghans. He wrote up a plan; how much it would cost to field a force of 500-1000 men with radios and transport and guns and bullets.[231] You could buy those and RPGs on the frontier. The cost was minimal; three to five million USD. That would have been enough to allow his former commander, Rocketti, to bring in the

Eastern Taliban forces and allow the collapse of Kabul and Ghazni. Gardez would have gone too. Because there was a real *fear* in Kabul of Tajik retaliation. Just look at the '95 to '96 Panjshir excess and the killings of Hazaras. There was a real memory of this and a fear. The US finally understood this by October and told the Northern Alliance not to take Kabul. But it was too late.

I remembered US and British Embassy staff complaining at meetings I'd attended in January 2002 how Sayyaff had all his guns pointed on Kabul from Paghman, even months after the City fell. Gunston continued:

In August 2001, Abdul met Commander Massoud in Tajikistan. He wanted to get him on side with his plan and did. Yet later, when the Brits were given a copy of it they chose to ignore it. Ultimately they just offered four satellite phones! But the window of opportunity was closing as the bombing was about to start. *That* was the *real* issue. Afghanistan and the temper of the Taliban and those who'd defected to Abdul and the King's side would change overnight. To understand why, one only has to remember Churchill's quote from the Malakand Campaign, 1898: 'Khan assails Khan, valley against valley, but all will unite against the foreigner'.

So, if you start throwing bombs into a country everything will change overnight. Particularly in a place like Afghanistan, which is only a geographical space, not really a country!

I remembered first reading about Haq in the London *Evening Standard*, when he was begging Blair and Bush not to begin bombing Afghanistan, to give him time first to put his plan in place first. Gunston had set out the reasoning for avoiding bombing in a fax (see Appendice III). He proffered it and I saw that it was addressed to 'General Lord Guthrie' and dated 13 October 2001.

The first page detailed the names and dates of contacts he and Seeger had had with British MOD, SIS and FCO in London and Peshawar. The last contact was 11 October 2001 and Gunston noted, 'call Michael Havelock, SIS, to say that we have returned (from Peshawar). Call as yet unreturned'. This note seemed to sum up the brush offs Gunston and Seeger were met with and in an effort to make light of this Gunston commented to Guthrie.

> This reluctance is probably for good operational reasons unknown to ourselves. Our concern is based on many years of experience working with the Mujahideen when fighting the Soviets, and the civil war that followed. This has led us to believe that there are no other credible Pashtun fighting commanders who can galvanise the many Pashtun tribes to rise up against the Taliban than Abdul Haq. Therefore we believe it is our duty to bring our concerns to your attention and those who may have a need to know.

He then proposed what he called 'The Solution': four major points aimed at 'achieving a terrorist free Afghanistan'. Firstly, the solution must be 'achieved from within by Afghans'.

> This would be the quickest, least damaging, least controversial and most long-lasting solution for achieving a terrorist free Afghanistan.

Gunston's note enlarged the reasons why:

> In contrast any attempt to impose a solution on Afghanistan from without – especially if by military force, carries a real risk of failure. Instead of widening the divisions amongst the different Afghan factions, it is likely to unite them against the foreigner and prolong the problem.

> It is also important to keep Pakistan's role in any solution to the minimum and /or strictly controlled. Her track record is not good. As a result she is distrusted and disliked by the majority of Afghan players.

> An inside solution should not be attempted by the mainly Tajik Northern Alliance alone. This would be resisted by the citizens of Kabul, surrounding Pashtun tribes and the Hazaras – all of whom have suffered at the hands of the Northern Alliance. But nor should it be attempted by such dubious Pashtun players as self-proclaimed 'General' Rahim Wardak who can spin a tell tale that sadly has little foundation in reality.

After making these three major points, Gunston's memo proposed what Haq could offer:

> 'In contrast, if discrete and immediate support was given to Abdul Haq, a fast acceptable inside solution could be obtained. He is known

and accepted as a proven operational leader and a man of principle with a trans-ethnic outlook. He would welcome the return of the King – but not his supporting 'Gilbert and Sullivan' cast. He has the support of old Mujahideen commanders from all the 7 old parties, current Taliban commanders both political & military as well as tribal leaders. He has been consolidating this support over the last three weeks and has a workable plan for capturing Taliban key cities of Jalalabad, Kabul, Ghazni & Kandahar. These cities form the main vertebrae of the Taliban's spinal cord. Their capture would render the Taliban paraplegic and allow the swift rounding up of the al Qaida network.

Because he is his own man, Haq is not a favourite of the Pakistanis and probably for this same reason, of the Americans either. It is precisely because of this that he has widespread trust and pledges of support from within Afghanistan. However he is not a Pashtun nationalist and has never espoused a greater Pushtunistan, which the Pakistanis would have reason to fear. At the cost of a few million dollars Haq could put a Pushtun field force into the area very quickly. This would become a focal point for Taliban defections and a counterweight to the Northern Alliance – both essential prerequisites for a fast, acceptable and lasting solution.

In the fax Gunston had finished off politely by writing: 'I do hope this has been helpful. The best number to reach me on …'

Today it is obvious that the British and US intelligence services did not simply cave in on all these points. They pointedly did *everything* they were warned *not* to do by Gunston's fax. Gunston continued:

The majority wanted law and order, peace and prosperity. Not the *Arabisation* of the government. But what our people *failed* to appreciate was that a lot of Haq and Khalis's former commanders had joined the Taliban so there was a closeness. For example, Din Mohammad's relationship with the Taliban was initially well meaning and respectful; unlike the US who wanted to cut deals with them for the oil pipeline. When Abdul died, Haqqani actually phoned din Mohammad to apologise. Though Din Mohammad would not do deals with the command one has to understand that Nangarhar is in a very difficult position with Kunar and Nuristan so close.

Gunston went on, 'I went to Rome and didn't speak to Abdul after. He went in on the Sunday'. Then, I asked what had been the threat to Western intelligence agencies of Abdul Haq. Gunston sighed heavily,

> In contrast to Washington DC, in Kabul Haq was seen as the greatest threat! Why? Because he was Pashtun. Because his vision was the antithesis to the way the Taliban had looked at Afghanistan. Because, despite that, he had a groundswell of support in their ranks. His vision was free of ethnic and religious hang ups. He was a true nationalist.

He also had the ability to pull people together, I reflected. Following Haq's death, Haji Qadir had asked Gunston to accompany him to the Bonn Peace Conference in November 2001 as 'advisor to the Eastern Shura' of elders. But, Gunston said, Qadir had ended up storming out of Bonn. Why? I asked. Gunston responded angrily.

> Well, it was *ridiculous*. Qadir was in an *extremely* difficult position. You see, he was there as a representative of the Northern Alliance. Yet when he realised *no* significant Pashtuns had been invited he began to get agitated. What could he do? Apparently the visas promised by Brahimi to Pashtun leaders failed to turn up leaving them unable to attend. So people like Din Mohammad never went and the whole event was dominated by Tajiks and the Northern Alliance. What could Qadir do? He ended up storming out. So Bonn just set Afghanistan on an inherently unstable trajectory.

He had also attended the installation of the new Afghan Government with Qadir in December 2001. Gunston rubbed his face in his hands.

> God! The whole thing was just like the second crowning of Shah Shujah. You *even* had men in CIA uniforms taking up the front ten rows. Supported by a Panjshiri chorus!

He shook his head wearily.

> Now the problem is you've got an unrepresentative court, a leader installed by the US, a Shah Shujah.[232] There's no *depth* to the present Government but unfortunately it's the only game in town. Forty-five percent of the population are not represented and the only single strong group is now the Taliban. It's the *direct* result of the US ignoring

Abdul and supporting the Northern Alliance as they didn't care what happened. One State Department person even admitted to me, 'The reason we chose Karzai was because he wears a suit and tie and talks like you and I'.

He sighed and stood up.

When Abdul died I was in Rome asking the King to write and in support of Abdul. When he was captured I flew into Peshawar and Din Mohammad told me he thought Abdul had been killed and broke into tears. With his leonine face, it was like a cat hiccupping. I think he's very straight. I was with Haji Qadir in '96 while Haji Din Mohammad was meeting the Taliban. That's why I don't believe he'll cut deal with them.

He paused, eyes downcast, and said slowly.

Listen. This family. This family gave their *lives*, provided the option for a peaceful Afghanistan. Now you have a country teetering on the edge of a resurgent Taliban and al Qaeda.

***

I went to Kenya to write. While there, I went to Lamu and found myself on a dow trip with an English couple. She a Blairite columist, her husband an ex-military man and, I later heard, possibly an ex-member of MI6. We were discussing a piece another journalist had written about the willingness of the then head of MI6, John Scarlett, to 'carry the can' for Blair over the 'sexing up' of the dossiers on WMD in Iraq.[233] I commented that the intelligence services seemed, as the author said, to have allowed themselves to become unduly politicised. As one of the chief cheerleaders in the press for the war in Iraq, she took fiercely against this view. Somehow the conversation got around to my interest in Abdul Haq. Her husband yawned lethargically, saying: 'Well what did it matter; he was dead within a couple of weeks anyway?'

CHAPTER THIRTEEN

'HE WOULD HAVE BEGUN A REVOLUTION, THAT'S WHY THEY KILLED HIM SO FAST'

In contrast to Washington DC, in Kabul Haq was seen as the greatest threat! Why? Because he was Pashtun. Because his vision was the antithesis to the way the Taliban had looked at Afghanistan. Because, despite that, he had a groundswell of support in their ranks.

SIR JOHN GUNSTON[234]

Kabul, January 2004

Towards the end of January 2004, I finally met the Taliban's Deputy Interior Minister, Mullah Khaksar. It was his boss, the Taliban Interior Minister, Mullah Razzaq, who had apparently given the orders for Haq to be killed.

The family told me that Khaksar had visited Haq in Peshawar after September 11 and helped him with his plan to overthrow the Taliban, intending to work with Haq in forming a broad-based government. The plan was for Khaksar to work with Khan Mir, another of Haq's jihadi commanders, in Kabul as Haq went into Afghanistan on his mission. The two would work on turning over several divisions of the Interior Ministry. In the event though, Haq had been killed and captured before the fall of Kabul.

I hooked up with Hanif. Khaksar had apparently turned himself over to the Karzai government following the routing of the Taliban and was now hiding out in a 'safe house'. At this stage there was still no Taliban Reconciliation Programme.

We headed in the direction of Khair Khana on a cold January day, the air thick with a winter freeze. Eventually we arrived at a rundown suburban house, stepped into a concrete hallway and were shown into a curtained room. The Mullah sat there alone. He had a shaggy dark beard, a voluminous dark grey turban and dark, spaniel-shaped eyes. I could see my breath in the cold air and was relieved when a young man arrived to stoke the *bukhari*[235] and bring us green tea and nuts.

Khaksar's dark looks were utterly incongruous with his quiet, high-pitched voice and the phone which periodically jingled 'happy birthday' from inside his *salwar kameez*. After some explanations of who I was, I asked whether, given the current situation, it might have been better for many members of the Taliban if Haq had not been killed? Khaksar replied, 'At the last days the friends of Haq in the Interior Ministry practically began a war. We were ready to act'. Haq had wanted a broad-based government, he said, even to the extent that he had met with the UN, the Arsala family and Massoud about this objective before September 11. Later, he had stayed at the Arsala house in Peshawar and spoken with Haji din Mohammad and Haji Qadir. He told me that he had known the regime would collapse two years before it did. I asked why Mullah Razzaq had wanted Haq dead and Khaksar said:

> He used his competence as it was an emergency situation. But he also said that, at this time, the Taliban still did not believe they would lose their power. They thought, rather naively, that Afghans would rise up against the foreign invaders in their support. They executed him as they thought the USA would rescue him and then he'd stand against the Taliban again. But the act [of killing Haq] was against human rights law and Shariat law. As he was killed without a fight and without a trial.

As to why the Taliban had killed Haq so fast, he said;

> If he was alive and his programme had been a success, then from my point of view he would now be President of Afghanistan ... If they had put him in jail the people would have been rising up and pushing for a revolution.

Again, his phone tinkled 'happy birthday' from somewhere deep within his *salwar kameez*. Fixing me with his bottomless dark eyes he added, 'A *lot* of people supported his plan, even in Khost, Paktia, Gardez and throughout Afghanistan'.

These were the same places Gunston had mentioned as being the backbone of the Taliban's hold over the south: the places which had fallen due to Haq's commanders and the willingness of the people who were fed up with the regime. Not due to some 'secret deals' made by MI6 who had been nowhere to be seen when help was needed.

His comments echoed Gunston's assessment of the sad irony that, in Kabul, Abdul Haq had been deemed a threat to the Taliban, yet in Washington and London, those charged with knowing better were just blithely unaware. I asked Khaksar if it was too late to include moderate Taliban in the government. 'Yes of course', he snapped. 'But if not 100% fruitful, it could be 20% at least'. It was a short interview. He had people to see, but he agreed to meet again the next day to talk more about the circumstances surrounding Haq's death.

The next day he told me that Razzaq had called him early one morning and told him to prepare to go to Hezarac. Khaksar had replied that he was sick. So Razzaq sent his personal bodyguards to kill Haq. Knowing the stature of Haq, I wondered if Razzaq had been too much of a coward to do it personally and asked why the Taliban inner core, those close to al Qaeda, had not thought it worth negotiating with Haq.

> They were not ready to talk then with anyone. They were just thinking of *their* power. Even Hikmatyar and the ex-King and Haq people came but they did not agree with any one.

'So they did not foresee the end? Did they not feel the US had power to get rid of them?' I asked.

'Not until the fall of Kabul did they think the regime would end. They thought people would fight with them', he replied.

Haq had realised it was hopeless trying to negotiate with the 'top flight' of the Taliban: Mullah Omar and those more closely allied with the Pakistani ISI. Instead he was targeting the moderates and, critically, the Afghan tribes and elders who were ready to throw in the towel with the Taliban. He understood that if the locals, and tribal elders, had agreed together to turn against the movement, it would be very difficult for the Taliban to stay. It was for this reason that he had likened the regime to a crystal that would crack finally once a small fissure had appeared in it. That fissure would be opened by the broad-based support that Haq could supply for an alternative to the Taliban; it was why the ISI, who knew the threat he had posed, had killed his wife and small son. Yet Haq had continued to open up this fissure with his meetings in Rome with tribal leaders, later in Peshawar and then within Afghanistan just prior to his death.

I had witnessed the fissure in support for the Taliban during the months I had worked in Kandahar in 2000. There were several incidents. Not only were Kandahari residents openly breaking Taliban edicts such as watching DVDs bought in Quetta, but kite flying had recently been reintroduced. I also remembered how – upon the capture of Taloqan in the North East – the staff in my office had celebrated. When I had asked them why and were not the Taliban a bad regime, they had said that they were happy the Taliban would soon win the war against the Northern Alliance, because then the Taliban would have to turn their attention to providing health and education services. There would be no excuse not to, once the war was finished. I remember too how my driver in Kandahar, himself an ex-mujahideen commander, had shown contempt for a group of Arabs who had quizzed him about who I was, particularly in terms of my nationality, during a trip to Kandahar's 'Gen'ral Post Office'.[236] I realised that the Arabs were regarded as – by ordinary Kandahari folk – not benefactors to the regime but as arrogant imposters.

After the fall of Kandahar, Mullah Razzaq had apparently escaped to Chaman: a desolate place of abandoned containers and smuggling depots in the midst of dust storms whipped up by the Registan desert. Its position between Kandahar and Quetta – prime Taliban territory – indicated to me the hardline nature of Razzaq's devotion to the Taliban cause. A point confirmed by Khaksar when he said, 'Razzaq was powerful in the Taliban Emirate, very hardline. These Taliban did not like to compromise, because al Qaeda did not want them to. They were not Afghans'.

What Khaksar said married up with what Gunston had stressed: that with the onset of the bombing, moderate Talibs had abandoned the fight, leaving the more fundamentalist al Qaeda[237] strand in charge. The more moderate Afghan commanders of the Talib battalions in the regions, the men Abdul Haq had once commanded during the jihad, were the fragile coalition he had needed to come over to his and the King's side. It was this fragile coalition which had needed the West *not* to bomb Afghanistan. As Ken Guest, stressed to me later, 'If the bombing hadn't started, Haq would not have felt the need to go back "inside" Afghanistan so prematurely'.

An interview given by Haq to *Newsweek*[238] magazine from Peshawar within a week of his capture illustrates what he meant by this. Of Taliban commanders, he said:

> We won't encourage them to defect. We say, 'Just stay there so we can use you. If you defect you're no use'. We plan to move in with our own commanders, with Taliban commanders, with tribal representatives. We'll just take down the Taliban flag and put up our own flag.

Then, Haq explained why the US bombing was so damaging to his plan and that of the Rome Process.

> Still soldiers and officials are already defecting to their homes, to their own camps; they're leaving in the thousands.

He had been talking to Taliban commanders by sattelite phone and they had come to see him at his home in Peshawar, where many of his relatives lived. Critically, he explained that, 'forty to fifty percent of the Taliban forces were former mujahideen. They will be with us if they don't have to worry about their own survival and security'.

The background to all this, he told *Newsweek*, was that he had left Afghanistan in 1992 saying he didn't want to take part in the destruction wrought on his country by civil war. Although the mujahideen had won the war militarily in 1992, they had lost it politically. Now, after September 11, he had returned to his country to finish a job he had begun when he had fought the Soviets. He argued that, as a military commander, he had a role to play, but he emphasized:

> No one can do it alone. We need teamwork. before September 11, there was a lack of united leadership to bring various tribes together. Now, after the former King has stated he'll return home, that helps us solve this problem. We can begin a national process, not based on ethnic groupings.

In terms of 'defections' he was aiming, he said:

> ... to the second level, to the division commanders and corps commanders. I'm saying to them, 'okay, the leadership is crazy. Why don't you and us and other tribes come together and work together?'

When asked if he could win over the Taliban leadership, Haq had replied;

> More than 50% are willing to accept a new government if they can be part of the process and if the Northern Alliance is not allowed to take power. They want the security to live as normal human beings. Most of the former mujahidin commanders who are with the Taliban, plus many Taliban commanders, are not happy with the leadership but also fear the Northern Alliance. They fear revenge killings if the Northern Alliance takes over. So we'll give them another option.

Today, Khaksar continued:

> When they executed Abdul Haq, I was in Kabul with one of Haq's commanders in the guesthouse [he was speaking of Khan Mir, Haq's former Paghman-based commander]. I gave him a gun and then the bodyguards came and told us they had finished Abdul Haq. I said to them, 'That is dreadful as he was a national figure in Afghanistan. And was famous Kabul commander during jihad'.

He looked down and folded a flap of his kameez over a knee.

> They told me Haq was killed at Charasyab and that Isatullah was killed where they captured him.[239]

I asked, 'Do you think Afghanistan would be better if Haq were still alive?' His reply was matter of fact.

> Undoubtedly! If his [Haq's] plan had happened there would be *no* opposition nor an insurgency by the Taliban. It would be a broad-based government with the support of the international community and UN. It would be a strong government with no opposition and the Taliban would be finished now.

CHAPTER FOURTEEN

'CAMP FOLLOWERS' IN KABUL

My head feels as if it might explode when I think about
the complexity of it all. And here is this idiot talking about
'milestones' and 'deliverables' and 'resource allocation'.

From *'Salmon Fishing in the Yemen'*[240]

Kabul and Jalalabad, January 2004– January 2005

Francesc Vendrell, an aristocratic white-bearded Spaniard, had
been the EU Special Representative in Kabul since 2002. He dressed
in immaculate Savile Row suits and now, like most diplomats,
travelled in a convoy of heavily armoured cars with an athletic-
looking posse of young men as his close protection team. I had
returned in November 2004 to work for him as a Political Advisor
with a remit to follow private security companies, counter-narcotics,
civil military affairs and disarmament. It was to be an insight into
the diplomatic community and NATO; a world that seemed very
removed from what I had experienced in Jalalabad.

The Presidential elections had taken place that autumn and
Karzai had been elected[241] with a large mandate, declaring he
would rid the country of warlords. Now there was chatter about
the selection of the new Cabinet. The Western diplomats tended to
prefer those Afghans who wore suits and had spent a long time in
the West. They lobbied Karzai about this repeatedly in meetings at
the Presidential Palace.[242]

One of the favourites was Hedayat Arsala, another was Rahim
Wardak, who - Gunston had told me - journalists covering the 1980s
jihad had dubbed 'the Brigadier'. Although Rahim Wardak - as a
former General in the Afghan army – held the title of 'Major General
and Chief of Staff of *Mahaz-i-Milli Islami* (the moderate party known
as NIFA) Robert Kaplan, an American journalist who had travelled

extensively in Afghanistan during the jihad, in his book described Wardak as a 'pompous exhibitionist' who;

> controlled no territory inside Afghanistan and rarely left Pakistani soil. He directed 'battles' across the border with a frequency hopping walkie-talkie given him by the Americans. But not even the Americans in Islamabad were fooled by him. Once, when Wardak claimed to have rained two thousand rockets on Kabul, a check by the U.S. embassy revealed that only eight rockets had fallen on the city that week. [243]

I had also heard references to other incidents, such as the one whereby Rahim Wardak had apparently orchestrated some so called anti-Soviet 'operations' which were filmed by an American tv news station. Dan Rather, who did the voiceover for the footage, was later embarrassed when it was discovered the operations had been faked, and actually occurred not in Afghanistan but Pakistan.

Now there were rumours that the very same Wardak was to be made Defence Minister. When I relayed this news to Haji Zahir, he snorted, '*Now* is time of having people like Rahim Wardak as Defence Minister!' It was a comment that passed judgement on the entire foreign intervention; the choices that had been made, the strategies (or rather the lack of them) followed, and the personalities selected to fill influential positions.

The meetings I had to attend in Kabul, in particular the civil-military roundtable meetings were particularly frustrating. Bizarrely, civil society organisations and NGOs – those who might have challenged the *raison d'etre* of the PRT model and the difficulties likely to be thrown up by the militarisation of aid – were excluded and relegated instead to a separate lesser forum. So here, in the confines of the Ministry of Interior or the Coalition Forces Command (CFC) 'Alpha' compound in Shar-i-naw, young Western soldiers put up Powerpoint presentations. These consisted mostly of bullet points indicating the 'milestones' to be achieved before an 'exit strategy' could occur. But the 'milestones' being used by the soldiers – building courthouses, for example – bore no relation to the political solutions – such as the absence of a justice system – so manifestly lacking. Getting this message across to soldiers who were often very young and whose faces changed every other meeting due to the fast, often-maximum six-month turnover, was not easy.

Recently, the Provincial Reconstruction Team (PRT) 'steering group', at the behest of the American General Dan McNeil, had decided that 'governance reform' was now a key domain of the military. Yet there was no explanation – beyond the holding of provincial elections – of how soldiers would achieve this.[244] To the military, 'governance' was simply another 'milestone' to be achieved like the building of courthouses and schools. Never mind that to be credible it needed to be owned by the Afghans (and not just those corrupt members of the Karzai regime) and it also needed a longer-term view. Hitherto, it had been the domain of the UN and anthropologists, but it also – as my time in Kandahar and Jalalabad made me realise – required an understanding of Afghan tribal or cultural dynamics. Hence, I found these meetings, and those Powerpoint presentations, very disconnected from the world I had experienced outside Kabul.

That the military's model of 'governance' seemed overly concerned with building physical structures like schools was alien to the work I had done with the UNCHS (UN Habitat) during the Taliban period, when we had worked on projects to re-build the civil society institutions which had been destroyed by two decades of war. These were known as 'community forae' (CF) projects. The CF projects had taken months if not years of emphasising 'process' as a basis for Afghans to work together. Only when the Afghans had accepted and understood this 'process' was the UN able to work successfully with the communities as its local partner in implementing physical and infrastructural - or (as with the women) public health awareness - projects. The CF that UN Habitat had worked to set up in cities throughout Afghanistan participated in both the selection and running of the development projects (in our case the rebuilding of water supply in Kandahar and Herat) hitherto undertaken by foreign workers. Ultimately the involvement of the CF enabled the projects to be more durable because when UN funding ceased, the people sometimes decided to continue them in their communities, funding them with Islamic taxes. The system, which was further developed and came to be known as the National Solidarity Programme (NSP) in 2002, has made a lot of headway in the north, although it is essentially only at village level. Due perhaps both to tribal dynamics, but also lack of funding, it has not been so successful in rural areas of the south, the prime location of the insurgency.

I also discovered upon my return in November 2004 that although the recent election was being trumpeted around the globe as a major benchmark in Afghan democracy, in Jalalabad people were more pragmatic. There I learnt that Karzai's support owed a significant amount to the Arsala's campaign for him with the tribes. Discussion between the Arsala family representatives, principally din Mohammad and elders, had resulted in 'block votes' for Karzai throughout the east, the south and amongst the refugee population still in Pakistan.

However, this loyalty was lost on the international community in their sealed compounds in Kabul, worlds away. In Kabul in December 2004, I attended a press conference where a member of the American Drug Enforcement Agency (DEA) and British officials publicly castigated Haji Din Mohammad as a 'criminal drug dealer'. When I asked British FCO / MI6 staff working on drugs if they had evidence to support this, they looked at me as though I were mad. 'But everyone knows it!' they chanted confidently. Their views seemed focused entirely on the 'conventional wisdom' of their peers or the Americans. They showed no curiosity as to why a former freelance journalist and Political Advisor to the EU might have an alternative viewpoint.

Perversely though, the Americans had pressed for the appointment, in late 2004, 'General' Mohammad Daoud, a Fahim ally and alleged druglord of the north-east, as Deputy Interior Minister and anti-drugs 'Tzar'. Yet in May 2004, several pieces in the *Los Angeles Times* had focused on Daoud's significant relationship with the poppy trade.

In Jalalabad, the locals told me that the British rarely visited from

Kabul. Perhaps this explained their obliviousness to the balancing act din Mohammad was doing to keep the tribesmen of the eastern provinces 'on side' with the Karzai government. And the fact that in the years from 2003, Nangarhar saw the largest decreases in poppy production due – in no small part – to the interventions of Din Mohammad and Baryalai.

At this time, in 2004, many eastern tribesmen were convinced that mystery US aircraft was spraying their poppy. Coupled with continuing incidents of American troops bursting into their houses, it brought local anger to fever pitch. This eventually found its expression in May 2005, when anti-American demonstrations broke out in Jalalabad and spread throughout the country. Locals shouting 'Death to America' smashed up international humanitarian buildings and burnt Din Mohammad's offices, accusing him of supporting Karzai and the US.

A final irony of this story between the British and the Arsala family was evident in 2005 when, despite their accusations toward din Mohammad and Zahir, the DEA (partnered by the British) opened a new office in Jalalabad aimed at controlling poppy production. The place they rented, for a colossal $35,000 USD per month[245] was none other than the hugely ostentatious fortress of Qadir's that Haji Zahir had just finished building. Zahir had always been the main target of their accusations and I had often warned him against playing into their hands by continuing to build such an opulent building. But it was ironic that they would actually rent it from him. I wondered how long the family could maintain its hegemony and whether – as the US built larger bases along the Pakistan border – it would take the Pathans, with their close network of ties, long to outwit the foreigners as they had the British during the nineteenth-century.

If Karzai was being compared to the British puppet, Shah Shujah, the US Ambassador Zulmay Khalilizad[246] was now the ill-fated nineteenth-century British envoy McNaughton whose behaviour had contributed to Shujah's downfall and the disastrous (for the British) retreat from Kabul in 1841. Today, Khalilzad scuttled imperiously between the Presidential Palace where he had his own office and met with elders, and the US Embassy, making little attempt to hide the fact that it was essentially he and not Karzai who was running the country. He might have benefited from the advice of Lord Roberts of Kandahar who, during the second Afghan war had said,

> We must not be afraid of Afghanistan and would profit from it by letting it be the master of its own fate. Maybe it is not the more attractive solution for us but I feel that I am right in asserting that the less they are able to see us, the less they are likely to hate us. Even if we suppose that Russia will attempt to invade Afghanistan and through it to obtain control of India, we will have much greater chance of getting the Afghans on our side if we abstain from any interference in their internal affairs whatsoever.

Patience with the US-backed regime of President Karzai was running low. Since Bonn, it had been thought unrepresentative of the Pashtun majority, with Karzai merely a figurehead of US interests. Increasingly though, the regime was also viewed as patently corrupt; the majority of Afghans now viewed it simply as a kleptocracy unable to respond to their needs. As Afghan civil society groups, and the Afghan Independent Human Rights Commission (AIHRC), pleaded with foreign donors to apply 'conditionality' to aid receipts, to force the government ministries to show a tangible output of 'services' to the Afghan people. Too much was simply 'lost' as corruption grew exponentially, publicly and shamelessly. For example, in 2003 General Fahim parcelled up government-owned land at Sher Pur, near the old British cantonment in Kabul, and gave it to his allies. Local people were forced off the land and vast kitsch palaces grew up. But still, several foreign aid agencies, including IOM, then rented the palaces built on this illegally-acquired land.[247] The pleas for conditionality on aid receipts fell on deaf ears. 'Conditionality' was, according to OECD guidelines, apparently deemed colonial.[248] Hence, aid money went direct to the government, from where it could be directed into the vast network of patronage and sinecures being built up by the President. In one donor round table support group meeting in 2005, I suggested that before increasing budgets to the Afghan National Police (ANP) in an effort to increase numbers, donors should think about conditionality because there were increasing reports of violence and corruption.[249] My words were met with an atmosphere of outraged surprise and the head of USAID said coldly that there was 'no evidence' the police were corrupt.

However, our office had a catalogue of examples. This was 2005, and with some regional police chief posts already selling for tens of thousands of dollars, the wilful obliviousness of donors to the ground level reality of where their taxpayers money was (not) going in Afghanistan was dismal.

By late 2004, our EU office was privately compiling reports of the number of drug hauls NATO soldiers in the south were being forced to 'let go' because they were associated with Karzai's brother or family allies. A recent piece in the *New York Times*[250] had named several of Karzai's allies in Kandahar, including Arif Noorzai, as key drug dealers. On its publication a huge row ensued. Karzai was infuriated and the female British Ambassador was forced to leave Afghanistan for a while. Karzai had apparently accused her of feeding the 'false' information to the *New York Times*.

Another issue was the seeming disconnect between donors and their capital cities. One European diplomat informed me he needed to disburse several million euros to one province prior to the election of a regional shura who might ensure some type of accountability, in order to fit in with datelines required back in his capital city.

Despite what Afghans told us about the corruption of the government, this fact was ignored by donors and the international community until after the charade of the 2009 presidential elections. Yet I frequently heard Afghan civil society groups begging donors to apply conditions to aid so that they could see some delivery of the services promised.[251] This request was consistently ignored and the Karzai government seemed unassailable. To illustrate, I refer to an encounter I had early in 2005 with a man who was visiting the country for a couple of weeks on one of those prescribed trips where visitors are wheeled around the same predictably small circle of government officials and so-called 'representative Afghans' - often the very people benefiting from the status quo and unlikely to have a challenging viewpoint! The man, a middle-aged German, overheard a conversation I was having with a British security consultant over dinner one night at Gandomack Lodge. We were talking about the corruption problem. The German leant over from the next table to interrupt our conversation angrily. President Karzai, he asserted aggressively, was 'completely clean' and there was 'no corruption' in Afghanistan. I found his arrogance disconcerting, particularly when I later discovered that he was head of a well known anti corruption organisation whose very raison d'etre was to know what was going on below the surface.

The warnings of other, more recent humanitarian interventions were not heeded. Speaking of Bosnia, Lord Ashdown had been quoted:

> Crime and corruption follow swiftly in the footsteps of war, like a deadly virus. And if the rule of law is not established very swiftly, it does not take long before criminality infects every corner of its host, siphoning off funds for re-construction, obstructing the process of stabilisation and corrupting every attempt to create decent government and a healthy civil society. This, above all was the mistake we made in Bosnia. We took six years to understand that the rule of law should have been the first thing. We are paying the price for that still.[252]

CHAPTER FIFTEEN
THE KING'S GROUP AND 'ROME'

If our leaders advise that we bomb our way through rather than think our way through, we must question the wisdom and the value of such leaders and suffer the pains of their mistakes.[253]

Kabul, December 2004

I had been told by an Afghan friend to interview a woman who had worked closely with Abdul Haq in Rome. So upon returning to Kabul I contacted her. I was directed to a street in Wazir Akbar Khan where she was staying at the time. A maid showed me into a room furnished with antiques, fine china and rugs. I sat down on a green velvet sofa and presently, a petite woman with dark eyes and a rounded face framed by thick dark hair came into the room. For her own privacy, I prefer not to name her here.

'You are interested in Abdul Haq?' she asked challengingly, seating herself to my right. I explained why, asking if it were true she had known him from Rome. She had, she said, because she had been working in the King's office. When I asked when he first became involved with the King and the Rome Process she cut in sharply, 'Have you interviewed Rahim Wardak and Hedayat Arsala?' I was thrown by her sudden interjection and asked if we were talking of the same Arsala who was a cousin of the family in Jalalabad. We were and she said again that she would be *very* interested to know what he and Wardak would say. When I asked why, she said that it was Arsala who first brought Abdul Haq to Rome in April 2001. In fact, this conflicted with Ritchie's account, because he told me that Haq had been involved earlier. She added that at this time there was a 'process' going on in Rome, where the King was based, and there was discussion about usurping the Taliban.

She said that Arsala had arrived, saying, 'I'm bringing Haq and he has a great plan'. She admitted that she had been the *last* to be convinced.

> Arsala thought Haq should be the military leader, the King the symbolic leader and himself the Prime Minister. There was a *lot* of rivalry around the King about who would take the position of PM. But when Haq realised Arsala's objective he said, 'No, I'm not working for one person. The people have to decide'.

She explained that Haq of course realised the King was essential to the plan as Afghans are inherently conservative. The King was needed as a rallying point. But Haq was adamant that who the King and who the Executive Council choose is 'their business'. Haq thus proposed having a Loya Jirga convened to decide who would take positions. She continued:

> The point was Arsala had assumed Haq would do the military stuff to rid the country of the Taliban and then place *him* in position as the PM. But Haq said, 'I'm *not* working for you as you're my cousin'. Arsala was unhappy about this.

Hands held limply together in her lap, she shook her head.

> After September 11, I went to DC on behalf of Haq and tried to convince Zalmay Khalilzad to help. But wherever I went, I was told that Arsala and Rahim Wardak had been there before. They claimed that *they*, not Haq, were the representatives of the King and that Haq was not recognised by the King as one of the group. They had really talked him down, working in *direct* opposition to what I tried to do. And both had connections with the CIA and so on. Arsala is a Pashtun who has *no* respect among Ghilzai Pashtuns as he lived in the USA too long. He told Khalilzad stuff like 'Haq can't raise an army', etc.

She looked drained.

> The key is that as soon as Arsala realised Haq would not work for him, to place him in the position as PM of a new Afghanistan, he stopped supporting him.

So, it seemed, Haq had not just been betrayed by the CIA, for whom he had fought and beaten the Soviets, and by the British, who were too ignorant to understand his potential value, he had perhaps even been undermined by a member of his own family.[254]

> And Khalilzad and the Americans wanted an insignificant tribal leader who couldn't raise an army to challenge them. *That's* why they chose Hamid Karzai.

'And what about the Northern Alliance? I asked. 'Were they on board with Haq's multi ethnic idea?' She nodded.

> Yes, absolutely. Haq travelled to Dushanbe[255] in July 2001 to see Massoud. He told him, 'You can no longer do everything alone and expect everyone to follow'. He was frank with him and said, 'You're a war criminal in the eyes of the Afghan people. If things get back to normal you'll be hung, so this is a chance to redeem yourself. Let's be part of a team'. Haq told me he'd said this. At that point he and Massoud were alone, having talked all night. He said to Massoud, 'We know each other'.

Also present at the meeting between Haq and Massoud at Dushanbe in July 2000 was former Ambassador Peter Tomsen, US Special Envoy to the mujahideen during the jihad. Tomsen later told me:

> Yes, Abdul and Massoud did agree to work together at the Dushanbe meeting. My impression was that they had separately both been in touch with Rome on a political approach involving the King. The meeting in Dushanbe allowed them to discuss modalities and to create the basis for future cooperation in creating an anti-Taliban network. I would take any comments on Abdul by agency officers with a grain of salt. The Agency remained critical of Abdul before and after Dushanbe. Abdul was in touch with Hamid Karzai in Pakistan but I never learned to what degree they were coordinating.[256]

Ritchie had also mentioned the Dushanbe meeting that July which had occurred only six weeks before Massoud's assassination and September 11. At this stage I did not realise that Ritchie had also been present and that his views on it differed to those of Tomsen. The Dushanbe meeting was extremely significant for not only did Haq have senior Taliban and tribal leaders on board with his plan, he apparently also had word from Massoud that the Northern Alliance would work with him under the King's banner.[257] Critically,

Massoud agreed to accept former King Zahir Shah as Head of State and wanted him in the alliance.

She brushed a tranche of shiny dark hair off her face and said, 'But what really did Haq in was his insistence in keeping Kabul demilitarised'. She explained that this was why Haq had been against the bombing campaign. For he *knew* it would result in the Northern Alliance forces breaking through Taliban lines. So when the bombing began he had to leave Peshawar *fast*. His plan was to build a security belt around Kabul with local commanders.

> He said it would be disastrous if the Northern Alliance descended upon Kabul. Today, as you see, we are suffering the consequences of that. He thought it essential to keep Kabul demilitarised and to hold a Loya Jirga and form a Government *without* military pressure from the Panjshiris.

Her words also echoed those of Sir John Gunston. I thought back to the Loya Jirga and the disappointment with it. The secret deal to disbar the King. The anger of my colleague, Nils, when he realised Brahimi and Khalilzad had struck a deal with the warlords. How, even in January 2002, British diplomats in Kabul had complained about Sayyafs' men being armed and just outside the city, effectively giving him the whip hand. How even fairly conservative Afghan women, including two national figures, had told me that Brahimi was a fundamentalist. Haq had foreseen the importance of keeping Kabul demilitarised: without that, there could never be an equitable settlement for all Afghans.

Although Dushanbe was significant, Massoud had not always kept his word. There had been anger when Massoud had broken the agreement made between mujahiddeen leaders in 1992 to *not* rush into Kabul as the last communist government fell. In a letter to Peter Tomsen,[258] Haq explained why this had been such a tragedy for Afghanistan (see Appendix V) that Massoud had allowed his forces to break the agreement under which the city was to be secured.[259] The chaos which ensued had lasted four years, and cost the lives of well over 25,000 civilians and the displacement of millions more from their homes. It also set the scene for the rise of the Taliban, who replaced this chaos with their brand of extreme law and order. 'So', she went on, '*That's* why he realised Kabul must be kept demilitarised'.

She looked suddenly delicate and vulnerable, as she whispered.

> He was a *remarkable* man. What I liked was partly his vision and courage and also the fact he acknowledged his past mistakes and weaknesses. I've met *no one* who was around during the jihad who did that!

I nodded as she spoke, fingering her scarf.

> Haq was *very* frustrated with the King being so slow to let him do his plan and in July 2001 said to him in front of me and Princess Homaira, 'What *type* of leader do you want to be, a Shah Shujah or an Ayoub Khan?'

She chuckled, 'He was very direct'. But I was thinking that if the King hadn't dithered, maybe there would have been no September 11. I asked her about Hamid Karzai and she frowned.

> He already had a plan with the Americans but was very insecure about Haq. Didn't like him being the 'number two'. Since then he's cut me out as he knows I was for Haq. My support for Haq has caused me a lot of problems. I can't get any sort of job in the administration.

This was no surprise. Karzai, despite his lack of form during the Soviet war, appeared extremely ambitious. A UN colleague who had been based in the south during the Taliban period told me how, when he'd organised meetings between the UN and tribal leaders back in 2000, Karzai had always tried to insist the meetings should be at his house rather than the UN offices.[260] There were rumours that at a certain stage after September 11, Karzai had stopped attending the meetings in Rome.

> You know often people didn't like Haq because he was a strong character and could be opinionated. He wouldn't change his mind on things. But he'd *always* win the argument ultimately. And he was *right'*.

She said these words with clarity and finality.

Before I left she asked me if I knew where she could find a job.

She needed the money she said. I felt how vulnerable she must be, despite her fierce intellect. She had been 'on the inside', close to people like Khalilzad. Now, she was an outsider because of her faith in Abdul Haq and because she had held onto her opinions, despite the fact this might lose her the jobs and money of American largesse. She was a female version of Haq: strong, opinionated, with vision, intellect, sensitivity and, above all, courage.

CHAPTER SIXTEEN

FROM JIHADI COMMANDERS TO TALIBAN

Through Unity, Peace. Through Peace, Stability.
Through Stability, Prosperity.

MANTRA OF ABDUL HAQ

Kabul, Sarobi, Faizabad and Jalalabad, 2004-5

I had interviewed two of Abdul Haq's former commanders: Khan Mir who had been Haq's Paghman-based[261] commander during the jihad and was to have worked alongside Mullah Khaksar in bringing battalions of the Interior Ministry over to Haq's side. The other was Mullah Malang, a well-known commander mostly based in Kandahar who had worked alongside Haq during the jihad. It was Malang's former 'Muj' commanders who were now reputed to be providing the circle of bodyguards around Mullah Omar.[262]

However, I had not yet met the man John Gunston had emphasised I must see: Aga Jan, who was based in Sarobi and had been with Haq when he was captured by the Taliban. Gunston had trumpeted him as:

> One of Haq's most significant Commanders, controlling the road from Jalalabad to Kabul. Even managed to close it off for ten days once, cutting off the Communist supply route. A *hell* of an achievement!

I got my opportunity to meet Aga Jan in January 2005. It was about to be *Eid ul Kuruban* and I decided to spend it in Jalalabad. One of our office cars was taking a colleague back to the Pakistan border and he offered me a ride. The only condition being that he needed to spend an hour or two talking to people in Sarobi on the way.

We left Kabul at dawn, driving through banks of snow in the still, blue-ish morning light. At the suburb of Micro Royan, a mass of concrete blocks built by the Russians for civil servants, we picked up a lady called Hafiza who had once worked with my colleague.

She was around forty, with her hair held down by a scarf and wearing thick woollen gowns around her *salwar*. It was very cold, particularly as we descended the Kabul pass beyond the last Pul-I-Charkhi checkpoint.

Sarobi, situated on the road between Peshawar and Kabul, with routes running up to the north via the Panjshir, was always reputed a dangerous place when driving to or from Pakistan. It was also one of the most strategically important places in the country to hold. Traditionally, it was a Hikmatyar area and Zardad, one of his commanders, had terrorised travellers and returning refugees as they passed his checkpoint here during the early 1990s, when the mujahideen ran riot across the country. The purpose of my colleague's stop in Sarobi was to interview local people about the infamous Zardad. Hafiza told me:

> I remember driving through here in '94. They almost pulled our car over but instead chose a bus. It was horrible. They used to take boys and put them in cells below ground.

We were driving across open ground, at the top of a windy hill from where one had a 360-degree view of the distant mountains of the north-east. Containers were scattered around amongst half-destroyed stone buildings. Now it was a scruffy police checkpost. Hafiza continued, 'They were horrible men, like animals, with long matted hair, carrying lots of guns and bullets'.

Zardad was about to go on trial again in Britain. Like many of the (now recently returned) former mujahideen commanders he had sought political amnesty in London when the Taliban arrived. The British, naively, had supplied it. Other Afghans were furious. It was only later when Peter Jouvenal, making a documentary with John Simpson on the Taliban, brought the issue to light. I told Hafiza an anecdote I'd heard about this:

> They were interviewing Mullah Muttawakil[263] and Simpson challenged him saying, 'Why are you giving shelter to OBL?' But Muttawakil's reply came swiftly, 'And why are you British giving shelter to Zardad?' Simpson, thrown, turned to Jouvenal and asked, 'Who on earth is he talking about?'

'That is a very strong reply', Hafiza commented.

The result was that Jouvenal made a documentary about Zardad, after which the British, embarrassed, attempted to try him. They failed first time for it was too difficult for the jury to untangle the complexity of the Afghan situation.[264]

The car was climbing now, from the bottom of the Kabul gorge to the last hills before Sarobi. To our left, the sky over the Panjshir was marshmallow pink. A shaft of sunlight moved across snow-covered mountaintops. We passed a small hut to the side of the road. The morning was bright in Sarobi, and we drove past *karachi* carts laden with crimson pomegranates. My colleague instructed the driver to pull over outside a scruffy chemists on the main thoroughfare and I asked directions to Aga Jan's house. The chemist led us around a road to the back of the village to a lonesome farmhouse which looked out over distant mountains. A grey turbaned old man sat against the stone wall surrounding the compound and girls wearing the bright pink dresses of pomegranate dye played in the yard. We descended the car and the chemist explained our business to the man.

Moments later, a squat man wearing a dark *pakhaul* hat came out, followed by two teenage boys. Aga Jan was shorter than I expected. When the chemist said Abdul Haq's name, his eyes filled with tears and he clasped his hands. I hadn't anticipated the depth of emotion he still felt for Haq. We had barely said hello.

We sat on a rug outside, tea and sweets were brought and Aga Jan apologised for his tears. His son translated. Aga Jan had just been to another Shaheed ceremony for Abdul Haq in Jalalabad. The son retrieved the documents relating to the ceremony and also brought some old photographs and a letter dated August 2003 from John Gunston. It was a job reference for Aga Jan. In the cold winter sunshine, I explained to him my interest in Abdul Haq. Aga Jan became still, then he turned and indicated with an outstretched palm the landscape around us and said:

> When the Soviet war started, all this was occupied by USSR. But Haq held all the mountains. Our friendship began in 1357, that is over twenty years ago. When I was only eighteen years old.

His whole face lit up and his eyes sparkled with his recollections.

> On every operation against USSR, I was with Haq. Abdul Haq was a different sort of leader, one who wanted a humanitarian government, for people to live in peace, to value education and culture. Pashtun, Tajik, Uzbek, Turkman, he got along with them all and with each was to them like their group.

As he spoke, he often said *dushman*, the word for 'enemy'. He had remained here during the Taliban and after September 11 travelled to Peshawar to see Haq.

A Toyota Corolla bounced up the path, full of noisy children. 'They're bringing food for Eid', the son explained.

I wanted to clarify if there was any basis for the slurs made in the two *Private Eye* pieces which had alleged that Haq had deliberately targeted civilians during an operation to blow up airplanes. Aga Jan told me that the airplane in question had been carrying military advisors back to Moscow at the end of their deployment and not children, as *Private Eye* had claimed. Haq had destroyed the military advisors plane using rockets sent from the top of Chakarlai mountain, next to the hill bearing the shrine of Khaja Sikander Babur. 'I was there', he said, 'I'd been in Tazin and Haq called me to come'. He had written down the dates but lost them with his papers when the Taliban burnt down his house. But he knew it was during Barbrak Karmal's[265] time. 'Whenever Haq did important operations it was during Karmal's time', he said.

On another occasion, he and Haq had distributed leaflets to children, who were being taken to the USSR for re-education. The leaflets carried messages explaining why they should help the Muj and not go to Russia. So, there had been no operation against schoolkids on a plane. I called the editor of *Private Eye* and then wrote an email asking who had submitted the piece. I was stonewalled. In relation to the allegations Gunston wrote:

> I knew AH from 1983 onwards and began working with him from 1984. I have never heard of this incident. I similarly have never heard of any such scurrilous slur made against AH throughout the period that I have known [him]. I have heard many other accusations but I

have never heard of any operation or attack that was based around the murder of his opponents let alone school kids.[266]

Considering that at the time of publication there were elements here in London who needed to slur AH to save their own professional positions for having allowed such a gallant patriot to die without Brit / US help. AH never took a life unless it was necessary ... This piece alludes to an interview some years after the alleged attack. I defy anyone to produce such a piece! The question is who planted it? You need to track the previous issue down to see if this gives any further clues to the source of this appalling calumny.[267]

He mentioned that one journalist who could have planted the story was someone alleged to have formerly worked at GCHQ, the headquarters of British intelligence. Another piece that had sparked Gunston's ire was published on 8 December 2001 in the London Times. The headline was "British Spies played key role in forcing collapse of regime" and within the piece MI6 were praised fulsomely for their 'apparent' role in "the negotiations which led to the handover of many of (Afghanistan's) cities". See my note on this.[268]

In Sarobi that morning in January 2005, I returned to the issue of 'Qarga' and the blowing up of the largest Soviet munitions dump just outside Kabul, an operation so strategically brilliant that – in 1987 – some said it had turned the war in favour of the mujahideen and, ultimately, the US. Yet inexplicably, as Gunston said, the CIA station chief, Milton Beardon, had said: 'It could have been any commander ... they all claimed credit for it'.[269]

Certainly one who had apparently not lost the opportunity to claim credit for the operation was the present Defence Minister, Rahim Wardak. I asked Aga Jan for his view about Qarga and whether Haq or Wardak had been responsible? He sighed and then spoke animatedly, looking alternatively at me and his son. But his answer was not immediately about Qarga. He talked of another successful operation carried out by Haq on the Sarobi to Kabul road, the major Soviet supply route from Jalalabad to the capital. Haq's mujahideen had managed to close it for ten days. I listened and soon understood why Aga Jan referred to this.

We got control of Sarobi for ten days. Haq was on top of the mountain. There was a rumour in Kabul that Sarobi was out of government control. Of course, the other Muj parties, particularly a commander of Rahim Wardak, Dr Sharok, tried to claim this. When Haq distributed warm clothes to the people Dr Sharok came up behind us pretending the clothes were from Wardak. But the people knew it was Abdul Haq … In fact this Dr Sharok wouldn't even talk in front of Haq, he was so shy.

Aga Jan then returned to the issue of Qarga.

So you see, it was the same thing with Qarga, with Wardak claiming the Operation for himself.

He explained how Haq had achieved the Qarga operation which reputedly took six months to plan and had blown seven underground stories of Soviet munitions.

They established a secret relation with an army officer who gave us the coordinates. So Haq could see from the map. Then we fired around fifty *Sahar shash* (Sahar six) rockets and it blew the thing.

Hanif Sherzad, my interpreter, had said of Qarga:

You could read the newspaper from the fire it threw up … Abdul Haq had also warned the British High Commission about the operation in advance. They filmed it from the roof of their building.

I continued to drill Aga Jan because I felt he was an honest man and I wanted to cut through some of the conflicting stories spread by those who had not been present at key events. 'Were any civilians deliberately killed by Haq?' I asked. His reply was tinged with annoyance,

Look, he used to plan what was city and what was military target with the map … We only followed Haji Abdul Haq's plan and *no* civilians were killed!

He related a story illustrating how Haq tried to avoid killing civilians. One day Aga Jan and Haq were sitting by the Abrasian road (the Kabul-Laghman road). There were around thirty Soviet checkposts and every week a car full of Russian ladies used to come down and meet their men who manned the checkposts. The ladies always came in a yellow car. And one of Haq's commanders came to tell Aga Jan the ladies had arrived and suggested they hit them. But Haq's reply was that it was against their culture to attack women, that they should aim for the officers instead. Jan said, 'When Qadir and Haji Zahir also closed the Sarobi-Kabul road a while later, they captured the women but let them go'.

The Arsalas were not simply Ruffian bullies. They were aware of and tried to follow international humanitarian law. Haji Zahir had once even lectured me once about following the 'rules of Geneva' when I had naively asked him why his soldiers didn't simply kill Pakistani soldiers who had transgressed onto Afghan territory during the border dispute? Aga Jan went on: '

> Haq's habit was that when he saw children he was sad they were not being educated and he was good with women. He avoided firing and airplanes thinking they could fall on women.

I then asked him if he could tell me the story of what happened on Abdul Haq's last mission. There was a pause. He looked silently into the hills and I noted his anorak and diamond-patterned jersey. After a while, he began speaking, his voice lower than before as he told me the story of Abdul Haq's capture at Tera Mangal, Hezarac.

***

My Irish colleague came to find me at Aga Jan's compound. We were late and our driver hurried the 4x4 along the narrow pass above the river towards Jalalabad. My colleague needed to reach Torkham before the border closed at five o'clock. But we got stuck behind several white Landcruisers which kept swerving across the road in front of our 4x4 to prevent us passing. At one stage, our car was almost pushed off the road. With several hundred metres down to the riverbed, that would have meant certain death. But the cars in front were going absurdly slow and finally I lost patience, urging the driver on. It was a dangerous manoeuvre because the road surface was loose with dirt and stones but he pressed his foot

235

determinedly and we swept past. Two hours later and we were in Jalalabad. Baryalai was not home, but Mahmoub and 'General' scuttled around me, bringing a *bukhari* stove with a steaming kettle of green tea. Abdul Haq's colonial desk, teak with slim drawers and a felt top, was at one end of the room. Over the next days I sat at it writing for hours by candlelight.

As dusk settled, Zahir sent a driver to fetch me and I found his compound jammed with Landcruisrs and bodyguards. Waiting for me on the doorstep was Haji Zahir. I asked what was going on. 'It's din Mohammad's people, and also Hedayat Arsala is here', he said, looking churlishly towards the door. Moments later he directed me inside and there in the gloom, with his back to the window, was Haji din Mohammad, smiling. Opposite on the floor sat another, large man who I initially took to be an American. Sitting, I realized there was a tension pervading the room.

'This is Hedayat Arsala', Zahir chuckled. He was the cousin who had moved thirty years before to Washington DC. I was surprised to find him here for several people now had told me the family were not close to him. Gunston had said 'Qadir had no time for him'. Arsala looked gruffly at me. He had small, dark eyes and a pallid white skin. I congratulated him on his recent re-appointment as Vice President and asked if he was the cousin who lived abroad. 'I studied in the USA, then worked for the World Bank for eighteen years, then returned for the jihad', he snapped, as I took in his tiny white goat beard. 'Actually I've been Vice President before. And was Foreign Minister in Dr Rabbani's government in exile. Then I was Minister, in the ...'

He droned on, listing title after title and position after position he had held during the foggy years of war; many of the titles held being during the mujahideen years of fighting in Kabul. He spoke distantly, as though to impress upon the interlocutor that here was somebody with a superior, if not a 'royal' presence.

By now he was listing the titles he had held during Karzai's recent interim government. His eyes bore an air of dissatisfaction, as though he didn't particularly wish to be in Jalalabad. I wondered what he was doing here, sitting on the floor in Jalalabad drinking green tea from a mug and surrounded by locals, rather than circulating in Kabul with foreign ambassadors who drank whisky from cut glasses.

I asked if he had known Haq. To my right, din Mohammad seemed to relax; evidently he seemed happy with the question. Now I remembered Gunston telling me that Arsala had not worked with Hizb, the rough and active party of Haqqani and Khalis, which the rest of the Ghilzai and *Arsala khel* had supported. Rather he had allied himself with the party journalists had dubbed the 'Gucci muj', Pir Gailani's party, the National Islamic Front for Afghanistan (NIFA).

He had, of course, known Haq he said. 'And did you leave the Mujahideen Government when Haq did?' I asked. Arsala paused, the room was silent. Din Mohammad leant forward, straining to catch Arsala's reply. At this stage I was unaware of the significance of my question for the family. 'Well, soon after', Arsala frowned.

Abdul Haq had left the country in 1992 when it became obvious the mujahideen were just fighting one another for the spoils, and killing tens of thousands of civilians in the process. He told his family that he had not fought to eject the Soviets from Afghanistan in order to become involved in a civil war afterwards. Meanwhile Arsala stayed and took on the first of what would become many government positions.

From Peshawar and later Dubai, Haq began writing to foreign diplomats and dignitaries entreating them to recognise and act upon the problems of warlordism and fundamentalism which were already shaping up in Afghanistan and the region.

Later that evening, I asked Zahir why there had been such an 'atmosphere' in the room when I had arrived. Zahir sneered.

> He is just here because he needs us now. But the people are not stupid, they know he was in America during the war.

I asked why Arsala behaved like this and he replied with a wave of his cigarette hand. 'When I am leaving this compound and going to Kabul Nadder is acting like he is King here!' Nadder was Haji Zahir's driver. Zahir went on. 'Look, yesterday I took him into my room where all elders was gathered'. Zahir was talking of the old sewing factory which he had converted into a room for meetings. Its walls were lined with some thirty sofas and occasional tables for tea and nuts. 'When the elders came in, Arsala was trying to sit in that chair!' Zahir said, jabbing his wrist towards an armchair which was placed throne-like at the end of the room.

> But I took the chair for myself. And Arsala, he is arguing with me, saying, 'But I am your elder'. He is *begging* me, saying, 'Why are you behaving like this, in front of *arl* elders?' And then I say to him, 'When my father is alive, *no one* is sitting in that chair but him. And when he is *not* live (if Din Mohammad is not here), then *I* am sitting in that chair'. And so I *sat* in chair! And he takes chair next to me, but complained, 'Why are you speaking like this to me, in front of elders?' And then I shout at him, 'In Kabul, you may have upstairs position, but remember, I am controlling de downstairs!'

His anecdote indicated much about what was wrong with the West's strategy in Afghanistan. For despite seeing himself as US-educated, and apparently superior, Arsala had come to Jalalabad because he needed support for the Presidential elections. He probably hated having to leave his grand office in the Presidential Palace to kowtow to his less elegant relatives in Jalalabad. But he at least – if not the Kabul-based community of foreign soldiers and diplomats who were attempting to foist a Western-style democracy on Afghanistan – understood the necessity of this. Especially when Zahir, although thirty years younger, was able to reassert the point that in Afghanistan real power came not from fancy positions essentially awarded by foreign-backed governments, but from the 'downstairs', in other words the tribes themselves.

Two weeks later, I interviewed another member of the former King's group. In a house in Wazir Akbar Khan, I was shown into a room whose floor was covered in rugs with the elegant *zahir shah* pattern. Around these were dotted small occasional tables boasting bowls of nuts and *kishmish*. The man had greying hair, was eloquent and dressed in a suit. I came to my point, asking whether Wardak and Arsala really had turned against Haq in Washington DC after

September 11. 'Yes absolutely', he said, eyebrows knitted in anger. He had also been in Jalalabad during Eid and told me:

> When we went to the Governors' Palace, one of the elders said to Arsala, 'We have seen your name on the list of the Cabinet. We don't know who most of them are. But anyway after your name it says "Senior Advisor". So tell us why the Americans are allowed to enter our houses at night to search without even the permission of the Governor?"

Then he said 'But the people are not stupid. They know he did only returned from the US in 1988. The war ended a few months later'.

Like others I spoke with, it seemed to me that this man clearly resented Arsala, feeling he had made little sacrifice during the war against the Soviets, only coming back late in the day to pick up the prizes of titles and positions dealt to him by warring mujahideen factions.

CHAPTER SEVENTEEN
RETURN TO KANDAHAR

Finally back to Kandahar, its dust, its crazy black turbaned boys on their flashy pick-ups, its famous tea and Pepsi saloons ....The modern Far West or maybe Mad Max's world ... I still don't know.

Email from my housemate, Denis, in Kandahar, February, 2001

Kandahar, 2005

'This is US soil!' the American soldier screamed when someone asked why we had to be contained in the vehicle. We had been here an hour on the airstrip at Kandahar where it was 40-degrees centigrade. My first visit here since I had left in November 2000, at the time of al Qaeda's attack on the USS Cole.

'They lose it every week', commented an Afghan passenger wryly. He was talking about the key to the civilian gate, apparently 'lost' by the US soldiers. If the key was found we would ride the UN bus for two hundred yards to our vehicles beyond the perimeter fence. Until then we must wait for we were not allowed to walk.

Earlier, our bags had been laid on the ground while sniffer dogs climbed over them and the soldiers screamed, 'Don't look!' The Afghans who had travelled with us on the humanitarian plane maintained a composed outlook. It got worse when I flew back days later, for the American soldiers made me stand – legs apart – in front of Afghan and foreign men while a phallic-shaped wand was frisked around my inner thigh. With such extreme disregard for cultural norms and even basic etiquette, it did not seem too far fetched to think of Afghans boiling with hatred beneath their composure. This behaviour was worlds away from the habits of decorum my former colleague had taken such pains to ensure I understood prior to my first deployment to Kandahar, in 2000: decorum which could, in a tricky situation in this conservative place, save your life. Today at the airport, when I asked some of the Afghans what they felt about this lack of consciousness or respect about these norms an elderly man admitted, 'Yes, for these reasons we can *never* travel with our wives by plane to Kabul. We must take the road'. A seven-hour drive and the risk of ambush was preferable to this humiliation.

We drove into Kandahar, fearful of roadside bombs which had doubled in incidence since the previous year, 2004. It was the first time I had returned to Kandahar since my departure across the Registan desert in a taxi to Quetta after the bombing of the USS Cole. When I had arrived in August 2000, I had come here to work for the UN.[270] Mullah Omar's house had been several hundred yards away from ours. I remembered the dust and the wild dogs running the streets after dark. The remains of eighteenth and nineteenth century style royal palaces had stood like cardboard cutouts in compounds still littered with landmines. Now the place looked more like Dubai. There was even a ferris wheel. But still, little development was evident upon the city's fringes.

I visited the compound I had shared with staff from Handicap International. The place still had the faded elegance of an old palace but there was an air of sadness. The foreigners had left for security reasons. Our old servant, Gulum, was still there, happy and amazed to see me. A 4x4 pulled into the compound as we chatted. The vehicle halted in a haze of dust, men got out and began pulling 'Handicap' signboards out of the back. Someone said:

> They're bringing all the signs back from Zabol. We have to stop work on our projects there now. The insecurity is too bad since the Americans are out there fighting the Taliban.

It was the first time they'd had to stop work in ten years, which was ironic given that, despite the heavy US presence at the airport, security had decreased since 2001. An old Afghan hand and writer, Jolyon Leslie, attributed the increasing insurgency in Zabol province to the fact so little development had taken place there between 2001 and 2004.[271]

At the UN Centre for Human Settlements (UNCHS), I saw our former office chief. Prior to September 11, he had always worn a black turban and had been openly Talib. He was rumoured to have undertaken English translations for Mullah Omar, been involved in mediations between the Taliban and the international community when an Indian airlines hostage crisis unfolded at Kandahar airport over Christmas 1999. He had apparently been awarded the position of Taliban Ambassador to Saudi Arabia in the summer of 2001. That he was also relatively urbane, kept us up-to-date on security issues and was in charge of our entire Southern Region Operation was a clear sign to me that those who saw the fight against the Taliban as a case of the good guys versus the bad guys[272] were ignorant of – and sadly often disinterested in – the complexity of the south.

The UN was only now, in 2004, belatedly trying to set up some sort of reconciliation programme for moderate Taliban willing to be reconciled with the new Afghan government. This, of course, had been a central plank of Abdul Haq's plan. My former office chief was rather muted and when I asked him if the reconciliation with the Taliban, a process rumoured to have begun under the auspices of former President Mujaddidi, was having an effect. He just indicated that he hoped it would take off soon so that his brother could come in from the cold.

At this stage though neither of us knew that the coalition was to continue with its self-defeating phenomenon of 'killing Taliban, smoking em out' then listing the numbers of dead at its Bagram press conferences for another five years, as though this was a means of measuring 'success' when the battle was actually not a physical one but one of perception. The local chief of the UN Office for Drugs control (UNODC) said, 'We don't want your democracy if all it brings is insecurity and corruption'.

The Karzai family were stuffing the administration with members of their tribe, the Popelzai, and family allies. Which was, he said, why people were turning back to the Taliban. He thought it absurd that the UN was now so 'politicised' that UN staff '*even* travelled in military vehicles'. He fumed, 'And then they wonder why they are becoming targets!'

During the Taliban period, UN staff had been advised never

to travel in vehicles with guns. To do so was considered this an inducement to becoming a target. Nevertheless security had been such that it was rarely a problem to travel outside Kandahar to conduct aid projects in rural areas. I had even made the six-hour journey over destroyed roads to Quetta by local taxi and road trips to Farrah and Herat were considered normal.

In line with this 'integration' between the UN – or aid and development workers – and military, there was increasing pressure for all aid work to fall under the mantle of the military, under the guise of the PRTs which were proliferating across the country. To me, this was a worrying development, in line with the military's domination in the triumvirate of 'diplomacy, development and defence' (an idea which came to be known as '3D').

To have the military essentially 'leading' on reconstruction and even development projects was certainly a contrast to the 'Community Forae' (CF) system set up in urban areas throughout Afghanistan during the Taliban[273] by my agency, the UN Centre for Human Settlements (UNCHS). This was part of the Poverty Eradication and Community Empowerment Programme (PEACE) launched in 1997 by the UNDP with:

> A US$33 million budget to address humanitarian and developmental needs, and to build up social and economic infrastructures in the context of the breakdown at all levels of governance in Afghanistan.[274]

The former UN Humanitarian Coordinator for Afghanistan described the programme thus:

> The community elects a development committee following the traditional Afghan shura principle, which is responsible for representing local points of view, for working out how activities are carried out, and finding people to take part in them. In this way, the programme hopes to create a sense of community ownership for rehabilitation and reconstruction initiatives and enhance people's ability to rebuild over the longer term without external assistance.[275]

For the UNCHS, more focus was placed on 'process' than on 'output'. The CF system recognised that 'outputs' could only be valued and hence self-sustaining if Afghans were central to the decision-making about projects and procedure. The aim was to fill much of the vacuum in local governance lost during the war when various phases of the conflict had seen elders and community leaders targeted and ancient systems of consensus-building wiped out.

To undertake CF projects, a 'pump priming' fund was given by the UN to set up separate community forums for men and women keen to be involved in civil society. The community forums would select development committees who would then work with the UN to select projects that would be beneficial to the community. An agreed formula was used to ascertain the most vulnerable, in other words, those who should be direct beneficiaries of the projects. Hence, when I arrived in Kandahar, at the height of a four-year drought, the CF and UNCHS had selected a project for the people of Kandahar and Herat city who were affected by drought. Hence we did a project to improve water supply and to clean the city's drains.

The CF approach could hardly have contrasted more with that of the PRT, which had been set up in 2003. Based on the Provincial Action Team (PAT) model from the Vietnam War, PRTs had average set-up costs upwards of 15 million euros, notwithstanding military and ongoing costs. And the PRT approach was essentially top-down and capital-intensive. The idea was for PRTs in the regions, staffed by mostly foreign military with a smattering of civilian staff, to extend the remit of central government to the regions. Not only was this something that undermined the traditionally delicate balance of autonomy between the centre and regions, but the PRTs had no common mandate. Neither were they a cost-effective way to undertake development projects. Rather than using the military to conduct such projects, it would have been far more efficient to use the agencies hitherto specialised in say, water supply and sanitation, like UN Habitat or the ICRC to run those projects.

As such, beginning in 2003, and at huge cost, international soldiers started to conduct most of the physical reconstruction work, while locals remained unemployed and angry. It was a contrast to the CF approach which was a bottom-up means of governance and development, where Afghan civil society was the primary focus, objectives were transparent and local people maintained a sense of 'ownership' over projects. Thus, crucially, a sense of dignity had prevailed.

Instead, there were stories about PRT projects being undertaken so that PRT commanders could 'buy off' the goodwill of local strongmen, normally close to the provincial capital in order for their soldiers to cross territory safely. Such projects were not about meeting the 'needs' of locals. Thus, stories circulated of wells being built without geological surveys nor reference to village disputes, causing long lasting problems. Instead 'reconstruction' was all about force protection (for the foreign soldiers) and 'physical output' (allowing them to tick the boxes of those 'milestones') in isolation of any meaningful engagement with Afghans.[276]

From 2004 to 2005, I attended the PRT 'Working Group' in Kabul and made visits to most of the PRTs which then existed in Afghanistan. Incredibly, the PRT Working Group excluded civil society groups and NGOs (both Afghan or international), relegating them to a separate lesser forum. In this 'lesser' forum, civil society groups struggled to maintain a dialogue with young NATO or coalition soldiers, who were being rotated out every three to six months; well before they had got to grips with the issues or the complex array of Afghan warlords, strongmen and key personalities.

The dominance of the PRT model by the military, was such that even a former ISAF soldier,[277] who now worked with the UN, said frustratedly in 2005: 'PRTs need an "engagement strategy" before they can have an "exit strategy"'.

***

On this day in Kandahar in June 2005, I was to meet with Karzai's brother, Ahmad Wali. Although he had no official position, Ahmad Wali was considered the 'real' Governor of Kandahar. From interviews with other interlocutors, we had heard of his association with – among other things – land seizures on the city outskirts. Then there were the drug rumours. The street had been cut off for his benefit, with concrete blocks, in the way of American private security companies or the CIA office in Jalalabad. My interpreter hung back. Although his family had known the Karzai family during the jihad years and he had admired Karzai's father, today he had no wish to shake Ahmad Wali's hand.

At the end of the meeting, Ahmad Wali Karzai offered me 'protection' –armed guards – for my journey the following day to the notorious poppy-growing area of Helmand. I had already travelled to the area when working in Kandahar in the year 2000. Afghan colleagues and I had driven across the desert, inspected the hydro power plant at Arghundab built by the Americans during the 1960s, and then made our way up the Helmand river where we had spent the day with a picnic among the reeds.

Today though I was advised by UN security that I must travel with guards. It was common knowledge that the area remained unstable, with skirmishes, hijackings and ongoing 'mopping up' operations by the Americans. My aim was to visit a US company based in Lash-kah-gah under contract to the State Department to undertake income generation schemes in an effort to persuade people away from poppy.

I was also interested in Helmand because there were rumours the British would be sending troops there the following year, 2006, to undertake a 'peace-keeping' operation and to take over the Southern Command of NATO Operations. This was surprising, in the light of a how a friend at a leading international humanitarian organization commented in June 2005: 'I don't see how it can be a "peace-keeping" operation when there's been ongoing conflict there since 2001'. The conflict he spoke of was part of the general insurgency that had gathered pace in the south since 2003. He added:

> Oh well, the Americans aren't stupid. They know this is failing. They'll hand it to the British, retreat and blame them when failure becomes obvious.

Unsurprisingly, the following morning I was forced to cancel the trip when the UN Security Chief informed me that twelve of the Chemonics staff I was due to visit that day had been killed overnight, targeted in a double rocket and IED attack.

It was hard to know whether this was Taliban insurgents or drug dealers, because there were powerful people making a lot of money out of poppy for whom continued insecurity was an advantage. A triumvirate of strongmen in the south – including Ahmad Wali Karzai in Kandahar, and Karzai family allies; the Governor's Haji Akhanzada in Helmand; Aga Jan in Urozghan and Assadullah Khaled in Ghazni - were rumoured to be operating together in a drug ring that also included Governors in other southern cities such as Ghazni. For such people, insecurity was crucial to enabling them to continue their operations. And the conflation by much of the media and military of such attacks as being associated purely with the 'Taliban' was a gift to the criminals and drug gangs. 'The family are traders', an English agricultural consultant, who had travelled in the south for decades, said of the Akhanzadas. 'And as they're traders their main concern is the drug trade. That's how they make their money'.

In any case, within months Tony Blair declared that Britain would send two battalions of soldiers to Afghanistan. When, that September 2005, I met with a Pashtun tribal leader from the Gailani family, to discuss his candidacy for the parliamentary elections, he told me in exasperation:

> The British may have forgotten their history in Helmand but the Kandaharis have not. Why do they not send the Spanish or French soldiers instead?

He knew that Afghans would be galvanised to fight, not simply as Taliban, but to repel the foreign 'infidel' invader like their forefathers during the first three Afghan wars and the campaign in Waziristan. Like the elder I had met along the border, who had proudly invited me for tea so he could show me the skull of a British soldier killed generations earlier by his grandfather, or those Pashtuns in Jalalabad inspired by the poem about Malalai, this man was hinting to me that these people – rural and simple as they were – retained a proud appreciation of their history, even if the British, whose ambassador had effectively told me he did not much care for Afghan history books, did not.

CHAPTER EIGHTEEN

GOVERNANCE AND TRADITIONAL STRUCTURES

In Afghanistan we look for answers inside our forts (largely reliant upon kinetic energy) when the answers actually lie in the hills, reliant upon the tribes. This was the core of Abdul Haq's message. The one we were incapable of listening to.[278]

Jalalabad & Faizabad, 2004-5

As far back as 1973, the American anthropologist Louis Dupree had identified how, in Afghanistan, tensions were developing between the concept of 'nation state' and that of a traditional society based on 'kinship' (in other words, something more tribal).

In his tome, *Afghanistan*, published in 1973,[279] Dupree described the concept of 'nation state' as follows:

> In the Western sense ... more a set of attitudes, a reciprocal, functioning set of rights and obligations between the Government and the governed – with emphasis on the individual rather than the group.

By contrast, he said, 'tribalism' tended to come in;

> In non-literate societies ... when kinship replaces government and guarantees men and women born into a specific unit a functioning set of social, economic, and political rights and obligations.

In the 1960s and '70s, Dupree recognised that Afghanistan was attempting to create a 'nation state' out of what he called, 'a hodge podge of ethnic and linguistic groups'.

Yet, looking back at what happened from 1973 onwards after the King was ejected, this tension in Afghan society – between 'centre and periphery' and between 'modernisers and traditionalists' – set in motion the series of coups which turned Afghanistan from a monarchy into a republic and ended in the chaos of the jihad and the inter-factional fighting which followed. Since Dupree wrote this, almost thirty years of war has destroyed much of Afghanistan's former social fabric and undermined traditional governance systems. In particular, the Soviets and the mujahiddeen (particularly Hikmatyar) have systematically murdered many of the elders and intellectuals who provided the 'glue' for jirgas.

The great irony, when one considers this history, is that since 2001, the international community has replicated this same tension by attempting to create a nation state in Afghanistan. Yet, writing in 1998, Amin Saikhal depicts how local governance and political order still functions in Afghanistan:

> In Afghanistan, political order and governance have always largely rested on a mixture of personalised, clientalistic politics, and elite alliance and elite settlement, legitimate through traditional mechanisms of consensus building and empowerment, such as the Loya Jirga (Grand Assembly).[280]

In their excellent paper, 'Integrating Tribal Structures into the State-building Process; lessons from Loya Paktia', Susanne Schmeidl and Massoud Karokhail assert that:

> ... networks are less orientated around ethnicity (e.g. Pashtun) than along smaller entities such as tribes, sub-tribes or smaller communities or solidarity groups such as quams in Pashtun society.[281]

> Tribal structures should best be understood as complex clientalistic networks where the importance of family and kinship overrules interest orientated associations. Such networks tend to be 'non modern' forms of authority (e.g. patriarchal and neo-patrimonial as described by Max Weber) where there is no 'public sphere'.[282]

Saikal's quote depicts 'how local governance and political order' functions in Afghanistan; outlining clearly that 'governance was never much centralised but depended heavily on local politics and elites'.[283] In this way, neither the Safavid nor the Moghul empires of the sixteenth- and seventeenth-centuries, nor later the Durrani rulers of the eighteenth- and nineteenth-centuries 'managed to preserve their rule permanently or extend state structures beyond the few urban centres'.[284] Schmeidl and Karokhail's paper goes on to explain how the lack of a state, 'or even thinking in state terms', has been further intensified by the war because during conflict, the 'accountability of local leaders towards the general population declines, focusing only on the needs and desires of very small groups'.[285]

Among other observations made during the introduction to their paper, Schmeidl and Karokhail emphasise how in a participatory approach to state building, 'security at the district and provincial levels is guaranteed by agreements among tribes, and between the tribes and the government'.

This was the core of what I'd learnt Haq had been working on when he was killed. It was also partly why Baryalai was driven to work on rebuilding traditional structures of consensus. The consultative shura which Baryalai had been working on since I had first known him in late 2002 was called the Council of Nangarhar Communities. In dari, this translates as 'shura e Mashwarati e Nangarhar' and in Pashtu, 'da Nangarhar Mashwaraty shura'. The inception and background to this Council is outlined in the endnote.[286]

I had seen how much care Baryalai had taken – since I had first known him in 2002 – over consulting on the evolution and eventual form of the Council of the Nangarhar Communities. There had been months of discussion as to the objectives for the shura and how best to attract members who wanted to serve their community, to work on the shura for no material gain, as was traditional amongst Afghan leaders. The stated objectives of the shura included discussing issues of unity between the tribes, security, economic development, women's issues and rights, the selection of locals for the Afghan National Army (ANA) and the facilitation of better relations with Pakistan. Another issue that would later gain their – and Baryalai's – attention was reconciliation with the Taliban. Because the issues were discussed in an Afghan forum, American generals increasingly saw the shura as a useful vehicle for bringing about the goals the West wished to pursue in Afghanistan. As Baryalai had said, however, the problem was who, despite the 'cloak of shura', was really making the decisions.

By 2004, it seemed the foreigners were also keen to start shuras across Afghanistan. The National Solidarity Programme (NSP) was taken up in 2001 by the World Bank, as an extension of Habitat's 'Community Forum' programme, which I had originally worked on in Kandahar during the Taliban. The programme would be rolled out from urban to rural areas and locally elected Community Development Councils (CDCs) would be set up. The PRTs which had extended their original remit – which was to provide security – into reconstruction and were now expanding further into governance.

I visited the US Provincial Reconstruction Team (PRT) in Jalalabad in December 2004. Its commander was interested in and responsive to local dynamics but soon a female civilian advisor arrived with the intent of starting a shura. Apparently, she showed little interest in what Baryalai had been doing and when she bypassed his Council of Nangarhar Communities he commented:

> The problem is when foreigners come here to start shura – like the PRT starting shura to hand out money 'via the shura' – these shuras are not attracting people who want to do good for the community. They are attracting strongmen and those who want to use the shura to make money. So this is unbalancing the structure of the traditional shura.

A German NGO had recently arrived in Jalalabad with the objective of working on counter-narcotics and shuras, and typified the view of the international community when they said, 'We don't like the traditional shuras as the old men make all the decisions'. So said one of the two grey-haired men who had come to set up the programmes. 'We prefer to use the National Solidarity Programme [NSP] system as it has a secret ballot'.

It seemed that the NSP, which had worked well in urban areas during the Taliban, was to be rolled out into rural areas and become a vehicle for bringing democracy into the villages of Afghanistan, bypassing traditional structures. I had worked on the precursor to the NSP project in Kandahar during the Taliban. Of course, the participatory aspect was very good, but the idea that use of a 'secret ballot' vote would automatically lead to democracy in this complex tribal society was naïve.

When in late 2009, I wrote to Baryalai asking how things were progressing with the 'parallel shuras' being set up by the foreigners, he said that the Americans wanted to work with shuras but so far did not have the right approach. The foreigners' shuras would not work because they did not accept the *traditional* concept of shura, but wanted to do it in 'so-called modern way, which was not compatible with the traditional way'. He was talking about the NSP which had been rolled out countrywide from 2003 onwards. The NSP shuras, he said, were now 'everywhere' in Afghanistan, but were '*not* the traditional shuras; members of these shuras are *not* leaders of their communities'. Indeed, he said, these members were only authorised by their communities to decide about the spending of the money allocated by the government for the projects in their areas and monitor and observe the implementation of these projects. By contrast, the traditional leaders were representatives of their communities in *all* issues related to their communities and were indispensible in interfacing between government and community - important in Afghanistan where rural areas remain so traditional, so distant from the centre. It was also important in solving disputes and conflicts. He added that the 'members of NSP shuras don't have that mandate'. Finally, he said, 'the NSP exists only on the village level, not the district or province level. Our shura operates on all three levels'.

Astri Suhrke,[287] writing on the dialectic between 'traditional' and 'modern' government structures, assessed the limitations of the Bonn Agreement, with its focus on 'modern government structures'. It was, she said, an approach which did not allow traditional elements a central role[288] and meant that these elements have thus had to compete for space and power. In particular, the promulgation since September 11 of the NSP into rural areas was thus an attempt to replace traditional structures with modern ones (in this case, the village-based 'democratically elected' Community Development Councils or CDCs).[289]

Baryalai's assertions about the limitations of NSP as compared to other, more traditional structures, were backed up in other studies. In 2008, a nationwide assessment of the NSP project was published.[290] It concluded that although the programme functioned very well, it often functioned either alongside traditional structures or was infiltrated by more traditional elements. It had a limited role to play in dispute resolution, for example, as compared to the role played by traditional leaders. Nixon says:

> ... mandating a single governance role for CDCs would produce mixed outcomes, due to the observed variation in how CDCs commonly function and in relation to customary structures. While there is evidence of fruitful governance improvements linked to CDCs this is often achieved through the implicit recognition of pre-existing governance patterns, not wholesale attempts to replace them.[291]

Schmeidl and Karokhail indicate:

> Even those shuras at the village level that are set up by NGOs or the councils of the government's National Solidarity Programme are generally appointed by the major tribal shuras within a given province.[292]

Unfortunately in the post Bonn state-building exercise there has been a fear that, 'collaboration with tribal elites may strengthen a parallel power system that opposes or at minimum is an obstacle to, the creation of a strong modern state'.

Suhrke, Schmeidl and Karokhail assert that such:

> ... zero-sum game approach to centre-periphery relations (with the centre being modern and desirable and the periphery (Provinces) traditional, backwards and undesirable), is 'unconstructive' in state-building exercises in countries where tradition and traditional structures still matter a great deal to the local population.

Dupree wrote about this tension in 1973:[293]

> Unfortunately, many of the national leaders in the non western world have been educated in the West and have the individualistic conceptions of nation-state. These leaders look on attempts to perpetuate tribal prerogatives as anarchistic, archaic and anti-unity.

Given the interest since 2004 in local governance, I wondered whether Baryalai's alternative model – the Council for Nangarhar Communites – was now being asked to be a vehicle to assist in the implementation of government policy from the bottom-up. There had been some initial interest by the Ministry for Reconstruction and Rural Development (MRRD), but he said that the effectiveness of the shuras and traditional structures of leadership in Afghanistan was being 'systematically ignored' by both the government, which felt challenged by what the shuras represented, and by the international community, which saw the NSP as a panacea in bringing democracy. Both, he said, had tried to eliminate or 'go around' the traditional structure, or 'not to involve [it] in the decision making process', or to 'replace the traditional leadership in an artificial way that doesn't work in Afghan society'.

In a direct reference to NSP, with its secret ballot and more democratic emphasis, he went on to say:

> When government and international community try to impose new leaders on the communities, it doesn't work. [The] Soviets tried this, [the] mujahideen tried this, [the] Arabs and our neighbours tried it. It didn't bring a [good] result and Karzai and his allies tried it. They all could not see the result.

One of the main problems for the Germans whom I had met in Jalalabad was that they had arrived, like the American PRT, with the goal of organising a parallel structure. They had spent several months doing up their compound and had now started work gathering data in the villages. The first time I had met them – when they had outlined their objectives to me – they had been confident and ebullient. Six months later, I found them frustrated and bitter. They were having implementation problems and were unable to get much of the community in the areas they had selected to participate. I asked if they had contacted the Governor. They sneered, presumably because they assumed that din Mohammad represented a certain limited franchise here. Maybe he did, but the comment about the secret ballot and their subsequent frustrations indicated that the Germans were trying to make a structure more in line with a Western democratic vision – with themselves as moderators – in a predominantly tribal society whose dynamics are necessarily fairly opaque to westerners more used to the concept of 'nation state'.

Since 2001, Afghans complained to me that relationships of trust between tribes had been further fragmented as the coalition had fostered hostility between groups. I had witnessed this myself in Jalalabad, as strongmen like Ali were favoured – with weapons, cash and the legitimacy conferred through working with the US and government – over tribal leaders with more historic legitimacy. Overnight, such actions had changed patterns of power and kinship and caused instability.

The importance of working with the tribal system was something that Abdul Haq had understood and in a letter to Jimmy Carter, dated 6 January 1992, he wrote:

> Today elections are impossible so I suggest we try and resuscitate the traditional system once again. Today the elements of power and tradition are Ulema; tribal leaders, resistance commanders; intellectuals and political party leaders and good muslims in Kabul. Each have shuras and committees.

Abdul Haq was talking of the Qawm, which is:

> Essentially ... a community of interests, local and traditional, cemented by kinship, tribal or other ties ... a solidarity group (encompassing family lineages, clans, tribes or sectarian, linguistic or ethnic groups) that is politically self governing and economically self sustaining. This traditional mode of community governance has proved remarkably resiliant. It has survived despite the efforts of successive rulers and bureaucracies in Kabul to bring it within the strait-jacket of a modern nation state, on the questionable assumption that the European construct of the nation-state was a *summum bonum*, a kind of political form of organisation that is self evident, a 'natural' culmination of all societies.[294]

Haq described how foreign interference had damaged such structures during the jihad;

> In helping create the political parties, America and other foreign nations built up anti-democratic Afghan fundamentalist groups which are now almost out of control. But by building on our own traditions, Afghans may yet be able to overcome these dangerous ideologues and restore peace and security.

In terms of how, in Afghanistan, 'personalities' rather than political parties in the Western sense of the word had more relevance, Baryalai explained that direction comes ultimately from the rural areas, from the people and from the tribes. For the Arsala family, this meant the tribes of Hezarac, Khoghiani and Shinwar, among other tribes of the Eastern Provinces: 'They are the ones whose support we can count on. We can mobilise them as we have spent time with them'.[295] The Arsala family had, for the most part, produced the types of 'chief' whom the British General Rawlinson had recognised as those who were able to hold together 'tribes ... of unequal power and divergent habits'.[296]

I had seen for myself how the people looked to the Arsala family as their representatives in Kabul and how they also came to ask the family for mediation of their problems. They came to discuss land and border disputes, issues with the American occupation or to plan how the tribes would mobilise themselves to ensure the re-election of Karzai, who was still seen as a Pashtun bolster against the Tajik-dominated Northern Alliance power. To ensure that bolster, the family, and its *quam* had supported the concept of a more heavily Presidential, as opposed to a Parliamentary, system when the new Afghan Constitution was debated and agreed in 2003/4.[297]

When Baryalai explained how the tribes organised themselves for the elections it indicated how little the West understood about Afghan-style democracy. For din Mohammad had discussed the presidential elections and its candidates with the tribespeople who told him that as they did not know the candidates personally they would look to him for advice. The result was hence a tribal 'block vote' for Karzai. In other Pasthu areas, there were reports of a disproportionate number of 'phantom' women being registered to vote. Others would probably never see the ballot, which was decided along tribal lines or by bribery, or in many places intimidation by local commanders who had made deals, possibly with regional strongmen or warlords. Especially for those whose illicit incomes depended upon their maintaining powerful positions in the local hierarchy.[298]

***

Sometime in February I visited Faizabad, a traditional Northern Alliance stronghold in the north-east and from where former President Rabbani originated. Other NATO countries were complaining the Germans were not doing enough from their PRT. This was a major poppy growing and trafficking area. I wanted to assess the impact of their PRT on local development efforts.

I flew in with our office interpreter, Najib. The plane headed into the vast confluence of the Hindu Kush and Pamir, finally making a dramatic landing on a tin runway installed by the Russians. We climbed into a scruffy yellow taxi organised by Najib and bumbled along the rutted road into town. The driver was clearly a poor local man. I asked what people thought of the PRT and he shouted: '*Why* do the foreigners come here only to *support* Nazir Mohammad?! All Nazir Mohammad's men are now working for the German PRT, even guarding its perimeter fence.'

He went on to explain that Nazir Mohammad was the most powerful strongman here, the leading drugs dealer, expropriator of property and even children. 'Everyone', our driver said, was 'scared of him'. So, as we arrived arrival at the outer perimeter of the German PRT, I asked the Afghan guards who they worked for. They chanted, 'Nazir Mohammad'.

Once inside the PRT (which had a set-up cost of around 15 million euros), comprising mainly of plastic cabins and vast steel containers sited on a flank of mud to the back of the airport, we met first with the civilian chief, an earnest German. He was amazed that the EU had allowed me to travel in a local taxi, concerned for my security. Ironically, it was the proximity to the locals conferred by travelling in a taxi – something diplomats, soldiers and intelligence officers who preferring convoys of armoured vehicles avoided – which had armed me with my first question for the PRT's civilian chief. Was it true, I asked, they were using the guards of a warlord to guard their perimeter? He sighed, confirmed it were so and admitted it annoyed him. The decision had been taken by the joint 'military chief' and had something to do with 'force protection'.

Later, we visited the local head of the Afghan Independent Human Rights Commission who affirmed the stories about this same warlord, Nazir Mohammad, kidnapping small children as well as local fears about his possible paedophilia. Not only, he told us, did Nazir Mohammad have the PRT in his pocket, he also controlled the police department. In fact, as we visited the police department the next day, Mohammad's cortege was arriving as we left.

The PRT appeared to be spending far more on its set-up and running costs than it would ever spend on the development of Badakhshan. It brought to mind what Haji Zahir had recently said about the 'running costs' of foreign soldiers:

'They are importing bottles of mineral water at $2 a bottle from Dubai for these guys, when Afghan soldiers are only paid 25 cents a day.'

Still, the PRT was paying lip service to the idea of consulting with locals. The Danish Commander told me enthusiastically, 'Yesterday we got pictures of local elders'. He showed me the photos. 'Tomorrow we'll go back to dig the wells!' Now, although well meaning, this all seemed absurdly simplistic when compared to the very impressive work already being done in Badakhshan by the Aga Khan Development Network (AKDN), who had been in region many years and among other detailed anthropological studies, had conducted income studies on the relative attractiveness for locals of working on the poppy harvest.

When I distributed my report on the Faizabad visit to EU Embassies, the German Ambassador denied angrily the PRT had a warlord guarding its perimeter. Yet four months later, in summer 2004, I returned and found Nazir Mohammad's men *still* there. I heard from the Afghans that whenever NATO chiefs, including the then British commander, flew into Faizabad, their first stop was apparently, lunch with Nazir Mohammad![299] Unfortunately, this emphasis on putting the PRT's interests above those of the locals made a mockery of the idea of NATO forces coming to Afghanistan to protect the locals and to manufacture 'security'. In the same way that the 2001/2 Faustian 'bargain' made by the West with Afghan warlords had allowed them to continue with their illicit and intimidating activities, this state of affairs had also inevitably brought insecurity in its wake. It also seemed contrary to the lofty ideals of 'human security' and the 'right to protect' (R2P) under discussion as a UN objective. Because on the ground and despite their superior firepower, the prime concern of NATO chiefs was 'force protection'. Other PRTs had made similar alliances in the south.[300]

The same conciliation to strongmen had made the international community unwilling to engage[301] in disarming illegal militias, most of which were associated with the strongmen who since September 11 had become its allies. Around 1,700 illegally armed groups existed nationally in Afghanistan. They would continue to terrorise the local population, steal their children, their property, run the drugs trade and intimidate people into voting the way they wanted during the parliamentary elections due to be held in Autumn 2005. Yet I witnessed both NATO and coalition representatives squirm in meetings with the Afghan government and other stakeholders when asked about the possibility of disarming them in a programme to be called 'Disarming Illegal Armed Groups' (DIAG).

There had also been the 'Disarm, Demobilise and Reintegration' (DDR) programme, whose meetings I attended each week in Kabul at the MOD. The DDR programme offered remuneration to soldiers in the so-called 'official' Afghan army in return for their handing in their more aged weapons. It was thus effectively a huge subsidy to those militias of the Northern Alliance – mostly General Fahim – who had taken over the Afghan National Army units from the departing Taliban in November 2001. Many of these scruffy, newly demobilised militias were now simply reintegrating into what were now dubbed 'illegal armed groups'[302] or, as a wry journalist observed, 'reintegrating into the drug trade'. These groups, led by the strongmen the West had made stronger, would never be taken on by the coalition or NATO. Even as the first DDR programme was initiated in 2003, shipments of Western arms had continued to arrive in the north from the US, to be given to the strongmen who had become our 'allies'.[303]

This was the precisely the state of affairs Haq had foreseen and desired to avoid through achieving a more equitable political settlement, avoiding the return of warlords to Afghanistan and not allowing the Northern Alliance to take Kabul. It was also why UN political officers such as my colleague, Nils, and some European ambassadors, had despaired of the 'peace versus justice' deal made with the warlords by Khalilzad and Brahimi on the eve of the 2002 Emergency Loya Jirga.

One of the 'disappointed' UN officers – who had worked in Afghanistan both pre- and post-September 11 – wrote to me in 2008.

> Last year [2007] I accepted another assignment [in Afghanistan]. I was so disappointed that I quit the job this July. All the mistakes that we had warned Brahimi[304] about have now grown to a fully dysfunctional state. Corruption, poverty, criminality, massive abuse of human rights, I felt very sorry for my Afghan friends, who had such high expectations after 9/11. Now many of them turned away from the international community and just expect them to leave. And frankly they might even be better off - much of the international assistance is barely more then window dressing.[305]

By 2005, the insurgency had strengthened and it was obvious that the international community was not delivering the building blocks required to stabilise the situation. There was a continued lack of coordination among different international actors and a failure of donors to respond to the requests by Afghans for conditionality on aid receipts (to ensure some delivery of services by this corrupt government to the people). The presumption by the military that – despite their lack of experience in state building, development or reconstruction – they should be the lead actors in the entire operation, often chiefly for the short-term benefit to themselves of 'force protection, seemed counter-productive. In late 2005, there had also been the bizarre decision of the European Union's Chief Election Observer, Emma Bonino to toe the Bush-ite line of dubbing the 2005 parliamentary elections 'free and fair' in contravention to what our team's election observers – and others – were saying from the field about intimidation of candidates, about security in the run up to the election and vote rigging on the day of the election and about fraud in the counting of ballots.[306] [307]

With the 1,700 armed militia groups still roaming the country intimidating people into voting the way strongmen preferred, many more strongmen – or their proxies, some of whom were women – were thus elected to the parliament in 2005. They quickly pushed through an Amnesty Law against future prosecution for the mass human rights violations many had carried out in the past.[308] The anger of Afghan women over this state of affairs was expressed by the brave Malalai Joya, who had risen to fame when she spoke out against the warlords at the Constitutional Loya Jirga. For her forthrightness, she had been expelled from that Loya Jirga and one strongman had recommended that she be raped. Elected during the parliamentary election as MP for her province of Farah, she continued to denounce the presence of the warlords in the new 'parliament' and was again expelled by them soon after. Since then, under death threat, she has had to remain in hiding.

The lack of a respected and decent Pashtun leader as an alternative to Karzai was becoming evident already in 2005. There were too many individuals wanting to be 'King' but failing to work together to form coalitions to topple Karzai's deeply corrupt government. By 2004, the international community had burgeoned and Kabul was full of foreigners, aid workers, private security companies and diplomats. Behind them came alcohol, arms dealing, brothels and loud parties. Roads were closed off with concrete barriers and in the streets of the Kabul district of Shar-eh-Naw, where the US private security Dyncorp company had offices, even schoolkids had to put up with the humiliation of being 'frisked' on their way home.

CHAPTER NINETEEN
THE UK HAQ EFFORT – PART II

> Periodically the British forget that you can annex land but not people. Whilst military strategy is required to occupy territory, a political strategy not reliant upon explicit military force is invariably needed to pacify and appease the population.

> WARREN, *The Fakir of Ipi*

London and Geneva, 2009

Back in Europe, I followed up with others who had played a part in Haq's last weeks. My aim was to ascertain the extent of the UK effort to promote Abdul Haq and his strategy in 2001, why it failed and the outcome of that failure. What I discovered has, I believe, major implications for our assessment of the competence of British intelligence agencies in the wake of September 11.

I had met Ken Guest briefly in Jalalabad in 2002, when he was working on the documentary for the BBC about Abdul Haq.[309] The next contact I had with Guest was in late 2008, by which time he was living in Kabul and had been involved with Afghanistan for twenty-nine years. He was described to me by Seeger as someone who:

> ... probably spent more time inside Afghanistan, living and working with the Mujahedin, than any other Western witness to that (Soviet) conflict. A sizable part of this time was with Jalaludin Haqqani, who now runs the Taliban campaign on the South Eastern border. He has also drunk tea and discussed religion with Osama bin Laden. As a result of that past, he has a first hand knowledge of not just how the ordinary Afghans thinks, but how the Taliban and Al Qaeda think and act.[310]

Jere Van Dyk who spent time with Ken Guest in 1981, while the two travelled with Jalaluddin Haqqani's front in Paktia, said of him in his excellent book about that period;

Ken was an Englishman. He had been here for four months, wandering from one guerilla group to another, in the Panjshir valley, in Kunar, Nangarhar, Logar. He was skinny like a marathon runner, with long black hair to his shoulders, a beard, gaunt features; and he wore a Soviet winter army jacket under his blanket. He had three cameras, a small cassette player, a New Testament, and a thousand stories to tell. He had been a British Royal Marine. He had not had a bath in a month.[311]

Ken Guest had served with 4 5 Commando Royal Marines, and during the 1980s he went on to make some forty-two trips into Afghanistan. After that he covered other wars in places varying from Liberia to Bosnia, Cambodia and Lebanon.

After 9/11 Guest became quickly disillusioned with what he was reading in the press. He wrote an email about Afghanistan in reply to a question by his older brother, who had served for sixteen years with the UK's Special Boat Service (SBS). Soon after, Guest received a phone call from an old acquaintance, 'RAM' Seeger, who was similarly worried and had been discussing this on the phone with Paddy Ashdown. Guest sent Seeger a copy of the email he'd sent to his brother and Seeger sent it on to Ashdown, also putting him in touch with Ken. Ashdown liked the summary and asked Guest if he could use it as a basis for an article in *The Times*.[312]

Seeger's interest in and experience of Afghanistan stemmed from the early 1980s when he had made nine trips into occupied Afghanistan in order to give training and support to the mujahideen. Seeger had commanded the SBS in the 1970s, but had since left the corps and was working as a security consultant. It was Seeger, whom Gunston had mentioned to me as having travelled with him to Jalalabad in October 2001.

Paddy Ashdown said to me of Seeger,[313] 'there should be a biography written on him'. He described Seeger as follows in his own book:

> In my first year as a senior boarder, I had been a fag for a senior boy who asked me to do none of the things normally expected of fags, such as making his bed or cleaning his shoes. Instead, I had to join

him doing PT in the backyard with a pack full of bricks on my back, or running along the banks of the River Ouse in large boots and the heaviest clothes we could find.

His name was "RAM" Seegar and he remains one of the most extraordinary men I have met. He taught me the techniques of endurance and the importance of physical fitness and an active mind.

I followed him into the Royal Marines and ended up, like him, in Borneo during the confrontation with Indonesia in the 1960s. Ram won an MC. I also followed Ram into the SBS, the Special Boat Section (now Service)'.[314]

Having aroused Ashdown's interest, Guest and Seeger decided to widen their lobbying.

Initially our lobbying aim was to make available our considerable knowledge of the country and its peoples, warn against the consequences of a blunt and over heavy approach and point out the complexities of Afghanistan. Then as soon as we became aware of Abdul Haq's intention[315] and the opportunity that this offered for a quick and effective solution, we focussed on trying to obtain support for his cause.[316]

Ashdown assisted them with meetings and the first people they met with were at an MOD central staffs intelligence cell on 21 September 2001. On the way into the first meeting, Guest says they passed a room in which there was a large wall map of Afghanistan and adjacent to it, a man standing on a ladder 'sticking red arrows' onto it. At this stage, Guest was concerned that a bombing campaign had already been decided upon. The meeting was with two staff officers, one of whom was a Marine. They had a file with some intelligence on Afghanistan. Guest nervously asked if he could know what that intelligence was. 'Of course', replied the officer and reached behind him to get it.

Writing to me in 2009, some eight years later, Guest told me:

When that file was opened and I was looking at what I was being told was the best intelligence they had at that point in time, the best insight from the furthest scout ... it still shocks me.[317]

For the 'intelligence' on Afghanistan produced at this meeting was little more than *The Times* article written by Guest himself! He added:

> We were planning to go to war and people with nothing against us [who] would die in large numbers and our youth would follow commands given in our name and die there too. And the best we had was from some former General Duties[318] Marine, who bought a camera and a one-way air ticket and went to Afghanistan and simply walked a lot and paid attention, and chance and fate led him to Haq, Haqqani, Massoud and bin Laden, and did it on invisible freelance budgets because he thought it mattered. And that source hadn't been back since 1989 and there I was being told, 12 years since I was last in Afghanistan and lacking any resources but what I recalled off the cuff ... I was being told (although they comfortably assumed it was Ashdown [who wrote the piece] as they appear to believe what they read in the press!) ... [that] I was the best they had!

Guest added:

> It was in that meeting I first proposed Abdul Haq's name ... and proposed to RAM I bring in someone I knew who had all the right credentials in social entry to ensure a very wide and senior network of contacts.[319]

That person was Sir John Wellesley Gunston and after a phone call from Guest, he came immediately to meet them in a Whitehall pub. Gunston then called Abdul Haq on his mobile, and they learnt that Haq was in Rome. And that he *already* had a plan.

A further meeting was arranged that evening in Knightsbrige, at the Special Forces club where Seeger, Guest and Gunston met with MOD staff officers to pass over the news about Haq's plan with the King. The following day, 22 September, Gunston travelled to Rome to meet with Haq. Other meetings fielded by the three, and described already to me by Gunston, were with various Tory grandees, Ming Campbell and Paddy Ashdown. Gunston's report from Rome was summarised by Seeger and sent to Ashdown, who passed it to No 10 Downing Street on 26 September, but to no avail.

Ashdown informed them that the PM had said that 'this is exactly the sort of thing that we are looking at', but that British intelligence has 'other resources'.

Guest reacted to this with disdain:

> For any well informed source it was *not* a multiple choice puzzle. *Nobody* was close to Haq in value to West and Afghanistan. If we were seriously looking at the situation this was obvious.

He added that either the PM was partially to blame: 'I strongly suspect from his determination to back the US unconditionally'.[320] A few days later the news was worse. Guest recalls:

> Paddy Ashdown called me and said, 'Ken, you must accept there has to be a fireworks display, a significant fireworks display, the Americans are demanding it and not until after the firework display can we continue the debate'.

Guest replied to Ashdown:

> Paddy, if that is to be the strategy we are to set ourselves upon, there can only be one certain casualty of this path, the death of rational debate. No good can come out of it. After the bombing begins we will not be able to have debate in any rational sense.

> This was a certain fact to me, not based on hindsight but understanding the dyanamics.[321]

> Our intelligence services were totally blind. En mass decamping to [the] USA [and] in the process ... infected with the spirit ... within the US intelligence services ... through these channels we heard such things as the 'Haq has baggage' comment which was to me a haunting call from the past ... as I knew who was speaking to me, Hamid Gul[322] .... For his voice to have carried through all the doors ... in order to reach me meant that the corridors of our intelligence services were empty, leaving the voice of ISI free passage to echo through from the 1980s. Christ, enemy were in our camps and welcomed there. It was chilling to know this.[323]

> Having seen the wall map in DIRA before the DIS meeting and the later one in the pub with DIRA I knew the absolute probability was we were going to war in Afghanistan, [with] at the very least a serious bombing campaign.

> I left the meeting in a ... state of shock ... it clearly marked the path we were edging towards, kinetic force, the trap of the secondary arena

... I knew if we went to war [in Afghanistan] in a kinetic manner we would bury people we had no need to lose, barring the results of a marriage between ignorance and arrogance and the bastard child sired by those afflictions. That child is now eight years old.[324]

At this stage, Seeger was still a little more hopeful;

After the initial MOD meeting (which was only a start) we were still hopeful - excited even, that Abdul Haq offered the way ahead and that it would be quickly picked up. It was only after Paddy came back with the comments about 'other resources' and 'Haq baggage' and no one bothered to make contact with Abdul in Rome, that we realised there was going to be an uphill battle.

Days later, Gunston returned from Rome. Guest was already committed to filming part of a series from the trenches in northern France. So Gunston and Seeger visited Peshawar from 1 to 9 October 2001. Seeger wrote:

Where we assessed Abdul Haq's plan for overthrowing the Taliban with a Pashtun field force. Before leaving (and the start of the bombing on 7 October) we submitted a modest list of requirements to the British Embassy (at their request).[325]

In further summaries of their collective thinking, Seeger explained to Ashdown et al, what Haq was attempting to do:

AQ, estimated then to be a 10,000 man private army of Arabs and Pakistanis, of which 3-4000 of which were known to be the most aggressive troops in Afghanistan and had been used as the Taliban's shock troops in their war against the northern alliance. Even if the Taliban had wanted to give up OBL, it is highly unlikely they could have done so whilst at the same time fighting the NA.[326]

It would be better, they said, for the Afghans to be the ones to defeat AQ, and if:

... Afghans were not involved at all (or only one faction used eg the Northern Alliance), an already difficult problem would be compounded as the Pashtuns (or worse still the Afghans as a whole) might close ranks against the western invader and fight with al Qaeda instead of against them.[327]

It would be a mistake, they stressed, to use the Northern Alliance to defeat the Taliban as:

> ... this would be resisted badly by the citizens of Kabul, surrounding Pashtun tribes and the Hazaras – all of whom have sufferred badly at the hands of the NA. The leaders of an inside solution must be pashtuns (the largest ethnic group – approx 44% of the population in contrast to the tajiks, the next largest group who are about 25%). While the Taliban could easily fragment (for reasons given earlier) they would be most unwilling to surrender or defect to the NA or western invaders. An adequately backed Pashtun field force would be a different matter. This could trigger large scale defections, build an alliance with the Northern tribes and facilitate the building of a widely accepted broad based government.[328]

Sadly this did not happen. In the report he made of that visit to Peshawar[329] before Haq's last entry to Afghanistan, he said of the bombing campaign:

> We have probably lost our best chance of achieving a peaceful, lasting and relatively bloodless solution. This would have been for Abdul Haq to have marched on Kabul, destroyed (mainly through defections) the Taliban and then possibly in conjunction with the Northern Alliance defeated the al Qaida Arab army.

Seeger and John Gunston left Peshawar on the 9 October, hoping to push this message in London. Seeger later wrote:

> Meanwhile no support had been given to Haq although a derisory offer of four sattelite telephones had been made by the British (Haq had already bought a large number of these in Dubai and what he really needed - and as was made clear by us in our submission[330] - was proper secure military radios). Realising that no serious help was forthcoming, Haq opted for a quixotic gesture and entered Afghanistan on October 21st from Parachinar to work with the tribal leaders and village headmen in the Azrow/Hisarak area[331]... when challenged by the Taliban border guards at Terimangul he told them who he was. The Taliban then put in large forces led by Arabs to converge on Azrow. Haq ran into these on the night of Thursday 25 October. There was some confused firing and then Haq tried talking

to a small deputation. This was joined by an arab who on hearing who Haq was, cocked his rifle and arrested him. Haq and his chief of staff Sayed Hamid were led away and shot the next day Friday 26 October in Rischoor barracks Kabul by arabs and Pakistanis. His nephew Isatullah, a bright young man of 23 who had been a great help to us in Peshawar and who had recently married into the Chitral Royal Family, was captured and shot the following Tuesday in Azrow and had his body thrown into a well.[332]

Guest, like Ritchie who had told me, 'No one can hold a candle to him', said of Haq's death:

And then … the impossible blow that Haq was dead and with his passing went out the last flaming hope for a good result. The scale of the needless tragedy was clear and yet so far hidden from common understanding it was not appreciated then and is little understood now. For me it was a moment such as I have never heard so eloquently expressed elsewhere about the coming storm of war as Sir Edward Grey on 3 August 1914. The lamps are going out all over Europe; we shall not see them lit again in our lifetime.

Seeger later summarised what had happened between September and December 2001.[333] Under the title, 'Why no attention given to Haq?', he writes,

Despite his offerring of a possible early solution, Haq never received any serious western attention. We lobbied hard on his behalf but to no avail. It seemed that Haq was distrusted or thought incapable of the task and / or other Pashtun leaders were preferred. Rumours were spread about his business interests, his involvement with Russian tarts and his penchant for insubstantial showmanship (Hollywood Haq). To anyone who knew him or had operated with him, these were absurd.[334]

Guest, commenting on these allegations and what Ashdown had said about Haq 'having baggage' said;

ISI do not indulge [in] idle gossip. We did. Anything ISI said had an agenda … So what exactly was the 'baggage' in the views expressed by ISI chief Hamid Gul in the '80s and echoing back in 2001? Haq's independence of spirit and word? When Haq's 'baggage' was put to me by Ashdown as a hurdle to advancing Haq, I did not hesitate in my response. I asked him to return to source and find out what this 'baggage' was and he would then find the charge would vanish like mist on a windy day … He called me back a couple of days later and said, 'You were right, there is nothing specific attached to the baggage allegation'. I suggested 'nothing specific' meant 'nothing at all' as if there had been a shred of support, rest assured, there would have been no hesitation in presenting it. Nobody could as it didn't exist.[335]

Such allegations were intended to promote the view that Haq should not be supported because, as Seeger concluded:

He was his own man. As a consequence he was never a favourite of the Pakistanis and perhaps for the same reason therefore of the Americans also. Yet it is precisely because of this that he had such widespread trust and pledges of support from Afghans.[336]

Seeger says somewhat ironically,

His one real failing was that he did not like to ask for anything that he thought might be refused.[337] Even worse than this disparaging of and reluctance to work with Haq was the possibility that an inside Pashtun solution was not wanted at all or thought to be unnecessary (i.e. a solution could/should be obtained by American arms and the Northern Alliance alone).[338] Or perhaps it was just a failure of the Coalition leaders to understand the complexities of the situation and the need for speed. Early backing of Haq and/or a Pushtun field force could have overthrown the Taliban without recourse to bombing. Once the bombing started it became a race against time. A strong convincing anti-Taliban Pushtun field force had to be in place before Pushtun feelings inside Afghanistan had hardened irrevocably against the coalition and/or the arrival of Northern Alliance troops at Kabul and the inevitable hardening of tensions that this would bring.[339]

As to the 'other resources' mentioned to them by Ashdown it became clear:

… that the American and British favourite was Hamid Karzai, chief of the Popalzai tribe … Although essentially a good man (who Haq might also have wanted/backed as a Premier) he was not a proven field commander with the potential to act as a counterweight to the

Northern Alliance. This was subsequently shown by his failure to capture Kandahar (despite US SF support).

Seeger's note continued:

But even if he had been able to capture Kandahar, this was hardly enough to balance the Northern Alliance. The key was Kabul and a Pashtun leader had to take this. In this respect Karzai never stood a chance, while Haq of course did.

When I asked Seeger why in his opinion so little attention had been shown to Haq, he said that he thought it was because British Intelligence just wasn't interested.

Some attempt was made to talk to Abdul, but those tasked to do so always seemed to arrive too late: just after Abdul had moved on, from Rome to Dubai, then Dubai to Peshawar. Abdul was finally seen in Peshawar by someone from the British Embassy but nothing of note came of this, apart from the derisory offer of 4 satcom telephones.

Yet significant amounts of money and support had been offered to other players whose names they seemed to have received very quickly.

Guest was more direct:

The truth is our systems were inadequate and utterly failed on intelligence. Why? How could they miss a collosus like Haq? What happened?[340]

***

I asked Guest, who explained to me that the problem in the West's battle against the Taliban was one of perception, to clarify what he meant when he spoke of the various 'generations' of warfare. For this was the bedrock of why this war was one of perception. He wrote back:[341]

1st Generation – we grapple hand to hand and batter each other with rocks.

2nd Generation – we wise up, use spears and bows to batter each other from a distance using some force delivery system.

3rd Generation – we complicate the whole thing by adding manoeuvre. Manoeuvre warfare can mean cavalry, tanks, aircraft and the mobility compounds all the problems

4th Generation is where conventional force mass (mostly 'state v state' but inclusive of civil wars and guerrilla warfare) is not confronted by an opposing state or force of a similar nature and where conventional strategy is confounded by the abstract nature of the resistance.

In 4th Generation the prime arena is psychological and the application of conventional force mass out of sync with the combat arena. Where you attempt to resolve a physiological frontline with conventional force the more force you use the worse the result can be.

This made sense, particularly when he added:

Taliban is a concept not a conventional force mass … Where we attempt to strike it with conventional means we flounder. Can this be proved? Yes. Look at the other side and reason how they achieve a better result with considerably less mass and resources. They primarily fight in [the] prime arena, mastery of the physiological front. It is a war of perception. This means our best weapon is being smart. Do you think we have been smart so far? Dis-regarding the distasteful nature of the opposing side, do you think they have fought a smart campaign? Based on results (they tend to lose tactically but win strategically, which is what matters) I would say they are very smart.

To win against an idea and a battle for perception you must have a smarter idea and the capacity to implant that as the best option. To do this effectively you must understand the local dynamics and the nature of the oppsing side. I would argue, based on how the West approaches the problem, the West do not understand the dynamics or the other side.

We … [have fallen] into [the kinetic arena] as we had that capacity and it was our 'comfort zone of understanding'. However the prime arena was not kinetic, it was psychological.[342]

As Guest, Ritchie and Abdul Haq had understood only too well, the key of Abdul Haq's message was the need to avoid resorting to kinetic warfare from the outset. For Haq knew that anything kinetic would immediately change the dynamics.

***

So what was the outcome of those decisions taken in September and October 2001? Guest remarked:

> We have been warring in Afghanistan two years longer than it took to win world war two and we are nowhere near that point Churchill described after the 'Victory at El Alamein in 1942 as 'the end of the beginning' where costly but marked achievements had been attained, the path was still rough but it was defined. [Today] we are still searching for our path and doing it without scouts.

> What does this have to do with Intelligence warfare and Afghanistan? Ponderous corporate mentality in a fast moving environment where your best arm is not kinetic, it is intelligence and flexibility. Probably because of that significant post cold war re-shuffling, where jealous bureaucrats, always the majority, ousted the field veterans. Result, slowly moving, safety seeking career seeking, career minded bureaucrats seize total control. Where the bureaucrats win we get spin .... it can be hard realising ... we've lost because of all the smoke and mirrors involved. Does it begin to sound like where we are now?

> So back tracking, British Intelligence were unable to take things on board as they were poorly informed, inflexible in motion, resistant to alternative views and comfortably corporate in mentality. Not at all the dashing image we like James Bond to be.

> If our leaders advise ... that we bomb our way through rather than think our way through we must question the wisdom and the value of such leaders and suffer the pains ... of their mistakes. Thucydides wrote, 'The state that separates its scholars from its warriors will have its thinking done by cowards and its fighting by fools'.

> In 2001 there was a far better option on the table that offered an honest and strong Afghan leader, the use of the tribes, sealing the border to prevent escapes and virtually no US footprint, other than discreet use of Special Forces as observers for report back needs. In effect an Islamic rejection of terrorism as un-islamic, exactly what we, in the West, should have been looking for and supporting.[343]

In 2001 the West advanced without proper contextual understanding … We favoured wide bombing, often wide of the mark, ever expanding US / Allies ground force deployment, installing a weak leader, resulting in no government capacity and massive corruption. What we got, is what you see now. It isn't pretty but it was all perfectly predictable, and it is the sort of thing that happens when we fail to properly consider all the options. Not ensuring we have sound strategy and full tactical support is a betrayal of trust our youth will pay for in blood.[344]

… Tactically it may have felt like victory, with things being bombed and blown up. This was the fire works display demanded at the time and as such it worked fine, merely lacking any capacity to deliver the strategic objective.

CHAPTER TWENTY

WHEN DID THE US REALLY CHOOSE KARZAI?
A PRIVATE US EFFORT TO SUPPORT ABDUL HAQ
(PART II)

> The cure was so simple. Do not rely on single source intelligence, and the US did, they relied on ISI, fundamentalists with political agendas.[345]

Geneva, July 2009

That there had already been another plan running alongside Abdul Haq's – a plan that was not just a reaction to September 11, but something that had been fostered for many months before – had by 2009 become obvious to me. The other plan was one that it seemed the Bush administration might have concocted early on with the Karzai family.

In summer 2009, I contacted James Ritchie again to clarify some issues that had arisen during the course of my research. These included the Rome process that the Ritchie brothers had largely funded, the meeting which had taken place between Haq and Massoud in July 2001 (which James Ritchie had also attended along with former US Special Envoy to the mujahideen, ex-Ambassador Peter Tomsen). I also wanted to discuss the apparent betrayal of Haq by other members of the Rome group,[346] and at what stage the US really selected Karzai as their 'man' in Afghanistan. During 2001, Karzai had apparently turned his back on Haq and the Rome process, culminating in what one former US diplomat described as the 'disgraceful two am phone call' from Khalilzad where he pressured King Zahir Shah 'to declare himself uninterested in restoration'.[347]

I also read the transcript of an interview of Joe Ritchie, who had rallied support for Haq alongside his brother James.[348] Although I had met with James Ritchie alongside Baryalai several times, after our initial interviews and prior to leaving Afghanistan, I was a little nervous about contacting him again, given the anger he had directed at me during our last interview. So I emailed James Ritchie some questions and eventually heard back from him when he returned to the US from Afghanistan. We spoke by phone in June 2009 and he told me how he had been involved with King Zahir Shah since 1996, trying to promote a Loya Jirga. Then he became involved with the Rome process.

Ritchie confirmed that he had met Abdul Haq in 1998 at a conference organised at Bonn, Germany which Ritchie had funded: 'The decision that came out of Bonn was to promote a Loya Jirga under the auspices of the King and he – Zahir Shah – would head it up'.[349] The Bonn meeting of 1998 had, according to Ritchie, come out of several other meetings of Afghan exiles including Istanbul and Frankfurt. Ritchie had been involved with them all. He was very proud of the original Bonn conference, which had 250 attendees and which he had funded.

> I made a tape [of the meeting] and had it distributed to all members of Congress. I even handed it to Hillary and Bill.

I asked about the apparent betrayal of Haq by other members of the Rome Process. Was it true that Wardak and Arsala went to Washington DC and rubbished Haq to people there after September 11?

> Yes! Absolutely they did. It was just *shameful*. I was sitting in Rome in late September 2001 at the Hotel Flumming where all the group hung out. There was a sidewalk café. I walked past Wardak and Arsala talking to a reporter. They were sat four tables behind. After they got up the reporter came and sat with me and said, 'Man what do these guys have against Haq?'

He sighed and went on:

> There was a group in Rome that betrayed Abdul Haq and Karzai was part of it. Other people were jealous of Abdul Haq's capabilities and *no one* measured up. Next, they misinformed Haq about why they were going to DC just then. 'Wardak has to close on a house deal', they said. But some days later I happened to be in the lobby of the hotel in Rome

when Wardak returned. I knew he'd been to Washington and bashed Abdul Haq, saying Rome wasn't supporting him and that he [Wardak] was in charge of the military operation [for the Rome group].

If this were true, it seemed incredible that Arsala, when I had met him in January 2005, had gone back to the family in Jalalabad, to request their assistance in getting the tribes to rally around his own re-election campaign. Had he, I wondered, really undermined Haq in Washington, as the woman from the King's group and now Ritchie were implying? Could he *really* have told people Haq was incapable of raising an army to fight the Taliban and that Wardak not Haq was the King's commander? It seemed odd, but then again I'd met plenty of Pashtuns who would all, given the chance, have been King.

Ritchie continued:

So in the lobby I said [to him], 'How did all your meetings go?' He immediately said 'I wasn't there' and turned his back on me. He didn't want to talk.

Ritchie then recounted an episode that had occurred several months before September 11.

At this stage Abdul Haq was *the* military guy of that group, The *only* man with the capability. All had agreed that. But Rahim Wardak didn't like that as he always wanted to be the commander of the Rome group. So one night Abdul Haq says, 'If you don't like my plan, you do it and make a plan yourself'. Everyone was fed up with him so they all told him, 'Yes, you do it'. But it was a joke, as he couldn't do it! The time passed, we were all sitting, meeting with Helena Malikyar and Princess Homaira. We wanted to do something quick so I asked Wardak for a deadline on his plan. Say one or two weeks. But the only thing on his mind was, 'Now I'm the Rome Commander'. He was incoherent. Every time I'd try to push him to set a deadline he just ran at the mouth. He'd never address the subject.

Ritchie sighed down the phone then said quietly, 'It was *disgraceful*!' What James Ritchie said about Wardak having been selected as military commander of the Rome group had been underpinned by a note from John Gunston. When he was in Rome on 19 October 2001, he had reported back to Seeger that he had met with Princess Homaira and Fatima Gailani.[350] Both ladies had told him that Abdul Haq – and by implication not Rahim Wardak nor anyone else – should be supported as the 'King's man' in the field. But they also told Gunston they believed the US were already supporting Hamid Karzai.

After that James had returned to Peshawar and eventually Afghanistan. Bud McFarlane, former Reagan-era National Security Advisor, had facilitated a lot of meetings for the Ritchie brothers in Washington and was assisting them in their lobbying effort. Ritchie said. 'He had good contacts in Washington, the CIA, etc.' Was the CIA, I wondered, the main block? 'That's my opinion. Yes'. Ritchie said.

A major issue of interest was the meeting between Haq and General Massoud in Hoja Baudin. 'Massoud's place outside Dushanbe', James said, confirming that he had been there, even filming and taping the meeting. When I asked whether he thought, given what had happened in 1991 when Massoud had broken the agreement between the mujahideen not to go into Kabul, whether Massoud would have kept his word, James said:

> I can't answer that. In the meeting we had with Massoud I asked him three times, one after the other, why we should think he'd continue to work on this thing in a joint effort. Each time he gave an answer that I didn't think was satisfactory like, 'I'm working with Dostum', when a month earlier he'd attacked Dostum. Then Tomsen, who was also there, got mad at me for asking him so many times.

Evidently James had been irritated by Peter Tomsen. Confused about why Tomsen was there and just who had organised the meeting with Massoud, I asked Ritchie to elaborate.

> Look, Abdul Haq had organised this meeting.[351] It's very ironic. There's a whole lot to this meeting. I believe Karzai had gone to see Massoud *before* this. Tomsen and Kayum Karzai had come to see me in Colorado. I contacted Peter [Tomsen] and said I should be involved in their attempts to do a Loya Jirga. But Abdul Haq had already had a

meeting with Massoud which he'd had to postpone once. I convinced Abdul Haq he should come talk to Peter at my place in Colorado. Kayum Karzai also came.

'What role did he play? I asked.

That's the key question! Tomsen wanted to bring Kayum Karzai. He wanted to 'start' something; I don't know. Tomsen said jokingly, 'Let's start the Meeker process'.

'Meeker?' I said.

That's where I live in Colorado. Abdul Haq was going to see Massoud so Peter said, 'We should all go together'. Abdul Haq was smart enough to realise there was more to this. Finally he says, 'OK, you guys can come'. Then they said, 'We can't come as you're going'. Abdul knew they were playing a game, which they were. Tomsen was *already* friends with Karzai.

When I asked Ritchie why he thought Tomsen should be supporting the Karzai family, he said:

It's like…. …these guys [diplomats] don't know *anything* about these people. If they're so easily graceful with them its like, 'It's okay, *they're* the people'.

The phone crackled but he went on:

So Tomsen tries to get Abdul to postpone the meeting. Abdul finally agreed to re-do the meeting but was not happy. So we set it up for Peter [Tomsen] and Kayum to come. I got to Washington. We had to get Uzbek and Tajik visas. The night before we're going Kayum says, 'I can't go. Someone pulled the plug on my fridge. I have to stay and sort out all the food in my restaurant'.[352] So when we get to Dubai and meet Abdul in a taxi, he says 'What happened to Kayum? Someone steal a steak or something?' At this, I heard Ritchie snigger and say, 'I had to laugh'.

When I wondered out loud what was the relevance of this Ritchie said:

I think Karzai had *already* made a deal with the US at this point *and* with Massoud. He wanted to send Kayum to make sure Haq didn't do a deal with Massoud behind his back. So Karzai had a plan. Probably with the Bush administration by this point. Only thing that matters is whose is the plan with the big guy?

'The big guy?' I asked.

Khalilzad. He and Karzai were buddies and they cut Abdul Haq out. I think they'd been working on something with Massoud. They cut Abdul Haq out. They did [that] *all* the way".

'Who?' I asked. 'The CIA?' Ritchie answered:

I assume. It's a very dark prism. He paused, then said, 'The stuff I'm telling you is first hand'.

CHAPTER TWENTY-ONE

ABDUL HAQ AND CIA STRATEGY IN AFGHANISTAN

The State that separates its scholars from its Warriors
will have its thinking done by cowards, and its fighting by fools.

THUCYDIDES

Abdul Haq's story is important because it is symptomatic of a wider
– and in many ways more important – story. This was hinted at in
Whitney Azoy's tribute piece in November 2001:

> Back to 'maybe he was, maybe he wasn't'. If Abdul Haq wasn't actively
> supported by the United States, why wasn't he? Because he was too
> independent? Because our Pakistani 'allies' didn't trust him – as, with
> excellent reason, he didn't trust them? Or perhaps because our own
> planners didn't think of it first? Our Afghanistan planners haven't
> been too good at their task for quite some time...[353]

The USA's 'Afghanistan planners' were, of course, the CIA.
Although there are numerous intelligence outfits that make up the
US government – so many in fact that 'they operate in an anarchy
of chaos, competition and disunity'[354] – it was primarily the CIA
who were responsible for the failure to recognise the value of what
Abdul Haq's 'Afghan Solution' represented.

In many ways the squandering of the opportunity that Haq
could have provided, and the suppression of the warnings he had
made reflects a continuation of the CIA's policy in the region since
the 1980s.

For example when I had asked Guest to clarify whether Kaplan
had been correct in asserting that Haq's performance with Reagan
had been instrumental in the procurement for the mujahiddeen of
stinger missiles, his reply said much about what was wrong with
CIA policy during the anti-Soviet jihad. Initially he referred to

281

Charlie Wilson's War, which had recently enjoyed huge success as a book and film in the US.

> I really enjoyed *Charlie Wilson's War* as entertainment, the relationship depicted between Wilson and the CIA was priceless. Is it history? No …

> In the film, Charlie Wilson was pushing for Stingers for Massoud. And yet, at the time Massoud was not favoured by US/CIA and remained in that sad state of neglect by them through to the end of 1989. The same barrier to understanding his value applied to Haq and the barrier was a two bar gate, ISI agendas and CIA lack of understanding; a result of their bunkered down Fort Apache approach, in the rear with the beer and wholly reliant on secondary sources, the prime part of which was ISI.

> Abdul certainly wanted Stingers, but not being favoured by CIA, he was not recognised as an outstanding commander and so not supplied with them…. as far as Milton 'Milt' Beardon, CIA Head of Station 1986–91, was concerned, Abdul Haq was not the finest Pashtun guerilla commander of the war, the *only* Pashtun commander to evolve into the secondary phase of guerilla warfare (mobility), the *only* one to have strategic reach to his planning, the commander of the most *spectacular* operations: destruction of the 40th Army Ammunition Dump at Karga, blowing up of the power lines to Kabul, attack on the Sarobi damn – every bit as daring as the Hollywood WWII film *The Guns of Navarone*. To Milt, Abdul Haq was nothing more than a simple, minor Commander. Less in fact; to Milt he was 'Hollywood Haq'. It was long Milt's proud boast that he coined that ignorant view, one he delighted in repeating *ad nauseam* to journalists. Having a grassroot view rather than a gin glass view of what was really going on inside Afghanistan, I have always felt the view expressed by Milt was not only inaccurate, it was profoundly distasteful and damaging to mujahideen needs.

> Milt and his like were so blind, they did not take what Haq had to say seriously. Abdul certainly wanted Stingers and had a good idea how best to use them as well. He argued he would not waste them in ones and twos all over the mountains, he wanted to deploy them where they could do the most harm, in and around Kabul airport, making every hit not only painful but highly visible. He was right.[355]

Guest was not the only journalist to have noticed that the CIA seemed to rely almost exclusively on the ISI for their intelligence. Robert Kaplan recalls a visit to Kandahar in 1988, when he discusses seeing Soviet aircraft – at that stage supposed to have taken hits from the mujahideen and departed – still flying in and out. He was confused because US intelligence reports from Islamabad continued to put out reports that, 'heavy mujahideen presence' had deterred all enemy aircraft from landing or taking off from Kandahar airport during the entire period of my visit'.[356] Kaplan asked whom the Americans were relying on for their information, and said, 'I was stunned to learn it was their liaison in ISI'.

Possibly Kaplan was 'stunned' because he knew that the ISI's strategic objectives for Afghanistan were not the same as those of the US. ISI was, he says:

> ... intent on creating a fundamentalist Afghanistan in Zia's image, wanted Kandahar to fall only if the credit and the spoils could go to commanders like Hekmatayar and Rasul Sayyaf (the leader of another fundamentalist mujahideen party that, like Hekmatayars, depended on outside support and was thus easily manipulated by ISI).[357]

Kaplan concludes:

> The awful truth seemed to be that the only sources of information the United States had about the fighting in Kandahar, and anywhere else in Afghanistan during the later stage of the war, were there own satellite photographs and what ISI chose to tell them.[358]

Other journalists covering Afghanistan during the 1980s were also critical. Peter Jouvenal told me:

> The Americans did and still do favour Hikmatyar . Even as recently as last year [2008], the CIA tried to weedle Hikmatyar into the present government. During the 1980s, and until the election of Benazir's widower, Asif Ali Zadari, the US listened too much to Pakistan. It was this blind obediance by the Americans to the ISI and support for Hizb-i-islami [Hikmatyar] which in my view contributed to 9/11. The attitude [of the Americans] was very short-term in the 1980s, very much 'let's get even for Vietnam'. Because the US didn't really care long-term, [they] encouraged the Arabs to come as thought it would give more legitimacy to the jihad.

In a book which has been as under-recognised as it was prescient, John Cooley[359] discusses the 'devastating consequences for world peace' of CIA support for radical Islam. Cooley notes that by 1988, Sayyaf had built a huge Arab-funded development near Peshawar to house forty thousand[360] people. He adds that this opulent lifestyle depended on the largesse of ISI and President Zia al-Haq (and ultimately the CIA, which, he says was unable to control the flow of its funds until after the death in a plane crash of ISI Chief General Akhtar and President Zia in 1988, in other words, as the jihad was ending and the Russians leaving.[361]

So, given that the CIA had apparently ignored, undermined and even interfered with Abdul Haq's plan, the question remains what *was* the strategy used by the CIA in Afghanistan after September 11? Afghan analyst Barnett Rubin throws some light on this when he says that in National Security Council (NSC) deliberations between Bush and the NSC on how to respond to September 11, the single focus was:

> ... the type of intelligence and military operations that would destroy al Qaeda and the Taliban regime. When the talk dealt with Afghan actors, the only questions were whether they would fight the Taliban and al Qaeda.[362]

As with Iraq, Rubin says there was no mention of post-war scenarios.[363]

Ironically, while Abdul Haq was meeting defecting Taliban commanders in Peshawar, the CIA were planning their own assault on Afghanistan. Rubin relates how on Saturday September 15, President Bush met with his war cabinet at Camp David. There, the CIA Director George Tenet presented the CIA's plan for striking terrorist bases and overthrowing the Taliban with a combination of air power and Special Operations. A week later Tenet was: 'planning the alliance of Afghan forces that would make this a US-assisted Afghan operation against foreign occupiers'.[364] Within three days of September 11, the CIA were already planning a bombing campaign. This was still ten days before Guest would see the wall map with its red arrows at the MOD in London.

Further tactics – such as 'buying off' Northern Alliance warlords – are revealed in published accounts by veteran CIA operatives. For example, Gary Shroen[365] recounts how in late September 2001, he carried $3 million USD in cash into the Panjshir valley, meeting with Engineer Arif, Massoud's intelligence chief. Shroen informed Arif of the US intention to overthrow the Taliban, although 'officially' President Bush was awaiting a response to his ultimatum that they give up bin Laden. Shroen then explained to Arif that, in order to act as:

> ... an honest broker in a post-Taliban Afghanistan ... the US would disburse money directly to commanders ... The CIA would control funding and arming [of] commanders separately through small CIA teams to assure that Afghans followed a strategy made in Washington.[366]

Yet CIA operatives like Schroen failed to foresee how their initial empowerment of these strongmen would soon become a runaway horse. For, as Rubin adds, 'these were only a few of the figures whom these funds and arms empowered more effectively than any election'.

Shroen gave Arif $500,000 USD cash and told him to stress to Fahim that much more money was available for purely military purposes. The following day Shroen met General Fahim and gave him $1 million. Schroen then travelled to Charikar where he gave $100,000 to Sayyaf. A few days later, the CIA's Counter Terrorist Centre delivered a further $10 million. Shroen says he left the four cardboard boxes containing the cash in a corner of the office that Arif gave him and he and Arif later had a 'good laugh' when Shroen gave Arif $22,000 for two trucks of helicopter fuel that somehow never materialised.[367]

Rubin says, 'The amount of cash given to commanders by the CIA in this manner ultimately amounted to several hundred million dollars'. The commanders, Rubin adds, changed the dollars quickly into local currency because the value of the US dollar sank as the local Afghani currency was flooded with CIA cash. The dollars' deflation became an incentive for these commanders to turn it into profitable investment. With the price of opium so high after the Taliban's recent ban, these Northern Alliance commanders quickly recycled the money into loans to farmers to finance the next spring's poppy crop.[368] Arif then built a four story house which looked like the kitsch marble mansion of a Pakistani drug dealer and which I had seen when undertaking election monitoring in the Panjshir. But this was small fry when compared to General Fahim's investment in numerous properties and a $30 million gold market in Kabul.

James Ritchie said to me of Fahim, 'by 2004 the IRI[369] told an Afghan friend of mine that he had accumulated $1 billion in wealth. $500 million in cash and another $500 million in business interests. Now he looks to be the next Vice President. I have personally seen him confiscate millions in real estate from our foundation.[370]

Meanwhile Sayyaf was in a large villa in Paghman, just west of Kabul where he ruled the district with his private militia, seized land and sent raiders into western Kabul, as he had during the early 1990s when he had apparently played a key role in the Afshar massacre. Today, he was still terrorising both locals and rivals alike. He had also, I learnt from British Embassy staff in January 2001, broken through Taliban front lines against the wishes of the coalition in order to storm into Kabul. Later, he continued to have his rocket launchers aimed on the city.

Ironically, back in September 2001 in Washington DC, the day before Schroen's arrival in Afghanistan, the State Department were demanding receipts from the King's group for a few thousand dollars. Yet, in the Panjshir, as described by Shroen himself, Afghanistan's future was playing out on a very different and utterly unaccountable trajectory. The interesting thing though about Schroen's account is how consistent the book is with previous accounts written by ex-CIA operatives, such as those of Beardon. This consistent misinformation – as Guest told me[371] – indicates why the past thirty years of CIA policy in the region have ultimately failed. For example, Schroen recounts that Abdullah Abdullah was aware that Abdul Haq was in contact with people in Washington. Shroen says:

Abdul Haq had always opposed Massood and the Tajiks. His popularity with key officials at the State Department and within the NSC was troubling, because he would certainly be pressing the same negative line about holding the Tajiks back from Kabul and focusing on the Pashtun south.[372]

Either ignorance or plain mischief must account for what Shroen says next:

Abdullah was convinced that if he could visit Washington to meet with senior policy makers, he would be able to clearly articulate the political policies of the Northern Alliance and, he hoped, reduce the distrust and fears of those who did not understand Afghanistan and its tortured history of these last twenty-plus years. I agreed that his visit to Washington was important.

Here the CIA infer – rather bizarrely – that Abdul Haq 'already' had support in DC and that they had to 'fight' to get support for the Northern Alliance route. He also thoroughly discounts the unpopularity of the Northern Alliance given their role in the inter-factional fighting of the early 1990s that laid waste to Kabul and made the countryside as insecure as it is today. His assertion that Haq already had support also conflicts with the many accounts given of US policy: from National Security Council reports, to the accounts of the Ritchies, to that of the former Reagan National Security Advisor, Bud McFarlane, who had been lobbying for Haq in Washington DC since well before September 11.

Critically, Shroen unwittingly shows that the CIA had failed to appreciate the need for a genuine Pashtun response to September 11. Instead he parrots the taunts of his colleague, Milton Beardon, when describing Haq and the Ritchie effort:

Within the CIA he became known as 'Hollywood Haq' and from then on, he did all his fighting with his mouth. He played no role in the mujahideen interim government of 1992 to 1996, so I thought that the effort to try to build him into a political figure who could challenge the Taliban was a waste of time. Haq had no tribal base of support to which he could attach himself (unlike Hamid Karzai, whose roots in the Tarin Kowt area north of Kandahar were strong and deep).

I predicted that if Abdul Haq moved into the Jalalabad area without an established base, he would be killed by the Taliban. Now that scenario was being played out in deadly earnest.

Here Schroen not only discounts Haq's leadership as 'the' foremost Pashtun commander,[373] he also twists the reason why Haq had honourably quit Kabul in 1992, as well as thoroughly discounting the role Haq had played in the Rome Process in the years leading up to September 11. It is bizarre that he makes so much of Hamid Karzai's roots in Tirin Kot because – although Hamid Karzai's father, Ahad, was well thought of – Hamid was not a well known figure during the jihad or nationally.

Guest had this to say of CIA management of the Soviet-Afghan War:

> The CIA was trusted with monitoring the Soviet Afghan War at close quarter, but was happy to … do nothing even marginally beyond the norm, accepting as gospel all that ISI told them. This betrayed the trust of the true heroes of the Afghan-Soviet War, among whom Abdul Haq, that they would rise to the needs of the hour, and do everything in their power to ensure the men doing the fighting and the dying were fully and properly supported … In my view, having spent time where the dying was done, that was a betrayal of trust not only to the men doing the dying, the Afghans, but also of the essential needs of the US to watch and learn, in order to increase their understanding of regional dynamics on the ground. This failure is where the root of all our present troubles are embedded. It mattered then and it matters now that we understand the dynamics. Incredibly, CIA contributed nothing to that understanding. In my view, that was a failure that set the path towards the future we now endure. If the lesson is not learned nothing changes.
>
> … [Yet] the cure was so simple. Do not rely on single source intelligence, and the US did, they relied on ISI, fundamentalists with political agendas.[374]

One of the prime examples of the CIA's failure to accurately report the actuality of key events occurring inside Afghanistan at the height of the anti-Soviet war was the issue – which I have already recalled – of the Qarga operation. In the documentary on Haq, *Afghan Warrior*,

Malcolm Brinkworth, the presenter, asked Beardon about the attack on Qarga dam. Who was the commander? Guest, who was behind the camera filming, recalls:

> Milt had no idea at all. He blustered that it was important, that lots of people claimed credit, that it did not matter. Actually it did matter. He had described this event as the most important thing in his career, it had occurred soon after his arrival as CIA head of station in Islamabad and he said he was showered with congratulatory messages and lorded as the hero of the hour. He said it 'made me'. And as the head of CIA station, charged with understanding the war and accurately reporting it and advising upon it, with all the funds and resources at his disposal (the largest ever American 'covert' operation) surely, who was the brilliant young Mujahead Commander in charge of the operation was worth knowing. A man to mark as one to support. People inside Afghanistan knew the name of the Commander, every Pashtun boasted about it as the Commander was Pashtun. That man was Abdul Haq. The man Milt beastly claimed credit for dubbing 'Hollywood Haq'. The man so denigrated, repeatedly, by Beardon. The man ISI did not like.[375]

Guest had written a book in 1996 naming Abdul as the commander[376] and told me: 'Yet in 2002, Milt *still* had no idea'.[377] This assertion is supported by Beardon's own book,[378] where he says dismissively of the Qarga operation:

> I never did find out who launched the attack – a dozen commanders insisted they were responsible – so I just decided to believe all or all or none of their claims. Kharga was smoking, and the mujahideen had a hundred new heroes. That was enough for me".

Guest added;

> Later, the interview done and as the camera kit was being packed away, I casually asked Beardon, if he might have the telephone number of a man named Hamid Gul. Beardon rattled out the number off the top of his head. It confirmed to me what I expected it to, for there was nothing chance about the asking. It betrayed, that Beardon was, apparently, still in steady communication with Hamid Gul. It was exactly what I expected to hear and was useful to know.[379]

CHAPTER TWENTY-ONE

On this fact, Guest noted:

> Of interest to me was the suggestion that in 2001, with panic the order of the day … [the] CIA turned to their former 'experts' of the region, like Beardon, for advice. And having not paid much attention when they had the opportunity they had very little to contribute other than seeking the views of their prime source before: ISI. The could be cause enough to have Beardon calling Hamid Gul often enough between Sept 2001 and 2002 to be able to rattle out his phone number off the top of his head in 2002 despite not having been deployed to the region since early 1989.

Guest, like most journalists covering the jihad, knew that Hamid Gul, despite no longer being ISI chief, in reality remained very influential on 'policy'.

Guest had met Gul during the course of filming the Haq documentary. He said of him:

> Now, although I do not agree with his political view (dressed up as Islamic ideals), there was no doubt that Hamid was a very intelligent man. More than able to run rings around Milt whilst standing on one leg blindfolded and juggling hand grenades, and, of course he did that during the Soviet-Afghan War.

> During the Soviet-Afghan War, and repeated now, we allowed reliance on systems that lacked practical understandings to work through the Afghan puzzle. As a result, lacking sure foundations to set a viable strategy upon, we now largely rely on kinetic force to bomb our way out. That this is a strategy of desperation is not lost to the opposing force and affords them outstanding propaganda value. Result: where once there were clear paths through the maze, the way out is now far more complicated. To escape, we need less kinetic force and more scouts.

It was possibly this type of gullibility by the CIA which had led to the border problems I had witnessed at the Durand Line, when in 2003 Pakistan began making incursions onto Afghan territory, supported by the Americans.[380]

Moreover, despite the assertions of Schroen and the CIA about the worthlessness of Haq, their opinion failed to appreciate the wider dynamics of the USA's post-September 11 engagement in Afghanistan. Yet others – not just the Ritchies, Guest, Seeger and Gunston – had foreseen the problems. In the November 2001 tribute to Haq, veteran US diplomat and writer, Whitney Azoy had declared, and some might now admit, with tremendous prescience

> Only by such efforts as Abdul Haq's – this much is increasingly, glaringly clear – can US objectives be achieved in the nexus of Afghan national power south of the Hindu Kush. Bombing can't. US troops can't. Northern Alliance troops (non-Pashtuns) can't. Turkish troops (ethnically more akin to the hated Northern Alliance Uzbeks) can't. Only the Pashtuns themselves – the groups from which the Taliban sprang and which now harbour Osama bin Laden – can get this job done.[381]

***

Joe Ritchie was also interviewed for the documentary, *Afghan Warrior*, in 2003 and in this he says more about the Rome group, and what the Ritchies and Abdul Haq had been doing, as regards formulating an alternative plan to finish the Taliban, in the run up to September 11. It also shows Joe Ritchie's view of the CIA and their role.

Joe began by saying that he and his brother had wanted to do something to help Afghans get out of 'the twenty-five years of hell' they had suffered. The key was, as far as they were concerned, to find an alternative to the both the Taliban and the Northern Alliance warlords.

> The Taliban was bad but not necessarily worse than warlords. The Afghan people were capable of kicking the Taliban out given an alternative which hadn't been given to them. The former King, because his name was gilt-edged, and because he was associated with a much better time, and was known to be a guy who was not power hungry and that actually kept the tribal balance ... was the potential ... alternative if he could be gotten into play.[382]

So the Ritchies worked on the King and on the concept of Loya Jirga. During the process Joe also got to know Haq and soon appreciated the need for a military component to the plan. Haq was, he said, 'The key guy there who was capable of ... putting together the commanders that were needed to make this militarily playable'. He had 'instantly connected' with Haq.

> As I got to know him I realised the dimensions of this guy that he was extremely brilliant, sophisticated, liberal in a good kind of way ... gentle, sensitive ... and he had a leadership ability that he could bring Afghans together ... Afghans are extremely fractious people, this was a man that could bring Afghan commanders together ... because commanders are even more fractious and he just led by virtue of the fact that he was the man with the vision and everybody realised this, he never pushed himself forward, he just ... was present and ... would wind up leading whatever group he was in by virtue of ... of his merits.

Even before they had the King in play, Haq had taken a trip in early 2001 to Peshawar and realised that the Taliban had only weak support then in Afghanistan. He said to Joe, 'This fruit is ready to be picked, the Taliban can be taken out now'.

At this stage Joe said that because of Haq's assets (in terms of commanders who knew and trusted him), there was the potential to go in with or without the King's help.

> This was a man who – in a situation where it was virtually impossible not to have baggage – this was the man whose hands were clean. He said to me at one time, 'I would favour a trial at the Hague of all the people involved in this, and I'll be the first one to go stand trial.

Joe talked of Haq's integrity and how this had led to the murder of his wife and son in Peshawar 'after it became known he was involved in the Loya Jirga concept'.

In the years and months prior to September 11, the Ritchie brothers had – with Bud McFarlane – brought Haq's plan to the attention of The White House, the State Department, the CIA and the Defence Department.

To lay out who Abdul Haq was, well they knew that pretty well already, but what his plan was, who the people, what the network was that he had available both inside and outside the Taliban, inside and outside Afghanistan, a lot of these people were in Peshawar, a lot were in Europe, a lot were in the US, a lot were inside Afghanistan ... Thinking that ... when they saw a network like this that they would be pretty eager to find a way to help out. ... prior to 9/11 they just couldn't seem to focus on that enough to actually want to do anything and then post 9/11, they wanted to do it another way.

Jo Ritchie said of Haq's ability:

... this guy was a master at slipping into a place and setting up, er, contacts, sources, ah plants ... at totally demoralising an enemy ... he'd rather have a hundred guys up against ten thousand, but where the ten thousand knew that among them, there were some guys who were on the other side but they didn't know who they were ... he had a sense for that kind of warfare and ... he would create a sense of momentum and inevitability that ... would make an enemy feel defeated. Long before it was technically defeated ...

But sadly:

There were some people who would, we're talking pre 9/11 now, who recognised this to be a wonderful thing ... but ... it wasn't their job to make it happen. The group that was in charge of making it happen, the CIA, had this problem with Abdul Haq ... [they said] 'This wasn't a man you could count on to stay on message' ... There were times when he'd stood up and told the truth in spite of the fact that they didn't want him to say those things. [So] they accused him of being 'Hollywood Haq'. I mean, this was the least Hollywood guy you ever met, I mean when he did get in the press incidentally, he did it at my insistence, for our people in Washington had finally said, I mean, he went to Peshawar and no press knew he was there, everything was totally under cover until finally the people in Washington said, 'Your're never going to get any help from them unless he goes public', and I called him and said, 'Abdul you gotta go public'. Basically the problem was, he wasn't a totally reliable puppet.

Joe explained how he had persaded Haq to come to Rome in order to persuade the King's group to sign onto the Haq Plan.

> The King and the folks around him, his executive committee, recognised that nothing was happening, nothing had happened for years, there was nothing on the horizon that was going to happen, with one exception. Abdul Haq had a plan.

Haq went to Rome and went through his plans with the King's Executive Committee, at the end of which, after they had grilled him with questions, he asked them whether 'they' had an alternative. They did not.

> So they unanimously voted to back what he was doing and … that's when the King, after twenty, almost thirty years in exile, signed onto something that … were maybe some people were going to get hurt which I think he didn't like at all, but, he recognised it was the only hope for his country, and so he, and the executive committee signed onto Abdul Haq's plan.

With this two-pronged strategy – Haq and the King – now in hand, the Ritchie brothers assumed people in Washington would take an interest.

> But it just didn't happen, I mean there was still the same lack of willingness to actually step in and help out … and so by late July [2001] or early August, Abdul was saying to me, 'Joe, save your time, save your energy, it's not going to work … we're just going to have to do it on our own'.

Within weeks the terrible thing, the 'cataclysmic event for the West' predicted by Haq back in 1991, happened. On the morning of September 11, Joe Ritchie and Bud McFarlane were due to meet the Secretary of State for South Asia. The meeting was cancelled and Joe Ritchie went to Rome, 'to encourage the King to get into play, which he did'. Joe then returned to DC:

> … thinking that now we were in essence at war, it shouldn't be a problem to get people to focus, on this [problem] of knocking off the Taliban … The problem then was that … they wanted to do it in their own way, without help from Abdul Haq.

At this point, Joe Ritchie said, he felt like a guy walking down the street seeing some men trying to break into a safe:

> ... and I happen to have the key ... and say, 'here's the key' ... how could you have a more golden opportunity to take something that's been prepared for years and served up on a platter ... people can't possibly ignore it ... But apparently the obvious fact is that the CIA didn't work with the man who couldn't be relied on to say exactly what they wanted, I mean ... this guy was too courageous, this was a man who would stand up and, if things were being done too wrong ... there's a risk he would say it publicly ... that one risk was just too great for them to deal with ...

Brinkworth asked Joe Ritchie just who in the US had recognised Haq's potential.

> I think people in the White House did recognise it ... I think people at Central Command recognised it ... but ... It's not their job to pick, I mean, it's the CIA's job to pick who we're going to work with.

But after Haq's death, the Ritchies had contact with Central Command.

> Because we explained that there were still a huge number of extremely courageous competent capable men in the field that weren't being talked to at all, they ... talked to us. And we found the uniform men terrific patriots, the right attitude, the right will, I thought they had it all correct, but again, they don't make those choices, those choices are made somewhere else and ... its basically CIA people making those choices and they're the ones who, I think, stopped the train from going down that track ... because the partners down that track weren't necessarily totally buyable.

Like James, Joe Ritchie explained how the commanders had been due to gather in Rome for a meeting that had been scheduled prior to September 11. The call had gone out in August but many had visa problems getting there and so proceeded in dribs and drabs.

> They were overtaken by events and, so instead of being able to do this on a schedule that they had worked out, Haq felt he had to get back quickly, and he went to Peshawar in late September by himself. They couldn't all follow because they had visa problems so they followed

piecemeal later on, and he headed to Peshawar and began collecting the ... local folks there to go ahead with the ... so he had to go ahead on a hurried basis. He didn't really have the time to get everybody in place because he felt he needed to get there fairly quickly to prevent the Northern Alliance taking over Kabul and leaving Afghanistan with a long-term problem.

Joe continued trying to get help from Washington: 'but we kind of ran out of luck there'. Haq told Joe to give up saying they weren't going to get help from there:

> ... but I thought if we could get something so small as a helicopter ride across the border ... we don't need any weapons, don't give us any money, no material supplies but if you can give Haq and a few guys a helicopter ride across the border, if you can take weapons that he has purchased in Peshawar and just drop them ... at a given point ... [That would] increase his chances of pulling this off, but it didn't work out.

At this stage Abdul Haq was in Peshawar and meeting with key members of the Taliban.

> His compound was 'Grand Central Station' in Peshawar. There were Afghan commanders from Peshawar, from Pakistan and from Afghanistan, but there were also these Taliban commanders who would sneak out of the country, come in and work out the arrangements and the understandings and ... be given a satellite phone and they'd go back in and so they were in pace ready to defect at the appropriate moment ... that's one of the reasons the East fell easily ... I think without a shot being fired, when his network started barking the signals ... after like the day the Northern Alliance moved in Kabul.

> He had to get in, with almost no one with him and virtually no arms, and first get a foothold, its like, you know, a beachhead, he had to get that done before he got snuffed out.

Joe said that it was he who had encouraged Haq to do the interviews in Peshawar on his strategy.

> The strategy was simply that, it finally encouraged him to do that on the grounds that my advice ... in Washington was ... it was the only way we were going to get the Americans to focus on him ...

Jo added that a couple of 'agency' guys in Peshawar were:

> ... amazed at ... what he had built up as far as a following and a network and ... they were totally bewildered at why he, why someone in Washington wasn't reaching out a hand to help him.

When Brinkworth asked if there was a real level of ignorance in the CIA about who the players were, Joe said.

> You know, let me distinguish between inside and outside the CIA. Within the CIA its hard to imagine that they, they couldn't have known who the players were ... But I think it was that knowledge that kept them going the way they were going. They knew who could ... who the ... who the whores were and who ... who the men of stature were and didn't want the men of stature. Outside the CIA, I think there was the problem of not knowing enough about the players, because if they had known more, the ... folks in the White House for example, and in some other places, I think they would have put some pressure on the CIA to use these guys. That was my sense of it, that when you got to the CIA guys, they ... knew who the players were and they didn't, and they wanted the guys they could buy, when you got outside the CIA they were less knowledgeable and then they would say, well the CIA guy tells us that Abdul Haq's got baggage. Ah. And they, they didn't want to pick a fight, you know, they didn't want to go twist the arm of the CIA ... whose responsibility it was to make these calls.

Regarding the final chat with ISI:

> We weren't expecting any help from them ... we figured that they were likely to try to betray him when he went in ... we knew that they had been continuing to supply the Taliban with weapons.

At the end of the day the Brits 'offered' Abdul Haq four satellite phones. The Ritchies had given him sixty, which were being spread to Taliban commanders. He was offered four by the Americans, which Joe Ritchie said:

> ... he respectfully declined, that was one thing he didn't need, and he assumed that was probably offered so that they could track him more easily ...

> Abdul Haq is the symbol of giving Afghanistan back to the people. Massoud is the symbol of giving it back to the Tadjiks ... to the Panjshiris.

297

> He [Haq] said the bombing rallied people to supporting the Taliban, it meant people came in from outside [mostly Pakistanis] to fight on side of Taliban who had not been there. But once it was viewed as an American action it made it a lot tougher from the standpoint of real Afghans that wanted their country back ... as now there was this split feeling about who were the good guys and the bad guys

> He thought it was a mistake ... because the country could have been taken back by the Afghans and that was the real problem. Had they been allowed to do it, and it wouldn't have taken long to find out whether they could or not, if they couldn't, then then go back to the bombing plan but ... if it could have been taken by this indigenous movement, then you had an Afghanistan in the hands of real Afghan patriots who believed in a broad-based multi-ethnic government. And if you weren't willing to let that happen then you would up with, well, what we wound up with. And that's why it was terribly important and that's why he was in such a hurry to get in there and, ah, give the men a chance to do this.

After Haq's death, with his guys already inside Afghanistan armed with sattelite phones, Ritchie reiterated what I had heard from Gunston and Guest about Haq's commanders in the South (which again demonstrated as 'false' the claims made in the British press that MI6 had somehow engineered the fall of the south).

> They were in place, ready to go ... he unfortunately got killed before the whole thing got rolling but they were still there, and they proceeded to take huge chunks of land, this wasn't widely reported but it's all there on the record ... the whole east, which was his, the kind of core of his home territory, fell without a shot being fired ... as far as I know, all the way from Sirobi clear to the border, which blocked the NA from coming further east, and then the first major town to the south, Ghazni, was taken by one of the men in his network, Ahrif Shah Jehan, a guy armed with a satellite phone and ten thousand dollars cash total to get the job done, but this was the guy that was the leader of the Hazaras ... in Ghazni province, and so ... these men, it was like he had said would happen. They stood up and took huge swathes of territory with very little fighting after his death.

CHAPTER TWENTY-TWO
CONCLUSIONS AND WAYS FORWARD

The USA betrayed Haq, by pretending to the outside that they'd supported him, but of course Haq was a nationalist and so they decided Karzai was the one.[383]

MEMBER OF THE AFGHAN ROYAL FAMILY

Abdul Haq's importance is that of a visionary. For he provided answers to the questions that the West is only now – after nine years in Afghanistan – beginning to pose. He was also a leader with a history of excellence in asymmetric warfare who was able to bring disparate groups together - even from across the ethnic divide – while not seeking a position for himself. These are qualities that those charged with running the Afghan conflict today are challenged to find, as they struggle to find an alternative to Hamid Karzai.

I have written this book not just as the account of a dispassionate observer of the post-September 11 conflict, but in an attempt to show why Abdul Haq's plan still matters. And why it ought to be informing the West's Afghanistan Strategy today.

The book has also shown how our own political masters, intelligence agencies and military strategists committed the West to an unwinnable war in a country that has repelled foreign invaders for centuries. They did so despite the fact that an alternative to war existed. They also did so seemingly in ignorance of the history and culture of Afghanistan, of the region and of the key players likely to be involved.

In contrast to the approach the West chose to adopt, Haq's 'solution' *did* include all parties,[384] did *not* rely on an imposed occidental-style central government with an 'Afghan National Army' to back it up, but rather on agreements between tribes. It would also have provided a Pashtun alternative to Pakistan's favoured warlord, Hikmatyar and to the Taliban. Ironically for Pakistan, not supporting Haq was actually an 'own goal' since he had never been a Pashtun Nationalist pushing for an independent Pashtunistan with a re-configuration of the Durand Agreement. In short, Abdul Haq had the potential to provide the most pragmatic and least costly means of stabilising the situation and an 'internal solution' to boot. Despite this, the CIA, MI6 and Pakistan's intelligence agencies chose to ignore, even to belittle him.

Ironically Donald Rumsfeld, at whose feet much of the blame must be laid for the military strategy chosen, writing an Op Ed in the New York Times in November 2008 about the need for a 'surge' in Afghanistan, said;

> 'What's needed in Afghanistan is an Afghan solution, just as Iraqi solutions have contributed so fundamentally to progress in Iraq. And a surge, if it is to be successful, will need to be an Afghan surge'.[385]

Though Rumsfeld was advocating a kinetic 'surge', he could have had an 'Afghan Solution' to 9/11.

Although there is finally much talk of 'talking to the Taliban' today, there is no respected figurehead to whom senior Taliban might reasonably switch sides. For senior Taliban will never, I believe, 'reconcile' with the government of Hamid Karzai, which is perceived by Afghans as a narrow and self-serving criminal kleptocracy. Nor will they reconcile with the 'foreign invader' who since 2001 has squandered so much local goodwill and been party to such hubris in the region.

Despite the lack of faith by Afghans in Karzai, his bizarre visit to Washington DC in May 2010 – to be feted by Obama, Clinton and Biden in spite of Obama's apparent fury over Karzai's earlier remarks about 'joining the Taliban' – indicates that the West is now stuck with a strategic partner whom even the US Ambassador to Afghanistan had described in November 2009 as 'inadequate'.[386]

There is a strange irony to the fact that Karzai, a man who was initially described by Afghans as a 'Shah Shujah', had by 2010 built his family an empire characterised by 'oligarch gangsterism' and today seems to have Obama's administration over a barrel.[387] The 'barrel' in question is the West's inability to exit the war in Afghanistan with a shred of pretence that it has 'won'. As ever since 2001, Afghan policy continues to be shaped by 'external' considerations such as US domestic policy rather than the needs of Afghans. Yet despite this the government of President Karzai, supported to the hilt by the West, looks increasingly unsteady as Karzai's behaviour itself becomes more erratic.

Although there begins, in 2010, to be talk about 'tribes', but there is still confusion about traditional legitimacy and customary (also known as 'hybridised') governance mechanisms.[388] For example, Western officials and journalists continue to conflate the terminology of 'tribal leaders' with the strongmen and warlords whom the West has empowered since 2001.[389]

The alternative would be to reconfigure Obama's so-called 'new' strategy, which is essentially no different from the course of action set in 2001 of working with illegitimate proxies. The 'surge' could have been an opportunity to begin a process of accountability: a disempowering of local power holders and reorienting of the strategy so that Western troops support ordinary Afghans, many of whom have expressed their desire for justice. Instead, the West continues with its short term policy of working with regional strongmen; a policy which undermines attempts at State-building, as these men are legitimised and enriched (often with lucrative contracts, for example to provide militia forces to work alongside NATO / coalition troops).[390]

The 'surge' – with its imperative of gaining 'leverage' over the Taliban on the battlefield in order to 'force' them to the negotiating table – demonstrates incomprehension about the nature of Afghan notions of honour and pride. For the Taliban have shown their prowess in asymmetric warfare and winning the battle of perception. They cannot thus be browbeaten into surrender with kinetic leverage from the 'surge'. Virtually every invader who has been to Afghanistan has made the same mistake. The surge will ultimately prove to be simply another example of Western hubris.

There is also a residual non-willingness by donors and intervenors to accommodate or even seek to understand concepts of traditional and / or charismatic legitimacy (such as that engendered by Abdul Haq and intrinsically important to his Peace Plan) or of alternative (eg 'customary' or 'hyridised') governance mechanisms (such as those I witnessed Baryalai seek to build through his shura). As such the West has lost the possibility of potentially useful levers for assisting governance, stability and accountability[391] at the local level. This is particularly the case in the Pashtun belt, the heartland of the insurgency. Partly this is because the phenomenon seems to the Western observer to be too complex, time consuming, anti-modern and repressive to women.[392]

Whereas many in the West saw the quick toppling of the Taliban regime as an end in itself, Abdul Haq recognised that the window of opportunity for 'stabilising' Afghanistan was minutely short. Which is why he said, 'It doesn't matter if I get killed. I just want to get the "structure" in place so it can go on without me'.

It is hard to know whether Abdul Haq had succeeded to get Jalaluddin Haqqani on board with his plan in 2001. Veteran Afghan journalist Kathy Gannon stated, "Had he wanted to, Haqqani could have handed the entire al Qaeda network to the US on a plate".

Ultimately Haqqani met with the ISI in October 2001 and eventually threw in his lot with Pakistan.[393] His network continues to lead an anti Afghan Government front from North Waziristan. However it is likely that the Haqqani's - with whose front Haq had fought early on in the jihad – visited Haq at some stage at his office in Peshawar in the aftermath of 9/11. We shall probably never know because – as Sir John Gunston had told me – the meetings with defectors were kept very secret, even from him and James Ritchie. When I asked Baryalai to confirm whether Haqqani had agreed to come over to Haq's side after 9/11, he reiterated that the two had known each other since the early days of the jihad and that Haqqani held Abdul Haq in high esteem.[394] It is my feeling that Haq would certainly have been in touch with Haqqani about his plans, that Haqqani would most likely have come on board with the type of structure and government (ie not overtly foreign backed) that

Haq proposed. And that Haqqani probably threw in his lot with the Taliban and the Pakistani ISI following Haq's death and the emergence of Hamid Karzai.

When I wrote to former Ambassador Peter Tomsen, the former US Special Envoy to the mujahideen, asking for a letter written by Haq to him in 1992, he wrote back to me:

> Abdul's detractors in the US and Pakistani governments have managed to emasculate his great contributions and his intellectual foresight when that remained a scarce commodity, including in the US great departments of government, and as you know, this attitude and with the ISI I fear even worse, contributed to his tragic death. You can fill up this blank space which is really a historical gap in what happened.
>
> Best regards, Peter.[395]

The bedrock of Haq's plan should remain our objective if stabilisation is to have any chance in Afghanistan, though the challenge today is far more complex and challenging than it would have been in 2001. For the purposes of concluding this, I will make some brief points about the West's mistakes in Afghanistan as they relate to what Haq proposed. These should inform the West about the way forward.

The bedrock required includes all those areas where, so far, we have failed to appreciate the requisite dynamics. To move ahead, we will need focus on an 'internal' solution, a process of account-ability for past abuses, a focus not on military security but on genuine people-centred governance and legitimacy, a recognition that Karzai is the wrong man for the job and there must be a new political settlement, the need to focus more on alternative governance structures and a need to be realistic about the adequacy of Pakistan as a strategic ally.

The seven major areas where the West has failed so far in its 'strategy' for Afghanistan include:

1. The absence of an internal solution

I remember how, in 2003, an Afghan-Australian *al Jazeera* journalist commented, 'This is just a short interlude of peace in an otherwise ongoing civil war'.

In 2001, the West failed to understand this fact as it allowed Northern Alliance warlords to dominate the government 'power' ministries. Today – with the Afghan National Army estimated at some sixty percent Tajik and defections running at some twenty-five percent – the West has clearly not learnt from its mistakes. Indeed that the ANA has failed to incorporate Pashtuns, who make up the majority of Afghans, indicates a policy of, at best, benign neglect by the international community.

The decision to focus on building up Afghan security forces as a means for the West to 'exit' Afghanistan is an attempt to impose an occidental external solution on a traditional society. It is unrealistic and, given the economic crisis, financially unsustainable for the West which would have to pay for it. It is also ill-suited to the Afghan context and culture. An internal solution, forged along traditional lines, and in the context of a more just political settlement than that conceived at Bonn, which failed to include the Taliban, would have been preferable.

This is why Haq was against the bombing, and undoubtedly would have been against the Obama-McCrystal 'surge'. In an interview with *Newsweek* in the week before he died, Haq said:

> I did tell someone [in the US] that if you hadn't bombed for two more weeks maybe there would have been no need to bomb. We could've had a solution. But Washington went ahead to satisfy the American public. And Afghanistan has to lose hundreds of lives. Afghan blood is cheaper than anything.[396]

Haq foresaw the danger of allowing the Northern Alliance warlords (who both Haq and many Afghans[397] had expressed the desire to be indicted for their past crimes) to control Kabul. Haq recognised the danger of an imbalanced political settlement (driven by so-called 'realpolitik') whereby the majority Pashtun, including moderate Taliban, found themselves voiceless and unrepresented even as their traditional foe – the mostly Tajik Northern Alliance – took control of the significant ministries in Kabul.

In 2001, Abdul Haq provided the only political strategy 'not reliant upon explicit military force' in Afghanistan that we are likely to see in a generation. He also had all parties to the conflict under his umbrella. Unfortunately, those charged with making these decisions, were either too blind or too ill-informed to realise. For as Joe Ritchie said in 2003:

> I couldn't have imagined a platter more *ideally* loaded for what the folks in Washington needed. I mean, here you had, *the* Afghan Commander who had pulled together more other commanders than *anyone* in the history of the war ... he'd shown the *most* courage, he had been the best at, at this kind of behind the lines warfare by far. He had a plan that didn't involve risking a *single* American life, the Afghans themselves were taking all the risks, he wasn't asking for any weapons or any financing, this was entirely resources brought by *his* men, *their* commitment, *their* lives. And he provided a huge counter-balance to this Northern Alliance force, which if it took Kabul, was going to lead to a long-term problem for Afghanistan and likely civil war again. And here it was, all in one place, it was credible, it was exactly as the doctor ordered ... but it had just one defect. The leader was, was not a man who could be bought, he was a man of courage and principle, and therefore the CIA couldn't 'own' him, and I think that was his, I think that was the fatal problem that ... kept him from getting the backing he needed to pull this off, and to leave Afghanistan in a ... long-term stable situation, which as we know ... now, it's not.[398]

2. The failure of the 'Peace versus Justice' Strategy

The ninth century Islamic scholar Ibn Qutayba wrote:

There can be no government without an army,

No army without money,

No money without prosperity.

And no prosperity without justice and good administration.[399]

In its post-September 11 intervention, the West has also failed to understand that in Afghanistan, a society based on notions of honour, for stabilization to be sustained, there must be justice. While there has been limited reform of the Justice Sector (led by the Italians), there has been no attempt to implement 'Transitional Justice' – ie accounting for past abuses. Instead the policy chosen was that of 'realpolitik', in other words to make an accord with brutal warlords who had been in exile and to dub this betrayal 'Peace versus Justice'. Warlords and strongmen, and not ordinary Afghan people, would be the West's key allies. This was the central plank of the strategy in 2001 and it remains so as I write this. Not only was this distinctly unethical it has also been a 'home goal'. For as the 'justice deficit' has grown, so too has the insurgency. Why?

Firstly, it has been fed by the type of political alienation I witnessed amongst the Pashtuns in Jalalabad. Secondly, it has been fed by what I would call the growing 'crisis of impunity'. This is characterised by those in positions of power being able to grab property and positions, and, when this is not punished, to move further and to kidnap or murder their local and political opponents. The resultant fragmentation of security, and growing disaffection with the government and the international community, which has shown itself unwilling to address the justice deficit, nor to protect people, has left Afghans with only one choice: to re-embrace the Taliban. For the movement *has* shown itself capable of providing a localised system of shariat justice.

The US and UN diplomats, who in 2002 boasted of 'Peace versus Justice' and 'a light footprint', failed to understand how the dangers of not protecting the interests of ordinary people – with respect to security, jobs and justice – would provide the Taliban with a huge strategic advantage. 'Peace versus justice' created an environment of impunity which has been ruthlessly exploited by the strongmen whom the West empowered militarily in 2001 and politically in 2002 at the Emergency Loya Jirga. As such, networks of illegal activities (such as trade in poppy, expropriation of property, protection rackets and the kidnap of children) have flourished.; headed by the strongmen we failed to indict at the outset. For example, the network of Ahmed Wali Karzai in Kandahar and throughout the south, described at length in a report by the Institute of War.[400]

Ironically, many of these men are the same personalities who represented the mujahideen factions which carved up Afghanistan during the early 1990s, leading the population to become so fed up that they accepted the arrival of the religious zealot Taliban. Meanwhile international actors, such as the Western civil society leaders I met at a conference in Geneva in 2009[401] cry, 'Afghans have a different level of human rights' or 'we had to work with the Northern Alliance warlords 'because they were the existing power'. Not only does this betray ignorance about the structure of Afghan society, it also implies that Afghans did not merit justice. This is a curious view given that the 2001 'invasion' was sold as a 'humanitarian intervention'. Also given that in many surveys such as one done by the AIHRC,[402] Afghans indicated their desire for justice. An absence of justice has led to further human rights violations as strongmen have been able to abuse positions of power and authority over a population which has no recourse to due process or redress. This factor, more than most, has fanned the insurgency.

Why for example, did the West bring to account the perpetrators of atrocities in, for example, the Balkans, but not in Afghanistan? When I asked him this question, Nader Nadery, Deputy of the Afghan Independent Human Rights Commission told me; 'basically there has been no political will by the international community nor the Afghan government for transitional justice in Afghanistan'.[403]

The West not only failed to appreciate these dynamics at the outset, it also failed to help the Afghans to build a viable state. We talked of democracy but simultaneously ensured this could not occur for we failed to support President Karzai to govern with the rule of law.

One means of supporting the rule of law (among others) was, of course, for Western troops to disarm the 'illegal' militias – which became known as 'illegally armed groups' scattered across the country; militias which did not exist in Afghanistan during the Taliban period, having been driven out. Instead the US led Coalition and eventually NATO armed them and used them to achieve short-term tactical objectives (for example, protecting the perimeter fences of our PRTs, or serving as private militias to 'work' alongside NATO soldiers). In so doing, the West won a few small battles, but lost the most significant battle in this conflict; that of perception. For in empowering the strongmen (possibly irreversibly) we have lost the support of ordinary Afghans.

In Afghanistan, after the shock of September 11 and twenty-three years of war, the West ought to have set out, as it did in Bosnia and in Sierra Leone, with a 'heavier footprint'. There was an opportunity to do so. The Northern Alliance warlords had fled outside of Afghanistan during the Taliban years, driven out by the Taliban for their criminal behaviour during the early 1990s. Indeed by September 11, most were still in exile. They returned as they saw the spoils to be had. Sadly, instead of taking this opportunity to indict the criminals and rights abusers who had scarred Afghanistan's past the West allowed them to hijack the democratic process, beginning with their military takeover of Kabul and its power ministries in November 2001 and compounded by their political hijacking of the Emergency Loya Jirga in 2002.[404] This has impacted on the rule of law, and ultimately – with the cash, weapons and impunity we extended to them – allowed them to seize the state. Meanwhile, Hamid Karzai's government, like that of Shah Shujah, 'proceeds smoothly against a backdrop of British bayonets'.[405] Karzai who initially had no power of his own, had been forced by the West's 'light footprint' and 'no boots on the ground' approach to Afghanistan to barter power with the warlords in order to remain in power. The result? A government so mired in corruption and polluted by the tentacles of criminal and mafia networks that it has very little credibility with ordinary Afghans, who are often thus impeded from something as basic as a livelihood. Paddy Ashdown put the conundrum in a nutshell when he said:

> Unless and until the rule of law is established and the corrupt are brought to justice, especially those at the very highest level in Afghanistan's power structures, there can be no safe democracy, no trusted government, no successful economy and no security for ordinary citizens.[406]

Yet so far neither Karzai, the international community, NATO, the UN or the Americans has shown any real interest in the importance of the rule of law in establishing a functioning state which – through their access to justice and redress – has legitimacy and relevance for local people.

In 1797, French political philosopher Benjamin Constant wrote in *Des Effets de la Terreur*: 'Nothing on earth can ever justify a crime, if you grant an amnesty to the past, you are corrupting the future'. Today that future spoken of by Constant has arrived in Afghanistan and it does not look pretty. Nor is it easily reversible.

3. The focus has been on military security at the expense of genuine governance

Jochen Hippler describes as 'imperial nation building' the phenomenon of focusing on military security. He recognises as problematic the urge to use:

> Local power structures, militias, warlords and even criminal gangs as auxiliary troops without considering their overall representation within society, the impact on the local population, and further political development.[407]

'Imperial nation building' has characterised the West's post-September 11 Afghan intervention. It has been vastly expensive: 'The US military currently spends $35 billion a year in the country, nearly $100 million a day; yet USAID spending for 2008 is $1.6 billion, some $4.4 million a day'.[408] This was before the troop surge in late 2009. This militarisation of aid and development has also ultimately become counterproductive both to the objectives of the international community as well as the 'imperative' of 'humanitarian intervention' in Afghanistan. In Kandahar now:

> Traditional tribal leaders have little influence at the provincial level, as political authority in Kandahar today is closely linked to militias and wealth.[409]

And the 'King' of the tribal militias in Kandahar, apparently closely supported and protected by the CIA and now NATO – which has been provided him with a revenue stream by financing his militia groups – has been President Karzai's half-brother, Ahmad Wali Karzai.[410]

The militia group controlled by the President's half-brother has been implicated in the murder of Kandahar's Police Chief, as well as rape and extortion.[411] Hence we have a situation where:

> ISAF has simultaneously strengthened those forces that undermine and manipulate Kandahar's formal government.[412]

> ISAF strategy of subcontracting and paying local militias is totally at odds with building a credible local governance.[413]

This situation is similar to what I witnessed in many PRTs and coalition bases that I visited around the country between 2002 to 2006. It was also present in the attitude of NATO and Operation Enduring Freedom representatives at the meetings I attended in Kabul on Security Sector Reform, on disarming illegal armed groups, at the PRT 'Working Group'.

In Kandahar, the problem has been that the 'power dynamics' have since early 2002 been engineered by Ahmad Wali Karzai with the sole objective of bolstering the kleptocracy of the Karzai family and its allies.[414] Nationally, the international community has failed to work with different elements of Afghan society. With its almost exclusive focus on military actors, the 'international community and the Afghan government alike ignored the fact that "village communities, clans, tribal groups and religiously defined communities formed the most important reference points for political identity and action" in the past'.[415]

Forster's paper also mirrors the concerns of James Ritchie who – in his first interview with me – had expressed concern about the lack of information traffic among the international community, but also the various departments of US Government (especially between the CIA and the Pentagon). Forster says, 'This paper illustrates the divergent tactics and interests of the international community in resolving the Afghan problem'. For example, Forster cites the fact that in Kandahar, 'the PRT was not aware of how much US Special Forces or CIA supported Ahmad Wali Karzai'. He added that, 'Ahmad Wali Karzai has benefitted enormously from these divisions'.

The proliferation of NATO and coalition contracts for strongmen (whether the hiring of land which is often illegally appropriated, contracts for guarding compounds and roads) has been a phenomenon since 2001. While this has met the short term objectives of individual base and PRT commanders of 'force protection', the effect has unsurprisingly been to massively empower regional strongmen at the expense of the central government, the rule of law, human rights, ordinary Afghans and ultimately democracy: an absurd contradiction in policy.

4. Karzai : the wrong man for the job

Sadly, what Joe Ritchie said, as far back as 2003, has come to pass.

> Karzai, he said, was like 'Shah Shujah', something that was … put in by the British long ago and therefore regarded as somebody else's, a puppet … and so when the Americans come in and bomb and … this is viewed as something brought in from the outside, that's not native, and it has huge effect on the ability of what's been installed from the outside to feel legitimate and to be able to govern.

Several people had indicated to me their inclination that Karzai had been 'chosen' by the US well before September 11. It was the episode whereby Haq had gone to meet General Massoud with James Ritchie and Peter Tomsen that really ignites questions as to when the US had 'chosen' Karzai. It indicates that the Bush administration was probably already working with Karzai by early 2001. Just what promises had been made and why is uncertain. This question is for others to follow up.

However, what is known about Hamid Karzai is that he had very little personal history: little action during the jihad, no power, no party and little record of bringing disparate groups together. Hence, after September 11 he had no leverage with Afghanistan's strongmen and with the US. It is not entirely his fault that to maintain his position since 2001 he has had to give out sinecures and positions to these 'strongmen' to buy their favour so that he could continue to rule. After all, the US and its allies were unwilling to either indict or to disarm these men. That Karzai was ambitious, we know. That he gradually stopped coming to meetings with the King's group, who had chosen Haq as their military commander, we know. We also know that he had previously worked alongside Zulmay Khalilzad, possibly for the US pipeline company UNOCAL. This was perhaps a factor in choosing him to lead Afghanistan. It is only since the disputed and highly fraudulent 2009 Presidential elections that the international community has finally fallen out of love with Karzai. Yet the signs were there long ago.

Joe Ritchie said of Karzai and his ambition back in 2003:

> By compromising and letting the Northern Alliance hold the guns, he gets to be President, it's kind of an interesting three-way deal between him, the Northern Alliance and the US, which purchases temporary stability. Long term though, I don't think it'll work for Afghanistan but, I think this is a tough temptation for Karzai to resist … this is a three-way deal. You think about it. It's a perfect deal: the US gets what they want; Karzai gets what he wants; the Northern Alliance get what they want. And the Afghans get screwed.

5. Democracy and traditional structures

The way out of the mire is for the West to recognise that Afghanistan remains a predominantly tribal society and that we must work with traditional structures, rather than the warlord militias that the coalition / NATO has created since 2001 to serve its short-term needs. Afghanistan's central government has never enforced its writ to the periphery; governance has been more a matter of a balance between the centre and localised, normally tribal, structures (though in the north such structures are more 'clan-like'). Although many traditional, tribal structures have been altered and in cases alterred by jihadi structures, they do still exist locally. To bring about an end to the conflict and regain stability the emphasis must be local. There must be a focus on traditional structures in fostering local solutions – in other words, 'agreements' between tribes – rather than the use of government, Special Forces or CIA-run 'tribal militia forces'.

This is consistent with what Angelo Rasanayam concludes in his tome on Afghan history:

Nation building policies and the related reconstruction efforts will have to be guided by the past. From 1747 to 1973, the old tribal structures were the basis of a crude but workable federalism headed by a King whose central authority was seldom very strong. These structures have survived after two catastrophic decades of war and anarchy.

But it is important not to conflate 'traditional tribal' and 'warlord' structures which many commentators often do. Rasanayagam recognises the importance of making this distinction when he says:

> But the tribal mindset based on patronage – warrior prowess and the dispensation of favours from the top down – has also survived. It would run counter to the implementation of policies, fostering a civil society and free-market mechanisms, that would be required to construct a viable and modern state.

Thus he says, for a modern state to flourish:

> The population has to be first disarmed and the warlords put out of business, and secondly, a federal system established under which tribes and ethnic groups become the partners, and not the rivals, of a national government.[416]

Since 2001, the West has dealt with Afghanistan catastrophically badly. A Peacemaker in Geneva commented to me that he felt the Afghan intervention was possibly the most badly handled of recent decades. With the leak in July 2010 of some 90,000 pages of classified military documents to the website, 'Wikileaks' much of the hubris, incompetence and cowardice of the international community in Afghanistan since 2004 will be on record. The importance of this book though is that it has catalogued what happened at the outset of the so called 'engagement'. I believe that what we see in Afghanistan today is a corollary of that.

Initially, the Bonn blueprint dealt with Afghanistan as though it would become a nation state. But we have made the mistake of dealing mainly with those Afghan technocrats who were educated in the West and forgetting that Afghanistan remains an agrarian, patriarchal, illiterate and predominantly traditional rural society.

It is ironic that the international community has often disdained the idea of more patriarchal, tribal forms of governance in Afghanistan (primarily due to their association with the repression of women) yet it has done virtually nothing to promote human rights in general, beginning with a process of accountability for past abuses, since September 11. This would have provided the most effective means of advancing the situation of women in Afghanistan.

We should allow the rural people and tribes to take more of a lead in democratising Afghanistan through the traditional Jirga system and recognize more traditional forms of legitimacy. Although the NSP is a good programme, it needs to acknowledge the traditional structures too. Although weakened during the mujahideen and Soviet-era, the tribes in the Pashtun belt continue to make up the majority of the population. They are also located, critically, where the heart of the insurgency is taking place. And, due to their important location along the Pakistani border, it is they alone who can provide a bulwark against the 'leaking' of insurgents coming from safe havens in the tribal areas or Pakistan.

Once again though, the West's failure to understand and work with traditional structures of governance in Afghanistan has led to another 'own goal' as the Taliban – who *do* understand the importance of utilising tribal and traditional networks – have been able to exploit this wretched situation by setting up a parallel (and arguably more effective) system of justice and governorships. By 2009, these reached into twenty-three out of twenty-four provinces.

6. Dealing with the neighbourhood

Other studies have dealt with the region in greater depth and I am not going to replicate those. However suffice to say that, in dealing with Pakistan, which is perhaps the most relevant neighbour when we talk of Afghanistan's immediate stability – and has been recognised as such by the depiction of the conflict as a double theatre called 'Af-Pak' – the West has recognised too late that Pakistan's strategic objectives in Afghanistan are not in line with its own.

As this book has shown, our intelligence agencies (predominantly the CIA and MI6) showed naivete (at best) in their excessive reliance on the ISI for information, as the CIA had done throughout the

1980s jihad. That the Pakistani intelligence and military have for a long time been powers unto themselves has been well documented in other books and articles. Today it remains questionable how much influence the government of Asif Ali Zadari has over its own intelligence and military outfits. This over-reliance by the West on ISI for information and strategic direction appears to have continued well into the current engagement in Afghanistan. Now the West (and Afghanistan) is paying the price for that.

This false sense of security as regards the nature of Pakistani politics has also come at a cost, not just to the West but also to Pakistan, whose government seems unable to maintain security or even a monopoly on power, as is shown by the Taliban's audacious torching of some fifty NATO supply trucks on the night of 9 June 2010 on the outskirts of Islamabad!

Elsewhere, the US Central Command (CENTCOM), who deal with the Afghan theatre, held a conference portentously entitled 'Afghanistan-Pakistan: the art of the possible' in Florida in June 2010. The conference title alone indicates a desire to change the goalposts of its original objectives in 'Af-Pak' such that the West can withdraw. Here, Pakistan was discussed in the context of the challenges presented by Tehrik-i-Taliban, the Punjab based insurgents, and the apparent ISI support for the Haqqani network, who form a major part of the Afghan insurgency. The fact that someone mentioned the difficulty that the US is having with ISI over visas for staff of the State Department, USAID, military and contractor staff indicates the difficulty of relying excessively on Pakistan as a viable strategic partner. Obviously the US is unable to change the geography of Pakistan's location. But the West and the US in particular ought to have recognized the need to be tougher. For example, conditionality of aid receipts might have meant they were used for reforming the madrassah system and development projects instead of being redirected to military spending by the Pakistani government for the purposes of its main strategic purpose, which is to curtail Indian might in the region.

***

The question remains then: why was military action chosen above Abdul Haq's 'Afghan Solution' which – by its nature being internal – had more chance of attracting support from disparate groups who have since pitted themselves against the Western backed government of Hamid Karzai. This question is relevant when one considers how so many armies have been vanquished over the centuries in Afghanistan. So why did we choose the path we did?

Firstly, polls after September 11 showed that the American public had 'desired military action', even if it meant civilian casualties.[417] Perhaps the shock of September 11, the first significant terrorist attack on US soil, made people want to 'lash out'. Military action, however blunt an instrument for resolving the problem, was a means of doing this. Sadly though, it has shown itself to be an expensive and ineffective way of resolving what is essentially a problem of state failure. The West's reaction to September 11 was essentially an emotional one.

Abdul Haq foresaw the problems inherent to the military strategy chosen in Afghanistan in 2001, which is why he sacrificed his life trying to prevent it. His thinking was similar to that of Tzu Tzung, who wrote over two thousand years ago, that the 'intelligent General' sought ways to *avoid* battle with its uncertain endgame and spiralling costs in blood and treasure.

Colonel Douglas MacGregor (retired)[418] writes of the dangers for a state associated with ill-thought-out military action:

> Failure to strategise and to avoid military action at the outset [of a conflict] can have devastating costs associated with ongoing military operations leading to loss of life and capital. This can have devastating consequences on a nation, and, as was the case with WWI, it even accelerated the end of the British Empire.

> While US provided training, equipment and advisors can significantly improve a partner state's capabilities, there *must already* be an indigenous force to equip, indigenous fighters to train and a senior leadership echelon to advise.

Interestingly he goes on to say, of the types of governments the West assists to take over in failed states.

> Legitimacy is not exclusively a function of elections. Legitimacy is also defined by a government's competence to win and hold power in ways that benefit American and allied interests.

Yet in Afghanistan, the West chose to work with the Northern Alliance and avoided the indigenous cross-tribal group comprised of senior Pashtun tribal leaders, Taliban, and the King's group of tribal leaders.

While the Northern Alliance may also have been an 'organised indigenous force', their historical track record was never going to enable them to be regarded as legitimate with the Afghan people.

> Had any of these questions been raised and accurately addressed within the purpose/method/end-state framework, it is doubtful American military action would have followed the course it did after September 11.[419]

In evidence given to the Department of Defence early in 2002, Joe Ritchie said:

> The essential variable in determining whether Afghanistan returns to warlordism/civil war, or to a healthy civil society is not the amount of money that it receives (which is likely to actually be detrimental). The key variable is the fair inclusion in the power structure of the local community leadership.[420]

He said the 'temporary arrangement' which left the power ministries in the hands of the Northern Alliance was 'totally unacceptable'. The only reason it was temporarily tolerable was that Afghans had been promised a Loya Jirga in June.

However, I witnessed what happened at that Loya Jirga and how, after a series of successful district and regional level elections of delegates who were to shape the country's future, the international community opted in favour of warlords much derided by Afghans themselves. Joe Ritchie commented:

> Afghans can handle hardships of all kinds: they can handle famine, plague, natural disasters, sickness, war, etc, but they cannot handle a

master. In Afghanistan, more than any place on earth, illegitimate rule means war.

In other words, in 2003 Ritchie recognised the problem of the 'justice deficit' which was implicit to the Bonn Settlement, to the CIA policy of co-opting unpopular warlords, to the ELJ in 2002, and still today in President Obama's 'surge'.

> Yet the current arrangement seems to portend exactly that. The Northern Alliance (or a small subset thereof, the Panjshiris) have capitalized on their military position (including their possession of Kabul), and on the pressure felt by the West to produce a consensus government in Bonn, to land in a position where they are the warlords of the entire country, with international approval. This arrangement has the short-term advantage for the West of appearing to have stabilized the situation, at least until the media withdraws; but the medium- and long-term outcome for the Afghans looks bad, unless the West is prepared to do the hard work of facing down the Northern Alliance later. This is not to say that we have set this up cynically, but the simple realities of the situation in Bonn led naturally to this arrangement. It made Karzai happy, because he became number one; the Northern Alliance were happy, because they got the guns; and the West was happy, because, by promising the Afghans a representative government in six months, the tough showdown was postponed, thereby enormously reducing the political embarrassment if things don't work out.

> Afghanistan is more than ready [for democracy]. Before the recent conflict, the monarchy then in place clearly derived its authority from the consent of the governed, as expressed in Loya Jirgas, which had been held for centuries. These Jirgas were not precisely our idea of 'ballot box' democracy (this would have been logistically impossible). They were simply representative government and the government resulting from these Loya Jirgas was regarded as fair, and had enormous popular support. This is the situation which must be recreated.

Today, as the number of 'fragile' and 'failed' states around the world proliferates, the West cannot hope to achieve its objectives by simply arming one faction against another in distant wars. This has failed in Afghanistan, which requires far more complex, long-term and serious political commitment if its problems are to be resolved. It has also failed in Somalia, where since 2006 the US has backed Somalia's traditional enemy, Ethiopia, in ridding the country of the Union of Islamic Courts. The result is a far more fundamentalist regime, al Shabab, which is overtly providing a safe haven to al Qaeda in Somalia.[421]

Instead of realpolitik, we now need more intelligent, more engaged, more just and more long-term ways of enabling the local people in these countries to build their states in line with their own culture. Military force, as the British used in Sierra Leone, might simply be needed to pressurise and capture local warlords at the outset before bringing them to justice. In Afghanistan that would have been equivalent to a 'surge' or 'heavier footprint' at the outset. However, if Abdul Haq's plan had been allowed to fly there would have been no 'space' for these men to return and operate.

As this book has shown, it can no longer be assumed that Western intelligence agencies are unimpeachable. The veil of secrecy behind which it is assumed they must operate should be lifted more often so that they can be subjected to greater scrutiny and their integrity, competence and ability to operate in the longer term strategic interests of the citizens of those countries they claim to represent must be continually put to the test. The same must be said for taking at 'face value' their claims of apparent 'success' in theatres of operations.

MacGregor goes on:

> Treating conflict avoidance as a declared strategic goal should give pause to those in Washington who think counter-insurgency is something American military forces should seek to conduct. For outside powers intervening in other peoples' countries as we have done in Iraq and Afghanistan, so-called counter-insurgency has not been the success story presented to the American people. Making cash payments to buy cooperation from insurgent groups to conceal a failed policy of occupation is a temporary expedient to reduce US casualties, not a permanent solution for stability.

... But unlike Britain's resources in 1914, American resources today are not unlimited. Years of easy tactical military victories over weak and incapable nation-state opponents in the Balkans, Afghanistan and Iraq have created the illusion of limitless American military power. This illusion assisted the Bush administration and its generals in frustrating demands from Congress for accountability; allowing politicians and generals to define failure as success and to spend money without any enduring strategic framework relating military power to attainable strategic goals.

In a report commissioned by Senator John Kerry into the failure to capture bin Laden at Tora Bora,[422] the costs of the Afghan conflict since 2001 are outlined:

For American taxpayers, the financial costs of the conflict have been staggering. The first eight years cost an estimated $243 billion and about $70 billion has been appropriated for the current fiscal year – a figure that does not include any increase in troops. But the highest price is being paid on a daily basis in Afghanistan and Pakistan, where 68,000 American troops and hundreds of US civilians are engaged in the ninth year of a protracted conflict and the Afghan people endure a third decade of violence. So far, about 950 US troops and nearly 600 allied soldiers have lost their lives in Operation Enduring Freedom, a conflict in which the outcome remains in grave doubt in large part because the extremists behind the violence were not eliminated in 2001.

Despite this, and although the war is obviously now heading in the direction of an intractable mire, some groups have benefitted from the runaway military spending that is a central plank of the strategy. Questions need to be raised on, for example, whether the West's so-called 'exit strategy' ought to have been dependent upon increasing the force size of the Afghan security forces (the ANA and ANP)? Or adding so called 'Tribal Militia' forces into that equation? And just who will continue to supply these growing forces with weaponry? Currently the ANA is being supplied with US manufactured M16s and Humvees; an arrangement which is hardly sustainable for Afghanistan. We need to thus ask questions about which groups or corporations are benefitting from the war in Afghanistan.[423] At the beginning of 2010, there are 150,000 foreign troops in Afghanistan and almost the same number of foreign contractors (who remain a 'hidden' force in terms of their numbers and requirement for weapons).[424]

There is also the 'revolving door' problem between those who benefit financially and the politicians who set the policy framework.[425] Brezinski[426] has written on how continued war in the Middle East is in the financial interests of the USA. Others have written about the interests of a key elite in 'continued war' because of, for example, the 'crisis of demand' endemic to capitalism. For example, the war resistors league[427] estimate that for the US total outlay of Federal Funds in 2009, military spending accounted for some 54% (of a total outlay of $ 2650 billion).

If such factors are considered, one is left wondering if Abdul Haq was overlooked because what he proposed did not suit the 'narrative' of various groups. Those who have rewritten their version of history – whether in the obituaries of Haq, in the *Private Eye* piece which alleged he was a 'terrorist', in accounts of how the South fell after the bombing began in 2001,[428] in the accounts by CIA operatives giving their version of events, in the responses of diplomats and MI6 operatives to the questions of journalists – prefer to uphold a narrative that defends their role in that history. Unfortunately though this does not serve either the Afghans, or the civilians being killed in this war, or the soldiers (both Western and Afghan) doing the dying on the battlefield, or the Western taxpayer. Neither does it serve the interest of the world's security for when the West finally extricates itself from Afghanistan, having first sought yet again change the goalposts of its original mission, it will leave behind fundamentalists who are strengthened with the vigour of knowing that they have managed to defeat not only the USSR, but now both the US and NATO in Afghanistan. This is no small feat. It will have major implications for reshaping the order of global security.

Those interest groups who continue to maintain an interest in this false narrative of history include the CIA, Britain's MI6, the Pakistani intelligence and military establishment, the warlords and strongmen of the Northern Alliance, the Karzai family and its allies, the 'military-security-industrial complex' for whom continued war has proven an unending pipeline to profit, and those Afghans who now benefit from a *status quo* which is characterised by instability, illegal activities, regional chaos and, internally, a climate of impunity, insecurity and ongoing civil war.

Why would Haq have been getting in the way of those groups? Perhaps because he had a track record of forthrightness, independence, legitimacy and the ability to bring disparate groups together. As he himself predicted in 1992;

> If these radical mujahideen elements take power in Afghanistan, there will be war forever. There will be no peace and security and we Afghans will have to beg for food and support for the rest of our lives.

APPENDICES

****

Rebel chief begs: Don't bomb now, Taliban will be gone in a month

A REBEL Mujahideen commander at the forefront of a new campaign to overthrow the Taliban made an impassioned plea to Prime Minister Tony Blair today to halt American plans for air strikes on Afghanistan.

Abdul Haq, one of the most powerful figures in an emerging opposition in the south of Afghanistan, told the Evening Standard: "The Taliban is collapsing from within — if the missiles strike, this will be delayed, even halted. Mr Blair has the influence to put the hand of restraint on America. I beg him to do it."

Dr Haq's appeal was made as Mr Blair left Moscow on the latest round of his diplomatic mission to shore up support for military action against terrorism, with Pakistan expected to be on his itinerary.

At a heavily guarded villa outside Peshawar, the former resistance leader spoke of a covert campaign to topple the Taliban, a process which he said could bring results "within a month".

As a Pakistani army unit kept watch and his own men patrolled with shouldered Kalashnikovs, Dr Haq spoke at length, for the first time since his return from exile abroad, about the secret war being waged against the hardline fundamentalist regime of Taliban leader Mullah Mohammed Omar.

"Every night I meet commanders who cross the mountains in darkness to brief me," he said. "They are part of the Taliban forces, but they no longer support them. These men will join us and there are many of them. When the time

AFGHANISTAN

From Keith Dovkants in Islamabad

is right, they and others will rise up and this Taliban government will be swept aside."

He said that while American and British help would be needed in the coming fight, it had to be a struggle in which Afghans took the leading role.

He acknowledged the contribution of the United Front (Northern Alliance) which is fighting the Taliban in the north of the country, but he said the Front represented only a narrow section of the population.

"I know my people," he said. "If they are bombed, they will close ranks. Don't forget the majority of the population has no access to news from outside — the Taliban banned television and what news there is is censored.

"People don't know what the war against terrorism is about. All they know is that when bombs fall, the Taliban will say 'The Americans are trying to kill us, we must fight'. They will fight.

"Despite everything the Taliban has done to destroy human rights, to destroy care of people's health, education, their livelihoods, they will fight.

"Afghans will always unite in the face of what they see as a foreign enemy and this will serve to strengthen the Taliban."

Dr Haq said his strategy centres on persuading the Taliban's own military forces

324

Abdul Haq: "The Taliban is collapsing from within. When the time is right, people will rise up and the Taliban will be swept aside"

Abdul Haq meets Prime Minister Margaret Thatcher in 1986

Northern Alliance fighters are trying to topple the Taliban

to turn against their leaders, a policy he claims will be effective. "The people are starving, they are already against them," he said.

"Many tribal leaders are with us, more will follow. With these pressures and the help of the world community, we will drive them out. The flag will be lowered and a new one raised."

Dr Haq envisages some difficult fighting, and the possible involvement of forces such as Britain's SAS.

He said the Taliban leaders and hardline loyalists, including Osama bin Laden, would retreat to mountain hideouts, bunkers created inside networks of deep caves.

"The terrorists will go with them," he said. "There are three to four thousand from Arab countries and five to six thousand from other countries. They will have to be fought. But what America — and your country — must try to understand is that they cannot be bombed. No one knows these mountains better than my people.

"We created those bunkers at the time of the Soviet occupation. We know where they are and what the weaknesses are. I assure you, there is no bomb smart enough to work its way into those places."

● Dr Haq, an academic who became one of the most respected Mujahideen commanders in the guerrilla war against Soviet troops in the Eighties, led an Afghan delegation to London in 1986, where he discussed the war with the then prime minister Margaret Thatcher.

Appendix II

Letter from Abdul Haq to Saudi Arabian Ambassador, dated 20 August 1991

بسم الله الرحمن الرحيم

HEZB-E-ISLAMI حزب اسلامی الغانستان
AFGHANISTAN

Province (	) ولایت
Front (	) جبهه
Date (	) تاریخ

20 August 1991

H.E. Yusuf M. Motabbakani
Ambassador
The Royal Embassy of Saudi Arabia
Chancery 1, Street 4
Islamabad, F-6/3

Dear Sir:

Kabul Province is the capitol of Afghanistan, the center of all political and military decisions. It is also the symbol of Afghanistan. Whoever controls Kabul controls the nation because there are the embassies and U.N. organizations, the major airports and military depots, the control and command force and the government ministries.

This is why Kabul is the major center for the struggle between Mujahidin and the regime. This is why, when Saudis come to Afghanistan, they go to Jihad in Kabul. This is why Sayyaff and Hekmatyar want more control in and around Kabul. From one side, they are poised to take political control, from the other side they bring most Arabs with them. From both sides they gain influence in Arab countries and get more financial support.

When most Arabs come to Pakistan they do not know about politics: they come in the name of Jihad. These radical Mujahidin elements have programs prepared for them. They take them from the airport to houses in Peshawar, afterwards they take them around Kabul to show them what they call the toughest, strongest and purest Jihad. They make the experience exciting.

Usually, these radical elements don't talk a lot about Jihad. Instead they talk about their politics and their radical brand of theology, how to bring revolution to their home countries and how to build support for what they call a "pure" Islamic state. They brainwash them. After their training, these visitors go home, defend their trainers, and act as ambassadors for these radical elements. Usually, once the visitors return home, they do three things: they work against their government giving speeches and agitating; they recruit more supporters for their cause; and they raise money for these radical elements in Afghanistan.

If these radical Mujahidin elements take power in Afghanistan, there will be war forever. There will be no peace and security, and we Afghans will have to beg for food and support for the rest of our lives. From the other side, people will come to hate the names of Mujahidin and Jihad throughout the world, and think that the word means only killing, destruction, disunity and terrorism. It will destroy the image of Mujahidin and Jihad. Moreover, the students and guests of these radical elements will find many supporters in your country and, if not

326

HEZB-E-ISLAMi
AFGHANISTAN

بسم الله الرحمن الرحيم   حزب اسلامى الغانستان

Province (ولايت)
Front   (جمهه)
Date   (تاريخ)

take full power, still engage in atrocities and chaos. This is neither good for you, nor for us, nor for Islam.

Meanwhile, foreign help is diminished these days and the radical elements turn to assistance from Libya, Iraq and their other friends in the Arab world.

I have designed a program and sent a copy to you already. We should take a decision, you and us, and work on it quickly. We have two types of activities in and around Kabul: 5,000 Mujahidin with guns and training around the city; and several thousand Mujahidin inside the city usually working for the government but really working for us performing sabotage, uncovering information, etc. This program will get houses in Peshawar, pick up our Arab guests at the airport, and send them to the real Jihad they came for, not propagandize them with political terrorist activities. When they return to their home countries they will talk only of Jihad. That way, the radical elements lose lots of friends. The Arab Mujahidin, when they return home, no longer act as ambassadors to these elements, no longer gain publicity for them, recruit supporters or raise funds. You will have fewer problems and so will we.

In the past, your publicity and support made these radical elements known as the leaders of the Afghan Mujahidin; now if you ignore all Afghan Mujahidin, these radicals will still be seen as the leaders. More sensible elements deserve your support so that people see them as leaders, for your interests, for those of Afghanistan and for Islam. We must strengthen Kabul so that the radicals cannot have it.

I appreciate your attention to these matters.

Respectfully yours,

ABDUL HAQ
Commander,
Kabul Affairs

John Gunston

facsimile

To:	General the Lord Guthrie GCB LVO OBE		
Fax:		**Pages:**	2
CC:		**Date:**	~~19/02/2001~~ 13·10·01
Re:	Commander Abdul Haq		

Thank you very much for coffee and your time this morning. I only wish we could have talked more about the Frontier.

Major RAM Seeger MC [late RM & OC SBS] and I have been over the last few weeks in trying to bring to notice to those who have an interest in solving the Afghan business, the potential of a remarkable Pushtun guerrilla commander, Haji Abdul Haq.

Our contacts with the MOD, FCO and SIS have been limited.

Friday, 21/09/01 Major Seeger & John Gunston met with Lt Col Philip Sampson, RM,
DIS – Counter Terrorism

John Gunston goes to Rome where Commander Haq has arranged a meeting between the former Mujahideen Commanders and King Zahir Shar. JG returns Tuesday – Haq to Pakistan via Dubai. Contacts with SIS were initiated through Lord Ashdown.

Monday, 24/09/01 Major Seeger meets with **Michael Havelock, SIS**
Wednesday, 26/09/01 John Gunston meets with **Philip Barclay, FCO, Counter Terrorism**
& Matthew Howland, FCO, Afghan Desk
John Gunston meets with **Michael Havelock, SIS**

The response was polite, though disinterested in Haq, as they [both FCO & SIS] are looking at other Pushtun assets. They will contact Haq if interested.

Major Seeger & JG fly out to Peshawar on Monday 1st October.

Reports of Haq's assets and intentions emailed securely to Lord Ashdown for dissemination on 3rd & 4th October. Response was that they are still looking at other Pushtun assets.

Friday, 05/10/01 Haq meets **William Astley, SIS**, in Peshawar. 1 hour meeting in which Haq explains that he has to know him well before he can brief him fully on his plan. Astley asks for his requirements. Avoids meeting with us. Major Seeger and JG had drawn up a brief summary which Haq faxed to him in Islamabad on 06/10/01

Tuesday, 0910/01 **William Astley** calls JG [now in Dubai on way back] and says that if we happen to be passing through Islamabad again to pop in for a chat.

Thursday, 11/10/01 call **Michael Havelock, SIS,** to say that we have returned. Call as yet unreturned.

This reluctance is probably for good operational reasons unknown to ourselves. Our concern is based on many years of experience working with the Mujahideen when fighting the Soviets, and the civil war that followed. This has led us to believe that there are no other credible Pushtun fighting commanders who can galvanise the many Pushtun tribes to rise up against the Taliban than Abdul Haq. Therefore we believe it is our duty to bring our concerns to your attention and those who may have a need to know.

THE SOLUTION
We believe that the quickest, least damaging, least controversial and most long lasting solution for achieving a **terrorist free Afghanistan** can be achieved **from within** by Afghans. In contrast any attempt to impose a solution on Afghanistan **from without** - especially if by military force, carries a real risk of failure. Instead of widening the divisions amongst the different Afghan factions, it is likely to unite them against the foreigner and prolong the problem.

PAKISTAN
It is also important that Pakistan's role in any solution is kept to the minimum and/or is strictly controlled. Her track record has not been good. As a consequence she is distrusted and disliked by the majority of Afghan players.

NORTHERN ALLIANCE & INSUBSTANTIAL PUSHTUN PLAYERS
An inside solution however should not be attempted by the mainly Tajik Northern Alliance alone. This would be resisted by the citizens of Kabul, surrounding Pushtun tribes and the Hazaras - all of whom have suffered badly at the hands of the Northern Alliance. But nor should it be attempted by such dubious Pushtun players as self-proclaimed 'General' Rahim Wardak who, when not in his cups, can spin a tall tale that sadly has no foundation in reality.

ABDUL HAQ
In contrast, if discrete and immediate support was given to Abdul Haq, a fast acceptable inside solution could be obtained. He is known and accepted as a proven operational leader and a man of principle with a trans-ethnic outlook. He would welcome the return of the King - but not his supporting Gilbert & Sullivan cast. He has the support of old Mujahideen commanders from all the 7 old parties, current Taliban commanders both political & military as well as tribal leaders. He has been consolidating this support over the last three weeks and has a workable plan for capturing Taliban key cities of Jalalabad, Kabul, Ghazni & Kandahar. These cities form the main vertebrae of the Taliban's spinal cord. Their capture would render the Taliban paraplegic and allow the swift rounding up of the Al Quaida network.
Because he is his own man, Haq is not a favourite of the Pakistanis and probably for this same reason, of the Americans either. It is precisely because of this that he has widespread trust and pledges of support from within Afghanistan. However, he is **not** a Pushtun nationalist and has never espoused a greater *Pushtunistan*, which the Pakistanis would have reason to fear. At the cost of a few million dollars Haq could put a Pushtun field force into the arena very quickly. This would become a focal point for Taliban defections and a counterweight to the Northern Alliance - both essential prerequisites for a fast, acceptable and lasting solution.

I do hope that this has been helpful. The best number to reach me is   , as my house is currently undergoing renovation. I am also emailing this to you at   .

Yours sincerely,

329

APPENDIX IV

3 OCTOBER 2001 SITUATION REPORT
(BY RAM SEEGER, SIR JOHN GUNSTON AND KEN GUEST)

RAM

SITREP 031001

INTRODUCTION

1. Haq's planned offensive against Kabul has huge potential but at present is over dependent on charisma and reputatation and the pledges of support from Taliban commanders. Through lack of material support it could easily bog down and unravel. The concurrent activity of the US and its allies could also have a critical effect.

THE PRIZES

2. The prizes to be gained from a successful outcome are:-

a. A relatively bloodless overthrow of the Taliban.

b. The capture of Kabul by Pushtoons.

c. The isolation of Al'Quaida (prior to its eventual removal).

d. An acceptable broad based government of all ethnic groups.

e. As a result of all of the above - a terrorist free Afghanistan.

3. Haq's plan is largely dependent on large scale Taliban defections and he has every reason to believe these are possible. Apart from the personal pledges of support from some major players, the regime is unpopular and in thrall to a disliked foreign army (Al'Quaida).

4. There is also the increasingly likely chance that a US backed Northern Alliance will be able to capture Kabul and impose a Tajik dominated government on the country. This would not be acceptable to the Pushtoon majority and to prevent it the Pushtoons would rally to the defence of the Taliban. This would prolong the civil conflict and strengthen Al'Quaida. On the other hand if a Pushtoon counterweight to the Northern Alliance was to emerge, there would be widespread Pushtoon support for this. This would ensure a better balance of ethnic power and increase the chances of being able to evolve a widely acceptable government. A further reason why the likely capture of Kabul by Northern Alliance forces would consolidate the Taliban cause is the memory of past Northern Alliance attrocities against the city's inhabitants.

5. Although Al'Quaida is able to control the Taliban Government by force of arms, its morale would be badly damaged if this government was to be overthrown. It would lose legitamacy and purpose and this would increase the possibility of disintegration from within.

OUTLINE PLAN

6. Haq's outline plan is to cross the border with two small hard-core groups of about 200 lightly armed Majaiedeen. Any larger initial group would arouse attention and provoke Pakistani interference. Once accross the border these groups would be quickly increased by groups of volunteers travelling independently from Pakistan or areas inside Afghanistan. The first of Haq's groups would start from the Mohmand tribal territories and after crossing into the Kunar valley converge on Jalalabad. The second group would start from Terrimangul and head for Teezine and Sorubi which are Hak's tribal homelands and from which he is confident he could draw much popular support. Large scale defections would be expected as soon as Taliban units were approached or confronted. Pledged defections by Jalalabad commanders would ensure the capture of this town and access to heavy weaponry (tanks and artillery) and uniformed soldiers. Areas of Arab resistence would be bypassed.

7. Simultaneously with the these two advances would be two uprisings from within Afghanistan - the area north west of Ghazni (Wardak) and and the area south of Ghazni but north of Kandahar.

8. Once he starts, Haqs sees his plan being completed quite quickly. It could all be over within 2-3 weeks. He will decide at the last moment which group he will travel with initially. All being equal he would probally opt for his home ground column (Terrimangul/Teezine).

AFGHAN SUPPORT FOR HAQ

9. It is not possible to guage the actual and potential support for Haq with any certainity but the indications are that it is real.

10. We have met and talked with two commanders from the areas around Ghazni - Mullah Malan (a renowned ex DRA former mujaiedeen and more recently ex Talib commander) and another commander from Wardak. We have also met and talked with two Talib commanders from Sorubi and Hesarak, the leader of the Mohmand border tribe and several other veteran mujaiedeen commanders.

11. Haq is acutely anxious of the need to get things right. He realises he has only one chance and as a consequence most of his efforts have gone into building alliances and establishing support. He is confident that he will attract more than enough men and that the problem may in fact lie in attracting too many. He is planning on a basic force of about 5,000 volunteers - this being the largest practical number he can control and supply. Defecting units of course would be additional to this.

OUTSIDE INFLUENCES

12. ISI. Haq has recently been visited by the ISI and is currently meeting with them again in Islamabad. He describes their mood as nervous and uncertain. They have expressed the desire to let bygones be bygone and the view that the Taliban has no future. They have not however (as yet) committed themselves to any sort of concrete support.

13. USA. American embassy personnel have visited Hak several times but according to him have not come up with anything concrete. Haq is worried that a deployment of American troops would result in increased support for the Taliban as Afghans closed ranks against the foreign invader. From what we have seen and heard we would support this view. At present the main foreign invader is Al'Quaid but this situation could change quickly. On the other hand, the threat of American action against the Taliban and Afghanistan weakens the government and encourages all moderate factions who want a peaceful Afghanistan to oppose them.

14. AL'QUAIDAR. It is understood that Al'Quaidar has purchased 15,000 camels and a large number of Kochi (nomad) tents. This suggests that they are preparing for a long march through inhospitable terrain. Bin Laden has been reported to have visited Jalalabad and has subsequently moved to Kandahar and is noe believed to be hiding in the mountainous area north of Kandahar and west of the Ghazni road. The same Taliban source also quoted Al Quaida members as saying that they had struck but one of ten planned targets. Mullah Malan expressed the view that if Haq was succesful and the Taliban were overthrown, the Arabs in Al'Quaida (less the obvious terrorists who would be arrested) would be invited to return to their own countries. NB. This would be the easiest course of action for a new Government to adopt but might not suit the USA. A possible quid pro quo for material assistance might be an undertaking not to do this.

15. THE EX-KING. While the King is still very acceptable as a figurehead for the creation of a new Afghanistan, his family and followers (with no recent experience of or feeling for Afghnaistan) are not. Haq intends to run his operation in the King's name for the cause of a united and peaceful Afghanistan. He does not wish to adopt a special name or cause specific to his efforts.

DIFFICULTIES AND DANGERS

16. Haq's operation will be running on borrowed money and a shoe string and very dependent on the resources he captures and/or are handed over to him by defectors. The uncertainity of this reliance is aggravated by the needs of his plan for speed, momentum and co-ordination. The dangers are that lack of transport and radios will result in poor co-ordination and delay. His men will also expect to be fed and clothed. To a lesser extent they will also want to be paid and it is possible that much of his potential support will fall away when it is realised that he has no financial backing.

17. Another problem will be the provision of civil administrations - most notably in Jalalabad and Kabul. Existing ones can probaly be used and adapted and in the case of Jalalabad, Haq's brother Haji Quadir would make a suitable provisional governor.

PROVISION OF WESTERN SUPPORT

18. Not to provide discrete support to Haq's enterprise would seem to be needlessly risking the huge gains that could result from a successfull outcome. The obvious needs are money, vehicles and radios and possibly some discrete specialist support (eg FACS (and stand off fire support), signallers, advisers etc).

i

Appendix V

Letter from Abdul Haq to former Ambassador Peter Tomsen (January 1993)

BEGIN TEXT:

DEAR AMBASSADOR TOMSEN:

I HAVE NOT SEEN YOU IN A LONG TIME, AND THOUGHT YOU MIGHT HAVE COME TO SEE US IN KABUL. HOWEVER, YOU HAVE REMAINED A GOOD FRIEND OF AFGHANISTAN, AND I WANT TO WRITE ABOUT TOPICS I COULD NOT EASILY DISCUSS BEFORE WHICH MIGHT HAVE BEEN MISCONSTRUED AS PETTY COMPLAINTS: ONE COMMANDER CRITICIZING ANOTHER OUT OF JEALOUSY. NOW IT IS EASIER TO SPEAK MY MIND. ALSO IT IS NOW CLEARER, TO THE OUTSIDE OBSERVER, WHICH ARE THE RADICALS AND WHO BELIEVES IN SELF-DETERMINATION.

WHEN THE MUJAHIDIN PARTIES WERE SOMEWHAT ARBITRARILY FORMED IN THE EARLY DAYS OF THE WAR, NO ONE MINDED THEIR FLAWS: WE NEVER THOUGHT THE SOVIETS WOULD LEAVE AFGHANISTAN, SO THE STRUCTURE OF THE RESISTANCE PARTIES WAS OF SMALL CONCERN. AFTER THE SOVIETS WITHDREW IN DEFEAT, AFGHANS BEGAN THINKING OF POLITICS. WE WATCHED THE PARTIES FORM INNUMERABLE FAILED ALLIANCES AND REALIZED THAT THEY HAD NO FUTURE APART FROM THE FRAGMENTATION OF OUR SOCIETY. THAT IS WHY WE FORMED THE NATIONWIDE UNITY OF MUJAHIDIN COMMANDERS: TO BUILD COOPERATION AND TRY AND TRANSCEND PARTY POLITICS.

IN THE EARLY DAYS OF THE COMMANDERS' SHURA, AHMAD SHAH MASSOOD AND HIS PEOPLE TOOK THE SIDE OF THE PARTIES AND OPPOSED THE SHURAS' POLITICAL DEPARTMENT. WE HAD NO POLITICAL DEPARTMENT

BECAUSE WE WANTED NO POLITICS: ONLY COMMITTEES FOR MILITARY COOPERATION, AND FOR PLANNING PEACE AND SECURITY. WE RELUCTANTLY AGREED TO MASSOOD'S REQUEST, AND THEY IMMEDIATELY STARTED HIRING, EXPANDING, AND BUILDING AN INTERNAL EMPIRE.

AIN WE ARGUED WITH MASSOOD AND HIS PEOPLE OVER OUR SUPPORT R THE UN PEACE PROGRAM WHICH AMERICAN AND OTHER DIPLOMATS AISED SO STRONGLY. TO US, THE UN PLAN EXPANDED THE NATION NCENSUS (SIC) BEYOND PARTIES AND EVEN COMMANDERS.

BOTHERED US THAT MASSOOD FORMED HIS SHURA OF THE NORTH AS A STINCTLY REGIONAL AND ETHNIC UNITY. WE FEARED IT WOULD BE HNICALLY AND GEOGRAPHICALLY DIVISIVE. WE MADE CERTAIN THAT E NATIONWIDE COMMANDER'S SHURA CONTAINED MORE HAZARAS AND RE NORTHERN MINORITIES THAN PUKHTOONS BECAUSE WE WANTED EVERY OUP TO FEEL SECURE IN A NATIONAL ORGANIZATION. ALTHOUGH SSOOD FINALLY AGREED TO SUPPORT THE UN PEACE PLAN, OUR NCERNS PROVED REAL. HE BROKE PROMISES HAD PURPOSELY BOTAGED THE UN PEACE PLAN AFTER ALLYING HIMSELF WITH DOSTAM, ME PARCHAMIS, SAYYAFF AND KHALIS.

TER WE CAPTURED SAROBI AND ALL THE POWER STATIONS, MY TROOPS D I WERE AT THE EASTERN EDGE OF KABUL ABOUT SIX KILOMETERS OM THE PRESIDENTIAL PALACE. MASSOOD AND HIS MEN WERE MUCH RTHER AWAY IN BAGRAM, BUSY FIGHTING HEKMATYAR'S FORCES. IT JULD HAVE BEEN EASY FOR MY TROOPS TO MOVE INTO KABUL, BUT I NTED COOPERATION AMONG THE MUJAHIDIN. I CONTACTED MASSOOD D ASKED IF HE HAD A SECURITY PLAN FOR KABUL: HE HAD NONE, ROMISED TO SEND AN EMISSARY TO LOOK AT MY PLAN, AND IN THE EANTIME PLEDGED NOT TO INVADE THE CITY UNTIL SECURITY COULD BE AINTAINED. THUS I DID NOT BELIEVE REPORTS THAT HIS MEN WERE OVING INTO KABUL THREE DAYS LATER. BY THE FOURTH DAY,

ASSOOD'S TROOPS WERE SPREAD OUT AND THE LOOTING BEGAN.

MY TROOPS WERE ALSO EAGER TO ENTER KABUL BUT I FORBADE THEM SO THAT THEY WOULD NOT CONTRIBUTE TO THE PROBLEM. AS YOU KNOW, MUCH OF THE CITY WAS DESTROYED AND MORE WAS LOOTED. MASSOOD'S OFFICIALS GAVE VOUCHERS TO SMALLER COMMANDERS, AUTHORIZING THEM TO SIEZE VEHICLES FROM ONE GOVERNMENT DEPARTMENT AFTER ANOTHER. ONE OF THESE VOUCHERS IS ATTACHED TO THIS LETTER (POST COMMENT: VOUCHER NOT ATTACHED TO ORIGINAL LETTER). WITHIN A WEEK, MOST GOVERNMENT DEPARTMENTS HAD NO CARS AND THE COMMANDERS HAD SOLD THE CARS THEY CONFISCATED. LITERALLY, SEVERAL TONS OF GOLD AND MILLIONS OF DOLLARS IN FOREIGN CURRENCY WERE TAKEN FROM THE CENTRAL BANK. EMBASSIES WERE LOOTED AS WAS THE MONEY EXCHANGE AND PARTS OF THE MUSEUM. HOMES WERE ROBBED AND HOMEOWNERS WERE SLAIN. BECAUSE OF A LACK OF COOPERATION, THESE MEN WERE LOOTING INSTEAD OF MAINTAINING SECURITY.
WE HOPE THAT BEFORE MUJAHIDIN ENTERED THE CITY WE COULD SUSTAIN ELECTRICAL POWER, MAINTAIN SECURITY AND THEN BRING SUPPLIES OF FOOD INTO KABUL WITH THE MUJAHIDIN. I WAS WORKING CLOSELY WITH UN ENVOY BENON SEVAN, ATTEMPTING TO SHIP UN FOOD INTO KABUL TO DISTRIBUTE TO THE CITIZENS AND RESTORE CONFIDENCE. THAT PLAN WAS THWARTED AS FIGHTING BROKE OUT BETWEEN HEKMATYAR'S AND MASSOOD'S TROOPS. SHORTLY THEREAFTER MASSOOD'S ORDERS (NOT PROFESSOR MOJADIDI'S) BANNED WOMEN FROM THE TELEVISION AND ISSUED EDICTS ON A FUNDAMENTALIST DRESS CODE AND HIRING PRACTICES.

TODAY IN KABUL, INFLATION RUNS RAMPANT. JUST PRIOR TO THE SHURA MEETING THAT ELECTED PROFESSOR RABBANI, A SHIPMENT OF NEWLY PRINTED BANKNOTES WAS FLOWN FROM THE FORMER SOVIET UNION

TO KABUL AND TAKEN STRAIGHT TO THE PRESIDENTIAL PALACE, BYPASSING THE CENTRAL BANK. THAT MONEY, BILLIONS OF AFGHANIS WORTH MORE THAN TEN MILLION DOLLARS, WENT TO BUY VOTES. AS THE PRINTING PRESSES CRANK OUT AFGHANIS, PEOPLES' MEAGRE SAVINGS ARE DECIMATED. FOR SEVERAL MONTHS, GOVERNMENT WORKERS HAVE RECEIVED NO SALARIES, AS AVAILABLE FUNDS WERE USED BY THE GOVERNMENT TO BUY VOTES. THROUGHOUT THE PAST TWO MONTHS, CROWDS OF GOVERNMENT WORKERS AND OTHERS GATHER EVERY SEVERAL DAYS, HOPING TO WITHDRAW SAVINGS FROM THE BANK. THEY ARE DRIVEN AWAY BY TROOPS AND TANKS BECAUSE NO MONEY REMAINS IN THE

BANKS, NOT EVEN PERSONAL SAVINGS, AND NO NEW MONEY ARRIVED

TODAY MASSOOD, ONCE PRAISED AS THE CHAMPION OF ETHNIC MINORITIES, IS ALLIED WITH SAYYAFF'S FUNDAMENTALISTS AGAINST THE SHIA MINORITIES. YET AVERAGE AFGHANS ARE COMING TO REALIZE THAT WHEN RABBANI AND MASSOOD PREACHED MINORITY RIGHTS, WHEN HEKMATYAR PREACHED MAJORITY RIGHTS, WHEN SAYYAFF AND KHALIS WARNED AGAINST THE SHIA AND MOJADIDI ARGUED FOR THE SHIA -- IT WAS NOTHING MORE THAN SELF-SERVING RHETORIC.

THIS GOVERNMENT IS NOT BROAD-BASED. IT USES MEN AND MATERIAL TO EXPAND ITS TERRITORY WHILE MAKING NO ATTEMPT TO BRING LAW AND ORDER TO THE PLACES IT ALREADY SUPPOSEDLY CONTROLS. AND IT CAN HARDLY BE DEMOCRATIC WHEN, AT THE SHURA, RABBANI STOOD AS THE SOLE CANDIDATE AND THE GOVERNMENT BRANDISHED MACHINE GUNS INSIDE THE SHURA TO SILENCE DELEGATES WHO TRIED TO COMPLAIN. MOREOVER, WHILE THE GOVERNMENT IS NOT BROAD-BASED, IT WILL NOT BECOME SO BY FORMING AN ALLIANCE WITH HEKMATYAR OR ANY OTHER POLITICAL FACTION PRIMARILY INTERESTED IN SHORT-TERM POWER AND LOOT. AS IN THE DAYS OF THE MISBEGOTTEN RESISTANCE PARTIES, ALLIANCES FORM AND BREAK UP AGAIN, RETAINING POWER FOR THEIR

LEADERS AND IGNORING BASIC RIGHTS OF SELF-DETERMINATION. FOREIGN BACKERS SUPPORT THEIR FAVORED FACTIONS, AND EACH FACTION NEEDS ITS ENEMY BECAUSE NOTHING BUT AN ENEMY JUSTIFIES ITS EXISTENCE.

DO NOT GET ME WRONG: I DO NOT OBJECT TO MASSOOD AND JAMIAT AS THE ONLY PEOPLE CREATING PROBLEMS, BUT THEY CHOSE TO FORM THIS GOVERNMENT AND ARE THUS IN POSITIONS OF RESPONSIBILITY.

TODAY THERE IS LITTLE CONTACT BETWEEN PROVINCIAL CAPITOLS AND KABUL, EVEN LITTLE BETWEEN DISTRICTS AND PROVINCIAL CAPITOLS. ON ITS CURRENT PATH, AFGHANISTAN RUNS THE RISK OF BECOMING FIFTY OR MORE SEPARATE KINGDOMS. FOREIGN EXTREMISTS HAVE BEGUN TO MOVE IN, BUYING HOUSES AND WEAPONS. AFGHANISTAN MAY BECOME UNIQUE IN BEING BOTH A TRAINING GROUND AND MUNITIONS DUMP FOR FOREIGN TERRORISTS AND AT THE SAME TIME THE WORLD'S LARGEST POPPY FIELD.

Lucy,   4/14/04
This letter was converted to a
cable by the consulate in
Peshawar; the consulate, I would
surmise, received the letter from
Abdul. The consulate cabled
it to the State Department. The
South Asia Bureau sent this
~~over in the EAP Bureau~~
copy to me about January, '02.
As noted in my letter, I was
in the East Asia Bureau. I
assume the consulate appended...

SOME US OFFICIALS HAVE ASKED JOURNALISTS I KNOW TO DOWNPLAY THE
PROBLEMS OF THIS GOVERNMENT. IT IS NOT AN ISSUE TO HIDE.
AFGHANISTAN'S POTENTIAL FOR POVERTY, DRUG PRODUCTION AND
TERRORISM IS A PROBLEM NOW; BUT IF IGNORED IT IS A CERTAIN
RECIPE FOR EMBARRASSING REGIONAL DISASTER. WE HAVE A PROVERB
ABOUT CAPPING THE CHIMNEY ON A STOVE: NOBODY SEES THE SMOKE OR
THE FIRE, BUT IT BURNS BELOW AND EVENTUALLY EXPLODES.

SIMILARLY, I DO NOT KNOW IF MASSOOD'S BEHAVIOR COMES AS A
SURPRISE TO DIPLOMATS WHO THOUGHT HIM A RESPONSIBLE MODERATE,
BUT THERE HAD LONG BEEN A DOUBLE STANDARD. WHEN, FOR EXAMPLE,
PIR GAILANI WENT TO MEET NAJIB, AMERICAN DIPLOMATS DENOUNCED
HIM SOUNDLY AND REFUSED TO SEE HIM: YET FOR YEARS MASSOOD'S

PEOPLE HELD TALKS WITH NAJIB AND THE SOVIETS AND THEIR
DISCUSSIONS WERE TERMED GOOD STRATEGY BY THE SAME DIPLOMATS.
THE FACT REMAINS THAT THE FOREIGN SUPPORTERS OF THE MUJAHIDIN,
IN CHOOSING WHOM TO GIVE WEAPONS AND SUPPORT, CREATED SEVERAL
MONSTERS. IT WOULD BE UNFAIR AND PERHAPS DISREPUTABLE OF THOSE
FOREIGN SUPPORTERS TO WALK AWAY AND LEAVE ORDINARY AFGHANS TO
COPE WITH THESE HEAVILY ARMED OPPONENTS OF SELF-DETERMINATION.

TODAY AFGHANISTAN'S POLITICIANS FOSTER MUTUAL HATRED TO STAY IN
POWER. YET THE COUNTRY'S PROBLEMS ARE NOT ABOUT SHIAS AND
SUNNIS, TAJIKS AND PUKHTOONS. THEY ARE ABOUT FOOD, SECURITY,
FUEL, EDUCATION AND HEALTH: THINGS DAMAGED BY THE WAR AND STILL
BEING STOLEN OR DENIED BY A SMALL CADRE OF POLITICIANS. I
STILL BELIEVE THAT THE UN PEACE PLAN MAY WORK WITH MINOR
ALTERATIONS, FOR THE UN PROGRAM FOCUSES ITS ATTENTION ON THE
LASTING AND TRADITIONAL CENTERS OF POWER: THE TRIBES AND

FAMILIES, THE RELIGIOUS LEADERS, THE INTELLECTUALS, AND THE
COMMANDERS. AS YOU CAN SEE FROM AN ATTACHED COPY OF AN OLDER
LETTER I SENT YOU, MY PREDICTIONS WERE UNHAPPILY ACCURATE (POST
COMMENT: COPY OF EARLIER LETTER BEING FORWARDED BY POUCH).
IT WAS DISHEARTENING TO VISIT KABUL AND WATCH PEOPLE SHOOTING
ONE ANOTHER LIKE WILD DOGS. IT SEEMED CLEAR THAT THOSE
CURRENTLY GRASPING FOR POWER ARE WILLING TO DO ANYTHING FOR
THEMSELVES. WE WERE WILLING TO ACCEPT THIS GOVERNMENT BUT THEY
REFUSED TO DO A GOVERNMENT'S JOB AND PROVIDE PUBLIC SERVICE.
MOREOVER THEY APPEAR TO FEEL THEY CAN ONLY TRUST THEMSELVES AND
SEEM UNWILLING TO SHARE AUTHORITY WITH OTHERS. I FINALLY
REFUSED OFFERS TO WORK WITH THE SOCALLED GOVERNMENT BECAUSE,
WHILE I WILL DO ANYTHING POSITIVE, I WILL NOT BECOME PART OF
THE PROBLEM.
SPEAKING POSITIVELY THEN, THE FIRST STEP TOWARD POLITICAL

RECONSTRUCTION IS BUILDING PUBLIC TRUST, AND THE KNOWLEDGE THAT
THE CURRENT AFGHAN WAR IS NOT AN ETHNIC WAR, BUT RATHER A WAR
OF POLITICIANS AND OPPORTUNISTS WHO ARE BLAMING THE PEOPLE FOR
PROBLEMS THE PEOPLE NEVER MADE. SEVERAL MILLION AFGHANS WORKED
TOGETHER IN EXILE, PEACEFULLY IGNORING SECT OR ETHNICITY. MANY
FORMED BUSINESS PARTNERSHIPS, OTHERS INTER-MARRIED. THE
LOGICAL OUTCOME SHOULD BE INCREASED UNDERSTANDING, NOT
HOSTILITY.

SLOWLY SOME OF US, FROM MANY GROUPS AND AREAS, ARE ESTABLISHING
CONTACTS AND DIALOGUE, FINDING WE AGREE ON MOST OF THESE
POINTS. AVERAGE AFGHANS ARE UNDER TERRIFIC PRESSURE WITH
FAMILY AND SECURITY CONCERNS, WITH WORRIES ABOUT DRUGS AND
ABOUT THE UNFAMILIAR FOREIGN EXTREMISTS COMING IN INCREASING
NUMBERS TO CITIES AND TOWNS. SLOWLY, THE WORD SPREADS THAT
AFGHANS CANNOT HAVE A STRONG AFGHANISTAN WITHOUT EACH OTHER,
AND THE AVERAGE MAN OR WOMAN IS NOT PART OF THE PROBLEM.

A NUMBER OF US ARE THUS TRYING TO DO SOMETHING, AND WHILE WE
HAVE NO COMPLETE PLAN YET THERE IS CAUSE FOR OPTIMISM IN AN
EMERGING CONCENSUS. ONE ACTIVITY YOU MIGHT CONSIDER IS MEETING
A WIDE VARIETY OF AFGHANS INSIDE AND OUTSIDE AFGHANISTAN, ALSO
IN CITIES APART FROM KABUL AND AWAY FROM GOVERNMENT AS SUCH.
IT WOULD GIVE YOU FRESH PERSPECTIVES AND ALLOW YOU TO MAKE UP
YOUR MIND BETTER THAN ANY LETTER. REGARDLESS, YOU ARE SOMEONE
WHO CARES DEEPLY ABOUT OUR COUNTRY, AND YOU'VE PROVED YOUR
SINCERITY MANY TIMES OVER MANY YEARS. WE WOULD APPRECIATE ANY
IDEAS OR SUGGESTIONS THAT YOU WISH TO SHARE.

SINCERELY YOURS, ABDUL HAQ.

ENDNOTES

1   There were three non fighting groups of Afghan exiles by 2000. The Rome group comprised the supporters of the ex King, Zahir Shah; the Bonn group was a splinter of the Rome group and the Cyprus group was made up of mostly Hazara and Pashtun Afghans who were against the re-instatement of the ex King and backed by Iran. Karzai was a member of the Rome Group (also known as the 'Rome Process').

2   For example in his book *Descent into Chaos*, (2008) Rashid says that – unlike his peers he argued in favour of an external military intervention in Afghanistan, seeing this as the 'only' way to 'save' the Afghan people from the Taliban .... and prevent the spread of al Qaeda ideology; he also says that he was 'intimately involved' with events - both 'as a reporter' but also as 'an adviser' and member of a what sounds to be a tight knit team of 'outside experts' which included Barnett Rubin (and a handful of other writers) and which had regular brainstorming sessions with UN officials (both pre and post 9/11) and which promoted their ideas to international organizations and western governments. Eg on p 55 Rashid discusses an initiative promoted by the then head of the UN Special Mission to Afghanistan, Francesc Vendrell. This was a concept paper produced in Spring 2001. Rashid notes: *"The paper called for the rearming of the Northern Alliance in order to deny the Taliban total victory. Along with Vendrell's initiative, the experts group began to promote a new thesis. Led by Barnett Rubin, we wrote a joint paper that was circulated widely ..."*. See pages XL1, XL11, 55, 405. And footnote 2 in Chapter Ten in *'Descent into Chaos'*. He also adds (p54) that this group 'brainstormed with Brahimi and other UN official several times a year' at the UN in New York but also in Berlin and Oslo. He adds 'all of us in the group had been good friends for a long time', all admired one anothers work and had enormous respect for Brahimi. In his acknowledgements (p405) he says that he and Rubin had become so close that he is not able to say whether the ideas in his book came first from Rubin or from himself. He also owes a great deal to Lakhdar Brahimi and Francesc Vendrell, who, as he says were, 'the architects' of the Bonn agreement (p 405).

3   See page 103 of Rashid's book, *Descent into Chaos*, (2008) where he explains that Barnett Rubin, who attended the Bonn Conference in November 2001, was given diplomatic status by the UN.

4   The other main branch of the Pashtun is the Durrani, associated with the former King and with Hamid Karzai.

5   As documented in, for example; Patricia Gossman, *Casting Shadows: War Crimes and Crimes against Humanity: 1978-2001*, Afghan Justice Project, 2005. Also reported variously by Human Rights Watch and by Afghan Independent Human Rights Commission in Kabul, *A Call for Justice: A National Consulation on past Human Rights Violations in Afghanistan*, Kabul, 2005.

6   For a period of eighteen months until the first presidential elections.

7   Dovkants, K. *The Evening Standard* 5 October, 2001

8   Gordon, M. and Weiner, T. 'A Nation Challenged: The Mission: A frantic call for US help that came too late'. *The New York Times*, 27 October 2001.
9   ibid
10 *Private Eye*, Issue 1040, 2 November 2001
11 Whitney Azoy, who also wrote an important work on Afghan Buzkashi.
12 W. Azoy, *The Bangor Daily News*, November 2001.
13 ibid
14 After the crucial battle of Taloqan in October 2000.
15 French MOD report.
16 Estimated at $236 billion so far by Eric Margolis in the *Toronto Sun*, 11 October 2009.
17 Cowell, 'US General Says'
18 From an unclassified memo quoted by Seth Jones, *Foreign Affairs*, May–June 2010 issue
19 D. Davis MP, *The Times*, July 2009.
20 on this point I differ with Ahmed Rashid, who argues in *Descent into Chaos*, "At the time of the invasion I broke with many of my colleagues by arguing that the war in Afghanistan was a just war and not an imperialist intervention, because only external intervention could save the Afghan people from the Taliban and al Qaeda and prevent the spread of al Qaeda ideology". PP XLIII
21 Public talk held on 26 May 2010 at the Geneva Centre for Security Policy.
22 Coll, Steve, *Ghost Wars*; pp 445
23 Rashid, Ahmed, *Descent into Chaos*, pp 87 'Haq's aim was to avoid the bloodshed that was sure to follow an American invasion'. Haq's apparent 'objective' for his mission as quoted to Rashid differs from what he tells other interlocutors and journalists as discussed in my book. Eg that it was important to put in place a 'structure' that could go on without him.
24 Barfield, Thomas. *Afghanistan; a Cultural and Political History*. pp288 and Rashid. A. *Descent into Chaos*;. pp. 87
25 Liu, M, *Newsweek*, 29 October 2001.
26 Conversation between Abdul Haq and Joe Ritchie (email from James Ritchie to author).
27 Email to author from Ken Guest, April 2009.
28 ibid
29 He and Massoud had made a pact to work together at Kulyab in July 2001, cited by former US Ambassador to the Mujahideen, Peter Tomsen (email to author, 2009) and by James Ritchie (telephone conversation, July 2009) both of whom were present. James Ritchie has video footage of the meeting.
30 W. Azoy, *The Bangor Daily News*, November 2001.
31 phone conversation between Peter Jouvenal and author, June 2009
32 A. Rashid, 'In Afghanistan, Let's Keep It Simple', *The Washington Post*, 6 September 2009.
33 Quoted by G. Arney, *Afghanistan*, Mandarin paperbacks, 1990, p.7
34 W. Azoy, *The Bangor Daily News*, November 2001
35 The projects were overseen by UNCHS but eventually became known as the National Solidarity Programme (NSP) when taken over by the IBRD in 2002.
36 Many of these relate to the reasons why the West should support Haq, and detail his 'peace plan', including its costings and its merits vis-a-vis the alternatives for stabilising Afghanistan and neutralising the Taliban.

37 Letter from Abdul Haq to Saudi Ambassador in Islamabad, 1991.

38 From a population of around 30 million.

39 In line with the military and political policy adopted by the international community in Afghanistan, the Under Secretary General to the UN, Mr Lakhdar Brahimi had insisted that a 'light footprint' would be the best way for the UN to operate here. As such, we were only twenty- seven international election monitors led by an Afghan Loya Jirga Commission.

40 In fact many Pashtun leaders were also excluded. I expand upon this later in the book.

41 Prior to their election, each Loya Jirga candidate was required to read an *afadavit* stating that they had not been involved in human rights abuses.

42 Zulmay Khalilzad, an Afghan by birth, was at this stage the USA's Special Envoy to Afghanistan.

43 Post-Loya Jirga discussion convened by The Asia Foundation at the Kabul Intercontinental hotel, July 2002.

44 'Amniyat' is the dari translation of 'security'. The other name for the Intelligence Police is National Security Directorate (NSD).

45 KHAD was the 'Khadimat-e-Atal'at-e-Dowlati', the state intelligence service set up by the Soviets following their 1979 invasion and built on the Kremlin model, which used the tools of Stalin's terror: secret denunciations, anonymous spies and confessions extracted by torture. It grew to 25,000 personnel by 1989.

46 *First In* by ex-CIA operative Gary Schroen recounts how General Arif and Fahim were given sackloads of cash dollars when the CIA entered the Panjshir valley in September 2001.

47 Another colleague had been fired when she had queried Brahimi as to which of the three warlords in Mazar-i-sharif, was the 'government' that the UN was supposed to support.

48 In the post-September 11 intervention in Afghanistan, the international community failed to make aid receipts conditional upon the incorporation of womens' rights, or human rights or indeed the 'output' of services the money was meant to be funding.

49 The mujahideen had rounded on Dr. Sima Samar at the Loya Jirga after she'd been elected as one of three Deputy Chairs. Partly this was because all three Deputy Chairs had been elected fairly by the delegates. As such, all three were from progressive, pro-democracy parties.

50 See Footnote 2.

51 Y. Fouda and N. Fielding, *Masterminds of Terror; the truth behind the most devasting terrorist attack the world has ever seen*, Mainstream, 2003.

52 The terror group in the Philippines allied to al Qaeda and responsible for many atrocities.

53 Although not in the Taliban leadership, a UN colleague described Mohseni as 'a well known extremist/fundamentalist from Kandahar'. He was also a subsequent force behind the infamous Shia female status law in 2009.

54 Eurasia.net

55 Reuters, 17 June 2002.

56 The Interior Ministry would be run by a Pashtun named Taj Mohammad Wardak, a weak 81-year old US-based exile, recently married to the teenage daughter of Dr Abdullah, a Panjshiri cabinet member. His appointment was symbolic, he would have no control over a ministry full of Panjshiris. Fahim remained Defence

Minister and also Vice President. Dr Abdullah remained Foreign Minister. Dostum was made a Vice President. Sima Samar, the progressive and lively Women's Minister was replaced, a surprise to many. The Pashtun community, who despite comprising somewhere between forty to sixty percent of the population, had effectively been cut out of government from the moment the Northern Alliance took Kabul. The Cabinet list decided by Karzai – the warlords, the UN and US at the ELJ – essentially entrenched the Northern Alliance hold on power.

57 Near Taimanee, in late May 2001.

58 K. Dovkants (Islamabad), *Evening Standard*, 5 October 2001

59 ibid

60 ibid

61 Najibullah was the last Afghan Communist President of Afghanistan. He was removed in 1992 when the mujahideen entered Kabul. For four years he took shelter in a UN compound, until he was killed by the Taliban, who castrated him and suspended his and his brothers bodies from a tank when they took Kabul in 1996.

62 The Afghan Red Cross is known as the Red Crescent, as in other Muslim countries.

63 One had four daughters and her husband, disappointed his wife had given him no sons, simply left for Pakistan. Another's husband, depressed by continual war, became a heroin addict. Others, having lost men to the ongoing war and disallowed from working during the Taliban had no option but prostitution.

64 As a *Sheikh ul Hadis*, he is deemed to know thousands of verses of the Holy Qaran by heart. Such credentials are more akin to a religious man than to they type of modernising legal expert able to able to reform Afghanistan's decimated judiciary to bring it in line with modern values. Dr Shinwari's training was solely in Shariat law and not Western jurisprudence. This would not have been adequate for a Chief Justice under the King's 1964 Afghan Constitution.

65 During August 2002.

66 Under the jurisdiction of the Supreme Court.

67 They began issuing edicts to ban women from singing on television and to ban the showing of the weekly Bollywood film on Kabul TV, much to the annoyance of most Afghans.

68 Ismael Khan is a member of the Northern Alliance.

69 Meeting with RAWA representative, Kabul October 2002.

70 Northern Alliance faction based in the Panjshir.

71 James Ritchie, in discussing this with the author in October 2009 said of Rahman's killing, 'it was an unbelievable display of brazen lawlessness'. A senior officer and Fahim ally in the Interior Ministry was reputed to be behind this most public act of violence.

72 The Afghan Independent Human Rights Commission was established as one of four commissions (the others being a Constitutional Commission and an Electoral Commission and a Loya Jirga Commission) as part of the Bonn Agreement.

73 Author interview in Kabul, 5 September 2002.

74 Following threats to her by the mujahideen after an article published in Dr Rabanni's newspaper *Payam-e-Mujahid*.

75 Dr Rabbani's newspaper, *Payam-e-Mujahid*, which represents the viewpoint of the Shura-e-Nazar, accused Sima Samar of blasphemy on the basis that she had said, during an interview with a Canadian magazine, apparently said that Shariat law

could be used in a modified format in some instances.

76   Author interview with Dr Kasim Fasili, concerning both Judicial and Constitutional Commissions, 29 August 2002.

77   ibid

78   In the context of security sector reform, different G8 nations took on different roles. Hence the Germans trained the Afghan Police, the US and UK the Afghan National Army, the British covered drugs policy and the Italians did reform of the Justice Sector

79   International Crisis Group.

80   Author interview in Kabul, 1 September 2002.

81   For the 32 Governors.

82   Gulbuddin Hikmatyar was an Islamicist warlord who the Americans now seemed intent on finding dead or alive, despite the fact that the bulk of US dollars directed at funding the Afghan anti-Soviet war during the 1980s had been directed to him, despite the warnings of, amongst others, Abdul Haq. Earlier that spring, the USA had sent a Hellfire missile into a convoy of vehicles thought to be carrying Hikmatyar in the Kunar Valley, but the assassination attempt had failed. Several Afghans had died but Gulbuddin had not been among them.

83   Younus Qanooni was subsequently made Minister of Education.

84   Author interview, September 2002

85   Despite this, Wazir Akbar Khan is still considered Kabul's 'embassy' district and, inhabited mainly by foreign NGOs and US military, has rents which at around $10,000 to 15,000 USD per month, would certainly match those of the more splendid suburbs of Washington DC.

86   From Jalalabad onto the Pakistan border at Torkham, Haji Qadir's picture adorned many checkposts along the way.

87   The Eastern Shura comprised representatives of the four eastern provinces of Nangahar, Nuristan, Laghman and Kunar.

88   Peter Hopkirk, *The Great Game*, Oxford University Press, 1990.

89   One of those killed had been an Italian woman. The bandits had tried to force her to come with them, alone behind a rock. She had refused and maybe at this stage there had been a panic followed by the deaths of all. It's likely the bandits escaped up the adjoining side-valley.

90   N. H. Dupree, *A Historical Guide to Afghanistan*, Afghan Air Authority, 1977.

91   Dupree, now in her eighties and living in Peshawar, and her American archeologist husband Louis, were Kabul's most well known international couple in the 1970s. She wrote several books on Afghanistan and he documented the treasures of the Kabul Museum, before it's looting by mujahideen factions after the USSR's 1989 withdrawal. Reams of Dupree's guidebooks were printed in 1977 when Afghanistan was still a favoured tourist destination. Two years later, the Russian invasion, which began the twenty-three year war, ensured that Dupree's books remain the uncontested guide of Afghanistan. Piles of her unread blue hardbacks were put away. They reappeared in January 2002, somewhat damp after years of storage away from the Taliban's edicts in some deep, dank cellar. Now they were being sold by small boys to journalists, aid workers and ISAF soldiers on Kabul's Chicken street, named after the birds once traded here.

92   Acquired during years as a refugee in Germany, where he had run a hotel during the 1980s when his brothers were fighting the jihad in Afghanistan.

93 'Remnants of an Army' by Lady Butler, Tate Gallery, London

94 The event was documented by Sir John Kaye in his *History of the War in Afghanistan*. (Bentley, 1857):

A sentry on the ramparts looking towards the Cabul road,
Saw a solitary white-faced horseman struggling towards the fort.
The word was passed; the tidings spread. Presently the ramparts
Were lined with officers looking out with throbbing hearts,
Through unsteady telescopes, or with straining eyes tracing the
Road. Slowly and painfully, as though horse and rider were in an
Extremity of mortal weakness, the solitary mounted man came
Reeling, tottering on. They saw that he was an Englishman. On
A wretched weary pony, clinging, as one sick or wounded, to its
Neck, he sat, or rather leant forward; and there were those who,
as they watched his progress, thought he would never reach,
unaided, the walls of Jellalabad. A shudder ran through the garrison.
That solitary horseman looked like the messenger of death.....The messenger was Dr
Brydon, and he now reported his belief that he was the sole survivor of an army of some
sixteen thousand men.

95 In Islamic tradition, prayers are said each Friday for five weeks after the death

96 Malalai had compared their behaviour to women 'playing with bracelets in their homes', instead of fighting to oust the foreign presence

97 APC means Armoured Personnel Carrier

98 R. Kaplan, *Soldiers of God*, Vintage, 2001.

99 ibid

100 Even Afghan refugees (there were two million in camps around Peshawar) had to join one of the six 'parties' in order to be eligible for aid handouts.

101 Hizb-e-Khalis (as it became known) was distinct from that of Hikmatyar , Hizb-e-islami. The two had split in 1979 when Khalis wanted to engage in more active combat against the regime.

102 Mullah Khalis was one of the oldest of the seven 'party' leaders, and had been educated at a private madrassah in the NWFP of British India prior to the establishment of a nationwide Afghan education system. Later, he taught in the Friday mosque of the Jabbarkhel (i.e. the Arsala family clan).

103 for descriptions of accompanying Jalaluddin Haqqani's Hizb-i-Islami front during the early 1980s, Jere Van Dyk's 'In Afghanistan; an American Odyssey' is a superb account.

104 Another leading commander of the party was Jalaluddin Haqqani, who became more radicalised and joined the Taliban. Haqqani is thought to have invited bin Laden to return to Afghanistan in 1996, upon his expulsion from Sudan. Qadir, as Governor of Jalalabad, greeted him upon his arrival.

105 B Ruben, *The Fragmentation of Afghanistan* ,Yale, 1990.

106 Generally the kuchi have found their traditional livelihoods eroded and so begun to settle on common pasture land. This plus the environmental pressures associated with a growing population and returnees coming from Pakistan after the war, has led to a proliferation of land and property conflicts throughout Afghanistan since 2001. The question is who resolves such conflicts: government, local tribal leaders or, increasingly, Taliban courts?

107 Qadir and Afridi had struck up a friendship over an incident involving Zardat, Hikmatyar 's notorious highwayman commander up at Sarobi. Afridi had bought

a fleet of six Pajero jeeps. Zardat's men impounded them at Sarobi and so Afridi turned to Qadir, then Governor of Jalalabad for help. After Qadir's intervention the cars were returned and a friendship was formed between the two men.

108 An Afghan who Qadir made intelligence chief in Jalalabad when he returned as Governor.

109 Torkham is the border between Pakistan and Afghanistan, at the Khyber Pass.

110 These were Qadir's bases for the Eastern Zone. They were not held by the Taliban but the Northern Alliance (under the auspices of Qadir). Also some bases in Laghman Province.

111 Dacca lies at the edge of the foothills on the Afghan side of the Khyber Pass. During much of the nineteenth century the British army occupied it as a forward base between the then India and Jalalabad.

112 A small valley between Jalalabad and the Kunar valley.

113 The MI6-backed warlord.

114 Qadir had also been Governor until 1996, when the Taliban had driven him out.

115 President Najibullah was the last Afghan Communist President of Afghanistan

116 Events subsequent to Massoud's move into Kabul are detailed in a letter Haq wrote to Peter Tomsen, the USA's former Ambassador to the Mujahiddeen (see Appendix V)

117 Six months after he made this comment, Hikmatyar joined forces with resurgent Taliban and Pakistani fundamentalists, and they called themselves 'Sword of Islam'.

118 Ambassador Yusuf M. Motabbakani of Saudi Arabia, based in Islamabad.

119 Kabul had not yet fallen to the mujahideen. It fell in 1991 and President Najibullah took sanctuary in the UN compound as the mujahideen factions began the fight for control of the city that was to last until 1996 when the Taliban came.

120 To Peter Tomsen, the USA's former envoy to the Mujahiddeen in Peshawar during the jihad

121 From the time of the 1973 coup which deposed King Zahir Shah, until the 1979 Soviet Invasion, Soviet-inspired reforms were introduced under several regimes.

122 R. Kaplan, *Soldiers of God*, Vintage, 1994.

123 Shaheed means Martyrdom. Haq is deemed Shaheed because he sacrificed himself for the cause of his country.

124 The Moghul Palace of King Akbar in India.

125 *Abdul Haq, Portrait of a Mujahid*, cultural committee of Kabul Mujahiddin Office, Peshawar.

126 Yet the circumstances leading to the fragmentation of Afghanistan's peace had their roots in previous decades.

The background to General Daoud's 1973 coup d'etat lay in the ascendancy of the Durrani dynasty. This part of the Pashtun tribe, from which came Afghanistan's Kings, had been ascendent over state and society since the end of the eighteenth century, but it had been weakening since King Zahir Shah's (1933-1973) father, Nader Shah came to power. Instead of making democratic reforms the two Kings continued to rely on Pashtun tribal and landed power.

By the late 1960s, several movements were emerging among the student population in Kabul. In parallel to the development of nationalist and communist parties, the Islamic movement had begun to emerge in the Sharia faculty of Kabul University. The Islamic opposition which fled to Pakistan at the time of Daoud's coup later took the shape of the Jamiat-i Islami, headed by Burhanuddin Rabbani, the Ittihad-i Islami, headed by Abd al-Rabb al-Rasul Sayyaf and the Hizb-i Islami, headed by Gulbuddin Hikmatyar. From Pakistan, they were able to launch an insurgency against Daoud's regime in Kabul. Interestingly, Peter Marsden gives some insight into how even then, the early resistance movement was ethnically divided. In his book *Taliban* he says the movement was initially comprised of Islamicist parties from the North, Uzbeks and Tajiks who had been forced to flee the Central Asian states at the time of the Bolshevik Revolution. The Pashtuns only joined en masse after the invasion of the Soviet Union. Marsden concludes that 'the early resistance was therefore, to a degree, a rising up of the element within Afghan society that had been marginalized by the ruling Pashtun establishment, with its tribal foundations'.

127 Although it was only later that Pashtuns joined the cause of the Islamicist parties, most having supported the Daoud friendly wing of the PDPA.

128 One effect of the Soviet invasion was to end the dominance over state and society enjoyed by the Durrani branch of the Pashtun tribe since the late eighteenth century. The resistance that followed the Soviet invasion of 1979 as well as the subsequent civil war allowed non-Pashtun ethnic groups to assert political and economic autonomy both from the state and from Pashtun dominance. From 1992 to 1996, the mainly Tajik Jamiat-i Islami party under President Burhanuddin Rabbani controlled the central government

129 The PDPA had two wings, Khalq and Parcham. Khalq was urban-based and Parcham more rural-based.

130 Haqqani went over to the Taliban early on and has remained with them.

131 Author conversations with Afghans in Jalalabad 2002-5

132 according to Antonio Giustozzi's paper '*Negotiating with the Taliban; issues and Prospects*' a Century Foundation Report (2010), unlike other Taliban fronts – such as the Pakistani Taliban – the Haqqani's have not pitted themselves against the Pakistani government or army but have remained focused on anti government activities within Afghanistan (in line with Pakistani strategic interests).

133 R. Kaplan, *Soldiers of God*, Vintage, 1994

134 With his brothers and their mujahiddin fighters, Haq and his men began to shape the caves at Tora Bora as a retreat from which to fight the Soviets. Later on, in the early 1990s, Osama bin Laden would base himself here, setting up training camps for extremists. It was from here that he slipped the noose of coalition forces in December 2001, most likely escaping across the border and into Pakistan.

135 which documents the covert operation of the CIA in Afghanistan during the 1980s

136 R. Kaplan, *Soldiers of God*, Vintage, 1994.

137 ibid

138 ibid

139 Even so, Haq realised the communist regime was not threatened by rural insurgencies and believed the fight must be taken to Kabul to hit the regime at its centre. He asked Khalis for arms and supplies but the old man refused, saying it was too dangerous and he too young and emotional. But Haq, determined, went anyway, transporting guns ahead, in the taxi of a friend. The guns never made it as the driver was caught and killed by the regime. So with three friends, Haq set out for Kabul by foot, journeying through the mountains to reach Tezin, on the city outskirts. They paused in the foothills to look at the city lights and once within the city contacted old friends and began building a network, being provided with

food, shelter and information about government activities.

From here Haq moved to Paghman, a valley to the North West of Kabul; an ideal base close to the city and Government installations and close to the refuge of the mountains. Haq's men cleared the area of agents suspected of working for government.

In Peshawar, the mujahideen headquarters continued to refuse Haq the arms and money needed to conduct operations. Finally though, during a trip to Peshawar to receive medical treatment and visit his family, Khalis recognised his resistance activities and agreed to support him.

Among his fighters, Haq enforced the principle that weapons belonged to the front, not to individual fighters. He even imprisoned some mujahideen for selling arms. Inside Kabul, he built a powerful guerrilla movement and an underground network, creating different cells of covert members under his command. The cells began with relatives and friends and people known to be anti-regime and grew to include trusted acquaintances. The network began to infiltrate the bureaucracy, the army and the Defence Ministry.

Kabul radio and TV, controlled by the communist regime, aimed to make Haq and the Kabul mujahideen a target of their propaganda. But Haq's network was so successful that the regime's frustration with it began to backfire. One day in 1988 Haq's Kabul front distributed resistance leaflets via a cell in the Defence Ministry. A leaflet was on each desk when personnel reported for work in the morning. But the Defence Minister was so angry that he chose three trusted officers to investigate. The officers were members of Haq's cell. So they identified several hardline Communists to the Defence officials and the men were severely punished. In this way, Haq's cells successfully formented problems between Khalq and Parcham, the two opposing factions of the Communist People's Democratic Party of Afghanistan (PDPA). They also distributed fake Red Star Soviet newspapers to the army, encouraging defection and disobedience.

Haq's tactical guerrilla fighting units around Kabul city operated in their own areas but united when necessary. From only four men Haq's command grew to over 5000, with units completely surrounding the city. In the longer term, Haq's military success was due more to foresight and the loyalty of his men than to a good supply of weapons.

140 P. Mishra, *What we think of America*, Granta 77, Spring 2002.

141 ibid

142 G. Crile, *Charlie Wilson's War: the extraordinary story of the largest covert operation in history*, Atlantic, 2003

143 Such was the US desire to defeat communism that the CIA even countenanced Pakistan's broader objective: to bring the borders of the Islamic world north of the Amu Darya (the river which forms Afghanistan's northern border with Russia). In an interview with the ISI chief, Pankaj Mishra says, 'Hamid Gul claimed his paper (on this strategy) went on to be read by high-placed officials in the CIA'. In fact, William Casey wanted the ISI to involve the Muslims of the Soviet Union in the jihad; he wasn't satisfied with the ISI-arranged smuggling of thousands of Qarans into what is now Uzbekistan and Tajikistan, or with the distribution of heroin among Soviet troops. An officer of the ISI I spoke to said the ISI received plenty of unofficial encouragement from Casey to attempt more damaging stuff, but nothing that could be traced back to the CIA or the government of the United States'.

144 A. Borovik, *The Hidden War: A Russian Journalist's Account of the War in Afghanistan*, 1990.

145 ibid

146 Pankaj Mishra, 2002.

147 A British journalist who was present, Jon Swain, witnessed what happened and told me of this incident.

148 I will describe more about what happened at Tora Bora later in the book.

149 This was the password.

150 The US coalition employed peshayee guards from Ali's tribe to guard their compounds in Jalalabad. To consider Hazerat Ali an ally of the Karzai government was short-sighted. On 4 October 2003 the shura-e-nazar party, led by Fahim and Rabbani, laid their cards firmly on the table, saying that they would run against Karzai in the June 2004 presidential elections. The irony of all this was that Haji Qadir, who the US and British distrusted, had been responsible for mobilising both Pashtun and Northern Alliance support for Karzai during the 2002 Loya Jirga, only weeks before his assassination.

151 Hizb-e-Islami, the Party of Younus Khalis, was the Resistance Party the Arsala family were associated with during the Jihad. It later split when Hikmatyar formed his own, more radical Hizb-e-Islami.

152 After the murder of their mother and another brother, Abdul Haq still had three sons and a daughter.

153 Author interview with Governor of Jalalabad, Haji din Mohammad, October 2002

154 At that time, very little of the reconstruction money promised for Afghanistan in January 2002 had arrived. Only $1 billion USD had been spent, and most of this on resettling returning refugees.

155 Professor Hasan Kakar

156 Much of the Arsala fortune has been made by importing spare parts for Landcruisers to Dubai.

157 The border areas around the Khyber Pass

158 Water catchment ditch.

159 A wise man.

160 In spring 2003, the issue of customs revenue being collected by Ismael Khan at the border, but not passed to central government, reached the press.

161 I could not be sure about this claim. For one day I had seen piles of cash pulled from beneath a bed by one of Zahir's staff. He claimed it was 'taxes' levied on the importation of buffalo from Pakistan at the Torkham border post. He also told me that using the cash to give to elders – presumably to buy their support - was 'Afghan rules'. Furthermore there was the issue of illegal logging and trucks carrying vast timbers which I guessed must have passed through the border post at Torkham which Zahir – as chief of the border guard - was controlling at the time. The timbers apparently mostly came from Kunar and Nuristan and were taken to Pakistan for processing.

162 Laying a price on the head of British and American nationals.

163 An edict banning the growing transportation and trafficking of poppy was issued by the Afghan Interim Government on 17 January 2002.

164 A UNODCCP report on Afghan poppy production (October 2002) showed a dramatic rise for the year. Production had surged from 185 metric tonnes (in 2001) to 3,400 metric tonnes (in 2002).

165 In September 2002.

166 Within the EU, farmers cannot receive area payments, for the amount of land area they owned, unless it was verified they actually owned or farmed the land claimed upon.

167 P. Hensher, *The Mulberry Empire*, 2002.

168 Like Afghan warlords, except blacked out windows were banned in Afghanistan in early 2002.

169 Incredibly, even by 2009, none of the FCO staff operating in Afghanistan spoke Pashtu (according to a House of Commons Foreign Affairs Select Committee Report on Afghanistan and Pakistan, July 2009)

170 WRC: Welfare and Relief Committee, a Pakistan-based NGO.

171 The eastern provinces which bordered Nangarhar.

172 The 'Eastern Shura' of which Qadir was nominally leader during his days as Governor of Jalalabad before the arrival of the Taliban, comprised the Provinces of Kunar, Nuristan, Nangarhar and Laghman.

173 During the Emergency Loya Jirga of June 2002.

174 Haji Zahir had taken 1000 soldiers and closed the bazaar and seized poppy paste at the time of President Karzai's April 2002 edict banning the growing and trafficking of poppy.

175 As documented by the UN and others and reported in the *Afghan Justice Project* report (Kabul, 2005) collated by Patricia Gossman.

176 Others in Jalalabad thought it possible Haji Zaman had taken money from Osama bin Laden in return for providing him safe passage over the mountains to Pakistan. They felt the British had 'chosen him' as Zaman was a man of the ISI despite the obvious flaws with relying upon Pakistani intelligence. Many believed Osama and key al Qaeda leaders simply used the route out through Parachinar, a town on the border with Pakistan. Unfortunately, Pakistan, the USA's key ally in the war on terror, was guarding that exit!

177 Haji Rohullah, a leader of the Salafi sect was arrested by the Coalition in August 2002, accused of being al Qaeda, and taken to Guantanamo Bay. His cousin, Wuli Wullah was the man Haji Zaman (and indirectly the British) selected to run the poppy scheme.

178 Had the British FCO consulted with our own Ministry of Agriculture in London, they surely would have informed that to run an area-based compensation payment scheme, such as is common throughout the EU, whereby the Integrated Arable Area Control system (IACS) underlies all area-based payments, You have to have a mapping of the land area first to prevent fraud.

179 Shown on Channel IV on the 25 May 2003 entitled: 'Here's One We Invaded Earlier'. Juniper Productions.

180 Part of the 'false narrative' as to when the Afghan insurgency resurrected itself must surely relate to the fact that so much attention was focused on Iraq from late 2002 onwards. It is for this reason, rather than the lack of cash spent on Afghanistan as has been cited, that people failed to notice the early strength of the insurgency. Instead many military commentators have estimated (wrongly in my view) that the insurgency only reasserted itself in 2004.

181 Gall, C. 'US Military investigates death of Afghan in custody' *New York Times* 4 March 2003 and Golden, T. 'In US Report, Brutal details of 2 Afghan inmates deaths' *New York Times*, 20 May 2005

182 Author conversation with two British war correspondents after they had reported on operations by British Marines in Afghanistan, June 2002

183 In *The Thin Blue Line: How Humanitarianism went to War* (Verso, 2009), Conor Foley argues that neither Afghanistan nor Iraq followed the blueprint of the humanitarian interventions of the 1990s.

184 While poppy production increased exponentially around Afghanistan 2003–2008, in Nangarhar it decreased.

185 *Afghan Justice Project* 'Candidates and the Past: The Legacy of War Crimes and the Political Transition in Afghanistan' (2005)

186 In the letters by Abdul Haq written to foreign ambassadors.

187 See among others; Fouda, Y., and N. Fielding, *Masterminds of Terror; the truth behind the most devasting terrorist attack the world has ever seen*, Mainstream, 2003.

188 Kate Clark, 2004.

189 In 2005, when many of them were elected to the parliament, they very soon passed a law giving themselves impunity for past rights abuses.

190 The International Crisis Group echoed these concerns about the Constitutional Commission when it said: 'the transitional authority (TA) and the UN have created a process lacking in transparency that accommodates the factions now in power in Kabul ... because the groups that dominate the TA, like the ethnic Panjshiri-Tajik shura-e-nazar heavily influenced the selections, few Afghans are likely to accept the Commissions as respresentative or neutral bodies'.

191 Even though the word democracy appeared in the 1964 Constitution.

192 Bill Rammell.

193 King of Afghanistan between 1880–1901.

194 I visited another place where incursions had been made in the Mohmand area. There the people told me the following:And so the next day I set out, accompanied by Majeed and Haji din Mohammad's second son, Khalil. We headed in the direction of the parched gullies and mountains skirting the Khyber pass. Eventually we arrived at a place called Goste in the Mohmand tribal area.

His added that the local Mohmand people (this is the Mohmand tribal district) are

Later, at a village called Anar Gai, men wearing an array of turbans crowded round us as we stepped from the vehicle. They were already stammering nine to the dozen, in an effort to get their concerns across. Above us, they pointed out three new Pakistani checkpoints in the hills above.

'The Pakistanis have come across the Durand line into our territory' was the essence of their concerns. 'This land is autonomous and though we will not be ruled by Kabul; the land is Afghan we as Afghans will fight to the death not to be part of Pakistan'.

An elder named Mangal pointed out rocks close by.

'The Americans arrived and stayed there. They came in twenty four Chinooks full of six hundred solders and fifty tanks/humvees. I went into their camp and asked why there were here? Their commander said, 'The Pakistani government told us that al Qaeda is operating in this area'.

The elder snorted, dismissively, 'But I told them, No they're not. Go into the villages and see how friendly the people are and drink tea'. The Americans had done so, distributing sweets to the children and after four days they left, one soldier having broken his leg and another being bitten by a snake.

195 He added that the local Mohmand people (this is the Mohmand tribal district) are taking up arms against the Pakistanis, attacking their checkposts with small arms fire at night. 'We'll fight to the death', they said.

196 The Durand Line was a creation of the British who negotiated a treaty with Amir Abdur Rahman in 1893, ceding a large swathe of formerly Afghan Pashtun territory to British India. The agreement was supposed to last hundred years but the conditions were so unfavourable that many Afghans have never recognised it. The British were keen to aquire this territory in order to split the unruly Pashtun people, with the hope of exerting some control over them. However, negotiations over the Durand Line have been a source of unceasing conflict between Afghanistan and Pakistan, particularly since the Partition of India in 1947. The squabbles were partly why Pakistan persisted in supporting brutal Pashtun warlord Gulbuddin Hikmatyar , in the hope that he would form a friendly pro-Pakistan Pashtun government in Kabul, hence obviating the need to renegotiate the Durand Agreement.

197 P. Marsden, *The Taliban: War, Religion and the New Order in Afghanistan*, Oxford University Press, 1998.

198 After the US had refused to sell arms to Kabul or provide loans with good terms, Moscow had equipped and trained the Afghan army and air force. Then the Soviets began to build large infra-structural projects such as the highway between Tajikistan to Kabul, linking the north with the capital and the Soviet empire with the ancient monarchy. It was clear to me when I visited the Salang pass in summer 2002, that such a vast engineering project must have been built with the strategic objectives of an invasion in mind. When I remarked on this to Baryalai as we drove to Peshawar in October 2002, he said 'the problem was that the Americans weren't helping us at the time, against Pakistan and so we had to look north'. The Soviets developed gas pipelines in the north of the country and built the huge military base at Bagram, now occupied by US coalition forces, to the north of Kabul.

199 See, for example, Kaplan, R. *Soldiers of God*. Vintage books, (p. 216) and Burke, J. *Al Qaeda; Casting a Shadow of Terror*. IB Tauris, 2003. (p. 76).

200 In June 2003

201 Ahmed Rashid, August 2004

202 McGirk, T, (Shkin) 'Battle in "the Evilest Place". *Time*, 3 November 2003

203 A. Warren, *Waziristan, the Faqir of Ipi, and the Indian Army: The North West Frontier Revolt of 1936–37*, New York: Oxford University Press, 2000.

204 ibid

205 ibid

206 C. Miller, *Khyber*, Macdonald and James, 1977.

207 Fletcher, *Afghanistan, Highway of Conquest*, 1965.

208 ibid

209 Isambard Wilkinson, *Daily Telegraph*.

210 Years later, I realised how this very factor underpinned the soundness of his personality. That Ritchie was here to do what he genuinely could for Afghanistan and had a deep and abiding love for this place and for its people and despite having his own family (who came with him to Jalalabad each year until security got so bad) he would be here for months at a time, nurturing his nursery saplings and agricultural projects. These projects were undertaken through the International Foundation of Hope, which Ritchie had founded and which by 2009 had planted over a million fruit and nut trees (in the eastern region) for more than six thousand farmers. It had also set up over fifty women's nurseries.

211 al Haq, President of Pakistan

212 He told Ritchie this in July 2002 when they met in Dushanbe.

213 General Franks was Chief of US Central Command, CENTCOM, when he retired from active service in May 2003.

214 It is to my regret that I did not speak with Benazir Bhutto about this before her death.

215 R. Kaplan, *Soldiers of God*, Vintage

216 ibid

217 P. Ashdown, *The Times*, September 2001. 'RAM' Seeger later says that he had shown Ashdown an email written by Ken Guest and that Ashdown had liked it and asked if he could use it as the basis for an article.

218 In Northern Ireland

219 Chairman of the Special Forces Club

220 Such as MI6, MOD, SIS, political players with leverage

221 There has even been a book written specifically on Malang's operations around Kandahar.

222 Ambassador Akram, GCSP, June 2010

223 Younus Khalis's son has since become part of the 'new' Taliban and this has been a problem for din Mohammad.

224 *Afghan Warrior,* Touch Productions, 2003 (made by cameraman and Afghan analyst Ken Guest and film-maker Malcolm Brinkworth).

225 M. Beardon and J. Risen, *The Main Enemy*, Ballantine Books/ Presidio Press, 2003.

226 G. Crile, *Charlie Wilson's War*, 2004.

227 This idea was later backed up by Haq's Kabul/Paghman-based commander Khan Mir who had been waiting for instructions. Mir had been 'embedded' with the Taliban Deputy Interior Minister who had several battallions ready to turn over to Haq's side.

228 Author interview with Khan Mir, 2004

229 He was speaking of the Rome Process, in which Haq had played such an active part in the six months prior to his death.

230 For most of the jihad, Haq and his family were associated with the 'party' of Younis Khalis, and the Arsala family were *khan khel* or the 'top' family of the clan.

231 As far as the 'plan' went, Seeger had written up a list of potential costings for weaponry, transport and equipment but stressed that the requirements would depend on how the enemy reacted and who joined the invading columns. Initial figures totalling 5,078,770.00 USD were based on the first 5000 men. ie. 45 groups of 100 men grouped into 9 larger groups of 500. If the force were doubled to a 10,000 man force this was estimated at around $10,441,490.

232 Shah Shujah, known by Afghans as the 'Puppet King', was installed by the British in 1837 and died in 1841.

233 S. Kiley, *The Spectator*, February 2004.

234 Interview with author, September 2003.

235 Stove heater.

236 Even during the Taliban regime it was possible to make an international phone call from the Post Office in Kandahar.

237 Also, Pakistani.

238 Interview of Abdul Haq by Melinda Liu of *Newsweek*, 29 October 2001.

239 Near Tera Mangal in Hezarac.

240 Pp. 58 by Paul Torday. Phoenix, London (2007)

241 He was technically elected for the 'first' time in September 2004 as since 2002 he had been President of Afghanistan's Interim Authority.

242 Author's diary, 2004.

243 Kaplan, R. D. *Soldiers of God: with Islamic Warriors in Afghanistan and Pakistan*. Vintage Departures Edition November 2001. New York. Pp 190 and 181

244 Coalition Forces Commander (2003–5), General Dan McNeil, felt that each regional PRT, rather than just being a vehicle to bring security, should also be the central focus point for 'governance' in the regions, instead of the provincial Governor being the central focus for 'governance'.

245 Author conversation with Haji Zahir in 2005, and also in report by the Senlis Council in 2006.

246 Zulmay Khalilzad, previously US Special Envoy, a former UNOCOL employee, a protégée of Condoleeza Rice and a member of the Rand corporation.

247 Such as the IOM who hired the office of the EU Election Mission on land at Sher Pur.

248 Contrary, therefore, to OECD guidelines.

249 Human Rights Watch report on Afghan police corruption.

250 C. Gall, *New York Times*, November 2004.

251 For example, in March 2005, at a meeting with donors and Afghan groups which had been organised by the Danish who were doing a report on aid delivery.

252 Paddy Ashdown, 'International Humanitarian Law, Justice and Reconciliation in a Changing World', The Eighth Hauser Lecture on Humanitarian Law, New York, 3 March 2004.

253 Ken Guest in email to author, September 2009

254 This issue, and an explanation its significance, is expanded upon later in the book in a conversation with James Ritchie.

255 To Hoja Baudin, also described in *Ghost Wars* by Steve Coll. But Coll only relates the story from the Massoud viewpoint, when it was Abdul Haq who orchestrated the alliance-led by the former King as a 'banner' to oust the Taliban.

256 Email from Peter Tomsen to author, 28 May 2009.

257 *Time*, August 2003

258 US Ambassador to the Mujahideen, 1988–92

259 Haq letter to Peter Tomsen dated January 1994.

260 The colleague worked for the UN Special Mission to Afghanistan (UNSMA)

261 Paghman is a mountainous area to the north of Kabul.

262 It was also Mullah Malang whom my colleague at EUSR was using as his main conduit into the Taliban in attempting to persuade moderates to defect. For this, President Karzai accused Semple of working with MI6 and had him thrown out of the country in December 2007.

263 Taliban Foreign Minister.

264 Zardad was the first person to be prosecuted under the Torture Convention in 2005

265 Babrak Karmal was the Kremlin's choice for President of Afghanistan from the time of the Soviet invasion, December 1979 to November 1986

266 Email to author, from John Gunston, February 2004

267 ibid

268 the piece in the Times by Michael Smith on 8 December 2001 stated "Britain's spies were heavily involved in the complex negotiations that led to the collapse of the Taliban across northern Afghanistan, Government officials said yesterday. The Secret Intelligence Service, MI6, reactivated old agents who had been in place during the Soviet occupation in the 1980s to take part in the operation. They also

used new agents developed before the September 11 attacks as part of operations against Osama bin Laden's al Qaeda terrorist network. One official said, 'They were used in highly imaginative ways to bring about the collapse of the Taliban in the North'". The piece – which sounded like PR for British intelligence agencies did not say which cities MI6 agents had apparently helped to fall. It went on fulsomely, "But officials claim that MI6 played a key role in the negotiations which led to the handover of many of the cities. 'MI6 officers waited until precisely the right moment and then used all their agents to press all the appropriate buttons', one said. The officials refused to give more details for fear of compromising the MI6 agents involved.

269 M. Beardon, *The Main Enemy*, Random House, 2003.

270 Although my contract was made by an NGO, ACTED, in order to circumvent UN rules which, at that stage, prevented British or Americans working in Afghanistan due to the threat from Osama bin Laden's 1998 fatwa against them.

271 J. Leslie and C. Johnson, *Afghanistan: The Mirage of Peace*, Zed books, 2004.

272 Eg the Italian politician Emma Bonino whose arrest by the Taliban alongside Christina Amanpour after apparently failing to heed warnings to stop filming in a women's hospital in Kandahar during the Taliban is described in Jolyon Leslie's book *Afghanistan: The Mirage of Peace*.

273 Following the intervention, the IBRD funded it and it became known as the National Solidarity Programme (NSP).

274 A. Rasanayagam, *Afghanistan: A Modern History*, London: IB Tauris, 2003.

275 Alfredo Witschi-Cestari, 'Coordinating aid in Afghanistan', Afghanistan info, October 1997, as quoted in Rasanayagam, A (2003)

276 B.J. Stapleton, 'A Means to what end? Why PRTs are peripheral to the bigger political challenges in Afghanistan', *Journal of Military and Strategic Studies*, Fall 2007, Vol 10, Issue 1.

277 Who then worked for UNAMA.

278 Email to author from Ken Guest, February 2009.

279 L. Dupree, Louis, New Delhi: Rama Press, 1973.

280 A. Saikhal, 1998, cited in Moshref 2002, 29.

281 S. Schmeidl and M. Karokhail, 'Integration of Traditional Structures into the State building Process: Lessons from the Tribal Liaison Office in Loya Paktia'.

282 ibid

283 ibid

284 Wimmer and Schetter, 2002, from S. Schmeidl, and M. Karokhail, 'Integration of Traditional Structures into the State building Process: Lessons from the Tribal Liaison Office in Loya Paktia'.

285 Rotberg, 2003, Goodson, 2001, Schlagintweit, 2002) in S. Schmeidl and M. Karokhail, 'Integration of Traditional Structures into the State building Process: Lessons from the Tribal Liaison Office in Loya Paktia.

286 The following note outlines its inception and background:
'The Nangarhar Community Empowerment Initiative was a process of democratic institution building that was expanded upon the traditional Afghan institution of the tribal council (Jirga) in order to provide a broadened democratic foundation for community empowerment and civic education in Afghanistan.
In late 2002, the traditional system, that was previously in place was non-existent. It was evident, at this sensitive juncture of time that the government was not in a position to establish Councils capable of empowering the community.

The Community Empowerment Initiative has effected the grassroots establishment of thirty-six democratically elected Community Councils throughout Nangarhar Province. The councils represent the people of each of Nangarhar's twenty-two administrative districts, the five precincts of the provincial capital city, Jalalabad, and nine other minority special-interest communities.
Since its inception in 2003, the stated purpose of the Council of Nangarhar Communities (CNC) has been to provide an interface between the people, the government, and the NGO community. Till now the CNC and its constituent councils have acted as advisory bodies only, serving as an experiment in local democracy-building and civic affairs management. The councils have had no formal authority to propose or enact governmental or developmental policy'.

287 Astri Suhrke, 'The Limits of State-building: The role of international assistance in Afghanistan', paper presented at the annual meeting of the International Studies Association, 2006.
288 As Schmeidl and Karokhail also assert.
289 S. Schmeidl and M. Karokhail, 'Integration of Traditional Structures into the State building Process: Lessons from the Tribal Liaison Office in Loya Paktia'.
290 H. Nixon, 'The Changing Face of Local Governance; Community Development Councils in Afghanistan', a report for the Afghan Research and Evaluation Unit (AREU), February 2008.
291 ibid
292 S. Schmeidl M. Karokhail, 'Integration of Traditional Structures into the State building Process: Lessons from the Tribal Liaison Office in Loya Paktia'. Schetter also makes this point.
293 L. Dupree, *Tribalism*, New Delhi: Rama Publishers, 1973.
294 N. Sharani, 'The State and Community Governance in Afghanistan', in Maley (ed) '*Fundamentalism Reborn?'*
295 Conversation with author, March 2005
296 Quoted by George Arney in *Afghanistan* (Mandarin paperbacks, 1990).
297 Author conversation with Haji Zahir Arsala, January 2004
298 Note that illicit activities which depend upon local positions of influence does not equate to 'tribal'.
299 Author conversation with British soldier, May 2005.
300 Author conversation with Carlotta Gall, 2005. Kate Clark also provides examples of NATO and Coalition troops working with local strongmen in her paper, '*Snakes and Scorpions: Justice and Stability in Afghanistan*' by Stephen Carter and Kate Clark (Kabul May 2010), an independent report produced for the Office of the High Commissioner for Human Rights (unpublished)
301 Or even be associated with the Afghan government undertaking.
302 The EUSR estimated there were around 1,700 of these illegal armed groups in 2005.
303 Anecdotal evidence from Afghan BBC journalists, amongst other sources.
304 At the time that Lakhdar-I-Brahimi and US Ambassador Khalilzad made the 'deal' with the strongmen to allow them not just to participate but effectively to negotiate the settlement of the 2002 ELJ in 2002, without the participation of the democratically elected delegates, (for this negotiation took place outside the main tent) some of the UNAMA officers had advised against this course of action, saying it would enable the stongmen to return to their fiefdoms stronger and to continue intimidation and illicit activity.
305 Email to author from former UNAMA political officer, Autumn 2008.

306 *A House Divided – Analysing the 2005 Afghan Elections* Andrew Wilder/AREU (December 2005)

307 As her Political Advisor, I challenged Emma Bonino on this when it came to writing up our official report on the 2005 Parliamentary elections. However in reality, as the EU's 'Chief Observer' on the Parliamentary Elections she was not independent and thus unable to pit herself against the steamroller of 'agreed' western policy. Among other things, the maintainance of a façade of 'democracy' in Afghanistan was necessary in order to persuade NATO countries to continue to send troops to Afghanistan.

308 Amnesty Law was gazetted in 2008 but did not come to Public Notice until end of 2009.

309 *Afghan Warrior*, Touch Productions, 2003.

310 Email from RAM Seegar to author, November 2008.

311 *In Afghanistan; an American Odyssey*. New York (Author's Choice). 1983 (pp 98)

312 Email to author from RAM Seeger, 26 September 2009.

313 Phone conversation with author, November 2008.

314 Paddy Ashdown's Autobiography (2009)

315 Note that according to a 'Dateline' sitrep prepared by RAM Seegar, they actually found out about Abdul Haq's initiative on 21 September 2001, when Sir John Gunston called Haq by phone.

316 'Afghanistan Summary' 16 January 2002, Sitrep prepared by RAM Seeger

317 Email from Ken Guest to author, March 2009

318 'General Duties' is the same rank as Private.

319 ibid

320 Email to author from Ken Guest, April 2009.

321 Email from Ken Guest to author, March 2009.

322 ISI chief during much of the jihad and blamed by many Afghans (to author) for the rise of the Taliban and the continuing insecurity in Afghanistan after September 11

323 ibid

324 ibid

325 'RAM' Seeger, Sit Rep 'Afghanistan summary' 16.01.02

326 ibid

327 ibid

328 ibid

329 See Annex – 'End of Summary Visit', Sitrep, 9 October 2001.

330 To the British Embassy in Islamabad on 6 October.

331 His family were originally from Hisarak so he would have a good reception there

332 RAM Seeger, Sitrep, 'Afghanistan summary', 16 January 2002.

333 ibid

334 ibid

335 Email to author from Ken Guest, March 2009

336 ibid

337 ibid

338 A, Rashid, *Daily Telegraph*, 19 October 2001.

339 RAM Seeger, Sitrep, 'Afghanistan summary', 16 January 2002.

340 email to author from Ken Guest, April 2009.

341 email to author from Ken Guest, August 2009

342 Email to author from Ken Guest, April 2009.

343 Email to author from Ken Guest February 2009.

344 Email to author from Ken Guest February 2009.

345 Ken Guest, in email to author, June 2009.

346 Ahmed Rashid discusses the meddling of ISI in the 'Pashtun equation' saying ISI wooed all sides in an attempt to manipulate the King's group and also the Peshawar group, which was led by Pir Syed Gailani and paid for by ISI (none of whose participants, Rashid says, wanted to fight the Taliban). Rashid adds that the New York Times and the Washington Post were manipulated by ISI into believing that ISI were trying to 'create moderates among the Taliban'. See 'Decent into Chaos' pp 72-3

347 Email to author from a former US diplomat to Afghanistan, June 2009.

348 Transcript of interview between Malcolm Brinkworth of Touch Productions and Joe Ritchie, in 2003

349 Note this is not to be confused with the post-September 11 'Bonn Conference' held in December 2001.

350 Daughter of 'Pir' Gailani, head of the NIFA party for which Wardak had previously been a commander. Also, Head of the Afghan Red Crescent Society, 2002 – present

351 This contradicts with what Steve Coll asserts in his book, *Ghost Wars: the secret history of the CIA, Afghanistan and bin Laden, from the Soviet invasion to September 11, 2001* (New York: Penguin Press, 2004). In other words, that Karzai and Tomsen had organised the meeting. It also differs from what Ahmed Rashid claims in his book 'Descent into Chaos', that Hamid Karzai had, in fact, attended a meeting with Massoud in summer 2001.

352 The Karzai brothers have a restaurant in Baltimore.

353 W. Azoy, *Bangor Daily News*, November 2001.

354 American citizen in Switzerland, September 2009

355 In this exchange, Ken Guest goes on to relate how he had seen what he believed to have been the first surface to air missiles (SAMs) that came into Afghanistan, delivered in 1982 to Malawi Jalaludin Haqqani's *markaz* (base) at Shahi Kot in Paktia.

356 R. Kaplan, *Soldiers of God*, New York: Vintage, 1990.

357 ibid

358 ibid

359 Cooley, J. *Unholy Wars – Afghanistan, America and International Terrorism*, Pluto Press, (London) 1999.

360 Cooley refers here to research by Christina Lamb.

361 ibid pp. 226

362 ibid

363 B. Rubin, February 2007

364 ibid

365 G. Schroen, *First In: How the CIA spearheaded the War on Terror in Afghanistan*, New York: Ballantine Books / Pressidio press, 2005.

366 ibid

367 ibid

368 ibid

369 International Republican Institute.

370 Email to author, 5 October 1999.

371 Email to author from Ken Guest, May 2009.

372 G. Schroen, *First In: How the CIA spearheaded the War on Terror in Afghanistan,* New York: Ballantine Books/Pressidio press, 2005.

373 Ken Guest email to author, August 2009.

374 Email to author from Ken Guest, September 2009.

375 Email to author from Ken Guest, June 2009.

376 K. Guest, *Flashpoint: at the Frontline in Today's Wars,* Arms and Armour, 1994.

377 Email to author from Ken Guest, June 2009.

378 M. Beardon, *The Main Enemy; the inside story of the CIA's final showdown with the KGB,* New York: Century, 2003.

379 Email to author from Ken Guest, September 2009.

380 Although the border incursions might have been initiated by the Pentagon.

381 W. Azoy, *Bangor Daily News,* November 2001.

382 Transcript of interview with Joe Ritchie for the documentary, *Afghan Warrior,* Touch Productions, 2003.

383 Conversation with author, spring 2005.

384 to the conflict. The Taliban have never admitted defeat. Hence did not participate in the Bonn conference.

385 D. Rumsfeld, 'Obama's challenges; One surge does not fit all', *New York Times,* 24 November 2008

386 Leaked Code Cable from Ambassador Karl Eikenberry, November 2009

387 As described in a report for the Institute of War by Carl Forster.

388 An exploration of 'Ways Forward' for the West in Afghanistan, in relation to the need to reconceptualise thinking more towards alternative governance mechanisms and concepts of traditional legitimacy are explored in the the author's paper titled; '*State-building in Afghanistan, a case showing the limits?*' published in the International Review of the Red Cross, Vol 92, Number 880, December 2010

389 As in the case of Mark Sedwill, NATO's Senior Civilian Representative, talking to Stephen Sackur on BBC World's *Hardtalk* on 18 May 2010.

390 D. Filkins, 'With US help, warlord builds empire', *New York Times,* 7 June 2010. This is a piece describing how warlord Matiuallah Khan heads up a private army (his own) earning millions of dollars for guarding NATO supply convoys that fight Taliban insurgents alongside US Special forces. The road runs between Kandahar and Tirin Kot. Khan reportedly now extorts from locals who attempt to use the road. "His militia has been adopted by US Special Forces officers to gather intelligence and fight insurgents. Mr Matiullah's compound sits about 100 metres from the US Special forces compound in Tirin Kot. A Special Forces officer, willing to speak only on condition of anonymity, said his unit had an extensive relationship with Mr. Matiullah. "Matiullah is the best there is here," the officer said. This has irritated some local leaders who say that the line between Mr Matiullah's business interest and the government has disappeared".

"Mr Matiullah's operation, the officials said, is one of at least 23 private security companies working in the area without any governance license or oversight......"

General Carter said that while he had no direct proof in Mr Matiullah's case, he harboured more general worries that the legions of unregulated Afghan security companies had a financial interest in prolonging chaos". (i.e in partaking in drug smuggling or enlisting Taliban or insurgents to attack those who did not use his security service).

Mr Matiullah was enlisted within a US intelligence report last spring as an associate of Ahmed Wali Karzai.

391 For such structures remain axiomatic to dispute resolution, as the Taliban understand so well.

392 Which is a matter of some complexity and not so 'black and white' as illustrated by anthropologist Anna Pont in *Rural Chickens and Social Animals* a study on rural Afghan women in Helmand published by Mercy Corps in August 2001.

393 Kathy Gannon, 2005

394 email from Nasrullah Arsala to author, August 2010

395 Email to author in April 2004, from Peter Tomson, former US Special Envoy to the Mujahideen,

396 Interview of Abdul Haq by Melinda Liu, *Newsweek*, November 2001.

397 Including the AIHRC which carried out a survey of the appetite by ordinary Afghans for 'transitional justice' entitled '*A Call for Justice: A National Consulation on past Human Rights Violations in Afghanistan*', Afghan Independent Human Rights Commission in Kabul, in 2005. This shows that Afghans hoped to have a process of accountability for past violations of human rights.

398 Transcript of interview for BBC documentary, *Afghan Warrior*, 2003.

399 From Schmeidl and Karokhail

400 C. Forsberg, *Politics and Power in Kandahar*, Institute for the Study of War, Washington DC, April 2010.

401 Global Humanitarian Forum conference, Geneva, June 2009.

402 *A Call for Justice: A National Consultation on past Human Rights Violations in Afghanistan*, Afghanistan Independent Human Rights Commission, Kabul, 2005, p14.

403 Email to author, June 2009.

404 One could also say 'military' role at the Emergency Loya Jirga when one considers the role of the intelligence police.

405 C. Allen, *Soldier Sahibs: the Men who made the North West Frontier*, Little Brown.

406 Paddy Ashdown speech, 2008.

407 J. Hippler, 'Nation States for Export? Nation building between Military intervention, crisis prevention and development policy' in *Nation Building: a Key concept for peaceful conflict transformation*, ed. Jochen Hippler, London, 2005.

408 M. Waldman, the Head of Policy for Oxfam International. '*Caught in the Conflict: Civilians and the International Security Strategy in Afghanistan*': a briefing paper by eleven NGOs operating in Afghanistan for the NATO Heads of State and Government Summit, 3–4 April 2009.

409 C. Forsberg, *Politics and Power in Kandahar,* Institute for the Study of War, Washington DC, April 2010, page 55.

410 Ibid. Also, Stephen Grey, http://www.guardian.co.uk/world/2010/may/16/afghan-prosecutor-arrest-warrant-us-officer, *Guardian*, 17 May 2010.

411 ibid

412 Carl Forsberg '*Politics and Power in Kandahar*'. Institute for the Study of War, Washington DC, April 2010, page 60.

413 ibid

414 ibid

415 Wimmer and Schetter, 2002, page 8.

416 A. Rasanayam, *Afghanistan, a Modern History : Monarchy, Despotism or Democracy? The problems of Governance in the Muslim Tradition*, IB Tauris, 2003.

417 The prospect of large numbers of innocent civilians being killed has driven support lower, but still the majority in favor of military force has been quite strong. Asking four times since the attacks, CBS/*New York Times* consistently found two-thirds saying that military action 'against whoever is responsible for the attacks' should go forward 'even if it means that innocent people are killed'. Likewise, ABC/*Washington Post* found on 27 September that seventy percent supported military action even 'if it meant innocent civilians in other countries might be hurt or killed'. Sixty-five percent favored 'attacking terrorist bases and the countries that allow or support them even if there is a high likelihood of civilian casualties' on September 27-28 according to *Newsweek*. CBS/*New York Times* used the phrase: 'What if … many thousands of innocent civilians may be killed?' and still found sixty-eight percent support. On October 7th (while the US bombing was underway) NBC News found seventy-eight percent saying that 'combating terrorism is worth risking civilian casualties in Afghanistan'. On October 17-18, Fox used strong language in a follow-on question ('even if it cost the lives of thousands of civilians in the countries we attack?') and still found sixty-two percent of the full sample in support.

418 *Armed Forces Journal*, April 2009

419 ibid

420 Written evidence passed to me by email from James Ritchie, July 2009.

421 al Shabab is thought to be hosting extremists from Pakistan and Afghanistan.

422 '*Tora Bora Revisited: How We Failed to Get Bin Laden and Why It Matters Today*', a report to members of the Committee on Foreign Relations, United States Senate, John F. Kerry Chairman, 111th Congress, first session 30 November 2009.

423 In 'The New American Foundation' (December 2008), F. Berrigan and W.D. Hartung, write: 'A new policy should not seek to reduce arms transfers as a goal in and of itself, but rather to strike a balance between short-term political and military considerations and long-term US interests in peace and stability. In many cases, seeking to enhance the role of human rights and conflict prevention in U.S. arms transfer policy will involve complex trade-offs, as in Iraq and Afghanistan, where massive 'train and equip' programs are central to the goal of reducing the direct U.S. military presence in those nations, although the new military and police forces in those nations have far to go in meeting basic human rights standards'.

424 Report by French MOD.

425 The problem of politicians who 'fix' the idea of going to war militarily yet who are subsequently offered Board seats with groups such as the Carlisle Group.

426 http://www.fromthewilderness.com/free/ww3/zbig.html

427 www.warresisters.org/pages/piechart.htm (last checked March 2011)

428 eg *The Times*,

ACRONYMS

AIHRC – Afghan Independent Human Rights Commission

ANA – Afghan National Army

ANP – Afghan National Police

CFC- ALPHA – Coalition Forces Command – ALPHA

CENTCOM – US military's Central Command

DDR – Disarmament, Demobilisation and Re-Integration

DEA – US Drug Enforcement Agency

DIAG – Disarmament of Illegal Armed Groups

DIS – Defence Intelligence Service

DFID – Britain's Department for International Development

DOD – US Department of Defense

ELJ – Emergency Loya Jirga

EU – European Union

FATA – Federally Administered Tribal Areas

G-8 – Group of Countries with largest economies

GCHQ – General Central Head Quarters (Britain's Intelligence Centre)

ICRC – International Committee of the Red Cross

IOM - International Organisation for Migration

ISAF – International Security Assistance Force

ISI – Inter-Services Intelligence Directorate (of Pakistan)

MI6 – British Secret Service (International)

MMA – Muttahida Majlis-e-Amal

MOD – Britain's Ministry of Defence

NA – Northern Alliance

NATO – North Atlantic Treaty Organisation

NIFA – National Islamic Front for Afghanistan

NGO – Non Governmental Organisation

NSD – National Directorate of Security (of Afghanistan). Also known as "Amniat"

NSP – National Solidarity Programme

NWFP – North West Frontier Province

PDPA – People's Democratic Party of Afghanistan

PRT – Provincial Reconstruction Team

RAWA – Revolutionary Afghan Women's Association

R2P - Right to Protect

RPG – Rocket Propelled Grenade

SIS – Secret Intelligence Service

UNAMA – United Nations Assistance Mission to Afghanistan

UNCHS - United Nations Centre for Human Settlements

UNODCCP – United Nations Office on Drug Control and Crime

USAID – US Agency for International Development

GLOSSARY *

Fez -   Prayer cap worn beneath turban

Kishmesh – Nut and fruit mixture

Pashtunwali (qaumi narkh) – the code of custom and honour governing pashtun tribes. This also functions as a body of laws for dispute resolution and a code of behaviour. The Pashtunwali may vary from tribe to tribe, each of which may retain distinct characteristics. Local elites and notables within and among tribes might use Pashtunwali as a means of providing a system of local governance. Pashtunwali is also a means to foster cohesions among major tribes.

Pashtun – The largest tribal society in the world which is around 15 to 25 million people who straddle the border between Afghanistan and Pakistan. Most Pashtuns are Sunnite Muslims and their language is Pashtu. Some Pashtuns now speak dari (a dialect of farsi) meaning there are less Pashtu speakers than the number of Pashtu ethnic group members. The reference for all Pashtuns is the Pashtunwali code of honour and custom, as well as the belief in a common ancestor, Qais Abdur Rashid. As such, Pashtuns believe in the idea of a social structure segmented by lines of descent from this common ancestor. The two major lines are the Durrani and the Ghilzai and these two groups account for over two thirds of all Afghan Pathans. These groups are then further divided into tribes, sub tribes (as demonstrated by the use of suffixes 'khel' or 'khail', or 'zai'), clans and extended families.

Patou – Large scarf or rug worn around the shoulders

Qaum – The word 'qaum' relates to the solidarity group that an individual feels they belong to. In pashtun society the word 'qaum' can be used to name tribal branches and sub-branches. Hence the word can be mixed up with the meaning of 'tribe' when in fact it relates more to a communal group, village, clan, extended family or professional network.

Spin Giri – The word spin giri means 'white beard'. Hence these are the most respected members of a community or within a tribe. A jirga is normally composed of spin giri and the influence of tribal elders is maintained by keeping the support of their constituency. Spin Giri can enhance their influence by having links with influential figures whether in government, or with important elders, khans or maliks of the region.

Ulema – Religious Leaders

Wakeel – a title which can be achieved by an influential khan or malik, eg by becoming a member of a Loya Jirga.

INSTITUTIONS

Jirga – This is the traditional decision making body in Pashtun Afghanistan. Jirgas are temporary bodies created for a special task, normally to solve disputes among tribes, sub tribes, clans, families, or individuals, as well as between government and tribes. The jirga is a means for negotiation and dialogue to take place so that stakeholders from different tribes and networks can engage with each other to solve disputes, gain resources, influence political processes or reach consensus on important issues. On a tribal level the jirga expresses the egalitarian ideals of Pashtun society.

Loya Jirga – A Loya Jirga (or Greater Jirga) is an extremely rare occurrence, is countrywide and is initiated by the central authority. It normally includes representatives of all ethnic and tribal groups, and regions. Previously, the Loya Jirgas were initiated by Afghan Kings. However in the wake of September 11 the Emergency Loya Jirga, held in June 2002, decided upon the Transitional Administration while the Constitutional Loya Jirga held in December 2003 / 2004 approved the new Afghan Constitution.

Shura – This term was once used for the gathering of Islamic dignitaries such as mullahs and ulema. But after the Soviet war the term began to be used for many types of gatherings, including those associated with the mujahideen. Hence the term began to compete with traditional Pashtun terms such as jirga. Today the term shura is used for all kinds of official gatherings and every tribe (both Pashtun and non Pashtun) has its own shura. Outside assistance is only then accepted when the tribal shura is unable to solve a dispute. Shuras are fairly stable structures which usually exist long term; more like a Council that has leadership and is comprised of influential people. More recently, shuras have adapted to government structures and can exist on village, district and province level. Often shuras are also set up externally (eg by NGOs) to assist in reconstrution projects. Like jirgas, shuras tend to be all male. Female shuras are newer and tend to be set up externally. Recently, groups we might in the west consider to be social or cultural organizations have also used the term shura. Eg Youth shura or Handicap shura.

*   with apologies to Conrad Schetter and Susanne Schmeidl

BIBLIOGRAPHY

BOOKS

Allen, C., *Soldier Sahibs: the Men who made the North West Frontier*, Little Brown

Arney, G., *Afghanistan*, Mandarin paperbacks, 1990

Barfield, T., *Afghanistan; a Cultural and Political history*. Princeton University Press, 2010

Beardon M. and James Risen, *The Main Enemy: the inside story of the CIA's final showdown with the KGB*, New York: Random House, 2003

Bergen, P. *Holy War Inc. Inside the Secret World of Osama bin Laden* London. Phoenix 2001

Borovik, A., *The Hidden War: A Russian journalist's Account of the Soviet War in Afghanistan*, USSR: International Relations Publishing House, 1990. Then by The Atlantic Monthly Press. USA, 1990

Brezinski, Z. *The Choice: Global domination or Global Leadership*. New York. Basic Books (2004)

Burke, J. *Al Qaeda: Casting a Shadow of Terror*. IB Tauris, London. 2003

Caroe, Sir Olaf, *The Pathans. With an Epilogue on Russia*, OUP Karachi, 2003 imprint (first edition printed by MacMillan in 1958)

Coll, S., *Ghost Wars; the secret history of the CIA, Afghanistan, and bin Laden, from the Soviet Invasion to September 11, 2001*, New York: Penguin, 2004

Cooley, J. K., *Unholy Wars: Afghanistan, America and International Terrorism*, London: Pluto Press, 2000

Crile, G., *Charlie Wilson's War: The Extraordinary Story of the Largest Covert Operation in History*, New York: Atlantic Monthly Press, 2003

Dupree, N.H, *A Historical Guide to Afghanistan*, Afghan Air Authority, 1977

Elliot, J., *An Unexpected Light: Travels in Afghanistan*, London: Picador, 1999

Fletcher, *Afghanistan, Highway of Conquest*, 1965

Foley, C., *The Thin Blue Line: How Humanitarianism went to War*, Verso, 2009

Fouda, Y., and N. Fielding, *Masterminds of Terror; the truth behind the most devasting terrorist attack the world has ever seen*, Mainstream, 2003.

Goodson, L., *Afghanistan's Endless War: State Failure, Regional Politics, and the rise of the Taliban*, Seattle: University of Washington Press, 2001

Griffin, M., *Reaping the Whirlwind: The Taliban Movement in Afghanistan*, London: Pluto Press, 2001

Guest, K., *Flashpoint: at the Frontline in Today's Wars*, London: Arms and Armour, 1994

Hensher, P., *The Mulberry Empire*, 2002

Hippler, J., (ed), *Nation Building: a Key concept for peaceful conflict transformation*, London, 2005

Hopkirk, P., *The Great Game*, Oxford University Press, 1990

Kaplan, R., *Soldiers of God: With Islamic Warriors in Afghanistan and Pakistan*, New York: Vintage, 1990

Kaye, Sir J., *History of the War in Afghanistan*, Bentley, 1857

Lamb, C. *Waiting for Allah; Pakistan's Struggle for Democracy* Viking 1991 (New Delhi)

Leslie J., and C. Johnson, *Afghanistan: The Mirage of Peace*, Zed books, 2004

Macrory, P., *Kabul Catastrophe: The Invasion and Retreat, 1839-1842*, London: Prion, 1966

Marsden, P., *The Taliban: War, Religion and the New Order in Afghanistan*, Oxford University Press, 1998

Miller, C., *Khyber*, Macdonald and James, 1977

Pont, A., *Blind Chickens and Social Animals: Creating spaces for Afghan Women's Narratives Under the Taliban*. Mercy Corps, Portland, USA. August 2001

Rasanayagam, A. *Afghanistan: A Modern History*, London: IB Tauris, 2003

Rashid, A., *Taliban: Militant Islam, Oil, and Fundamentalism in Central Asia*, London: IB Tauris, 2000

Rashid, A., *Descent into Chaos: How the war against Islamic extremism is being lost in Pakistan, Afghanistan and Central Asia*, Allen Lane, London. 2008

Rubin, B., *The Fragmentation of Afghanistan*, Yale, 1990

Rubin, B., *The Search for Peace in Afghanistan: From Buffer State to Failed State*, New Haven, Conn: Yale University Press, 1995

Schroen, G. *First In: How the CIA spearheaded the War on Terror in Afghanistan*, New York: Ballantine Books/Pressidio press, 2005

Van Dyk, Jere. *In Afghanistan: An American Odyssey*, New York: Author's Choice, 1983

Warren, A., *Waziristan, the Faqir of Ipi, and the Indian Army: The North West Frontier Revolt of 1936–37*, New York: Oxford University Press, 2000

ARTICLES

Azoy, W., The Bangor Daily News, 5 November 2001

Ashdown, P., 'Paddy Ashdown's Afghan Solution: Strategies for War' *The Times*, 20 September 2001

Bearak, B, Obituary: Muhammad Zahir Shah, Afghan ex-King, *New York Times*, 24 July 2007

Bearak, B, 'Taliban Executes a Top American-backed Rival', 27 October 2001, *New York Times*

Bearak, B., 'Who Betrayed Haq? Candidates are Many'. *The New York Times*, 27 October, 2001

Davis, D. (MP), *The Times*, July 2009.

Dovkants, K. (Islamabad), 'Rebel chief begs: Don't bomb now, Taliban will be gone in a month. *Evening Standard*, 5 October 2001

Filkins, D, 'Rule of the gun: Convoy Guards face an Inquiry', *New York Times*, 6 June 2007.

Filkins, D, 'With US help, Warlord builds Empire'., *New York Times*, 7 June 2010.

Gall, C., *New York Times*, November 2004

Kiley, S., *The Spectator*, February 2004

Levine, S, Wall Street Highflier finds Haq's death deals Two blows' *The Wall Street Journal*, 29 October 2001

Liu, M, 'I'm Sick and Tired of Bloodshed: But Abdul Haq died a violent death at the hands of the Taliban' *Newsweek*, 29 October 2001

Lorch, Donatella, 'Farewell to a Friend', *Newsweek,* 29 October 2001

Maniere de voir, le Monde diplomatique. 110 'Imprenable Afghanistan: l'histoire, les acteurs, les enjeux', Avril, May 2010

Margolis, E., *Toronto Sun*, 11 October 2009

McGirk, T, (Shkin) 'Battle in "the Evilest Place". *Time*, 3 November 2003

Mishra, P., *What we think of America*, Granta 77, Spring 2002.

Moore, M. and Khan, K. 'Taliban Claims to Execute Foe. Abdul Haq was recruiting Defectors' *The Washington Post*, 27 October, 2001

Novak, R., 'Abdul Haq's Last Hours', *The Washington Post*, 1 November 2001

Rashid, A., 'In Afghanistan, Let's Keep It Simple', *The Washington Post*, 6 September 2009

Rashid, A., *Daily Telegraph*, 19 October 2001

'The CIA's Intervention in Afghanistan: Interview with Zbigniew Brzezinski, President Jimmy Carter's National Security Adviser', *Le Nouvel Observateur*, 15 January 1998.

Smith, M. 'British spies played key role in forcing collapse of regime' *The Daily Telegraph*, 8 December 2001

Swain, Jon. 'Kabul's lost man of Peace'. *The Sunday Times*, 18 November 2001

Warren, M, 'Last of the Warlords keeps enemy at bay' *The Daily Telegraph*, 19 November, 2001

Private Eye, –(un-attributed), 19 October 2001 (Issue 1039) and 2 November 2001 (Issue 1040)

REPORTS AND JOURNALS

Afghan Independent Human Rights Commission in Kabul, *A Call for Justice: A National Consulation on past Human Rights Violations in Afghanistan*, Kabul, 2005

Patricia Gossman, *Casting Shadows: War Crimes and Crimes against Humanity: 1978-2001*, Afghan Justice Project, 2005,

Killing you is a very easy thing for us: Human Rights abuses in SouthEast Afghanistan, Human Rights Watch, vol. 15, no. 5, July 2003

Forsberg, C., *Politics and Power in Kandahar*, Institute for the Study of War, Washington DC, April 2010

Ken Guest, Lucy Morgan Edwards, 'RAM' Seeger. *The Tribal Path: Commanding the Prime battle Space. A more hopeful strategy for Afghanistan*. The Small War's Journal, 4 March 2010

Tariq, Mohammed Osman, *Tribal Security System (Arbakai) in Southeast Afghanistan* – Occasional Paper no 7', Crisis States Research Centre, December 2008

Steven Carter and Kate Clark. *Snakes and Scorpions: Justice and Stability in Afghanistan*, Chatham House, London. January 2011

Kerry, John F. (Chairman), *Tora Bora Revisited: How We Failed to Get Bin Laden and Why It Matters Today: A Report To Members of the Committee on Foreign Relations*, United States Senate, 111th Congress, first session, November 30 2009.

Lucy Morgan Edwards. *State-building in Afghanistan: a case showing the limits?* International Review of the Red Cross, Volume 92, Number 880, pp 1-25. December 2010

Lucy Morgan Edwards. *Defence, Diplomacy and Development (3Ds): A New Approach to International Relations?* working paper commissioned by and written for the Swiss Agency for International Development and Cooperation (SDC), 2008.

Lucy Morgan Edwards, *The Potential of Tribal Solutions in Stabilising Afghanistan* May 2009 www.the-beacon.info

Liaison Office, The (TLO), *Between the Jirga and the Judge: Alternative Dispute Resolution in Southeastern Afghanistan,* TLO Program Brief 1/2008, Kabul, 2008.

Liaison Office, The (TLO), *Land Based Conflict In Afghanistan: The Case of Paktia,* unpublished working paper, Kabul, 2008b

Schmeidl, S., and M. Karokhail, *Integration of Traditional Structures into the State building Process: Lessons from the Tribal Liaison Office in Loya Paktia.*

Astri Suhrke, *The Limits of State-building: The role of international assistance in Afghanistan,* paper presented at the annual meeting of the International Studies Association, 2006

Wisner, D, *Is Time ripe for Transitional Justice in Afghanistan?* The Fletcher Online Journal for SouthWest Asia and Islamic Civilisation, Fall 2008

Also various reports from the International Crisis Group

MISCELLANEOUS

Transcript of interviews with Milton Beardon, 7 September 2002, Touch Productions. London

Transcript of interview with Joe Ritchie, 9 September 2002, Touch Productions. London

Transcript of interview with Robert 'Bud' McFarlane, Touch Productions. London

Letters written by Abdul Haq to Jimmy Carter, (6 January 1992), to Ambassador Yusuf Motabbakani, (20 August 1991), to Peter Tomsen (dated January 1993), to Margaret Thatcher.

AUDIO AND VIDEO

Ritchie, James and Joe (producers), 'Afghanistan: A Plan for Peace. A background of Afghanistan's form of Tribal democracy', as presented to the US Congress in January 2009, CD

Malcolm Brinkworth and Ken Guest (2003) *Afghan Warrior* Touch Productions.